1993

# WORDS ON MUSIC

A Note about the Editor

Jack Sullivan, Associate Professor of English at Rider College, is the author of *Elegant Nightmares: the English Ghost Story from Le Fanu to Blackwood* and the editor of *Lost Souls: A Collection of English Ghost Stories* (both Ohio University Press). Dr. Sullivan is a regular contributor to the *New York Times Book Review* and the *Washington Post Book World* and has written for a wide range of other publications including *The New Republic*, *Harper's*, *New York Newsday*, and *USA Today*. His program notes and articles on music have appeared in *Keynote*, Carnegie Hall *Stagebill* and other publications, and he is Program Annotator for the New Jersey Symphony Orchestra.

# WORDS ON

# MUSIC

## FROM ADDISON TO BARZUN

Edited by Jack Sullivan

*OHIO UNIVERSITY PRESS* Athens

Translations of "Beethoven's Despair" and "Music as Science and Sentiment" by Hector Berlioz, copyright © 1990 by Jacques Barzun.

Introduction and Notes © copyright 1990 by Jack Sullivan

95 94 93 92 91   5 4 3 2 (cl. edition)

95 94 93 92 91   5 4 3 (pbk. edition)


Ohio University Press books are printed on acid-free paper ∞

Library of Congress Cataloging-in-Publication Data
Words on music : from Addison to Barzun / edited by Jack
Sullivan.
   Includes bibliographical references.
   ISBN 0-8214-0958-1 (alk. paper). — ISBN 0-8214-0959-X
(pbk. : alk. paper)
   1. Music—History and criticism. I. Sullivan, Jack, 1946–  .
ML160.W95   1990
780—dc20      89-72115 CIP   MN

For Robin, my C-Major chord

# Contents

# Preface

This book is a collection of distinguished writing on music for both the specialist and the general reader. Covering instrumental and vocal music from the medieval period to the present, it gathers together in one place a diverse range of pieces that are distinctive for their literary quality, readability, and ability to illuminate. Included is the work of novelists, composers, literary essayists, cultural historians, performers, and others whose quality of prose enables them to speak simultaneously to the novice and the seasoned music enthusiast.

The purpose of this book is to introduce a representative sample of these rewarding but often neglected writers and thereby provide an elegant, readable guide to the art of music. It is the assumption of the writers collected here that the pleasures of this art, like those of any other, can be heightened by good writing, that words can conjure sounds and help us to face the music. This is a literary genre that has the power to fuse two seemingly disparate art forms and enhance the enjoyment of both.

The book moves from an overview to an insider's perspective. Part I, an overture on the art of writing on music, includes an editor's introduction, a piece by Jacques Barzun that serves as a poetics for the subject, and a few feisty diatribes by George Bernard Shaw that boil music criticism down to its essence. Part II, the heart of the book, covers major composers and masterworks, from Gregorian chant to Pierre Boulez, arranged chronologically by musical period. Since many of the writers in this collection—Leigh Hunt, E. T. A. Hoffmann, Virgil Thomson, to name a few—have a remarkable ability to summarize the essence of a composer's contribution in a few paragraphs, this section comes close to constituting a concise survey of musical style. Part III features essays on such broad topics as opera, recordings, and musical emotion; these pieces tie together some of the volume's larger interdisciplinary concerns, especially the relationship between literature and music. Concluding the book on an informal note is a series of portraits and memoirs which evoke the personal, purely human dimensions of the musical life.

Each piece is introduced by a short headnote placing the subject in aesthetic or historical perspective and is concluded with a parenthetical reference to its original place and date of publication. These references, together with bibliographic citations in the introductions and suggestions for further reading at the back of the book, may help readers who are interested in finding further material by a given author.

I have tried to make variety a keynote of this anthology, not only in types of articles but in their length. The range of voices is wide, including the exuberance of Hector Berlioz and Leonard Bernstein, the cantankerousness of George Bernard Shaw and H. L. Mencken, the urbanity of Heinrich Heine and Cecil Gray, and the erudition of Jacques Barzun and Charles Rosen. Length is a function not of the importance of the subject but of the nature of the article and the sensibility of the writer. Heine's comparison piece on Rossini and Meyerbeer and Barzun's article on Liszt, for example, are quite long compared to Thomas Love Peacock's and Aaron Copland's pieces on Mozart; this is not, of course, because Mozart is less important than these other composers but because Heine and Barzun write from a broad cultural perspective whereas Peacock and Copland are interested in their subject's universality. Nevertheless, this book does have a general bias in favor of conciseness; the goal is to give the reader a brief but rich taste of a number of writers and subjects.

The emphasis on brevity has necessitated cuts, indicated by ellipses, largely of references to performers and personalities now of historical interest only. Exceptions include instances in which such an excision would mar the prose or weaken the texture of the argument. In a similar spirit, I have made minor changes in some of the older translations to conform to modern usage. Every effort has been made to produce the most readable book possible.

Space and editorial considerations also mean that this anthology cannot claim to be comprehensive. The work of several admirable writers, including Hugo Wolf, Ferrucio Busoni, Richard Capell,

Richard Taruskin, Robert Craft, Nicholas Kenyon, and Wilfrid Mellers did not quite fit into the scheme of this collection, although the reader is pointed toward books by these and other notable authors in Suggestions for Further Reading.

Another category not included here is negative criticism. Although the writers collected in these pages may occasionally grumble or make invidious comparisons, this book is a positive one, a celebration of great music by writers whose prose matches their enthusiasm. Readers who want to sample the malevolent delights of negative musical commentary—and music has elicited more purely destructive writing than perhaps any other art—should consult Nicolas Slonimsky's delightful *Lexicon of Musical Invective*. Indeed, that notorious volume might serve as a pungent companion to the present one.

# Acknowledgments

My first and greatest thanks goes to Jacques Barzun for his generous help, splendid translations, and seasoned advice throughout the preparation of this book. I am also grateful to Charles Simmons, Alan Williams, Helen Paxton, Art Paxton, Helen Ruttencutter, Joseph Horowitz, and Andrew Porter for their encouragement and ideas. A special thanks goes to my wife, Robin Bromley, who helped with every aspect of preparing the manuscript.

# Permissions

"Music into Words," "Literature in Liszt's Mind and Work," and "Why Opera?" by Jacques Barzun. Reprinted in revised form by permission of the author.

"The Miracle of Gregorian Chant" and "The Fatal Perfection of Palestrina" by Cecil Gray. Reprint permission granted by Rowan & Littlefield, Totowa, New Jersey.

"J. S. Bach: Three Glimpses: I, Bach the Colorist" and excerpts from "Varese: Skyscraper Mystic" in *Discoveries of a Music Critic* by Paul Rosenfeld. Copyright 1936 by Harcourt Brace Jovanovich, Inc. and renewed 1964 by Edna Bryner, reprinted by permission of the publisher.

"Scarlatti's Keyboard Quirks" by Glenn Gould, from *The Glenn Gould Reader*, edited by Tim Page. Copyright © 1984 by the estate of Glenn Gould. Reprinted by permission of Alfred A. Knopf, Inc.

"The Enchantment of Rameau" and "Moussorgsky's Vision of Child-hood" by Claude Debussy, from *Debussy on Music*, translated and edited by Richard Langham Smith. Copyright © 1977 by Martin Secker & Warburg Ltd. and Alfred A. Knopf, Inc. Reprinted by permission of Alfred A. Knopf, Inc.

"The Clarity of Haydn," "Schubert: Music's Great Heart," and "Music and Sin" by H. L. Mencken, from *H. L. Mencken on Music*, edited by Louis Cheslock. Copyright © 1961 by Alfred A. Knopf, Inc. Reprinted by permission of Alfred A. Knopf, Inc.

"At the Thought of Mozart" by Aaron Copland, from *High Fidelity*, January 1956 (Vol. 6, No. 1, P. 53). Reprinted by permission of *High Fidelity* Magazine.

# P A R T  I

## Writing about

## Music

# The Elusive Art

## JACK SULLIVAN

**M**usic is difficult to write about precisely because it transcends language. However one regards music, whether primarily as emotional communication or as architecture in sound, it is clearly an art that takes us to a world beyond words. In instrumental music, this point is perhaps obvious. But even vocal music transcends its text, often to such an extent that the most commonplace poem or prose passage immediately sheds its verbal weight and takes flight when treated by a Bach or a Schubert. The whole notion of composing words on music seems a daunting paradox. E. T. A. Hoffmann goes so far as to declare music to be an "unknown realm" of "inexpressible longing," one having "nothing in common" with the world of words and writing—even as he writes brilliantly about it.* Heinrich Heine declares that the "essence of music is revelation" which "permits no analysis" beyond that provided by two travelers he overheard in Marseilles arguing the respective merits of Rossini versus Meyerbeer by singing tunes at each other across the table: "Instead of a noisy exchange of insignificant phrases, they gave us most exquisite table music, and finally I had to admit that people should not dispute at all concerning music, or should do so in this charmingly realistic fashion." Yet Heine makes these remarks in the course of his own charmingly realistic piece on Rossini versus Meyerbeer, an essay that never once traffics in "insignificant phrases."

In his *Composer and Critic* (1946), a lively history of music criticism, Max Graf identifies Heine as the first writer on music to engage a wide audience in an accessible, nontechnical style, but we might want to extend that distinction back a bit, to Joseph Addison's

---

*All quotations are taken from the essays that follow.

biting opera articles from the early eighteenth century in the *Specta-tor* or Charles Burney's learned but lucid *General History of Music,* from 1776. For the past three centuries a wide variety of writers have taken on the seductive challenge of writing about music and describ-ing its significance in their lives and cultures. From Addison to Virgil Thomson, writers in and out of the music field, including composers, literary essayists, novelists, performers, and professional journalists, have written on music with precision and passion.

At its best, what this literature delivers is the exciting, somewhat eerie illusion of hearing the music being described. When we read Hector Berlioz on Weber or Leigh Hunt on Mozart, the words evoke not only thought but sound, sensation, delicious anticipation. If the music is familiar, our memories are stirred; if it is new or otherwise unfamiliar, we experience a sense of voluptuous curiosity and sus-pense that, in an age of recordings, can often be quickly consum-mated. Perhaps no other form of literature has quite this power, so peculiarly gratifying, of blending two art forms and enhancing the pleasures of both.

A recent example of the genre working at its peak is Desmond Shawe-Taylor's 1973 *New Yorker* article on Schubert's C-Major Quin-tet. A close look at this piece can perhaps give us a sense of what the musical essay is still capable of achieving. Beginning as a concert review in which the performance (by Isaac Stern and friends) is judged to be "good enough to evoke the customary magic," the article speculates on why music lovers for a hundred years have agreed on the Quintet's "disturbing beauty."

Part of the speculation touches on the mystery of art. Music, like all art, seems mysterious because "its values are incapable of the kind of proof that we recognize in other fields," and criticism is thus deemed useless by people who seem totally unruffled by so much else in their daily lives depending on "equally unverifiable judgments— on the quality of friends and acquaintances, for example. The Schubert Adagio might be called the musical equivalent of some person (luckily we have all met one or two such) whose sweetness and depth of character are instantly recognizable, and never fail us."

Recognizing that this personal assertion will not satisfy the in-quirer, Shawe-Taylor proceeds to "virtues more definitely musical," which he elucidates without resorting to technical analysis. In a kind of musical narrative depicting the three main instruments in the

Adagio pursuing "their grave, serene melody, while above and below them the two others fill a decorative role," we are led into the music's texture. As for melody, Shawe-Taylor writes that Schubert, "to whom a dozen immortal tunes often occurred in the course of a morning's work, here struck, in the last year of his short life, a new vein," a long-drawn idea "rising and falling as gently as the breath of a deep sleeper." The final paragraph connects the Scherzo's "repeated unison descents into the void" with Schubert, in this work from his last year, contemplating death.

This essay plays all the notes essential to first-rate writing on music. It is at once freely anecdotal and musically precise; it uses direct but imaginative language to make Schubert's textures and melodies unfold in our minds as it moves us toward larger meanings and associations. And it does all this without resorting to technical jargon. Anyone reading this article who has not heard the Quintet will surely not remain in this unfortunate state for long, just as anyone who knows the work will probably now hear it differently and more deeply.

For an earlier, somewhat different model, we go to George Bernard Shaw, whose columns from a century ago are still, by amazingly common consent, regarded as the most penetrating and pleasurable music criticism in English. The Shavian method is admirably illustrated in a pair of 1891 pieces from the *World* on the *Messiah*. Here, Shaw protests "the impossibility of obtaining justice for that work in a Christian country. Import a choir of heathens, unrestrained by considerations of propriety from attacking the choruses with unembarrassed sincerity of expression, and I would hasten to the performance if only to witness the delight of the public and the discomfiture of the critics."

The remainder of Shaw's musings consists of a dramatic series of statements describing how Handel's masterpiece *should* sound versus the "lumbering" reverence practised by generations of Handel singers who had "their Handel training in church." Instead of "the fiercely tumultuous *He Trusted in God,* with its alternations of sullen mockery with high-pitched derision and its savage shouts of *Let Him Deliver Him if He Delight in Him,*" we get, jogging along at half the proper speed, "an expression of the deepest respect and propriety, as if a large body of the leading citizens, headed by the mayor, were presenting a surpassingly dull address to somebody." Instead of

Handel's characteristic launching of a "whole mass of voices into florid passages of great brilliance and impetuosity" clearly meant "to be sung with one impulse from end to end without an instant's hesitation," we get a chorus "so dull that all the reputation of Handel is needed to persuade Englishmen that they ought to enjoy it, whilst Frenchmen go away from our festivals confirmed in their skepticism as to our pet musical classic." Shaw's rather depressing conclusion is that "a mood of active intelligence," were it to infect conventional concert-going habits, "would be scandalous."

Yet the total effect of Shaw's railing, far from being depressing, is exhilarating, for he shows us just how exciting even a chestnut like the *Messiah* can be. (He would probably be pleased to see how many of his injunctions about tempo and rhythmic energy have been adopted by the current "original instruments" movement.) Like Shawe-Taylor in his Schubert article, Shaw makes us hear the music in its ideal splendor. What is delightfully idiosyncratic about Shaw is that he needs a certain amount of bile to get him going: his pieces invariably contain a biting diatribe or two, even though the basic thrust of his writing is positive—indeed, ecstatic. Whatever his subject, Shaw wants us to recognize that the state of ecstasy and the state of music are one and the same, and he wants us to get furious at anything that dulls or conventionalizes or makes passive our experience of it.

Here then are two major writers on music who have contrasting tones but common overall goals. From them we might generalize by saying that the writer on music is someone who is able to evoke the sound and personality of a piece and connect it with a larger cultural, spiritual, or purely personal framework. We might add that as in the case of literary criticism, much of this writing exists in the form of reviews; as Wilfred Sheed once pointed out, the review is perhaps the last remaining marketable form of the literary essay, and this holds true (with the exception of program notes, which themselves are increasingly becoming corporate products) for musical essays as well. This is not necessarily a debilitating restriction: writing on music, like writing on books, is often clearest when most specific, and a review gives the writer a concrete launching pad for larger musings.

Different writers, of course, employ different strategies. Virgil Thomson, for example, favors homey metaphors (Haydn is an avuncular "old bachelor," Mozart a communal spirit whose "themes are like people"), while Paul Rosenfeld piles on elaborate adjectives (Varèse is a "skyscraper mystic," a creator of "incandescent manifestations of material entities in stellar space"). Yet despite differences in style and sensibility, the most stimulating writers in this field, from whatever time period, have one thing in common: the sense that music, as Andrew Porter puts it, is a "voyage of discovery" whose pleasures can be shared and intensified through the act of writing.

This sense of sharing is seen most strikingly in the work of composers who tackle the difficulties of the form as if they didn't exist. One reads certain pages of Berlioz and Schumann with the same joyful sense of expansion found in their music, as if language were being stretched beyond its limits and entering the composer's own sonic domain. This curious transliterary feeling is reinforced by a frequent similarity of verbal and musical style: Wagner, for example, favors cosmic generalizations in his writing, Busoni intricate convolutions, Ives collage-like digressiveness, Leonard Bernstein go-for-broke hyperbole. With these artists, words and music emerge as different aspects of the same sensibility and style of communication.

It is perhaps not surprising that composers, writing on music, are so often engaging. Just as some of the best literary essayists have been novelists (James, Forster, Lawrence, Nabokov, Updike, to name a few), some of the greatest writers on music have been those who create it. To the automatic advantage of an insider's knowledge, they frequently bring a largeness of vision, an ability to step back and see the creative stream of which they are part. In some cases, notably that of Berlioz, with his stabbing irony, and Copland, with his elegant lucidity, the verbal felicity is so keen that one can easily imagine these composers making writing their major careers. Indeed, in the cases of E. T. A. Hoffmann and Virgil Thomson, that is very much what did occur. This phenomenon is not always intentional: an interesting case is that of Ned Rorem, whose pungent essays and notorious *Diaries* are so scandalously entertaining that they run the danger of eclipsing his achievement as a composer. Nor should we forget monetary considerations: as regular music columnists, Berlioz, Schumann, and Debussy wrote more criticism than music, simply to make ends meet.

Another group of writers that has contributed splendid work to the genre is literary essayists. This category includes not only E. T. A. Hoffmann, George Bernard Shaw, Romain Rolland, Jacques Bar-

zun, and other men of letters whose work on music is highly celebrated, but also luminaries not always associated with music such as
Thomas Love Peacock, Leigh Hunt, and H. L. Mencken. For those
caught in the circle of writing words about other words, writing about
music holds a special enticement and fascination. The musical essays
of these literary expatriates exude an almost palpable sense of pleasure and release. When Heine writes on Liszt, or Peacock on Mozart,
or Edward Said on Glenn Gould, the style takes on a freedom and
fluidity not always found in these writers' other work. It is as if they
had suddenly hit upon a new love interest, free from inhibiting
patterns and associations.

Some of these literary figures have extensive musical back-
grounds: Leigh Hunt was an accomplished pianist and singer, H. L.
Mencken a pianist, Anthony Burgess an amateur composer, Cecil
Gray and Ethel Smyth ambitious composers whose work sank into
oblivion. But even in cases such as those of Mencken and Gray, men
who longed to be remembered for music rather than letters, this
literature rarely betrays the peevishness and competitiveness so
often displayed by literary critics who are frustrated novelists.
Rather, Shaw's work on Wagner or Mencken's on Haydn are labors of
love. This largeness of spirit is in no way belied by the negative
commentary so entertainingly prominent in this literature. When
these writers go on the attack—and no one attacks with feistier
abandon than Shaw writing on Brahms, say, or Mencken on Italian
opera—they do so out of a sense of genuine, almost naive outrage.
We get the sense (as noted in our examination of Shaw's *Messiah*
piece) that they are defending something which has directly enhanced their lives, something almost sacred, from mediocrity or
desecration.

Not surprisingly, a special momentum and vividness sparks the
work of fiction writers, who often cast their musical essays in a
narrative format. Well known are passages on music in novels by
Joyce, Mann, Forster, Proust, and others. Less celebrated is the work
of fiction writers who comment directly on music—George Eliot on
Liszt and Wagner, Romain Rolland on Handel and Beethoven,
Henry Chorley on Italian opera, G. K. Chesterton on Gilbert and
Sullivan, Anthony Burgess on musical influences, Thomas Mann on
Wagner, Paul Horgan on Stravinsky, Guy Davenport on Ives. The

energy of this writing is almost novelistic, as if the essayist is trying to explode the stereotypical formality of essay form.

Another enticing category of musical essayist is the performer with a gift for words. Several of these, including Liszt, Schumann, and Busoni, are now remembered mainly as composers. Recently, writers more clearly identifiable as performers, including Glenn Gould, Charles Rosen, and Gary Graffman, have written incisively, sometimes brilliantly, on a variety of musical topics. For reasons that seem genuinely mysterious, these performer-essayists tend to be pianists. Violinists, singers, and tuba players seemingly have not written as much. Another quirk is that all the recent writers in this category, despite their quite individual voices, share a common tone of cool elegance and wit that is consonant with their performance style. More heated, extroverted performers do not appear to write as often or as well. (Leonard Bernstein is an exception here, as he is in virtually all other matters.)

The best writing on music, from whatever source, tends to consist of odds and ends—scattered essays, reviews, program and record liner notes, memoirs, and chapters in books—rather than pieces from regular columns and academic journals. This is an art best approached on an occasional basis, when the writer's muse is visited by the right mood, the right confluence of thought and sound. The regular column, with its relentless politics and deadlines, and the academic journal, with its fetish for the unreadable, are not congenial formats. (Pieces on literature, where words must connect only with other words, are usually less vulnerable to these problems, although the amount of unreadable music criticism probably does not exceed the amount of unreadable literary criticism by much.)

As for regular music critics who can be read with pleasure, it is striking how many of them have a grounding, or at least a lively interest, in literature and the other arts. To read James Huneker on George Moore, Ernest Newman on Ibsen, Eduard Hanslick on wine, Paul Rosenfeld on modern art, Richard Gilman on Romantic poetry, Richard Capell on Goethe, or Andrew Porter on Melville is as stimulating as reading these writers' thoughts on matters musical. This phenomenon holds for much of the best writing in the field: great writers on music almost invariably reach beyond the special confines of the music world to make vital connections with the other arts.

In an earlier, less specialized age, before we needed academic labels like "interdisciplinary" to describe a perfectly natural cultural curiosity and connectedness, this broadness of sensibility was the norm. Debussy, for example, sprinkled his musical columns with lively appreciations of Conrad, Chesterton, and Mallarmé and preferred the company of novelists, painters, and poets to that of musicians, whom he considered narrow and provincial. His most obsessive enthusiasm was not for another composer but for Poe, with whom he constantly compared his life and art.

Indeed, until recently, virtually all writing on music was "interdisciplinary." To Schumann, Chopin's Opus 31 Scherzo is "so overflowing with tenderness, boldness, love and contempt that it may be compared, not inappropriately, to a Byron poem." To Paul Rosenfeld, the shifting colors in a Bach keyboard work are comparable to Tintoretto and Cézanne. To the most authoritative writers, art is seen whole, not as a series of confinements to academic boxes, each with its own alienating codes and jargons. Walter Pater's suggestion that all art should "aspire to the condition of music" is not so much the "art for art's sake" cliché it is often made out to be as an indication that all the arts are most naturally seen in relation to each other. Certainly composers see them that way: from Vivaldi to Elliott Carter, they have regularly based their works, instrumental as well as vocal, on literary and other extramusical "programs," no matter how many times critics have pronounced on the superiority of "absolute" music.

For reasons not always clear, some composers seem to inspire better prose than others. Mozart and Varèse, for example, have been written about again and again with wonderful vividness. Even though they are about as different as any two composers could possibly be, they do have one thing in common: a powerful, unmistakable musical personality, a purity and clarity of expression, onto which writers can project their most uninhibited prose. The perfection of the one and the sheer physicality of the other have proved an irresistible draw, one that discourages vagueness and pomposity.

Beethoven has inspired about as much writing as Mozart, but although some of it (by Berlioz, Shaw, Tovey, and others) is exciting, much is pompous and grandstanding. The cosmic scale of Beethoven, coupled with his heroic struggle against deafness, have been occasions for a kind of bombast and sentimentality from which even a normally reliable writer like Romain Rolland has not been exempt.

One of the most stimulating and original writers on Beethoven was Wagner, but Wagner himself has inspired more incoherent prose, both pro and con, than any other composer. In his case, the reasons are not mysterious: as the most polarizing composer of all time, he elicited writing that was often purely ideological—the kind of rant and pontificating that make for bad criticism in any art. As in so many other instances, Shaw provided a model that few were able to emulate; he was a true anomaly, a Wagnerite with a sense of humor. (Only in our own century, in writers ranging from Thomas Mann to Robert Craft, has criticism begun to come to terms with Wagner and his legacy.)

Musical politics, along with a curious propensity toward matters highly technical, also accounts for the relative lack of good writing on old music. Much of the recent work on medieval, Renaissance, and baroque music is either unreadably technical or consists of drum-beating propaganda for (and occasionally against) the "original instruments" movement. Readable pieces on Gregorian chant, Palestrina, or Bach are found most consistently in early twentieth-century writers such as Shaw, Debussy, Schweitzer, Rosenfeld, and Cecil Gray, or more recently in the work of Wilfred Mellers, Nicholas Kenyon, Glenn Gould, and Richard Taruskin—all writers whose love for the music exceeds their obsession with the vintage of the instruments performing it.

In general, nineteenth-century music has probably inspired more writing, both forceful and vapidly sentimental, than that of any other century. This is partly because some of the most natural writers—Hoffmann, Schumann, Berlioz, Liszt, Wolf—were themselves Romantic composers, intimately connected with their subject and eager to reach a growing middle-class audience. It is also because the music itself is highly amenable to verbal musing in a way that more impersonal or classical music is not: besides exhibiting the vividly individual personality already mentioned, it is often programmatic, coming with poems and prose passages appended to the score. This is music that almost demands to be written about.

The amount of writing on twentieth-century music is also prodigious, and although much (especially by composers who provide their own program notes for new works) is horrendously technical and dull, much is also first-rate. Bernstein on Mahler, Ernest Newman on Schönberg, Boulez on Debussy and Webern, Ned Rorem on Ravel, Constant Lambert on Sibelius, Virgil Thomson on Ruggles, Andrew Porter on Boulez and Britten, Wilfred Mellers on Bernstein—these are some of the most perceptive, exciting essays in the literature. The music of our own time, with its remarkable variety and range, exerts a strong pull on writers, even if it does not always do so with general audiences; indeed, if this literature were more widely known, it might help with the much-deplored audience problem: vivid writing on music, especially with the aid of recordings, has the power to seduce the listener into even the most "difficult" composer's world.

The way into that world is through directness and clarity, not technical obfuscation or abstraction. This is the message the great writers on music teach us, again and again. As Charles Rosen and others have pointed out, music is the most abstract art only in that it is the least representational. In every other respect, it is the most immediate, visceral, and sensual of the arts, and the writer who is willing to seize that immediacy and project it back to the reader is the most likely to succeed. The more specific the focus the better, which is why the best essayists tend to write sparingly on the aesthetics of music in general and more lavishly and consistently on particular composers, performers, and musical experiences, even when the piece is not a review. Wagner, for example, anchored much of his highly abstruse discussion of the "music of the future" to a series of passionate takes on the nine Beethoven symphonies; Berlioz described the "science and sentiment" of music in terms of personal physical responses ranging from nausea and dizziness to elation. Jacques Barzun, in his "Music into Words," (the following essay) has written lucidly on the general principles of this elusive but curiously emotional art. Suffice it to say here that these ground rules are not terribly arcane or rigid; they are very close, in fact, to the strategies involved in writing any elegant, readable criticism of the arts.

No music, of course, absolutely needs verbal overtures or codas, any more than any other art does. But perhaps we should heed King Lear and "reason not the need," for to do otherwise would be to suppress one of music's most luxurious pleasures. For when we read Albert Schweitzer on Bach, the cantatas and oratorios come alive in our imaginations with dramatic pictures; when we read H. L. Mencken or Desmond Shawe-Taylor on Schubert, that composer seems to sing on the page; when we read Paul Rosenfeld or Henry Miller on Varèse, the latter's "sound masses" screech and thunder like a subway at rush hour; when we read Heinrich Heine on Chopin or Berlioz, not only the composers but the Romantic epoch comes alive more vividly than in any novel. These literary experiences can only heighten the musical one. Our minds and hearts quicken, waiting to hear the real thing. Or, if we have just heard it, we are granted an occasion to turn it over once again, voluptuously, in our minds.

# Music into Words

## JACQUES BARZUN

*Originally a lecture delivered at the Library of Congress in 1951, this piece has been revised by the author as the opening essay for this volume, where it serves as an informal poetics and statement of principles. One of the most distinguished and wide-ranging cultural historians of our time, Jacques Barzun has enriched the intellectual life of the past half century with books ranging from* Darwin, Marx, Wagner *to* Berlioz and His Century, *from* A Stroll with William James *to* A Catalogue of Crime. *In "Music into Words," he unites a number of lifelong interests in a freewheeling disquisition on the relationship between music and the other arts—a central concern of this book—as well as on the more specific topic of how to write about music, on the large question of what criticism in general does as well as the more particular one of why words on music are useful, pleasurable, and inevitable. Jacques Barzun has always been dedicated to the proposition that essays on the arts, including music, should be directed to the educated layperson and written in ordinary language, with its infinite possibilities and nuances, rather than in specialist jargon. "Music into Words" is an admirable embodiment of that principle.*

Are there genuine connections between music and words, or only accidental associations, some of them tolerable but most of them forced or farfetched? Is it possible to describe music in ordinary prose, or is technical jargon indispensable? And if description is allowed—perhaps "translation" would be the fitter term—does its possibility imply that music conveys a meaning outside itself, like the arts of literature and painting?

On the answer to these questions a good many of our activities depend for their justification—the whole status and value of music criticism for one. Every concert goer is something of a music critic when he offers a judgment on what he has just heard. Or can it be that words are meaningless, that one is saying nothing with great vehemence? Again, the teaching of music is inseparable from comment, appreciation, and interpretation of styles. Are all the words of all the patient souls who push young talents through the mill so much gibberish? People say so even as they go on gibbering: they have been told so often that music is music; immaterial, elusive, absolute, and no words can apply to it.

Hence discourse about music must remain technical. If so it can only interest professionals, and it is limited to salient points within a piece. A bar-by-bar technical analysis of a large work would be unendurable even to professionals—in short, great works of music are unquestionably great but their greatness is as it were unspeakable.

Such is the prevailing view. It has an astringent quality which was no doubt needed when the looseness of gushing "appreciation" became general during the nineteenth century. But on reflection this self-denial about words appears a rather crude remedy, which I suspect is now used out of intellectual pride rather than reasoned reflection. Indeed it is childish to keep reminding the world that inarticulate sounds are not articulate. The formidable question remains, why the great musicians, the great critics, and the great public keep talking about music as if their words meant something.

This historical fact is unquestionable: there is a vast literature of stories, sketches, essays, confessions, letters, and anecdotes in every European language, which gives an excellent idea of what music is for, what it is like, how it lives and moves in the lives of those attuned to it. The authors include great composers from Monteverdi to Van Dieren; great writers from Cellini to Shaw; great performers (who might also be writers and composers) from Bach to Busoni. The cliché about music being undiscussable must be therefore deemed local and temporary. The older permanent truth is that music can be talked about like any other art; and perhaps it must be talked about if it is to give its devotees the full measure of enjoyment and significance.

But, what is remarkable is that no author or composer in the span of four centuries has tried to make rational the connection between his words and the musical experience that he discussed. All take the connection as self-evident, which must be because these literary and musical artists lacked on that point the benefit of modern skeptical thought. Given this skepticism, we are compelled to argue in favor of the position unconsciously taken in the past, though at the same time it would be foolish to neglect whatever may be found valid in the negative view.

To take off from that, we must first separate the upholders of it into musical people, who usually accept the antiverbal view without argument, and literary people, who feel vaguely overawed by music and who put forward the discrepancies between the two arts. The literary person proclaims that "he knows nothing" about music (though he listens with enjoyment) and says he is tongue-tied because of his ignorance of technicalities. His argument amounts to saying: "I am a man of words; if words could be used about music I should be able to produce them; I can't, hence music is an experience absolutely self-contained."

The rejoinder to this reasoning is that the "literary" listener has perhaps not sufficiently reflected on his own experience of music. How can a man "know nothing" about sensations he has undergone willingly, repeatedly, and pleasurably for years, for a lifetime? Obviously he is confusing the conventions of a trade with the bases of human knowledge. He is suffering from the modern error of supposing that knowledge and professionalism are synonymous; by which principle primitive man could never have learned to build bridges since there were as yet no schools of engineering.

Turn now to the professional or the accomplished amateur musician. Immersed as he is in performing and in judging performance, he has no need to search for precise critical language. Music for him is quite truthfully a self-contained experience. He can share it with his fellows by an almost bodily communication of sympathy. He is moreover so busy practicing or composing or coaching others—not to speak of putting up music stands and dog-earing scores—that he rarely has time to classify his impressions. The violinist who is also a reader senses that the Razoumowsky Quartets do not pertain to the Napoleonic Wars as does Tolstoy's *War and Peace*. Moreover, he assumes that he knows all there is to know about music and concludes that it is an art diametrically opposed to the so-called "representative" arts of literature and painting. If challenged, he would clinch his case by pointing out that each word in the language has a distinct meaning, whereas single notes or chords mean nothing, and thus may mean anything.

It is here that the counter argument must take hold and dispose of the platitudes about words. It is not true that words have intrinsic meanings; it is not true that meanings reside in single words. Turn to the dictionary and look up a common noun: the first striking fact about it is that it has eight, ten, a dozen, or a score of meanings. If someone bursts into a crowded room shouting "Chair!" it is impossible to tell whether he is asking for a seat or calling upon the chairman. He may be a mad professor who has been deprived of his post—for in a University a chair is a post . . . which is why it cannot be sat on. In an eighteenth-century novel a chair is a vehicle, and in a twentieth-century drawing room a chair is almost anything that is not a rug or a lamp. This last fact reminds us how wrong it is to say that a word automatically puts us in mind of an object. On hearing "chair" and being told that it means a seat, anyone will visualize something different; a thousand people will picture a thousand dissimilar objects. "Chair" is really that sound we can fill with meaning only with the help of other words and of knowledge that cannot be put into words.

In everyday life we can seldom understand the snatches of conversation overheard on the street, the quick undertones exchanged within a strange family, or the easy allusions of other men talking shop. In short, there is nothing mechanical about verbal meanings. All communication in words remains an art, no matter how habitual; and like every art it is made up of more elements than can ever be enumerated. Tone of voice, gesture, and facial expression, choice and placement of words, omission and superfluity of sounds, plus the indefinite sphere of relevancies that we call context, all play their role in the transmission of meaning.

Discourse about art and criticism forgets these basic truths. Speech is so common that we do not analyze its mysteries, and as a result comparisons among the arts are strangely distorted. The stuff of each art is assigned some flat, blunt attributes that supposedly exclude one another: words point to things and ideas; paint can reproduce the visible world of nature; music is pure form; architecture is machinery for living groups; poetry, dance, and music are time arts; the plastic and graphic arts are concerned with space— none of these aphorisms is without suggestiveness and importance, but not one of them is wholly and exclusively true. Thus, one can say that the two forms of sound called speech and music are alike in requiring the addition of extraneous elements before they can make a significant impression on a human mind.

And even so the comparison remains a little unfair to words, for the parallel drawn has been between the art of music and the merely workaday use of speech. If we pass from daily talk to literature proper, the force of all that has been shown is augmented manifold. Augmented and also complicated by the presence of what we recognize as artistry. The line between the utilitarian and the literary uses of speech cannot be drawn; it is circumstantial and shifting, and this variability is reproduced in all of the fine arts. A bugle sounding taps in camp says "go to bed" just as clearly as the vesper bell says "come to church." This is by context and convention, exactly as in articulate speech. But in an opera those same musical sounds would be quite transfigured and charged with new meanings. Again, certain pieces of music, for instance a jig or a Virginia reel, though they utter no distinct message, are nevertheless little else than invitations to the dance. The appeal to mind or spirit is slight, whereas the pull upon the legs is powerful. Yet a dance movement in a Bach suite or the finale of Beethoven's Seventh Symphony uses the same conventional rhythms and figures with wholly different effect.

It is therefore not the presence or absence of conventional forms and phrases that distinguishes art from messages of utility, or that distinguishes the art of music from any other. All we can say is that art differs from workaday communication in that it transcends the literal—not excludes it or denies it, for it often contains it—but goes beyond.

If this is so, then another imaginary barrier between music and the other arts disappears: no art denotes or gives out information. We can test this generality by considering a passage of literature, say the scene in Shakespeare where Hamlet finds Yorick's skull and says: "I knew him, Horatio; a fellow of infinite jest, of most excellent fancy. He hath borne me on his back a thousand times. And now how abhorrèd in my imagination it is! My gorge rises at it. Here hung those lips that I have kissed I know not how oft . . ." etc. Clearly these words are not to *inform* us that Hamlet knew Yorick. They do not answer the question that a lawyer might put: did you or did you not know and associate with one Yorick, deceased? Their purpose is quite other, namely to impress us with certain realities of death and thus to heighten the shock with which we shall soon see Ophelia's burial procession. Nor is this all. The words, while disclosing yet another aspect of Hamlet's character, suggest his constant harking back to the old days when his father reigned; moreover, the facts presented fit and sustain the brooding atmosphere of the whole play, so that the effect—as it is the purpose—of those simple words is to reverberate endlessly.

If, contrariwise, Hamlet came on and said: "Death really does dreadful things to the nicest, jolliest people," the gist of his remarks would be exactly what it is in the scene as we have it, but the impression made would be nil. The *meaning* that only art conveys would be blotted out. Meaning is altogether unlike information: notice the small but effective shift from Hamlet's "he" and "him," denoting the Yorick he remembers, to: "How abhorrèd in my imagination it is." It is at once Hamlet's recollection and Yorick turned to earth. This, if I may say so, is the secret of literature; the adjective "literary" means: doing this sort of thing with words; it does not mean using words to denote physical objects and familiar ideas.

For conceivably Shakespeare could have used many other objects, invented other details, to serve his same purpose in the same way. Hence we should never mistake the *literal* ballast of the sentences for the literary meaning of the piece. The play—any play—is not about the people, notions, or cocktail glasses that it juggles with; in a strict sense literature is not *about* anything, it *is*—precisely like music. And precisely like music, like any art, literature offers a presentment having significance. What kind of significance I will suggest in a moment; at this point it is enough to conclude that the things signified are not the things named.

If it should be objected that a poetic drama such as *Hamlet* is not a fair test (even though the passage chosen was common prose), I would remind the objector of a scene in *Madame Bovary,* a prose work notoriously designed to exhibit the prosaic in life. In the novel, Flaubert makes one of the principal love scenes take place in a cab that keeps driving aimlessly round and round the provincial city; the incident is in keeping with the rest of the story, but it is safe to say that anyone who believes in the literal circuit of that vehicle knows nothing about love, cabs, or literature.

Here, of course, one must beware of falling into the trap of symbolic interpretation: the cab does not "stand for" anything. Such an explanation would only be literalism at the second remove, duller still than the simple-minded sort. Let someone suggest that Flaubert's cab means the wild drive of the passions, or the vicious circle of sensuality, and the very thought makes one groan. Why? Because it is limiting and mechanical; it sets us to solving riddles instead of grasping meanings. Allegories are frigid for this very reason, that they seem to offer significance only to dilute it into information. Similarly, works of literature that communicate by means of broad generalities about love, death, fate or revenge are invariably tedious and, paradoxically, false. We cease to believe in propositions which in other contexts we should readily accept. And this in turn explains why it is fatal for an author to go directly after the eternal verities. He can state them, but the statement won't be art; for let me repeat at the risk of being tedious myself, literature does not reside in propositions; though it may say a great deal, it tells nothing; it thereby resembles music: it is a composition of meanings.

If this assertion is true we should expect that great works of literature, in spite of being verbally explicit, would give rise to different interpretations. This is exactly what we find. No two critics agree about the meaning of any given masterpiece, and the greater the work the greater the disagreement. This remains true after the most laborious reading of the text and the most honest attention to previous commentaries. From this one can infer what must be the unspoken differences that co-exist in the thousands of minds which have read *Hamlet* or *The Divine Comedy*. We get a glimpse of this chaos of opinion when we discover what an earlier century thought of a work that we think we know well: it seems like a wholly other treatment of the same subject—the movie we gape at after reading the novel.*

This divergence receives and strengthens the parallel between the art of words and the art of music. I have in mind the argument

---

*Note that within living memory Mozart has turned from a gay, superficial composer into a profound and tragic one.

that denies clear meaning to a piece of music because no two listeners give the same account of it. Yet, it will be said, no one will ever confuse what happens in *Hamlet* with what happens in *King Lear,* whereas your musical program hunter will hear the waves of the ocean in a piece which another takes for the Rape of the Sabine Women. Quite so, but this contrast is only superficially correct. The plots of Shakespeare's dramas are not likely to be confused because they are the skeleton, not the significance of the piece; whereas what the programmatizer hopes to tell us with his ocean or his Sabines is the significance, the upshot, the net effect. If we want in music the true parallel of plot we must look for the form of the work and its key relationships, a skeleton about which there will be no confusion either, assuming an educated listener.

Returning now to significance, we may grant that the inditer of programs is almost certain to fail; he fails, that is, to convince us that the piece is the same things as, or a true copy of, a storm on the ocean. He fails because he has tried to equate a work of art with a proposition or with the name of a thing or an idea; and we rebel against this either because we know equation to be impossible or, in less conscious moments, because we have a pet label of our own, which clashes with the other.

Thus when Sir Laurence Olivier produced his motion picture version of *Hamlet* he prefaced it with a short explanation—a few programmatic words—that defined the forthcoming action as "the tragedy of a man who could not make up his mind." My feelings were immediately up in arms against this hoary misinterpretation of a play in which the hero makes up his mind quickly, repeatedly, and brilliantly. But the play would not be more accurately described by maintaining the opposite of Olivier's view. Rather, we must give up these attempts at summarizing. Is Tolstoy's *War and Peace* a novel about Napoleon—no, certainly not; and yet . . . well, yes and no. Is *Don Giovanni* an opera about a Spanish libertine? Does the Ninth Symphony celebrate the brotherhood of man? Is Velasquez' "Surrender at Breda" an historical painting? Yes and no; yes and no; yes and no. The "yes" answer is correct in the same sense as the statement that the earth is one of the planets. It *is* one of the planets, but to an earth dweller it does not feel like one: there is so much more to say, a myriad qualities to add, which swamp the mere definition.

The analogy is one to which the critic of the arts must keep coming back: a great work resembles an animated realm that the beholder inhabits as well as perceives. It is various, extensive, treacherous, perfectly still and yet in constant motion. Like the moon seen from a vehicle, it follows one about while looking down with indifference. The masterpiece mirrors the mind of one man and of all men; it annoys, delights, instructs, and sometimes preaches, though it contradicts itself and other revelations that are equally true; it shapes the conduct of multitudes who have never so much as heard of it, and it is often powerless to improve the behavior of those who study and believe its message. It was created out of nothing, but pieces of other worlds lie embedded in it like meteorites; it is the cause of endless unimaginable creations after itself, yet its own existence is so precarious that its survival often suggests miraculous intervention through the agency of fools and thieves. It seems to have neither purpose not utility, though it commands veneration, it bestows money and prestige, and it arouses a hunger that some find insatiable.

This and much else is the fluid phenomenon named Art, which we try to decant into our little individual flasks of consciousness with the aid of words. The attempt must seem hopeless until we remember that it is quite like another task which we have no option but to perform—the task of organizing the experience of living. We begin this second task as soon as we learn to talk, and the volume of words which comes out thereafter shows how necessary we feel discourse to be, even about familiar acts. But the words by which we capture the flux of life were not given mankind ready-made. Hard as it is to believe, the best words, like the worst clichés, had to be invented; they were once strange and fresh; and the entire charting of our perceptions, from stomachache to religious ecstasy, had to be made bit by bit like a geodetic survey. The coverage is by now so extensive that we forget its historical growth, its slow progress towards sharper and sharper adequacy. We come to believe that every experience for which we have a word, be it heartburn, hypocrisy, or ambivalence, was a plain fact from the beginning. Nothing could be further from the truth. Each piece of reality had to be carved out from all its neighboring parts, had to be named, and the name elaborately explained until it became a commonplace.

If we agree to see art as a source of meaning, something like the carving and naming of experience is bound to take place about art also. Something *like* it, rather than the identical thing. For we have yet to consider the way art and life are related and the kinds of words that apply to each. Life, art, discourse form an eternal triangle within which it is difficult to avoid missteps. We can err about life and suppose that the experience of it has been pretty thoroughly charted. We know, for example, what anger is. Yet each angry man, each bout of anger, is in some respects unlike any other. The common words by which to mark those differences soon run out. We feel about our anger, or that of our friends, or about any vivid example of an enemy's anger, an inexpressible immediacy and richness that overflows the poor word. What do we do about that? We turn to art. We refer to Achilles' rage, to the furies, to Othello, or to any other creations that we have "experienced" as if they embodied those fireworks of feeling erupting from the abstract core of human anger.

But it is not because Shakespeare copies, it is because he discriminates and distills that we go to him for an extension of awareness. He—or any artist—enlarges the scope of our perceptions without throwing us back into the total stream. For one thing, the choice of a single medium, such as words or paint, brings clarification. Through it the artist gives us not life but equivalent sensations sorted out and organized. There is no anger in the stage Othello nor in ourselves watching him.

But contrary to a prevalent notion, it is not the organizing that is fundamental, or else we could take no pleasure in fragments of ancient sculpture. The fundamental thing is that the fragment can speak to us. In color and texture it is as unlike flesh as can be, but the equivalence intended by the human fashioner still holds for the human observer. In other words, the several arts compel the different materials at hand to serve the curious purpose of producing sensations that we recognize as commentaries on our existence. By convention some of these materials seem to be "closer" than others to the original impression of life, but this is an illusion. Stone is not closer to flesh than word is to thing. Just think of the immense diversity of words used in different languages for the same things, the great diversity of styles used in the graphic arts for the creation of lifelikeness, and the enormously rapid change in musical genres without much change in the effect produced on human beings. The means of artistic communication are infinite, and a tapestry is as lifelike as a ballet.

It would be easy to rely on logic and say that since all this is true of the arts and since music is an art, music must also present an equivalence of life. Many would continue to doubt the validity of the reasoning. Does music embody anger, or manifest hypocrisy? And was it not admitted earlier that music doesn't *tell*? Of course, literature doesn't tell either; what are we to think?

Perhaps an example will make things clear. In the introduction to the first movement of Beethoven's Ninth Symphony we are given sensations contrived in such a way that the ear—the thinking ear, that is—remains uncertain of the tonality, the direction, the fulfill-ment of the sounds. This is protracted until the tutti comes crashing down upon us in D Minor and all doubts are at an end. This is a favorite effect of Beethoven's, another instance being the transition from the Scherzo to the finale of the Fifth.

Now, why is it "an effect"—an affecting thing? Why do we re-spond to it, and respond to it, I should imagine, all alike even though it may cause annoyance to some and pleasure to others? The impres-sion as a whole has no name, and no good would be served by calling it Resolution of Uncertainty. Any such term is limiting, literal, and—one may properly add—unmusical. Just so: music is a medium through which certain unnamable experiences of life are exquisitely conveyed through equivalent sensations for the ear. As Mr. Roger Sessions has admirably put it: "Emotion is specific, individual, and conscious; music goes deeper than this, to the energies which ani-mate our psychic life. . . . It reproduces for us the most intimate essence, the tempo, and the energy of our spiritual being; our tran-quillity and our restlessness, our animation and our discourage-ment . . .—all, in fact, of the fine shades . . . of our inner life."

I would qualify this statement in one way, which seems to me all-important: although music is not like, nor about, namable emotions, being neither literal nor abstract, it has a way of interweaving itself with some of our perceptions that do have names, and so tempts us to tag the music with the experience of which we are reminded. This accounts for the programmatizing, the titling of pieces large and small, and the inevitable amateur comments about passages that are

"like sunset on the Matterhorn" or "like the kiss of an archangel."
Notice that these analogies are usually with the rare and the fanciful,
precisely because they are not readily namable in spite of their vividness and intimacy. If you should ask, "what is the kiss of an archangel
like?" you would probably be told, "It's just like the close of the
Siegfried Idyll."

The fact that music begins to speak to us at the point where
words stop accounts also for something rather more important and
certainly more aboriginal—the fact that articulate and inarticulate
sounds can combine to form one meaning: I refer to the fact that
songs can be composed and understood. If a good judge can say that
one setting of given words is better than another, it is not merely
because one tune is better adapted to the conventional accent of
those words, but also because it wraps itself more snugly around their
significance. We appreciate this in reverse when we remark that the
Star-Spangled Banner is a tune somewhat wanting in martial fire and
ill-adapted to the patriotic feeling of the words. When we know that
its traditional form was that of a convivial song "To Anacreon in
Heaven," we recognize its fitness to that theme and discover that the
awkward wandering of the notes turns from blemish to expressiveness.

Music's power to present the sensations missing from the verbal
signs of an experience explains why as a general rule the text of the
best songs and operas is inferior to the musical setting. A great poem
is complete in itself and needs no addition from another art. Great
music is complete in itself, and only a disagreeable overlap of intentions can result from its being harnessed to great literature. Fortunately, many musicians have shown a certain indifference to poetic
expression and thus have expended their powers on verse that was
literal and required to be made into art. We then enjoy both the
independent beauty of the music and the pleasure of its adaptation
to a rudimentary conception in words.

This rudimentary conception is present, of course, in instrumental music, to which we must return as the final test of our thesis.
For music has taken rank among the high arts by virtue of its relatively recent emergence as a presentment that can stand by itself: all
its claims to absoluteness and disconnection from life rest on the fact
that intelligent people will sit silent and motionless for twenty minutes while upwards of a hundred men blow and scrape "meaningless"

notes. But consider this strange institution. In order to find one's way in this supposed desert of significance, it appears advisable to distinguish "suspensions" of sound, "resolutions," cadences (or fallings) in appoggiaturas (or leanings), sequences (something like raised eyebrows), broken chords and what not other inarticulate suggestions of bodily experience. Again, the movements are called (in Italian, to be sure) gay, fast, walking, dying, joking, or retarded—all in defiance of plain fact, since nothing moves or dies, is suspended or resolved. Stranger still, there is often a madman, sandwiched between the performing and the listening lunatics, who is delegated to lead and interpret the meaningless sounds by means of a pantomime which is said to be as necessary as it is expensive.

When the noise and gestures have subsided, the audience are heard to say whether the new piece has merit and the old one was played right. Obviously they are comparing the flood of sensations with a preexisting pattern in their minds or memories, a pattern which they ascribe a value akin to revelation. The sensations offered are extraordinarily complex and the receiving mind must be extraordinarily acute, for it sometimes happens that all the notes of a familiar piece are played in the right order at the right speed, and yet good judges declare they could hardly recognize the work. It lacked force or coherence or was subtly bereft of its accustomed virtue. This fairly usual experience surely goes to prove that music communicates something beyond the relation of its audible parts. It conveys a meaning which some people catch and others do not; a meaning which is not in the notes, since these can be played correctly and yet meaninglessly; a meaning which is not universally intelligible, since listeners vary in their judgement of composers, of works, or performances; a meaning which like verbal meaning depends on a mass of previous knowledge and educated feeling.

This last thought is not merely one of common observation, it has also been the subject of experiment. The classic statement of the results is that of Dr. Philip Vernon, a British musician and psychologist, who sixty years ago subjected the Cambridge Musical Society to a series of tests proving conclusively that to consider music a purely auditory experience is contrary to fact. His report should be read and pondered by anyone who believes that, whatever vulgar souls may do, his own response to music is the contemplation of pure form. The facts are enlightening and amusing, both, and they prove how much that is commonly deemed non-musical goes into intelligent listening.

The reason for this paradox is that the artist-composer, even while he attends to the demands of his material or to his formal design, consciously or unconsciously endows the piece with qualities that correspond to his grasp of life as a whole. The order in which he puts things, the things he repeats and the things he avoids; the suggestions, emphases, and climaxes; the pace of his thought and the intensity of his will; the stops, the false starts, the crashes, and the silences—everything he does or leaves undone—is a signal that evokes in the listener the nameless features of life. The composer has no autobiographical intention; he may be a dramatist composing the wordless biography of some imaginary being, like Mozart depicting Figaro or the Queen of the Night; but the concourse of sounds is as surely the equivalent of a lived experience as are the lines of an expressive face or the gestures of an inspired actor.

The conclusion is inescapable that musical meaning relates to the existence of the creature that man is, not solely because music delights man, and not solely because he assigns to it a value beyond mere delight, but because it requires from him a special attention to particulars within and without his own mind. He must, as we say, understand the idiom, that is, he must record and relate the multitude of sensations aroused in him, and assimilate them: the very word shows the link between music and life.

It follows that what the artist has put together, the critic can take apart and restate in the foreign tongue of prose. In doing this, he does no more than account to himself and others for what he has undergone. The critic may, for example, ask himself how it is that some works using all the devices of the art according to rule are nonetheless dull, whereas others are not only agreeable but great? One composer, we say, has ideas, another has not. But this is to repeat the fact without explaining it. The ideas we refer to are obviously something other than clever tricks for linking the common elements of the medium, though this cleverness is not to be despised when, as we also say, there is a point to it. Bach is not a great composer because he was adept at counterpoint, but because he had a purpose in using it. Gluck is a great composer despite the clumsiness of his technique—if art that is successful can ever be called clumsy. When we perceive something we value, it is idle to carp at the means employed, art being the first and truest pragmatism.

But criticism immediately asks how a diversity of means can achieve similar results. This remains a complete mystery unless we admit the proposition to which our long argument has been leading, namely, that the "point" of speech or music or art is to summon up and give shape to the stuff of human experience. Anything we understand, we understand in the light of human experience, actual or potential. We must bring our little share of wisdom and remembered life with us, or else remain deaf and dumb to messages most heavenly, since neither words, nor paint, nor music nor science can unload at our feet the full cargo of reality.

For "potential experience" we have the word Imagination, and it is this faculty that the artist possesses in great strength and uses to spur our own. By a combination of instinct and design he so orders the elements of his art that the interplay of contrived sensations produces new meanings. Our attention is arrested and sustained. The stream of impressions holds us because it refers to our past and future being, to our conscious or submerged memories, to our anxieties and our purposes; it arouses and satisfies our expectations on all planes, from rhythmic sympathy with our heartbeat to the flattery of our ego by subtlety.

When I say that the work of art, the musical masterpiece, does all this, I mean that in any given instance it may do some or all of these things. At first, the very great work may appear to do none of them: it defies our expectations and unpleasantly disturbs our heartbeat. Our ego is flouted and our anxieties increased. We leave the concert hall muttering. But history has taught us that we should expose ourselves to the work again and again until one of two things happens: either we reject the alien vision for good, or we adopt it by adapting to it. It is to help acceptance by removing doubts and dispelling mysteries that criticism exists. The traditional belief that criticism is intended to separate the good from the bad seems to be a confusion between means and ends. It may at times be necessary to point out the bad, but only as a corollary to defining the character of a piece by imputing to it an intention that is bad, or an intention that is good but poorly executed. Again, those who maintain that criticism judges and gives grades for the sake of the artist's next performance mistake criticisms for teaching. Even the teacher might be said not so much to pass judgement as to show the pupil, like a critic, what the pupil's own work does and fails to do.

The role of critic then, is to act as go-between, as midwife, between the artist's conception and the beholder's recognition of it in the created thing. An undertaking so ambitious is never perfect or complete, which is why there can hardly be too much criticism—despite the artist's conviction that there are too many critics. The remedy to this excess is to improve the quality of criticism by making stringent demands on those who criticize. In music particularly we should be very exacting, and also very receptive, because music criticism is still in its infancy, and the clichés and prejudices I have discussed hamper its maturing. The composer and his admirers deny the possibility of translating "music into words," though the leap from the one to the other medium is the same for all the arts. It is the same because all the arts concern themselves with one central subject matter, which is the stream of impressions, named and unnamed, that human beings call their life.

Provided the critic is himself at home in life, in music, and in words, he will not blur in his reader's mind the difference between life and art and between words and music. His remarks will show that meaning lies beyond the thing said. Replace literalism by imagination and you have got rid of the bugbear of "programmatic" interpretation.

Remains the question of vocabulary. What words are appropriate to lead the listener into the neighborhood of musical understanding and give him the push that will make him land in the very center of perception? A full answer would amount to a manual of critical practice. Its most general principles are implicit in what I have said. First, the criticism of music, like that of the other arts, must be written for the layman; an educated layman if possible. Such a reader may be expected to pick up some few technical terms used simply to point to a part of the work. Just as in a painting attention is drawn to a "patch of cobalt blue in the middle distance," so the music critic may refer to the cadence, the tutti, the arpeggios, or the second subject. More complicated references must be reserved for the learned journals, exactly as the literary scholar reserves his discussion of acatalectic meters and double syllepsis. Such matters have importance for the trade, not for the public.

Having singled out what he considers noteworthy, the critic

explains what makes it so. Here he uses ordinary words and the range of possible phraseology is infinite. No one can predict what type of commentary will enlighten a particular mind, though it is safe to say that a critic ought to be aware of current doctrines and superstitions.

Nothing is excluded on principle. The facts of history, biography, psychology, poetry, architecture, or of any art or science may be equally relevant. Analogies may be drawn from the workshop or the boudoir, provided always that anything said makes a point and that the point relates to some precise part of the musical experience.

This is a tall order and the record shows that it cannot be carried out without recourse to analogy. The proposition need not be argued again, that things in this world are often alike, though no more than alike. We may therefore say A is to B as C is to D. The statement of a bold critic long ago that the overture to *Figaro* was like champagne means: the sensation in my palate when I drink the celebrated wine resembles the sensation in my ears when I listen to the celebrated overture. The analogy might of course be boiled down to the single adjective "sparkling," but words of this convenient sort tend to lose their sharpness by overuse. Hence the critical obligation to keep inventing analogies and employing their very strangeness to force attention.

Analogy is of course not without danger. It can impart an indelible character to the work or the passage it seeks to illuminate. Much nineteenth-century music suffers from having a certain kind of poetical character stamped upon it. The Moonlight Sonata, the Pathétique, the Appassionata, have themselves become trite through their label, as if the suggestiveness of the music were itself threadbare. Perhaps the most striking example is that of Berlioz's *Fantastic Symphony,* in which five movements differing markedly in atmosphere are heard and spoken of as if all were demonic like the last; the result being that the adagio, one of the loveliest of pastoral movements, hardly penetrates the mind-hardened eardrum. Such misconceptions are perhaps inevitable; they result from criticism, and better criticism is the only antidote.

The existence of apt criticism matters not only to artists and amateurs but also to society at large. In a civilization as old and changeful as ours there is a constant movement between art and social thought. Ideas, attitudes, models for the mind and the body come from the artist and are popularized by the critic. New forms arise as the old filter downwards. This is what Shelley meant when he called poets "the unacknowledged legislators of the world." And music's effect is surely as strong as poetry's, acting as it does on the nerves and the very bowels of mankind. But because the art in its higher reaches is wonderfully complex, its action is uncertain and diffuse. It takes the critic speaking the speech of the literate man to arouse in that man the desire for music new and strange, and to ease the road to pleasure through that desire.

The goal to keep in view is meaning. It is meaning that makes sensations cohere, meaning that rewards and justifies the groping eye, ear, mind. In our century we have assimilated, among other things, primitive sculpture and non-objective art; in the previous century, inanimate nature as a realm of art—the traditional god of thunder had long departed and the earth spirits were mute; but now the mountain echoes began to speak ethics and esthetics and to inspire masterpieces in their own image. There is no reason why hereafter the meaning of music should not become just as well understood as that of the eternal hills. If the critics seek the way, this civilizing effort will not prove a superhuman task. The language of criticism by which we assess literature was not found ready-made. It had to be invented, phrase by phrase and term by term. And so it must be for music. Once made and tested by public use, the critic's grammar and vocabulary are available to all. Music will then no longer be a thing apart, cut off from the sphere of pleasure and significance. Every literate being will feel as free to translate music into words as he now is to translate love, religion, the joy of living, or the spectacle of nature. It will then be a platitude rather than a heresy to say with Hazlitt: "We listen to the notes of a thrush with delight from the circumstance not only of sound, but of seasons, of solitude, the recollections of a country life, and of our own."

Finally, under that dispensation, the division with which we started, of two clans using the words "literary" and "musical" as terms of faint abuse or misplaced pride—that division will abolish itself, and all persons with artistic feelers of whatever kind will share equally the blessings of a common tongue.

(Extracted by the author from an address at the Library of Congress, October 23, 1951.)

# Three Diatribes

## GEORGE BERNARD SHAW

*With typical self-deprecation, George Bernard Shaw wrote in 1932 that only those interested in "dead Prima donnas" would ever read his music criticism. Since then he has come to be regarded as one of the great music critics in English, described by Andrew Porter of the* New Yorker *as "the delight and despair of anyone who tries himself to write about music," and by W. H. Auden as "probably the best music critic who ever lived." Though Shaw is best known as a playwright and polemicist, his writing on music may well be the most perfect specimen of his art. Here we find the celebrated Shavian wit in its most impish, undiluted form (the Brahms Requiem is "the work of a first-class undertaker"; the Mendelssohn "Scotch" Symphony "would be great if it were not so confoundedly genteel"); here we find the most lucid exposition of his egalitarian ideals and his hatred of pretention. Music was Shaw's first love, from his early stints as music critic on the* Star *(1888–90) and the* World *(1890–94) to his final words on the subject in 1950, the year of his death. To Shaw, music was the most basic of the arts: he was fond of saying that a knowledge of music was more important for an understanding of his plays than a knowledge of literature. Shaw expended far more energy writing music criticism than writing about it, but his few words on the subject in his regular column for the* World *are gems of pithy insight. The following passages, cast in characteristically Shavian modes of irony, speak volumes about the importance of lucidity and passion and the pitfalls of pretention and obfuscation.*

1

Although I have not, at the moment of writing this, seen Cavalleria Rusticana, my refusal to buy the score has not left me in total ignorance of the work. Do not be alarmed, I am not going to perpetrate an "analysis." Those vivid emotions which the public derive from descriptions of "postludes brought to a close on the pedal of A, the cadence being retarded by four chords forming an arpeggio of a diminished seventh, each grade serving as tonic for a perfect chord," must be sought elsewhere than in these columns. It is perhaps natural that gentlemen who are incapable of criticism should fall back on parsing; but, for my own part, I find it better to hold my tongue when I have nothing to say. Yet I cannot help chuckling at the tricks they play on their innocent editors. An editor never does know anything about music, though his professions to that effect invariably belie his secret mind.

I have before me a journal in which the musical critic has induced the editor to allow him to launch into music type in order to give a suggestion of a certain "fanciful and suggestive orchestral design" in Cavalleria Rusticana. The quotation consists of a simple figuration of the common chord of G sharp minor, with "etc." after it. If a literary critic had offered this editor such a sample of the style of Shakespear as

"Now is the," etc.

he would probably have remonstrated. But he is perfectly happy with his chord of G sharp minor, which is ten times more absurd. And yet that editor devotes a column of his paper to criticizing me in the most disrespectful manner. Can he wonder that my sense of public duty does not permit me to remain silent on the subject of his utter incapacity within my special province?

(*World*, October 21, 1891.)

———

2

Somebody has sent me a cutting from which I gather that a proposal to form a critics' club has reached the very elementary stage of being discussed in the papers in August. Now clearly a critic should not belong to a club at all. He should not know anybody:

his hand should be against every man, and every man's hand against his. Artists insatiable by the richest and most frequent doses of praise; entrepreneurs greedy for advertisement; people without reputations who want to beg or buy them ready made; the rivals of the praised; the friends, relatives, partisans, and patrons of the damned: all these have their grudge against the unlucky Minos in the stalls, who is himself criticized in the most absurd fashion.

People have pointed out evidences of personal feeling in my notices as if they were accusing me of a misdemeanor, not knowing that a criticism written without personal feeling is not worth reading. It is the capacity for making good or bad art a personal matter that makes a man a critic. The artist who accounts for my disparagement by alleging personal animosity on my part is quite right: when people do less than their best, and do that less at once badly and self-complacently, I hate them, loathe them, detest them, long to tear them limb from limb and strew them in gobbets about the stage or platform. (At the Opera, the temptation to go out and ask one of the sentinels for the loan of his Martini, with a round or two of ammunition, that I might rid the earth of an incompetent conductor or a conceited and careless artist, has come upon me so strongly that I have been withheld only by my fear that, being no marksman, I might hit the wrong person and incur the guilt of slaying a meritorious singer.)

In the same way, really fine artists inspire me with the warmest personal regard, which I gratify in writing my notices without the smallest reference to such monstrous conceits as justice, impartiality, and the rest of the ideals. When my critical mood is at its height, personal feeling is not the word: it is passion: the passion for artistic perfection—for the noblest beauty of sound, sight, and action—that rages in me. Let all young artists look to it, and pay no heed to the idiots who declare that criticism should be free from personal feeling. The true critic, I repeat, is the man who becomes your personal enemy on the sole provocation of a bad performance, and will only be appeased by good performances. Now this, though well for art and for the people, means that the critics are, from the social or clubable point of view, veritable fiends. They can only fit themselves for other people's clubs by allowing themselves to be corrupted by kindly feelings foreign to the purpose of art, unless, indeed, they join Philistine clubs, wherein neither the library nor the social economy of the place will suit their nocturnal, predatory habits. If they must have a club, let them have a pandemonium of their own, furnished with all the engines of literary vivisection. But its first and most sacred rule must be the exclusion of the criticized, except those few stalwarts who regularly and publicly turn upon and criticize their critics. (No critics' club would have any right to the name unless it included—but the printer warns me that I have reached the limit of my allotted space.)

(*World,* September 3, 1890.)

---

## 3

A man cannot go on repeating what he has said a thousand times about the way the Monday Popular quartet played Haydn in G., No. 12 of Opus 756, or about Santley as Elijah. I turn in desperation to the musical journals, and my hopes rise as I see the words, "Ignorant Misstatement." But it is actually not G. B. S. this time; somebody else, I suppose, has made a remark sufficiently obvious to shake the foundation of make-believe on which "art" of the usual professional type is built. The tenants of that fashionable edifice are always protesting that I am an impudent pretender to musical authority, betraying my ignorance, in spite of my diabolical cunning, in every second sentence. And I do not mind confessing that I do not know half as much as you would suppose from my articles; but in the kingdom of the deaf the one-eared is king.

The other evening I was looking into a shop-window in Oxford Street, when a gentleman accosted me modestly, and, after flattering me with great taste and modesty into an entire willingness to make his acquaintance, began with evident misgiving and hesitation, but with no less evident curiosity, to approach the subject of these columns. At last he came to his point with a rush by desperately risking the question, "Excuse me, Mr G. B. S., but *do* you know anything about music? The fact is, I am not capable of forming an opinion myself; but Dr Blank says you dont, and—er—Dr Blank is such a great authority that one hardly knows what to think." Now this question put me into a difficulty, because I had already learnt by experience that the reason my writings on music and musicians are so highly appreciated is, that they are supposed by many of my greatest admirers to be a huge joke, the point of which lies in the fact that I am totally ignorant of music, and that my character of critic is an exquisitely ingenious piece of acting, undertaken to gratify my love of mystification and paradox.

From this point of view every one of my articles appears as a fine stroke of comedy, occasionally broadening into a harlequinade, in which I am the clown, and Dr Blank the policeman. At first I did not realize this, and could not understand the air of utter disillusion and loss of interest in me that would come over people in whose houses I incautiously betrayed some scrap of amateurish enlightenment. But the naïve exclamation, "Oh! you *do* know something about it, then," at last became familiar to me; and I now take particular care not to expose my knowledge. When people hand me a sheet of instrumental music, and ask my opinion of it, I carefully hold it upside down, and pretend to study it in that position with the eye of an expert. When they invite me to try their new grand piano, I attempt to open it at the wrong end; and when the young lady of the house informs me that she is practising the 'cello, I innocently ask her whether the mouthpiece did not cut her lips dreadfully at first. This line of conduct gives enormous satisfaction, in which I share to a rather greater extent than is generally supposed. But, after all, the people whom I take in thus are only amateurs.

To place my impostorship beyond question I require to be certified as such by authorities like our Bachelors and Doctors of music—gentlemen who can write a Nunc Dimittis in five real parts, and know the difference between a tonal fugue and a real one, and can tell you how old Monteverdi was on his thirtieth birthday, and have views as to the true root of the discord of the seventh on the supertonic, and devoutly believe that *si contra fa diabolus est*. But I have only to present myself to them in the character of a man who has been through these dreary games without ever discovering the remotest vital connection between them and the art of music—a state of mind so inconceivable by them—to make them exclaim:

> Preposterous ass! that never read so far
> To know the cause why music was ordained,

and give me the desired testimonials at once. And so I manage to scrape along without falling under suspicion of being an honest man.

However, since mystification is not likely to advance us in the long run, may I suggest that there must be something wrong in the professional tests which have been successively applied to Handel, to Mozart, to Beethoven, to Wagner, and last, though not least, to me, with the result in every case of our condemnation as ignoramuses and charlatans. Why is it that when Dr Blank writes about music nobody but a professional musician can understand him; whereas the man-in-the-street, if fond of art and capable of music, can understand the writings of Mendelssohn, Wagner, Liszt, Berlioz, or any of the composers?

Why, again, is it that my colleague, W. A., for instance, in criticizing Mr Henry Arthur Jones's play the other day, did not *parse* all the leading sentences in it? I will not be so merciless as to answer these questions now, though I know the solution, and am capable of giving it if provoked beyond endurance. Let it suffice for the moment that writing is a very difficult art, criticism a very difficult process, and music not easily to be distinguished, without special critical training, from the scientific, technical, and professional conditions of its performance, composition, and teaching. And if the critic is to please the congregation, who want to read only about the music, it is plain that he must appear quite beside the point to the organ-blower, who wants to read about his bellows, which he can prove to be the true source of all the harmony.

(*World,* February 15, 1893.)

# PART II

## Composers and

## Masterworks

# The Miracle of Gregorian Chant
# The Fatal Perfection of Palestrina

## CECIL GRAY

*Cecil Gray was one of the liveliest and most urbane musical essayists in England during the 1920s and 30s. With his fellow composers Philip Heseltine (the real name for Peter Warlock) and Constant Lambert (see "Sibelius and the Music of the Future"), Gray founded the* Sackbutt *in 1920, a publication known for witty repartee and controversial opinion. As if to make up for the lack of attention received by his own music, Gray poured out a stream of prose on other composers, much of which can be enjoyed in his delightful memoirs,* Musical Chairs *(1945). The following excerpts are from his* History of Music *(1928), one of the most readable musical histories since Charles Burney's (see "Purcell, England's Master"). Both passages illustrate Gray's love of paradox and his ability to summarize a complex aesthetic in a few paragraphs.*

The origins, not only of modern poetry but of modern drama also, can be traced back to the wordless vocalise at the end of the Alleluia chant in the Mass. They have both sprung from the very heart of the music of the Catholic Church. The fact may not in itself be of intrinsic importance, but it certainly is symbolically significant in that it demonstrates more clearly than anything else could the truth of what was enunciated earlier in the chapter: namely, that music is the art in which the early Christian values are best expressed and embodied, and the one which is the model and archetype for all the others. And if to the enormous importance of the part which Gregorian chant played in the history, not only of music but of all the arts, we add that which it played in mediaeval life generally, and consider how, for example, the chant which was used on a particular day would be cited in statutes and chronicles as a means of dating an event; how official ceremonies and public observances of all kinds were celebrated to its solemn and majestic strains; how it accompanied the lives of all, noble and peasant, great and humble, rich and poor, cleric and layman, from the cradle to the grave—then indeed we begin to realize the overwhelming cultural significance of this great Roman fountain of song, as sweet and pure and inexhaustible as the Aqua Virgo of the Eternal City itself, and playing endlessly, day and night, throughout the centuries, as do the fountains in the Place of St. Peter before the sanctuary which is the heart and core of Christendom.

At the same time, quite apart from the important place which it occupies in the History of Civilization, it possesses a purely aesthetic appeal as great as that of any other form of art that has ever existed— an appeal which, however, triumphantly defies all attempts at analysis or definition. Wherein lies the secret of its irresistible glamour and fascination, of its immemorial power to move us? It seems, on the face of it, to be entirely devoid of every attribute of musical beauty which is commonly deemed essential. It has no determinate rhythm, no harmony or accompaniment of any kind, and its melodic scope is severely limited and circumscribed. Nevertheless, when heard in the appropriate surroundings and under fitting conditions, these simple unisonal chants take on a remote, magical, and disembodied quality—a grave ecstasy, radiant yet austere, impassioned yet serene—and glow as with a secret, inward fire. The voices themselves seem to undergo a curious transmutation and become impersonal, sexless, superhuman almost, giving expression to the inarticulate yearnings and aspirations, not only of the living, but also of the countless generations of the dead and the unborn. If we accept the definition of a miracle as a phenomenon contrary to or deviating from the laws of nature, then we may justly call Gregorian chant a musical miracle, for its beauty and appeal are not to be accounted for by any known laws or principles governing musical art, but exist in spite of them, in defiance of them.

# The Fatal Perfection of Palestrina

The super-eminent position that Palestrina occupies by universal consent among all composers of the sixteenth century is due not so much to his innovations—actually, like so many great composers, he invented very little, if anything at all, either technically or stylistically—as simply to his possession of a higher degree of genius than any of his colleagues, but of essentially the same order. If one is able to distinguish between his work and that of, say, the Nanini or Anerio brothers, it is not so much by virtue of any essential difference in mentality or any marked originality of style—although of course every creative artist has a definite individuality of his own to some extent—but simply on account of its superlative merit and its well-nigh flawless perfection. This absolute impersonality may or may not be a characteristic of the very greatest art: it is certainly, however, a necessary attribute of the greatest religious art. In the same way that the priest officiating at the altar ceases temporarily to be an individual and becomes a mere passive vessel or instrument of Godhead, so the fitness of music to the celebration of the divine rite depends largely on the extent to which the composer has been able to submerge his individuality and become an impersonal agent. And it is because Palestrina is more successful in fulfilling this condition and in achieving this state of compositorial humility and self-abnegation that he must be accounted the greatest of all religious musicians, with the possible exception of the anonymous creators of Gregorian chant. . . .

At least three distinct styles can be discerned in his work, as in that of so many other great artists. In his first book of masses, and in several other compositions published later, but probably written about the same time, he appears rather in the light of a disciple and follower of the Netherland school than as a practitioner of the method and manner introduced by Festa and Animuccia. They are highly complex and artificial, and as full of ingenious contrapuntal contrivances as the most elaborate productions of the Flemish school. His second period is characterized by a constantly increasing tendency in the direction of melodic suavity and harmonic clarity, culminating in the *Missa Papae Marcelli*—the most famous as it is likewise one of the best of all his masses—in which the utmost sensuous beauty is united to a great wealth and subtlety of technical resource, without, however, detracting from the profoundly devotional character of the music. Finally, in the work of his third period, the formal structure becomes more concentrated and precise, the polyphonic texture still more refined and simplified, and the harmonic and melodic idioms undergo a further process of clarification, resulting in the formation of a style from which every vestige of the old Flemish style has been finally eliminated.

The difference between the old and the new music might be compared to that between a trackless mediaeval forest with its gnarled and moss-grown tree-trunks and its thick tangled network of spreading branches through which no light can penetrate, and a cultivated park with neatly trimmed hedgerows, well-kept paths, smooth lawns and terraces, and swans floating serenely and majestically on ornamental lakes. In the later works of Palestrina one finds a deliberate and systematic avoidance of the modal asperities of the older music, and a definite inclination in the direction of modern tonality, resulting in a more vertical, harmonic style of writing, in which parts are continually disposed so as to produce full three note chords at the expense of interesting individual melodic progressions; and this tendency is further accentuated by a preference for syllabic declamation and conjunct motion of the parts within a restricted compass, which together inhibit the superabundant melodic flow, the energetic bounding leaps, majestic soaring sequences, and rich tonal arabesques that are such prominent features of the style of the great Flemish masters. Precisely the same change, it may be noted, takes place about the same time in French literature, when the rich, exuberant, vivid, and picturesque idiom of Rabelais and Montaigne gives place to the elegant, refined, and somewhat colourless language of Malherbe and Descartes.

It may safely be said without fear of contradiction, for it is one of the few points on which all critics are agreed, that in the works of his last period Palestrina comes as near to absolute perfection as is permitted to mere mortals—certainly nearer than any other composer who has yet lived. Nevertheless all our admiration for his marvellous art should not blind us, as it is naturally apt to do, to the fact that this perfection is the outcome of a narrowing and not a broadening of artistic resource. The man who aspires to artistic perfection, like the man who aspires to moral perfection, must take vows of poverty and divest himself of all his material possessions; and

Palestrina, in throwing away the rich inheritance of the Netherlands and stripping himself of all his artistic resources as it were, is a kind of musical St. Francis, and as such is entitled to our reverence and admiration. But it does not follow that we must all go and do likewise; indeed, for the majority the ascetic ideal is generally a fatal one to pursue, in art as in life. For one saint we get a horde of lazy, parasitic, worthless friars, and for one Palestrina we get a race of musical weaklings. In short, while one can only unreservedly admire the great personal achievement of Palestrina, it cannot be denied that the effect of his example on other composers led to the emasculation, impoverishment, and rapid decadence of contrapuntal art. Despite its undeniable beauty and sublimity the so-called Palestrina style is a delicate hothouse plant, carefully reared and nurtured in the close, incense-laden atmosphere of the church, and liable to wilt and wither away when taken out of its surroundings and brought into contact with life and reality. Its beauty is essentially cloistral; its absolute fitness to the purposes of the ritual is to a great extent attained at the expense of musical interest and vitality. For example, to hear the celebrated *Miserere* of Allegri, one of the most distinguished members of the Roman school after Palestrina, in its proper place in the Easter service, is a profoundly moving experience on account of its liturgical felicity; from a purely musical point of view, however, it is quite uninteresting—there is practically nothing at all there, in fact. And even in the work of the master himself we frequently encounter an extreme tenuity of musical substance which, however apt it may be to the ritualistic purposes, is hardly sufficient to hold our aesthetic, as distinct from our religious, attention.

It will be seen, therefore, that the Palestrina style, so far from being the culminating point of perfection and the unsurpassable model of the contrapuntal style, as it has generally been represented to be by musical historians, is, from a purely abstract point of view, a decadence and an emasculation of it. It may be the most perfect form of devotional art the world has ever known, but it is certainly not the ideal polyphonic style. It contained the seeds of death, and deprived polyphony of the strength and energy necessary to resist the continual assaults of homophony; it is the wooden horse in whose belly lay concealed the Greek monodists who laid siege to the Trojan citadel of counterpoint at the end of the sixteenth century.

(*The History of Music*, 1928.)

# Purcell, England's Master

## CHARLES BURNEY

*Charles Burney's monumental two-volume* General History of Music *(1776, 1789) is not only a landmark work of musicology and music history but a literary masterpiece as well. In a style both learned and anecdotal, elegant and abrasive, terse and chatty, Burney covers music from the ancients to the eighteenth century, with related commentary on poetry, places, manners, and the history of ideas. Burney wrote for a wide audience, one with an interest in general culture as well as music. The quality of his mind and conversation was such that even without a university education he was a favorite of the king and queen as well as a friend of Samuel Johnson, Edmund Burke, and David Garrick. In fact, volume 1 of the* History *carries a dedicatory epistle to the queen composed by Johnson, an appropriate choice given the meticulous Johnsonian balances in Burney's own assessments of art. Some commentators assert that the* History *is more enthusiastic and detailed, and therefore more valuable, in Burney's coverage of his contemporaries than of older music. That this is not always the case is demonstrated by his section on Purcell, whom he rated, despite Purcell's coming from a "barbarous" time, higher than Handel.*

In tracing the progress of English Music through the reigns of James and Charles I. the Protectorship, and chief part of Charles II. but few secular compositions occurred which could be heartily praised. Indeed, with respect to the objects of my particular enquiries, they seem so much the periods of dulness and insipidity, that the power of charming, by the arrangement and combination of musical sounds, may be said to have slept, and artists to have played and sung with as little meaning and animation, as if the art had been carried on by *Somnambuli*. I therefore feel a particular pleasure in being arrived at that period of my labours which allows me to speak of HENRY PURCELL, who is as much the pride of an Englishman in Music, as Shakspeare in productions for the stage, Milton in epic poetry, Lock in metaphysics, or Sir Isaac Newton in philosophy and mathematics.

Unluckily for Purcell! he built his fame with such perishable materials, that his worth and works are daily diminishing, while the reputation of our poets and philosophers is increasing by the constant study and use of their productions. And so much is our great musician's celebrity already consigned to tradition, that it will soon be as difficult to find his songs, or, at least to *hear* them, as those of his predecessors Orpheus and Amphion, with which Cerberus was lulled to sleep, or the city of Thebes constructed.

So changeable is taste in Music, and so transient the favour of any particular style, that its history is like that of a ploughed field: such a year it produced wheat, such a year barley, peas, or clover; and such a year lay fallow. But none of its productions remain, except, perhaps, a small part of last year's crop, and the corn or weeds that now cover its surface. Purcell, however, was such an excellent cultivator of his farm in Parnassus, that its crops will be long remembered, even after time has devoured them. . . .

Purcell is said to have profited so much from his first lessons and close application, as to have composed, during the time of his being a singing boy in the chapel, many of his anthems which have been constantly sung in our cathedrals ever since. Eighteen was a very early age for his being appointed organist; that is *maestro di capella* of Westminster Abbey, one of the first cathedrals in the kingdom, for choral compositions and performance. It was not likely he would stop here: the world is, perhaps, more partial to promising youth, than accomplished age; and at twenty-four, in 1682, he was advanced to one of the three places of organist of the Chapel Royal, on the death of Edward Low, the successor of Dr. Christopher Gibbons, in the same station.

After this, he produced so many admirable compositions for the church and chapel of which he was organist, and where he was sure of having them better performed than elsewhere, that his fame was soon extended to the remotest parts of the kingdom.

From this time, his anthems were eagerly procured, and heard with pious rapture wherever they could be performed; nor was he suffered long to devote himself totally to the service of the church. He was, very early in his life, solicited to compose for the stage, and chamber, in both which undertakings, he was so superior to all his predecessors, that his compositions seemed to speak a new language; yet, however different from that to which the public had been long accustomed, it was universally understood.* His songs seem to contain whatever the ear could then wish, or heart could feel. My father, who was nineteen years of age when Purcell died, remembered his person very well, and the effect his anthems had on himself and the public at the time that many of them were first heard; and used to say, that "no other vocal Music was listened to with pleasure, for near thirty years after Purcell's death; when they gave way only to the favourite opera songs of Handel."

The unlimited powers of this musician's genius embraced every species of composition that was then known, with equal felicity. In writing for the *church,* whether he adhered to the elaborate and learned style of his great predecessors Tallis, Bird, and Gibbons, in which no instrument is employed but the organ, and the several parts are constantly moving in fugue, imitation, or plain counterpoint; or, giving way to feeling and imagination, adopted the new and more expressive style of which he was himself one of the principal inventors, accompanying the voice-parts with instruments, to enrich the harmony and enforce the melody and meaning of the words, he manifested equal abilities and resources. In compositions for the *theatre,* though the colouring and effects of an orchestra were then but little known, yet as he employed them more than his predecessors, and gave to the voice a melody more interesting and impassioned than, during the last century, had been heard in this country, or perhaps in Italy itself, he soon became the delight and darling of the nation. And in the several species of *chamber Music* which he attempted, whether sonatas for instruments, or odes, cantatas, songs, ballads, and catches, for the voice, he so far surpassed whatever our

*He produced the overture and act-tunes for *Abdelazar,* a tragedy written by Mrs. Behn, and acted at the Duke's Theatre, in 1677, when he was only nineteen; to *Timon of Athens,* altered from Shakspeare by Shadwell, in 1678; and to *Theodosius, or the Force of Love,* by Nat. Lee, in 1680; the songs and processional Music of which are still performed.

country had produced, or imported before, that all other musical productions seem to have been instantly consigned to contempt or oblivion. . . .

The collection of his secular vocal Music, which did him the greatest honour, and long rendered his name dear to the British nation, was published by his widow two years after his decease, by the title of ORPHEUS BRITANNICUS [1698 and 1702]. Here were treasured up the songs from which the natives of this island received their first great delight and impression from the vocal Music of a *single voice*. Before that period we had cultivated madrigals and songs in parts, with diligence and success; but in all single songs, till those of Purcell appeared, the chief effects were produced from the words, not the melody. For the airs, till that time, were as unformed and misshapen, as if they had been made of notes scattered about by chance, instead of being cast in an elegant mould. Exclusive admirers of modern symmetry and elegance may call Purcell's taste barbarous; yet in spite of superior cultivation and refinement, in spite of all the vicissitudes of fashion, through all his rudeness and barbarism, original genius, feeling, and passion, are, and ever will be, discoverable in his works, by candid and competent judges of the art.

To this admirable collection are prefixed seven copies of verses to his memory, at the head of which is an ode, written on his death, by Dryden, which was set by Dr. [John] Blow, and performed at the concert in York Buildings. The Music of this ode was printed 1696, the year after our favourite musician's decease. It is composed in fugue and imitation, and is learned and masterly, but appears laboured, and is wholly without invention or pathos. There is, however, so much of both in the poetry, that it borders on bombast. . . .

There are few songs in the *Orpheus Britannicus* but what contain some characteristic mark of the author's great and original genius. The melody, however, will at first seem to many at present uncouth and antiquated; but by a little allowance and examination, any one possessed of a great love for Music, and a knowledge of our language, will feel, at certain places of almost every song, his superior felicity and passion in expressing the poet's sentiments which he had to translate into melody.

The favourite songs with Purcell's admirers, during my youth, were the following; and upon a late attentive perusal of the book, they seem to have merited particular distinction. "Celia has a thousand charms;" the first movement of this, like many of Purcell's songs, seems only *recitative* graced, or embellished with the fashionable *volate*, or *flourishes* of the times, which are now as antiquated as the curls of his own peruque, or the furbelows and flounces of Queen Elizabeth. The second movement, however, of this song, is plaintive and graceful; and at "I should my wretched, wretched, fate deplore," is still new and pathetic.

"You twice ten hundred deities," opens with what seems to me the best piece of recitative in our language. The words are admirably expressed throughout this song, by modulation as well as melody. And there is a propriety in the changes of movement, which does honour to Purcell's judgment, as much as the whole composition to his genius. The change of style and sluggish motion given to the notes at these words: "from thy sleeping mansion rise," is a model of musical imitation and expression. The modulation is still so excellent, that the best modern masters are obliged to adopt it on almost all great occasions.

Of the Music in King Arthur I shall say but little, as it has been lately revived, well performed, and printed. If ever it could with truth be said of a composer, that he had *devancé son siecle,* Purcell is entitled to that praise; as there are movements in many of his works which a century has not injured, particularly the duet in King Arthur, "Two daughters of this aged stream," and "Fairest isles all isles excelling," which contain not a single passage that the best composers of the present times, if it presented itself to their imagination, would reject. The dialogue in the Prophetess, "Tell me why, my charming fair," is the most pleasing and ingenious of all the compositions of the kind which the rage of fashion produced during fifty years. The first part of "O lead me to some peaceful gloom," is truly elegant and pathetic.

"From rosie bow'rs," is said to have been "set in his last sickness," at which time he seems to have realized the poetical fable of the swan, and to have sung more sweetly as he approached nearer his dissolution; for it seems to me as if no one of his productions was so elevated, so pleasing, so expressive, and throughout so perfect, as this. The variety of movement, the artful, yet touching modulation, and, above all, the exquisite expression of the words, render it one of the most affecting compositions extant to *every Englishman* who regards

Music not merely as an agreeable arrangement of combination of sounds, but as the vehicle of sentiment, and voice and passion.

There is more elegant melody, more elaborate harmony, more ingenious contrivance, in the motion and contexture of the several parts in the works of many great composers; but to the natives of England, who know the full power of our language, and feel the force, spirit, and shades of meaning, which every word bears according to its place in a sentence, and the situation of the speaker, or singer, I must again repeat it, this composition will have charms and effects, which, perhaps, Purcell's Music only can produce. . . .

And now, having heartily praised Purcell's extensive genius and talents, I shall not dissemble his defects. Melody, during his short existence, was not sufficiently polished by great singers; and though there are grand designs in his works, and masterly strokes of composition and expression, yet his melody wants symmetry and grace. And by writing on a given base, which forced him to submit to a crude, and sometimes a licentious and unwarrantable use of passing-notes, his harmony is not always so pure as it ought to be. . . .

An absurd custom prevailed in Purcell's time, which he carried to greater excess, perhaps, than any other composer, of repeating a word of one or two syllables an unlimited number of times, for the sake of the melody, and sometimes before the whole sentence has been heard. Such as no, no, no—all, all, all—pretty, pretty, pretty, &c. *ad infinitum.**

He was so little acquainted with the unlimited powers of the violin, that I have scarcely ever seen a becoming passage for that instrument in any one of his works; the symphonies and ritornels to his anthems and songs being equally deficient in force, invention, and effect. And though his sonatas contain many ingenious, and, at the time they were composed, new traits of melody and modulation, if they are compared with the productions of his contemporary, Corelli, they will be called barbarous. But Corelli wrote for an instrument of which he was a great master: and who ever entirely succeeded in composing for one of which he was ignorant? When a great performer on keyed-instruments condescends to compose for the violin,

---

*There is often equal redundance and absurdity in the use the Italians make, at present, of *sì, sì, sì,* and *nò, nò, nò,* in their songs.

upon which he has never been a good player, or the voice, without knowing in what good singing consists, the passages all come from the head and none from the hand, except the hand of a harpsichord player, which is ever unfit to suggest ideas either for a voice or for any other instrument than his own. Such a composer for the violin must inevitably embarrass the player with perpetual awkwardnesses and difficulties without effect, which discover an utter ignorance of the finger-board.

If Purcell, by travelling, or by *living longer* at home, had heard the great instrumental performers, as well as great singers, that arrived in this country soon after his decease, and had had such to compose for, his productions would have been more regular, elegant, and graceful; and he would certainly have set *English words* better than it was possible for any foreigner to do, for our feelings, however great his genius, or excellent, in other respects, his productions. But Purcell, like his successor, Arne, and others who have composed for the playhouse, had always an inferior band to the Italian opera composers, as well as inferior singers, and an inferior audience, to write for. . . .

Music was manifestly on the decline, in England, during the seventeenth century, till it was revived and invigorated by Purcell, whose genius, though less cultivated and polished, was equal to that of the greatest masters on the continent. And though his dramatic style and recitative were formed in a great measure on French models, there is a latent power and force in his expression of English words, whatever be the subject, that will make an unprejudiced native of this island feel, more than all the elegance, grace, and refinement of modern Music less happily applied, can do. And this pleasure is communicated to us, not by the symmetry or rhythm of modern melody, but by his having fortified, lengthened, and tuned, the true accents of our mother-tongue; those notes of passion, which an inhabitant of this island would breathe, in such situations as the words he has to set, describe. And these indigenous expressions of passion Purcell had the power to enforce by the energy of modulation, which, on some occasions, was bold, affecting, and sublime. . . .

It has been extremely unfortunate for our national taste and our national honour, that Orlando Gibbons, Pelham Humphrey, and Henry Purcell, our three best composers during the last century, were not blessed with sufficient longevity for their genius to expand in all its branches, or to form a school, which would have enabled us to proceed in the cultivation of Music without foreign assistance.

Orlando Gibbons died 1625, at forty-four.
Pelham Humphrey died 1674, at twenty-seven.
And Henry Purcell died 1695, at thirty-seven!

If these admirable composers had been blest with long life, we might have had a Music of our own, at least as good as that of France or Germany; which, without the assistance of the Italians, has long been admired and preferred to all other by the natives at large, though their princes have usually foreigners in their service. As it is, we have no school for composition, no well-digested method of study, nor, indeed, models of our own. Instrumental Music, therefore, has never gained much by our own abilities; for though some natives of England have had hands sufficient to execute the productions of the greatest masters on the continent, they have produced but little of their own that has been much esteemed. . . .

If a parallel were to be drawn between Purcell and any popular composer of a different country, reasons might be assigned for supposing him superior to every great and favourite cotemporary musician in Europe.

Carissimi and Stradella, if more polished in their style, were certainly less varied, and knew still less of instruments, than our countryman. They had both, perhaps, more grace and regularity, but infinitely less passion and fire.

The elder Scarlatti was more *recherché* and learned, but never so natural and affecting.

In Germany, if Keiser, during an active and much longer life, surpassed him in the number and excellence of his dramatic compositions, his productions for the church, could they be found, would, I believe, bear no comparison.

Lulli, blest likewise with superior longevity, composed also more operas than Purcell, and was the idol of the nation for which he laboured; but though his overtures long served as models, even to Purcell, as well as to the composers of all the rest of Europe, and his Music was performed by better singers and a more numerous band, supported by the patronage of a court, and all the splendor of ingenious and costly exhibition; it is easy to see that even his theatrical works are more *manierées,* monotonous, and uninteresting in themselves, than those of Purcell; but in relinquishing the stage, and stepping on holy ground, we should have found, even in France, during all his glory, and the enthusiasm he raised, none of his votaries who would attempt to put his sacred Music in comparison with that of our countryman.

Rameau, the successor of Lulli in court and popular favour, and who had more learning and theoretical knowledge in the art, than perhaps any practical musician of modern times; yet, in pathos and expression of words and the passions, he was Purcell's inferior, even upon the stage; and in the church, he had no claim to celebrity.

Handel, who flourished in a less barbarous age for his art, has been acknowledged his superior in many particulars; but in none more than the art and grandeur of his choruses, the harmony and texture of his organ fugues, as well as his great style of playing that instrument; the majesty of his hautbois and grand concertos, the ingenuity of the accompaniments to his songs and choruses, and even in the general melody of the airs themselves; yet in the accent, passion, and expression of *English words,* the vocal Music of Purcell is, sometimes to my feelings, as superior to Handel's as an original poem to a translation.

(*A General History of Music,* 1776, 1789.)

# The Roots of Bach's Art
# Bach's Tone Painting
# Bach's Brandenburgs

---

# ALBERT SCHWEITZER

---

*In addition to being a celebrated humanitarian and physician, Albert Schweitzer was an organist and musical historian whose great passions were Bach and Wagner. Schweitzer's classic J.S. Bach, le musicien-poète (1905) presented Bach not only as a master of counterpoint and harmony but as a vivid tone painter who chronicled the extremes of joy and despair. Schweitzer made a brave attempt to see Bach whole, as the "objective" culmination of his era and as a uniquely individual artist. Like his subject, Schweitzer had the rare ability to soar from small particulars to lofty abstractions with clarity and ease.*

Some artists are subjective, some objective. The art of the former has its source in their personality; their work is almost independent of the epoch in which they live. A law unto themselves, they place themselves in opposition to their epoch and originate new forms for the expression of their ideas. Of this type was Richard Wagner.

Bach belongs to the order of objective artists. These are wholly of their own time, and work only with the forms and the ideas that their time proffers them. They exercise no criticism upon the media of artistic expression that they find lying ready to their hand, and feel no inner compulsion to open out new paths. Their art not coming solely from the stimulus of their outer experience, we need not seek the roots of their work in the fortunes of its creator. In them the artistic personality exists independently of the human, the latter remaining in the background as if it were something almost accidental. Bach's works would have been the same even if his existence had run quite another course. Did we know more of his life than is now the case, and were we in possession of all the letters he had ever written, we should still be no better informed as to the inward sources of his works than we are now.

The art of the objective artist is not impersonal, but superpersonal. It is as if he felt only one impulse,—to express again what he already finds in existence, but to express it definitively, in unique perfection. It is not he who lives,—it is the spirit of the time that lives in him. All the artistic endeavours, desires, creations, aspirations and errors of his own and of previous generations are concentrated and worked out to their conclusion in him.

In this respect the greatest German musician has his analogue only in the greatest of German philosophers. Kant's work has the same impersonal character. He is merely the brain in which the philosophical ideas and problems of his day come to fruition. Moreover he uses unconcernedly the scholastic forms and terminology of the time, just as Bach took up the musical forms offered to him by his epoch without examining them.

Bach, indeed, is clearly not a single but a universal personality. He profited by the musical development of three or four generations. When we pursue the history of this family, which occupies so unique a position in the art-life of Germany, we have the feeling that everything that is happening there must culminate in something consummate. We feel it to be a matter of course that some day a Bach shall come in whom all those other Bachs shall find a posthumous existence, one in whom the fragment of German music that has been embodied in this family shall find its completion. Johann Sebastian Bach,—to speak the language of Kant—is a historical postulate.

Whatever path we traverse through the poetry and the music of the Middle Ages, we are always led to him.

The grandest creations of the chorale from the twelfth to the eighteenth century adorn his cantatas and Passions. Handel and the others make no use of the superb treasures of chorale-melody. They want to be free of the past. Bach feels otherwise; he makes the chorale the foundation of his work.

If we pursue, again, the history of the harmonisation of the chorale, we are once more led up to him. What the masters of polyphonic music,—Eccard, Praetorius and the others—strove after, he accomplishes. They could harmonise the melody only; his music at the same time reproduces the text.

So it is, again, with the chorale preludes and the chorale fantasias. Pachelbel, Böhm and Buxtehude, the masters in this field, created the forms. But it was not given to them to quicken the forms with the spirit. If all their struggles towards the ideal were not to be in vain, a greater man had to come, who should make his chorale fantasias musical poems.

Out of the motet, under the influence of Italian and French instrumental music, came the cantata. From Schütz onwards, for a whole century, the sacred concert struggles for its free and independent place in the church. People feel that this new music is cutting the ground of the old church service from under their feet. It forces itself further and further out of the frame of the service, aiming at becoming an independent religious drama, and aspiring towards a form like that of the opera. The oratorio is being prepared. At this juncture Bach appears, and creates cantatas that endure. A generation later it would have been too late. As regards their form, his cantatas do not differ from the hundreds upon hundreds of others written at that time, and now forgotten. They have the same external defects; they live, however, by their spirit. Out of the ardent will-to-create of generations that could not themselves give birth to anything durable, there has come for once a will equal to the ideal that hovered before the two previous generations, and that triumphs in spite of all the errors of its epoch, purely by the grandeur of its thought.

At the end of the seventeenth century the musical Passion-drama demands admission into the church. The contest rages, for and against. Bach puts an end to it by writing two Passions which, on their poetical and formal sides, derive wholly from the typical works of that time, but are transfigured and made immortal by the spirit that breathes through them.

Bach is thus a terminal point. Nothing comes from him; everything merely leads up to him. To give his true biography is to exhibit the nature and the unfolding of German art, that comes to completion in him and is exhausted in him,—to comprehend it in all its strivings and its failures. This genius was not an individual, but a collective soul. Centuries and generations have laboured at this work, before the grandeur of which we halt in veneration. To anyone who has gone through the history of this epoch and knows what the end of it was, it is the history of that culminating spirit, as it was before it objectified itself in a single personality.

## Bach's Tone Painting

The relation of Bach's music to its text is the most intimate that can be imagined. This is evident even in externals. The structure of his musical phrase does not merely fit more or less the structure of the poetic phrase, but is identical with it. In this respect we may contrast Bach with Handel. In the latter, the musical period of a long verbal passage consists of separate fragments joined together in the most masterly way, the verbal phrase, however, having to surrender something of its own natural form in order to accommodate itself to that of the music. There always results a certain antagonism between the rhythm of the two factors. We get the impression that if we were to let a Handelian theme fall to the ground, the tone-melody and the word-melody would separate under the shock; whereas a Bach phrase would remain unbroken and inseparable, his musical phrase being only the verbal phrase re-cast in tone. His music is indeed not so much melodic as declamatory. He is what Guido Adler maintains Wagner is, a product of the great music of the Renaissance.

The melodic impression his phrases make on us is due to his clear and consummate sense of form. Though he thought declamatorily, he could not help writing melodically. A vocal theme of Bach's is a declamatorily conceived phrase, that by accident, as if by a marvel perpetually repeated, assumes melodic form, whether it be a recitative, an arioso, an aria, or a chorus. His texts, regarded from the standpoint of form, were as unapt for music as any that could be imagined. A Biblical verse does not fall into any musical period, not even a verbal one, for it has its origin not in a rhythmical feeling but in the necessities of translation. It was no better with the original texts given him by his librettists. These again have no inner unity, being painfully pieced together out of reminiscences of the Bible and the hymn-books. But when we read the same sentences in Bach's music, they all at once fall into definite musical phrases.

The declamatory unity of tone and word in Bach reminds us of Wagner. While, however, it is self-evident in the latter, the verbal phrase itself being musically conceived, so that the music only adds the intervals, as it were, in Bach the phenomenon is more wonderful—the music seems to confer a higher vital power on the words, divests them of their lowly associations, and shows them in their true form. This marvel is so perpetually repeated in the cantatas and Passions that we come to regard it as a matter of course. But the more deeply we penetrate into Bach, the more we are filled with the ever-renewed and ever-increasing astonishment that the thoughtful soul feels in presence of those daily occurrences of nature that are at the same time the greatest marvels.

If we have once absorbed a Biblical verse in Bach's setting of it, we can never again conceive it in any other rhythm. It is impossible for anyone who knows the *St. Matthew Passion* to run over in his mind the sacramental words of the evening Communion without consciously or unconsciously giving the words the accents and duration that they have in Bach's declamation. No one who knows the cantata *Nun komm der Heiden Heiland* (No. 61) can ever again think of the "Siehe! Ich stehe vor der Tür und klopfe an" ("Behold, I stand at the door and knock") apart from Bach's phrasing of it. Even if he has forgotten the actual intervals, the musical ground-plan of the passage has become, after several hearings, so much the plan of the passage itself, that it is impossible to think of the one without the other. . . .

Everywhere, in fact, there is the same profound view and the same characteristic expression of the emotions and actions. Moreover, Bach now and then heightens the sentiment of his text in the most striking way; he turns contentment into exultant joy, and grief into violent despair. Not that he neglects the nuances of feeling even in thus intensifying it; his music expresses many degrees of joy and of sorrow. But all of them are surcharged with emotion. When he translates a feeling into tone, he voices it in its extreme form.

In the first chorus of the cantata *Ach, lieben Christen seid getrost* (No. 114), he expresses the "getrost" in terms of such overflowing joy that the music goes far beyond the text. There is the same joyous excitement in the resignation expressed in the first chorus of the cantata *Was mein Gott will, das g'scheh allzeit* (No. 111).

It is the same with the organ chorales. What the chorale-preludes "Mit Fried und Freud fahr ich dahin . . ." and "Wer nur den lieben Gott lässt walten . . ." express is joy of an animated kind, not the peaceful confidence of which the text speaks.

Bach is thus bent on making the music characteristically expressive at any cost. Before he decides simply to write beautiful music to a text, he searches the words through and through to find an emotion which, after it has been intensified, is suitable for musical representation. He remodels his text to suit the way he means to express it in music. The words are finally no more than a shadow-picture of the music. Bach's relation to his text is active, not passive; it does not inspire him so much as he inspires it. His music lifts the words to a higher power, bringing out in transfigured form what seems struggling for expression in the mediocrity or,—as often enough happens—the banality of the poem. . . .

We get the impression that the composer is even indifferent to the actual words of his text and their banalities, not merely because they have the same savour for him as for his contemporaries, but because he is conscious how little really remains of the words when he has poured his own poetic power upon them. It was a similar consciousness of strength that made him burden himself with the contemporary Italian form of the *da capo* aria; he was secretly aware that his musical declamation could vivify even a mere pattern of this kind.

There is a great difference between the respective attitudes of Bach and Mozart towards a poor text. Both of them make us forget it by their music, but for quite different reasons. Mozart's object is to distract our minds from the text by means of music that is beautiful in itself. Bach gives it a new profundity and a new form in his music. . . .

On the whole we can say that Bach only takes into account in his music the most salient episodes of the text, confining himself mainly to expressing the basic mood of it. Often this seems to him to reside in some contrast, which he will suggest by a conflict of two characteristic motives. The classical example of this is the introductory chorus of the cantata *Ihr werdet weinen und heulen, aber die Welt wird sich freuen* (No. 103). His fondness for sharp contrasts makes him particularly delight in texts of this kind. Even when the antithesis suggested in the poem is purely incidental, he will fasten upon it and make it the fundamental idea of his music.

# Bach's Brandenburgs

The Brandenburg concertos are the purest products of Bach's polyphonic style. Neither on the organ nor on the clavier could he have worked out the architecture of a movement with such vitality; the orchestra alone permits him absolute freedom in the leading and grouping of the obbligato voices. When we said, in another connection that Bach's mode of expression is to be conceived as a plastic one, and deduced from this certain principles for performance, there was a danger of our being misunderstood, as if our object were to try to re-introduce the old, stiff way of playing his music. But one has only to go through these scores, in which Bach has marked all the nuances with the utmost care, to realise that the plastic pursuit of the musical idea is not in the least formal, but alive from beginning to end. Bach takes up the ground-idea of the old concerto, which develops the work out of the alternation of a larger body of tone—the *tutti*—and a smaller one—the *concertino*. Only with him the formal principle becomes a living one. It is not now a question merely of the alternation of the *tutti* and the *concertino;* the various tone-groups interpenetrate and react on each other, separate from each other, unite again, and all with an incomprehensible artistic inevitability. The concerto is really the evolution and the vicissitudes of the theme. We really seem to see before us what the philosophy of all ages conceives as the fundamental mystery of things,—that self-unfolding of the idea in which it creates its own opposite in order to overcome it, creates another, which again it overcomes, and so on and on until it finally returns to itself, having meanwhile traversed the whole of existence. We have the same impression of incomprehensible necessity and mysterious contentment when we pursue the theme of one of these concertos, from its entry in the *tutti,* through its enigmatic struggle with its opposite, to the moment when it enters into possession of itself again in the final *tutti.*

In Bach we often have not one but several groups of solo instruments, that are played off against each other in the development of the movement. The wind instruments are used with the audacity of genius. In the first concerto Bach employs, besides the strings, a wind-*ensemble* consisting of two horns, three oboes and bassoon; in the second, flute, oboe, trumpet and violin are used as a kind of solo quartet against the body of the strings; in the third he aims at no contrast of *timbres,* but employs three string trios, all constituted in the same way; in the fourth concerto the *concertino* consists of one violin and two flutes; in the fifth it consists of clavier, flute and violin; in the sixth, Bach employs only the *timbre* effects to be had from the strings,—two violas, two gambas, and cello.

The study of Bach's nuances in these works is a continual source of delight. They are all so simple, and yet so full and rich. Observe, for example, how, in the first movement of the fourth concerto, from the twenty-seventh bar before the end, the *piano* comes down in a wavy line from top to bottom, following the line of the *forte* theme, that winds downwards and lies, as it were, in violent convulsions on the ground, till suddenly a bold *forte* of the whole orchestra puts an end to the unrest that began with the first entry of this subsidiary theme in the violins, and leads into the victorious conclusion.

(*J.S. Bach, le musicien-poète,* 1905; enlarged German edition, 1908; translated by Ernest Newman from the German.)

# Bach the Colorist

## PAUL ROSENFELD

*Although he made his reputation primarily as a champion of twentieth-century music (see "Varèse, Skyscraper Mystic"), Paul Rosenfeld was also an astute commentator on earlier composers. His pictorial, richly metaphorical prose style, as well as his background as an art critic in the 1920s, made him an ideal chronicler of color in music. As this passage on a little-known aspect of Bach illustrates, he often saw music in relation to painting, with exquisite and illuminating results.*

Belatedly enough, the discovery of the present writer that Bach was a colorist took place, in the April of 1934, in the rooms of the New Music School in Fifty-ninth Street in New York, tense with the presence of a deeply, studiously interested, eagerly receptive crowd of musicianly people. The medium of it was a young man looking like somebody grinding for a Ph.D. in English in the Yale Graduate School: Ralph Leonard Kirkpatrick, who is a Yankee from Massachusetts, and a magnificent artist. Equipped with a fine sense of style, a strong grasp of the form of the complex music he plays, and a reverence for that music's quality and meaning as well as a fine technical control of the clavichord and the harpsichord on which he performs it, he executed, on two memorable evenings, several of the preludes and fugues from the *Well-Tempered Clavichord*, a couple of the French Suites, a *Partita*, the *Chromatic Fantasy and Fugue*, and all the *Goldberg Variations*, magnificently upon the instruments for which Bach originally cast them. And while he played, he gave the writer, who isn't very highly educated but who on these occasions probably shared his experience with many of his fellow hearers, a glimpse into the immortal cantor's imagination in a way completer than any previously afforded him.

The experience a bit resembled that of some hypothetical, untraveled art-lover in the New England of a hundred years since who knew Tintoretto's paintings only through prints of them and found himself, magically transported, in the *antecollegio* of the palace of the Doges in Venice. Like the art-lover before the original Tintorettos, the writer was confronted by unexpectedly spacious, tridimensional objects. With voices and volumes surprisingly discrete and round, and strongly antithetical for all their delicacy, the polyphonic structures stood astoundingly up and out, the effect, here too, flowing from the actuality of the color. The melodic lines resembled fine gilt or lizard-green threads and wires; the individual notes were tiny sparks; while the sustained volumes hung in the air, so many golden clouds or colored shadows. Like the greatest Venetian, and his great Cretan pupil, and *his* nineteenth-century rediscoverer Cézanne, Bach had modeled, it was plain, in color itself, with antitheses not only of tones but of qualities of tones: playing timbre against timbre as well as note against note and distinguishing the various voices by means of color as well as pitch, a feat made possible by the fact that both the clavichord and the harpsichord are capable of producing great varieties of quality of tone. And like the amazed traveler in the famous anteroom, the writer had to recognize that he had hitherto incompletely conceived the medium in which his beloved artist had worked; that his conception of it had embraced merely one of its elements, that of design. In his case, the mistake had resulted from the circumstance that he had hitherto heard Bach's clavier works performed only upon the piano, an instrument valuable for its force of tone, but dull of timbre, and therefore able to give what to all effects amounts only to a black-and-white version of the work of a supreme colorist.

Since the writer preserves a nineteenth-century affection for the piano, he was relieved, later while reading up on the subject of J. S. Bach and his congruous instruments, to learn that the modern instrument is by no means so unserviceable in the performance of Bach as, during the excitement of the Kirkpatrickan revelation, he had momentarily thought it might be. Schweitzer, for example, called to his mind the comparative limitations of both the older keyboard instruments: that of the clavichord flowing from the fact that its tones are too weak to be distinguishable at a distance greater than twenty-five feet; and that of the harpsichord, which for the reason of its abruptness of attack and its incapacity to sustain single notes, remains incapable of doing justice to pieces requiring singing tones. Nonetheless, he cannot but feel that never to have heard Bach played on an old instrument by scholarly artists like Mme. Landowska and Mr. Kirkpatrick is to remain ignorant alike of the sensuosity of his imagination and of the exquisiteness of his power of definition; of the delicacy of the values, the oppositions and relationships of tones his representations of his world involved; and hence, not at all to know the wonderfully prismatic nature of those powerful forms of his which the piano must, to the best of its ability, somehow be made to body forth.

(*Discoveries of a Music Critic*, 1936.)

# The Capaciousness of Handel

## ROMAIN ROLLAND

*Like his contemporaries George Bernhard Shaw and H. L. Mencken, Romain Rolland was a literary man whose first love was music. In his work as novelist, playwright, biographer, art historian, and literary essayist, Rolland demonstrated the centrality and universality of music in the stream of human culture. His ten-volume novel,* Jean-Christophe, *winner of the Nobel prize in 1916, depicted the spiritual odyssey of a fictional composer; his books on Beethoven and Handel (two for each composer) viewed the former as the ultimate emblem of the individual overcoming adversity and the latter as the ultimate example of an individual embodying an age. Rolland's approach to writing on music was intuitive rather than analytical. As his contemporary Paul Rosenfeld pointed out, Rolland's prose seemed "moulded" on musical style. Some may find his writing on Beethoven to be a bit dated and heavy-breathing, but his work on Handel is a model of the reasoned passion which characterizes his writing at its best.*

No great musician is more impossible to include in the limits of one definition, or even of several, than Handel. It is a fact that he reached the complete mastery of his style very early (much earlier than J. S. Bach), although it was never really fixed, and he never devoted himself to any one form of art. It is even difficult to see a conscious and a logical evolution in him. His genius is not of the kind which follows a single path, and forges right ahead until it reaches its object. For his aim is no other than to do well whatever he undertook. All ways are good to him—from his early steps at the crossing of the ways, he dominated the country, and shed his light on all sides, without laying siege to any particular part. He is not one of those who impose on life and art a voluntary idealism, either violent or patient; nor is he one of those who inscribe in the book of life the formula of their campaign. He is of the kind who drink in the life universal, assimilating it to themselves. His artistic will is mainly objective. His genius adapts itself to a thousand images of passing events, to the nation, to the times in which he lived, even to the fashions of his day. It accommodates itself to the various influences, ignoring all obstacles. It weighs other styles and other thoughts, but such is the power of assimilation and the prevailing equilibrium of his nature that he never feels submerged and overweighted by the mass of these strange elements. Everything is duly absorbed, controlled, and classified. This immense soul is like the sea itself, into which all the rivers of the world pour themselves without troubling its serenity.

The German geniuses have often had this power of absorbing thoughts and strange forms, but it is excessively rare to find amongst them the grand objectivism, and this superior impersonality, which is, so to speak, the hallmark of Handel. Their sentimental lyricism is better fitted to sing songs, to voice the thoughts of the universe in song, than to paint the universe in living forms and vital rhythms. Handel is very different, and approaches much more nearly than any other in Germany the genius of the South, the Homeric genius of which Goethe received the sudden revelation on his arrival at Naples. This capacious mind looks out on the whole universe, and on the way the universe depicts itself, as a picture is reflected in calm and clear water. He owes much of this objectivism to Italy, where he spent many years, and the fascination of which never effaced itself from his mind, and he owes even more to that sturdy England, which guards its emotions with so tight a rein, and which eschews those sentimental and effervescing effusions, so often displayed in the pious German art; but that he had all the germs of his art in himself, is already shown in his early works at Hamburg.

From his infancy at Halle, Zachau had trained him not in one style, but in all the styles of the different nations, leading him to understand not only the spirit of each great composer, but to assimilate the styles by writing in various manners. This education, essentially cosmopolitan, was completed by his three tours in Italy, and his sojourn of half a century in England. Above all he never ceased to follow up the lessons learnt at Halle, always appropriating to himself the best from all artists and their works. If he was never in France (it is not absolutely proved), he knew her nevertheless. He was anxious to master the French language and musical style. We have proofs of that in his manuscripts, and in the accusations made against him by certain French critics. Wherever he passed, he gathered some musical souvenir, buying and collecting foreign works, copying them, or rather (for he had not the careful patience of J. S. Bach, who scrupulously wrote out in his own hand the entire scores of French organists and the Italian violinists) copying down in hasty and often inexact expressions any idea which struck him in the course of reading. This vast collection of European thoughts, which only remains in remnants at the Fitzwilliam Museum at Cambridge, was the reservoir, so to speak, from which his creative genius continually fed itself. Profoundly German in race and character, he had become a world citizen, like his compatriot Leibnitz, whom he had known at Hanover, a European with a tendency for the Latin culture. The great Germans at the end of that century, Goethe and Herder, were never more free, or more universal, than this great Saxon in music, saturated as he was with all the artistic thoughts of the West.

He drew not only from the sources of learned and refined music—the music of musicians; but also drank deeply from the founts of popular music—that of the most simple and rustic folk. He loved the latter. One finds noted down in his manuscripts the street cries of London, and he once told a friend that he received many inspirations for his best airs from them. Certain of his oratorios, like *L'Allegro ed Il Penseroso*, are threaded with remembrances of his walks in the English country, and who can ignore the *Pifferari* (Italian peasant's pipe) in *The Messiah*, the Flemish carillon in *Saul*, the joyous popular Italian songs in *Hercules*, and in *Alexander Balus*? Handel was not an artist lost in introspection. He watched all around him, he listened, and observed. Sight was for him a source of inspiration, hardly of less importance than hearing. I do not know any great German musician who has been as much a visual as Handel. Like Hasse and Corelli, he had a veritable passion for beautiful pictures. He hardly ever went out without going to a theatre or a picture sale. He was a connoisseur, and he made a collection, in which some Rembrandts were found after his death. It has been remarked that his blindness (which should have rendered his hearing still more sensitive, his creative powers translating everything into sonorous dreams) soon paralyzed his hearing when its principal source of renewal was withdrawn.

Thus, saturated in all the European music of his time, impregnated with the music of musicians, and the still richer music which flows in all Nature herself, which is specially diffused in the vibrations of light and shade, that song of the rivers, of the forest, of the birds, in which all his work abounds and which have inspired some of his most picturesque pages with a semi-romantic color, he wrote as one speaks, he composed as one breathes. He never sketched out on paper in order to prepare his definite work. He wrote straight off as he improvised, and in truth he seems to have been the greatest improviser that ever was. He wrote his music with such an impetuosity of feeling, and such a wealth of ideas, that his hand was constantly lagging behind his thoughts, and in order to keep apace with them at all he had to note them down in an abbreviated manner. But (and this seems contradictory) he had at the same time an exquisite sense of form. No German surpassed him in the art of writing beautiful, melodic lines. Mozart and Hasse alone were his equals in this. It was to this love of perfection that we attribute that habit which, despite his fertility of invention, causes him to use time after time the same phrases (those most important, and dearest to him), each time introducing an imperceptible change, a light stroke of the pencil, which renders them more perfect. The examination of these kinds of musical *eaux-fortes* in their successive states is very instructive for the musician who is interested in plastic beauty. It shows also how certain melodies, once written down, continued to slumber in Handel's mind for many years, until they had penetrated his subconscious nature, were applied at first, by following the chances of inspiration, to a certain situation, which suited them moderately well. They are, so to speak, in search of a body where they can reincarnate themselves, seeking the true situation, the real sentiment of which they are but the latent expression; and once having found it, they expand themselves with ease.

Handel worked no less with the music of other composers than with his own. If one had the time to study here what superficial readers have called his plagiarisms, particularly taking, for example, *Israel in Egypt,* where the most barefaced of these cases occur, one would see with what genius and insight Handel has evoked from the depths of these musical phrases, their secret soul, of which the first creators had not even a presentiment. . . .

The intimate sense of his works was falsified in the century which followed his death by the English interpretations, strengthened further still in Germany by those of Mendelssohn, and his numerous following. By the exclusion of and systematic contempt for all the operas of Handel, by an elimination of nearly all the dramatic oratorios, the most powerful and the freshest, by a narrow choice more and more restrained to the four or five oratorios, and even here, by giving an exaggerated supremacy to *The Messiah,* by the interpretation finally of these works, and notably of *The Messiah,* in a pompous, rigid and stolid manner, with an orchestra and choir far too numerous and badly balanced, with singers frightfully correct and pious, without any feeling or intimacy, there has been established the tradition which makes Handel a church musician after the style of Louis XIV, all decoration—pompous columns, noble and cold statues, and pictures by Le Brun. It is not surprising that this has reduced works executed on such principles, and degraded them to a monumental tiresomeness similar to that which emanates from the bewigged Alexanders, and the very conventional Christs of Le Brun.

It is necessary to turn back. Handel was never a church musician, and he hardly ever wrote for the church. Apart from his *Psalms* and his *Te Deum,* composed for the private chapels, and for exceptional events, he only wrote instrumental music for concerts and for open-air fêtes, for operas, and for those so-called oratorios, which were really written for the theatre. The first oratorios he composed were acted. And if Handel resolutely abstained from theatrical representation—which alone gives the full value to certain scenes, such as the orgy and the dream of Belshazzar, expressly conceived for acting—on the other hand he stood out firmly for having his oratorios at the theatre and not in the church. There were not wanting churches any less than dissenting chapels in which he could give his works, and by not doing so he turned against him the opinion of religious people who considered it sacrilegious to carry pious subjects on the stage, but he continued to affirm that he did not write compositions for the church, but worked for the theatre—a free theatre. . . .

One sees what a variety of forms and styles he used. Handel was too universal and too objective to believe that one kind of art only was the true one. He believed in two kinds of music only, the good and the bad. Apart from that he appreciated all styles. Thus he has left masterpieces in every style, but he did not open any new way in opera for the simple reason that he went a long way in nearly all paths already opened up. Constantly he experimented, invented, and always with his singularly sure touch. He seemed to have an extraordinary penetrating knowledge in invention, and consequently few artistic regions remained for him to conquer. He made as masterly a use of the recitative as Gluck, or of the *arioso* as Mozart, writing the acts of *Tamerlano* which are the closest and the most heartrending dramas, in the manner of *Iphigénie en Tauride,* the most moving and passionate scenes in music such as certain pages of *Admeto* and *Orlando,* where the humorous and the tragic are intermingled in the manner of *Don Giovanni.* He has experimented very happily here in new rhythms. There were new forms, the dramatic duet or quartet, the descriptive symphony opening the opera, refined orchestration, choruses and dances. Nothing seems to have obsessed him. In the following opera we find him returning to the ordinary forms of the Italian or German opera of his time.

Still less can we say that he held to a rigid form with his operas, which were continually adapted to the changing tastes of the theatre public of his age, and of the singers which he had at his disposal, but when he left the opera for the oratorio he varied no less. It was a perpetual experiment of new forms in the vast framework of the free theatre (*theatre en liberté*) of the concert drama; and the sort of instinctive ebb and flow in creation seems to have caused his works to succeed one another in groups of analogous or related compositions, each work in a nearly opposite style of feeling and form. In each one Handel indulged momentarily in a certain side of his feelings, and when that was finished he found himself in the possession of other feelings which had been accumulating whilst he was drawing on the first. He thus kept up a perpetual balance, which is like the pulsation of life itself. After the realistic *Saul* comes the impersonal epic of *Israel in Egypt.* After this colossal monument appear the two *genre* pictures, *The Ode for St. Cecilia's Day* and *L'Allegro ed Il Penseroso.* After the Herculean *Samson,* a heroic and popular tragic comedy sprang forth, the charming flower of *Semele,* an opera of romanticism and gallantry.

But if the oratorios are so wonderfully varied they have one characteristic in common even more than the operas; they are musical dramas. It was not that religious thought turned Handel to this choice of Biblical subjects, but as Kretzschmar has well shown, it was on account of the stories of the Bible heroes being a part of the very lifeblood of the people whom he addressed. They were known to all, whilst the ancient romantic stories could only interest a society of refined and spoilt dilettanti. Without doubt, these oratorios were not made for representation, did not seek scenic effects, with rare exceptions, as for instance the scene of the orgy of *Belshazzar,* where one feels that Handel had drawn on the direct vision of theatrical representation, but passions, spirits and personalities were represented always in a dramatic fashion. Handel is a great painter of characters, and the Delilah in *Samson,* the Nitocris in *Belshazzar,* the Cleopatra in *Alexander Balus,* the mother in *Solomon,* the Dejanira in *Hercules,* the beautiful Theodora, all bear witness to the suppleness and the profundity of his psychological genius. . . .

A great breath of nature passed over German music, and pushed it towards tone-painting. Telemann was, even more than Handel, a painter in music, and was more celebrated than Handel for his realistic effects. But the England of the eighteenth century had remained very conservative in music, and had devoted itself to cultivating the masters of the past. Handel's art was then more striking to them on account of "its color" and "its imitative effects." I will not say with Saint-Saëns that "there was no question of exotism with him," for Handel seems to have sought this very thing more than once; notably in the orchestration of certain scenes for the two Cleopatras, of *Guilo Cesare,* and of *Alexander Balus.* But that which was constantly with him was tone-painting, the reproduction through passages of music of natural impressions, a painting very characteristic, and, as Beethoven put it, "more an expression of feelings than painting," a poetic evocation of the raging tempests, of the tranquillity of the sea, of the dark shades of night, of the twilight which envelops the English country, of the parks by moonlight, of the sunrise in springtime, and of the awakening of birds. *Acis and Galatea, Israel in Egypt, Allegro, The Messiah, Solomon,* all offer a wondrous picture gallery of nature, carefully noted by Handel with the sure stroke of a Flemish painter, and of a romantic poet at the same time. . . .

But great painter as Handel was, he did not work so much

through the brilliancy, variety, and novelty of his tone-colors as by the beauty of his designs, and his effects of light and shade. With a voluntarily restrained palette, and by satisfying himself with the sober colors of the strings, he yet was able to produce surprising and thrilling effects. . . . All his orchestral art is in the true instinct of balance and economy, which, with the most restricted means in managing a few colors, yet knows how to obtain as powerful impressions as our musicians of to-day, with their crowded palette. Nothing, then, is more important, if we wish to render this music truly, than the avoidance of upsetting the equilibrium of the various sections of the orchestra under the pretext of enriching it and bringing it up to date. The worse fault is to deprive it, by a useless surplus of tone-colors, of that suppleness and subtlety of nuance which is its principal charm.

Let us consider his *Concerti Grossi*. None of his works is more celebrated and less understood. Handel attached to them a particular value, for he published them by subscription, a means which was usual in his day, but which he himself never adopted except under exceptional circumstances. . . . The form of his concerto, of which the principal movements varied from four to six, oscillated between the suite and the sonata, and even glanced towards the symphonic overture. It is this for which the theorists blame him, and it is this for which I praise him. For he does not seek to impose a uniform cast on his thoughts, but leaves it open to himself to fashion the form as he requires, so that the framework varies accordingly, following his inclinations from day to day.

The spontaneity of his thought, which has already been shown by the extreme rapidity with which the *Concerti* were composed— each in a single day at a single sitting, and many each week— constitutes the great charm of these works. . . .

Let us now come to that class of Handel's instrumental music to which historians have given far too little attention, and in which Handel shows himself a precursor, and at the same time a model. I refer to his open-air music.

This took a prominent place in the English life. The environs of London were full of gardens, where, Pepys tells us, "vocal and instrumental concerts vied with the voices of the birds." Handel wrote pieces especially intended for these garden concerts. Generally speaking, he attached very little.importance to them. They were little

symphonies or unpretentious dances, like the *Hornpipe*, composed
for the concert at Vauxhall in 1740. . . .

With the *Firework Music* the character of open-air music is even
more definitely asserted, quite as much by the broad style of the piece
as by the orchestration, which is confined entirely to the wind instruments. The composition is divided into two parts: an overture which
was to be played before the grand firework display, and a number of
little pieces to be played during the display, which corresponded to
certain allegorical set pieces. The overture is a sort of stately march in
D major, and has some resemblance to the overture of the *Ritterballet*
(Huntsman's Dance) of Beethoven, and which is, like it, joyful,
equestrian, and very sonorous. The shorter movements comprise a
bourrée, a *Largo a la Siciliana*, entitled *Peace*, of a beautiful, heroic
grace, which lulls itself to sleep; a very sprightly allegro entitled *The
Rejoicing*, and two minuets for conclusion. It is an interesting work
for the organizers of our popular fêtes and open-air spectacles to
study. If we have said that after 1740 Handel wrote hardly any other
instrumental music than the *Firework Music*, and the two monumental concertos, *a due cori* (for two horns), we have the feeling that the
last evolution of his thought and instrumental style led him in the
direction of music conceived for the great masses, wide spaces, and
huge audiences. He had always in him a popular vein of thought. I
immediately call to mind the many popular inspirations with which
his memory was stored, and which vivify the pages of his oratorios.
His art, which renewed itself perpetually at this rustic source, had in
his time an astonishing popularity. Certain airs from *Ottone, Scipione,
Arianna, Berenice,* and such other of his operas, were circulated and
vulgarized not only in England, but abroad, and even in France
(generally so unyielding to outside influences).

It is not only of this popularity, a little banal, of which I wish to
speak, which one could not ignore—for it is only a stupid pride and a
small heart which denies great value to the art which pleases humble
people;—what I wish to notice chiefly in the popular character of
Handel's music is that it is always truly conceived for the people, and
not for an élite dilettanti, as was the French opera between Lully and
Gluck. Without ever departing from his sovereign ideas of beautiful
form, in which he gave no concession to the crowd, he reproduced in
a language immediately "understanded of the people" those feelings
in which all could share. This genial improviser, compelled during

the whole of his life (a half-century of creative power) to address from the stage a mixed public, was like the orators of old, who had the cult of style and instinct for immediate and vital effect. Our epoch has lost the feeling of this type of art and men: pure artists who spoke *to* the people and *for* the people, not for themselves or for their confrères. Today the pure artists lock themselves within themselves, and those who speak to the people are most often mountebanks. The free England of the eighteenth century was in a certain measure related to the Roman republic, and indeed Handel's eloquence was not without relation to that of the epic orators, who sustained in the form their highly finished and passionate discourses, who left their mark on the shuddering crowd of loiterers. This eloquence did on occasion actually thrust itself into the soul of the nation as in the days of the Jacobite invasion, where *Judas Maccabaeus* incarnated the public feeling. In the first performances of *Israel in Egypt* some of the auditors praised the heroic virtues of this music, which could raise up the populace and lead armies to victory.

By this power of popular appeal, as by all the other aspects of his genius, Handel was in the robust line of Cavalli and of Gluck, but he surpassed them. Alone, Beethoven has walked in these broader paths, and followed along the road which Handel had opened.

(*Handel*, 1916; translated by A. Eaglefield Hull.)

# A *Messiah* for Heathens

## GEORGE BERNARD SHAW

*In addition to being the most broadly interdisciplinary of music critics, Shaw was also one of the most prophetic. These accounts of the real spirit of Handel's* Messiah *versus the Victorians' pious and ponderous distortion anticipate the recent revolution in "old music" performance, with its demand for clarity and rhythmic thrust. Shaw's call for "active intelligence" over stultifying "reverence" typified his writing not only on Handel but on all music—the art he loved best and was determined to rescue from dullness and convention.*

Christmas being the season of mirth, music, the great English killjoy, with its intolerable hypocrisies, is gladly put away until it is time to return to work and duty and mental improvement and other unpleasantness; consequently my critical machinery has got out of gear somewhat. I might have kept off the rust by attending the regulation Christmas performance of *The Messiah;* but I have long since recognized the impossibility of obtaining justice for that work in a Christian country. Import a choir of heathens, restrained by no considerations of propriety from attacking the choruses with unembarrassed sincerity of dramatic expression, and I would hasten to the performance if only to witness the delight of the public and the discomfiture of the critics. That is, if anything so indecent would be allowed here. We have all had our Handelian training in church, and the perfect churchgoing mood is one of pure abstract reverence. A mood of active intelligence would be scandalous. Thus we get broken in to the custom of singing Handel as if he meant nothing; and as it happens that he meant a great deal, and was tremendously in earnest about it, we know rather less about him in England than they do in the Andaman Islands, since the Andamans are only unconscious of him, whereas we are misconscious. To hear a thousand respectable young English persons jogging through *For He shall purify the sons of Levi* as if every group of semiquavers were a whole bar of four crotchets a capella, or repeating *Let Him deliver Him if He delight in Him* with exactly the same subdued and uncovered air as in *For with His stripes we are healed,* or lumbering along with *Hallelujah* as if it were a superior sort of family coach: all this is ludicrous enough; but when the nation proceeds to brag of these unwieldy choral impostures, these attempts to make the brute force of a thousand throats do what can only be done by artistic insight and skill, then I really lose patience. Why, instead of wasting huge sums on the multitudinous dullness called a Handel Festival does not somebody set up a thoroughly rehearsed and exhaustively studied performance of *The Messiah* in St James's Hall with a chorus of twenty capable artists? Most of us would be glad to hear the work seriously performed once before we die.

(*World,* January 21, 1891.)

Fundamentally my view of the Handel Festival is that of a convinced and ardent admirer of Handel. My favorite oratorio is *The Messiah,* with which I have spent many of the hours which others give to Shakespear, or Scott, or Dickens. But for all this primary bias in favor of Handel, my business is still to be that of the critic, who, invited to pronounce an opinion on the merits of a performance by four thousand executants, must judge these abnormal conditions by their effect on the work as open-mindedly as if there were only four hundred, or forty, or four. And I am bound to add that he who, so judging, delivers a single and unqualified verdict on the Festival, stultifies himself. The very same conditions which make one choral number majestic, imposing, even sublime, make another heavy, mechanical, meaningless. For instance, no host could be too mighty for the Hallelujah Chorus, or See the Conquering Hero. In them every individual chorister knows without study or instruction what he has to do and how he has to feel. The impulse to sing spreads even to the audience; and those who are old hands at choral singing do not always restrain it. . . .

But *The Messiah* is not all Hallelujah. Compare such a moment as I have just described with the experience of listening to the fiercely tumultuous *He trusted in God,* with its alternations of sullen mockery with high-pitched derision, and its savage shouts of *Let Him deliver Him if He delight in Him,* jogging along at about half the proper speed, with an expression of the deepest respect and propriety, as if a large body of the leading citizens, headed by the mayor, were presenting a surpassingly dull address to somebody. There may be, in the way of the proper presentation of such a chorus as this, something of the difficulty which confronted Wagner at the rehearsals of *Tannhäuser* in Paris in 1861, when he asked the ballet master to make his forces attack the Bacchanal in a bacchanalian way. "I understand perfectly what you mean," said the functionary; "but only to a whole ballet of *premiers sujets* dare I breathe such suggestions."

No doubt Mr Manns's three thousand five hundred choristers might better his instructions so heartily as to go considerably beyond the utmost licence of art if he told them that unless they sang that chorus like a howling bloodthirsty mob, the utter loneliness of *Thy rebuke hath broken his heart,* and *Behold and see,* must be lost, and with it the whole force of the tragic climax of the oratorio. Besides which, there is the physical difficulty, which only a skilled and powerful orator could fully surmount, of giving instruction of that kind to such a host. But I see no reason why matters should not be vastly improved if Mr Manns would adopt throughout the bolder policy as to speed which was forced on him after four on Selection day by the silent urgency of the clock, and persisted in to some extent—always with convincing effect—in Israel. Increased speed, however, is not all that is wanted. To get rid completely of the insufferable lumbering which is the curse of English Handelian choral singing, a spirited reform in style is needed.

For instance, Handel, in his vigorous moods, is fond of launching the whole mass of voices into florid passages of great brilliancy and impetuosity. In one of the most splendid choruses in *The Messiah, For He shall purify the sons of Levi,* the syllable "fy" comes out in a single trait consisting of no less than thirty-two semiquavers. That trait should be sung with one impulse from end to end without an instant's hesitation. How is it actually done in England? Just as if the thirty-two semiquavers were eight bars of crotchets taken alla breve in a not very lively tempo. The effect, of course, is to make the chorus so dull that all the reputation of Handel is needed to persuade Englishmen that they ought to enjoy it, whilst Frenchmen go away from our festivals confirmed in their scepticism as to our pet musical classic.

Again, in the beginning of *For unto us*, the tenors and basses told each other the news in a prosaic, methodical way which made the chorus quite comic until the thundering *Wonderful, Counsellor*, one of Handel's mightiest strokes, was reached; and even here the effect was disappointing, because the chorus, having held nothing in reserve, could make no climax. The orchestra needed at that point about twenty more of the biggest of big drums. Another lost opportunity was the pathetically grand conclusion of *All we like sheep*. Nothing in the whole work needs to be sung with more intense expression than *But the Lord hath laid on Him the iniquity of us all*. Unless it sounds as if the singers were touched to their very hearts, they had better not sing it at all. On that Monday it came as mechanically as if the four entries of the voices had been produced by drawing four stops in an organ. This was the greater pity, because it must be conceded to our young Handel-sceptics that the preceding musical portraiture of the sheep going astray has no great claims on their reverence.

(*World*, July 1, 1891.)

# Scarlatti's Keyboard Quirks

## GLENN GOULD

*The essays of visionary pianist Glenn Gould were often remarkably similar to his playing—quirky, unpredictable, lucid, contrapuntal in thought and texture, and utterly original. Since Gould's tragic death in 1982 at age fifty, his essays have come under new scrutiny and have occasioned the same kind of controversy that once attended his revolutionary interpretations of Bach, Mozart, and Schöenberg. In a recent* New Republic *article, Sanford Schwarz called his essays "polished," but also cold and "highfalutin." Leonard Bernstein, on the other hand, characterized his writing as "one long series of delightful and stimulating shocks." As Tim Page, compiler of* The Glenn Gould Reader (1984) *has pointed out, one thing is certain: Gould's vitality graced the world of letters with a species of music criticism largely absent since the days of Huneker, Henderson, and Thomson. Gould's program note on Scarlatti, written for the Canadian Broadcasting Corporation, is a good example of his writing at it most terse and jovial. The "irrepressible vivacity and goodwill" he finds in this composer is fully in tune with his own sensibility.*

Domenico Scarlatti's keyboard works were not, of course, conceived as piano music; yet few composers have ever written with such conspicuous flair for the keyboard—indeed, Liszt and Prokofiev are perhaps Scarlatti's only close rivals in the "maximum effect for minimum effort" department. And Scarlatti's shrewd tactile appreciation helps his six-hundred-odd sonatas transfer to contemporary instruments without the least disadvantage to their harpsichord-derived methodology, and to thrive while subjected to the least style-conscious of pianistic tricks. Yet it's not mute testimony to a latent *Augenmusik* potential—the sort of "write it really well and even a quartet of tubas can't do it harm" strategy that works for Bach, let's say—but a tribute, rather, to an extraordinarily farsighted deployment of the keyboard resource.

This is all the more remarkable because, despite their many offbeat gimmicks, Scarlatti's sonatas are far from formula-proof. Most of them are in one full-speed-ahead movement, observe the inevitable binary key change, and with but few exceptions foster their somewhat breathless virtuosity by a gabby two-part texture, which, notwithstanding octave doublings and triad fill-ins, enables Scarlatti to get about the keyboard with a dexterity and manual eccentricity matched by none of his contemporaries. Scarlatti does not develop ideas in that extensive, discursive way which was proper to his generation; he seems almost embarrassed when caught with a fugato on his hands or when embroiled with any but the briefest stretto imitation. Most of the contrapuntal devices which helped to formulate the imposing pronouncements of Bach and Handel are just baroque impediments to Scarlatti. He is at his happiest, and best, glibly scampering from one scintillating sequence to the next, one octave to its neighbor, employing the now current avant-garde trick of using marginal extremes in quick succession, and as a result his music possesses a higher quirk quotient than that of any comparable figure. There is a predictable discontinuity about Scarlatti, and, if his work is not memorable in the conventional sense, if his fantastic fund of melody doesn't easily impress itself upon the listener's memory, the irrepressible vivacity and goodwill of this music ensure that just about any suite of pieces culled from those six hundred sonatas will be one of the surefire delights of music.

(Program notes for a CBC broadcast, February 1968.)

# The Enchantment of Rameau

## CLAUDE DEBUSSY

*As a music critic, Claude Debussy sounded the same revolutionary note he did as a composer. Calling for a total liberation from old formulas, from the "false profundity" of the Germans to the "hysterical mysticism" of "Gounod & Co.," he championed very old and recent music. For Debussy, freedom of form and "beauty of sound" were the only absolutes. It is not surprising that he was a passionate admirer of Rameau. (See also headnote to "Moussorgsky's Vision of Childhood.")*

For many people, [Rameau] is merely the composer of the famous Rigaudon from *Dardanus,* and nothing more.

It's an example of a peculiarly French streak of sentimentality: we cling frantically to certain set ideas about art just as we do to certain styles in clothes—even if they do not suit us at all.

We all know about the influence of Gluck on French music. It was an influence that would never have taken place were it not for Marie Antoinette, the Austrian Dauphine. Incidentally, it was much the same in Wagner's case, for we owe the first Paris performance of *Tannhäuser* to another Austrian—Mme von Metternich. However, Gluck's genius was deeply rooted in the work of Rameau. *Castor et Pollux* contains in embryo the initial sketches for much that Gluck was to develop later on. On close comparison it appears that Gluck could not have taken Rameau's place in French music without immersing himself in Rameau's beautiful works and making them his own. But why on earth is the Gluck tradition still alive? His pompous and artificial way of treating recitative is enough to show us that it is, and there is also that habit of suddenly interrupting the action: Orpheus, having just lost Eurydice, sings an aria that is hardly in keeping with his sad state of mind. . . . But then that's Gluck all over, and everybody bows down to it. Rameau should have changed his nationality—it's his own fault that he did not!

We have, however, a purely French tradition in the works of Rameau. They combine a charming and delicate tenderness with precise tones and strict declamation in the recitatives—none of that affected German pomp, nor the need to emphasize everything with extravagant gestures or out-of-breath explanations, the sort which seem to say, "You are a singular collection of idiots who understand nothing and would easily believe that the moon was made of green cheese!" At the same time one is forced to admit that French music has, for too long, followed paths that definitely lead away from this clearness of expression, this conciseness and precision of form, both of which are the very qualities peculiar to French genius. I've heard too much about free exchange in art, and all the marvelous effects it's had! It is no excuse for having forgotten the traditions founded in Rameau's work, unique in being so full of wonderful discoveries.

But back to *Castor et Pollux*. The scene is the burial place of the kings of Sparta. After the overture, which makes sounds appropriate for the display of the flowing costumes in all their silken glory, we hear the lamenting voices of a choir intoning the funeral odes for Castor. At once we are enveloped in an atmosphere of tragedy. But it's still a human one—that is to say, it's not just an atmosphere of ancient Roman tunics and helmets. People weep, just like you or I. Then Telaira comes in, Castor's lover. There unfolds the sweetest, deepest lament that was ever wrought from a broken heart. Pollux appears leading some warriors who have just avenged Castor. Then the choir perform a wonderfully warlike interlude, with superbly powerful music and trumpet fanfares. And that finishes the first act.

In the second act we are at the entrance to Jupiter's temple, where everything is prepared for a sacrifice. It is simply a marvel, but one would have to quote it all . . . Pollux's solo aria: "Nature, amour, qui partagez mon sort" ("O Nature, O love, you who share my fate"), so unique in feeling and so novel in its construction that all sense of time and space is suspended. Rameau seems like one of our contemporaries whom we could congratulate as we left the theater.

It really was most disturbing! . . . The scene that follows, in which Pollux and Telaira are to sacrifice the greatest of loves to the desires of the Gods, sees the entry of the high priest of Jupiter and then Jupiter himself, who appears enthroned in glory. In his sovereign goodness he has compassion on the human torments of Pollux, the poor mortal whom he, as chief of the Gods, could crush at will. But, I repeat, one would have to quote it all. . . .

Then we come to the last scene of this act. Hebe leads the heavenly Graces in a dance, their hands filled with garlands of flowers with which to capture Pollux—Jupiter has commanded this magic to wean Pollux from his desire to die. Never has such a delicate feeling of the voluptuous found such perfect expression! It fills the heavenly air with such light that Pollux needs all his Spartan energy to withstand the spell and remember Castor. And, I must admit, *I* nearly forgot him for a moment.

To the end, this music preserves its fine sense of elegance. It is never affected, and it never uses dubious effects. Have we continued in such good taste? Or have we replaced it with our Byzantine locksmiths? I dare not say. Let us thank the Schola, MM. V. d'Indy and Bordes, and the artists they assembled for such a restoration of beauty.

I hope I will be forgiven for having written so much on a subject that is not really of our time. My excuse is first and foremost Rameau himself, who is well worth it. And moments of real joy in life are rare: I wouldn't want to keep them to myself.

(*Gil Blas*, February 2, 1903; translated by Richard Langham Smith.)

# The Clarity of Haydn

## H. L. MENCKEN

*Like George Bernard Shaw, H. L. Mencken was a master of language whose first love was music. There are other parallels as well: both men had intensive but sporadic musical training and were amateur pianists; both got their start as writers working as music reviewers for newspapers; both possessed an acrid wit that was strongest in their music columns; and both continued to use musical titles, metaphors, and forms in their work long after it became clear that their reputations would be made in other fields. Mencken's essays on music are not nearly as well known as Shaw's, but they meant more to him than perhaps anything he wrote. He regarded his inability to make music the center of his life as a personal tragedy. "My lack of sound musical instruction," he wrote in* Happy Days *(1940), "was really the great deprivation of my life. When I think of anything properly describable as a beautiful idea, it is always in the form of music. I have written and printed probably 10,000,000 words in English. . . . But all the same I shall die an inarticulate man, for my best ideas beset me in a language I know only vaguely and speak only like a child." This 1916 essay on Haydn has Mencken's characteristic zest and passion. Written during a period when the rage for Beethoven had virtually eclipsed both Haydn and Mozart, it illuminates Haydn's revolutionary clarity and "simplicity" with a force that makes it a forerunner of the current Haydn revival.*

Never having heard the Haydn symphony which Dr. Strube and his tone artists are to perform on Friday night, I am unable to tell you precisely what is in it, but all the same I offer my ears in wager that good stuff is there, and that no one will hear it without joy.

Old Haydn wrote so many symphonies that no one in the world has heard them all, but he never wrote one that lacked beauty, and he never wrote one that was not marked all over by his extraordinarily cheerful and ingratiating personality. Exploring them is an almost endless business and full of charming surprises. Some time ago, idling away a half hour at Schirmer's I happened upon one so crowded with loveliness that its relative obscurity remains astounding. A composition of such unusual beauties written today, would make a composer's reputation. But Haydn wrote dozens, nay scores, like it: and many of them are now moldering on the shelf and forgotten by all save compilers of thematic catalogues. . . . Among them all it is difficult to find a dull one, or one which does not show superb musicianship on every page.

The very clarity and simplicity of these great works has mitigated against a true understanding of their merit. Too often they are dismissed as hollow, as trivial, almost as infantile. In the shadow of the vast compositions of Beethoven they shrink to almost nothing. But a diligent study of them is all that is needed to rehabilitate them. Under the smooth and glistening surface there is seen a structure of the utmost complexity and ingenuity. They are magnificently articulated and thought out. They stand as unsurpassable examples of that exact and inevitable form which is the soul of all great music. There are ideas in them; the flow of beautiful sound never ceases for an instant; they have a beginning, a middle and an end; they hang together almost perfectly. One turns to them, from harmonic and emotional bombastics of modern orchestral music. . . .

But Haydn was more than a great composer of music; he was, beyond everything else, a great musical revolutionary. The orchestra as we know it today is his creation, or, at any rate, more his than any other man's. He put form and logic into the symphony, the most formal and logical of musical forms. He improved and gave direction to the solo sonata. Above all, he left the marks of his genius upon the string quartet. His principal quartets, even after all these years, remain fresh and vigorous; they still dispute for places on programs with the quartets of Beethoven and the vastly more complex quartets of a later day. In them, and for the first time, one finds that varied and resourceful four-part writing which is the secret of all the charm of the form, and that adroit use of polyphony which alone makes it possible. And in them, too, despite many a naïf touch, one finds a sound understanding of the capabilities and limitations of the four instruments, and an amazing skill at developing their beauties. The famous Kaiser quartet, as it stands, is so nearly perfect that the search for flaws in it can only lead to absurdity. Beethoven, true enough, wrote greater quartets, but he surely never wrote a greater one within those limits.

As for the symphonies, they are little heard today, not so much because they are empty of the wild emotion that music-lovers have been taught to look for, as because they are infernally difficult of execution. Their very simplicity, in fact, is what makes them hard to play properly; the slightest error in tone or dynamics sticks out like a sore thumb. Modern music, by its bewildering complexity, gives tone artists hedges to hide behind. Once in Munich, hearing "Electra" from the front row of the orchestra, I observed several of the first violins lose their places. A kindly brother in art hauled them up by stabbing them in the ribs with his fiddle bow. But though they had been playing *fortissimo*, it made not the slightest difference to the audience, and even the conductor was unaware of their mishap. A musician lately told me of a similar proceeding, deliberate this time, in the Boston Symphony Orchestra. During the performance of a celebrated tone-poem, much disliked by the men, a group of the first violins invariably played *"Fuchs, du hast die Gans Gestolen,"* or some other such sweet lullaby. But the audience never noticed it, and neither did Dr. Fiedler, the estimable *kapellmeister* . . . imagine that sort of thing in Haydn! The very ushers would scream!

Haydn was born in 1732 at Rohrau, a small town in Austria, near the border of Hungary. His father was the village blacksmith, and also practiced the science of a church sexton; his mother had been third cook in the household of Graf Harrach, a local magnifico. Mamma Haydn had 12 little Haydns, and after her death her successor had 5 more. Joseph was the second of the 17. At the age of 6 he was humanely rescued from this happy home by an uncle from the nearby town of Hainsburg, one Johann Matthias Frankh, a schoolmaster. Uncle Johann taught him the violin and harpsichord and discovered that he had a voice. One day this voice was heard by George Reutter, the court *kapellmeister* at Vienna, and in 1740 little Joseph was translated to the capital, where he was soon piping a shrill soprano in the choir of Old Steffel, the Vienna cathedral. . . .

It was Metastasio the poet who first set Haydn on his legs. How they met is not known, but Metastasio got him a pupil in Senorita Marianne von Martinez, a daughter to the Master of Ceremonies to the Papal Nuncio, and this connection brought him to the notice of various influential persons, and after engagements as orchestral conductor with Baron von Fürnberg, Countess von Thun, Count Hagwitz, Count Morzin and other members of the nobility, he began that long engagement with the Esterhazys which was to make his reputation and his fortune, and to color the whole stream of his life. The Prince Esterhazy of that time was Paul Anton, and like all his relatives he was an ardent musician. . . .

Prince Paul Anton died a year after Haydn got to Eisenstadt and was succeeded by his brother Nicolaus, a gaudy and Gargantuan personage. Nicolaus was the Diamond Jim Brady of his time. He spent his immense revenues upon gigantic fetes and shows, and wore uniforms heavily encrusted with precious stones. His notion of a good time was to go boar-hunting with a hundred companions, and then feast and carouse for two weeks. Nevertheless the family love of music was in him, and he seems to have treated Haydn with great respect. Not content with having music made for him, he essayed to make it himself, and so spent his rainy days practicing on the violoncello and the barytone, a somewhat smaller instrument of the same tribe, now happily extinct. Haydn wrote no fewer than 175 compositions for the barytone, including three concertos, and Nicolaus played them all. On this instrument, perhaps, the Prince was a competent performer, but he seems to have had difficulties with the 'cello, for in all of Haydn's trios the parts for it are very simple, and there is a legend that he made them so in order to please his patron. These trios suffer from the fact to this day, for 'cellists dislike them, and so their great beauties are seldom heard. Haydn himself played either the violin or the clavier parts: both are difficult and intensely interesting.

As I have said, Haydn remained with the Esterhazys, off and on for 30 years. Then he went to England as Händel had done before him. He was received with the highest respect when he got there, and became, indeed, the chief lion of London, but it took a lot of arguing to induce him to go. On the one hand, he was getting old and greatly disliked travel; on the other hand, he had many ties in Vienna. One hears of him struggling painfully with the English language, and longing sadly for the flesh-pots of Wien. The English victualry did not please him; he would awake in the night weeping for a basin of German *Linsensuppe* and a slab of the excellent coffee cake of his old friend Frau von Genziger. Worse, a widow of London, Mrs. Schroeter, tried to ensnare him, despite the fact that he was married. (He had been separated from his wife, a barber's daughter for 23 years.) All in all he longed to escape, and in 1792 he returned home. But two years later he was lured back and remained until the summer of 1795. Despite his discomforts, he wrote some of his best music in England. . . .

Back in Austria once more, he devoted himself wholeheartedly to composition, and among the fruits of his last years were "The Creation," "The Seasons" and the Austrian national anthem. . . . When the hymn was first sung on February 12, 1797, it made a colossal success, and Haydn became a national idol.

The composer himself ranked his hymn above all his other compositions. When the French bombarded Vienna in 1809 he seated himself at his piano every morning and played the melody amid the booming of the guns. In May of that year, only five days before his death, he arose from his bed and played it three times in succession. The air had acquired a lofty sacredness in his eyes. He was a firm patriot and its adoption by his people had moved him profoundly.

(*Baltimore Evening Sun*, November 23, 1916.)

# At the Thought of Mozart

## AARON COPLAND

*A remarkable number of American composers have been gifted with words. Among the more notable include Virgil Thomson, Ned Rorem, Leonard Bernstein, Charles Ives, Roger Sessions, and John Cage. One of the most felicitous of all is Aaron Copland, whose no-nonsense clarity, humor, and warmth have graced the American musical scene since midcentury. More than perhaps any other composer-essayist, Copland had the ability to write from a composer's insider perspective and make his insights totally comprehensible to the lay reader. Copland is known mainly for his articles on his contemporaries—Stravinsky, Bernstein, Chavez, Kirchner, and others both renowned and (until he championed them) unknown. That he was also a penetrating writer on older music is demonstrated by this editorial on Mozart, one of the most perfect pieces ever on this most perfect of composers.*

Paul Valery once wrote: "The definition of beauty is easy: it is that which makes us despair." On reading that phrase I immediately thought of Mozart. Admittedly despair is an unusual word to couple with the Viennese master's music. And yet, isn't it true that any incommensurable thing sets up within us a kind of despair? There is no way to *seize* the Mozart music. This is true even for a fellow-composer, any composer, who, being a composer, rightfully feels a special sense of kinship, even a happy familiarity, with the hero of Salzburg. After all, we can pore over him, dissect him, marvel or carp at him. But in the end there remains something that will not be *seized*. That is why, each time a Mozart work begins—I am thinking of the finest examples now—we composers listen with a certain awe and wonder, not unmixed with despair. The wonder we share with everyone; the despair comes from the realization that only this one man at this one moment in musical history could have created works that seem so effortless and so close to perfection. The possession of any rare beauty, any perfect love, sets up a similar distress, no doubt.

Mozart had one inestimable advantage as compared with the composers of later times: he worked within the "perfection of a common language." Without such a common language the Mozartean approach to composition and the triumphs that resulted would have been impossible. Matthew Arnold once put it this way: during such a time "you can descend into yourself and produce the best of your thought and feeling naturally, and without an overwhelming and in some degree morbid effort; for then all the people around you are more or less doing the same thing." It has been a long time since composers of the Western world have been so lucky.

Because of that I detect a certain envy mixed with their affectionate regard for Mozart as man and musician. Composers, normally, tend to be sharply critical of the works of their colleagues, ancient or modern. Mozart himself exemplified this rule. But it doesn't hold true for other composers and Mozart. A kind of love affair has been going on between them ever since the eight-year-old prodigy made the acquaintance of Johann Christian Bach in London. It cooled off somewhat in the romantic nineteenth century, only to be renewed with increased ardor in our own time. It is a strange fact that in the twentieth century it has been the more complex composers who have admired him most—perhaps because they needed him most. Busoni said that Mozart was "the most perfect example of musical talent we have ever had." Richard Strauss, after composing *Salome* and *Elektra,* paid him the ultimate compliment of abandoning his own style in order to refashion himself on a Mozartean model. Schönberg called himself a "pupil of Mozart," knowing full well that such a statement from the father of atonality would astonish. Darius Milhaud, Ernst Toch, and a host of composer-teachers quote him again and again as favored example for their students. Paradoxically, it appears that precisely those composers who left music more complicated than they found it are proudest to be counted among the Mozart disciples.

I number myself among the more critical of Mozart admirers,

for I distinguish in my mind between the merely workaday beautiful and the uniquely beautiful among his works. (I can even complain a bit, if properly encouraged, about the inordinate length of some of the operas.) I like Mozart best when I have the sensation I am watching him think. The thought processes of other composers seem to me different: Beethoven grabs you by the back of the head and forces you to think with him; Schubert, on the other hand, charms you into thinking his thoughts. But Mozart's pellucid thinking has a kind of sensitized objectivity all its own: one takes delight in watching him carefully choose orchestral timbres or in following the melodic line as it takes flight from the end of his pen.

Mozart in his music was probably the most reasonable of the world's great composers. It is the happy balance between flight and control, between sensibility and self-discipline, simplicity and sophistication of style that is his particular province. By comparison Bach seems weighted down with the world's cares, Palestrina otherworldly in his interests. Composers before him had brought music a long way from its primitive beginnings, proving that in its highest forms the art of music was to be considered on a par with other strict disciplines as one of man's grandest achievements.

Mozart, however, tapped once again the source from which all music flows, expressing himself with a spontaneity and refinement and breath-taking rightness that has never since been duplicated.

(*High Fidelity*, January 1956.)

# Mozart's Noisy Ghost

## LEIGH HUNT

*Although now known primarily as a literary essayist, political polemicist, and poet, Leigh Hunt was also one of the most vivid and engaging music critics of the early nineteenth century. As general editor of the radical London paper the* Examiner, *Hunt published a number of opera reviews between 1808 and 1821 that comprise a grand fusion of his interests in language, music, and theater. As a Romantic, Hunt disdained the "mechanical" literalness of neoclassicism and strove for a multiplicity of highly individual and metaphorical impressions. At the same time, being the editor of a popular newspaper gave his writing a clarity and directness that make him much more accessible to a modern reader than most of his contemporaries. His goal, he was fond of saying, was to "extend enjoyment" to the widest possible audience. Hunt was an ardent lover of Mozart, to whom he owed the realization that music could be as powerful as poetry, but he had a strenuous objection to the ghost in* Don Giovanni. *This 1817 elaboration of that complaint (the original having apparently caused quite a stir) is not only an argument about an opera but a major essay on the aesthetics of terror. The kind of understated ghost Hunt advocates here was eventually to find its way into everything from the tales of Le Fanu to the operas of Britten.*

We cannot mention *Don Giovanni* again without again expressing the delight it has given us. The Managers have shewed their taste, as well as a sense of their true interest, in getting it up so well, and repeating it so often. Our objections to the marble Ghost (always begging the reader to keep in mind that we speak with very unaffected deference on the works of this great Master) still remain; but it appears that some have mistaken the nature of them, and we cannot afford to let their error continue. It is the *noise*, and the noise only, of the music in which the Ghost is concerned, that we find fault with, not the chords, or the rest of the feeling. But to the noise we have very strong objections, and we think they are founded in reason, and in the practice of Mozart's brethren, the poets. We have not our former criticism by us, but we believe we there stated, though briefly, that loudness on such an occasion was contrary to the finest idea of the supernatural, which is that of power in its most powerful shape, and consequently its least vehement and assuming.

We ought therefore to have mentioned before that the first scene in which the statue speaks is that in which he affects us most. The cemetery by moonlight, the gleaming in it (which by the way is very finely managed) of the statue on horseback, the air of deathlike repose, the solemn and mute inclination of the statue's head, when *Don Giovanni* asks him if he will come to sup with him, and then the terrible words it utters—

Di rider finirai pria dell' aurora—
Thou shalt have done with laughter before morning—

in which every word is syllabled out with so awful a monotony, till there comes a drop on the *o* in *aurora*—present a combination than which nothing can be more grand or fearful; but then nothing at the same time can be more quiet, and full of a conscious power.

Now when Mozart got his statue off the horse, and set him in motion, it appears to us that he spoiled him; and we think Wieland or Schiller would have told him so, had he known and been in the habit of talking with them on his works; just as Raphael made use of his friend Ariosto, and Ariosto perhaps did of Raphael, when he wrote his picture of Alcina. All the great professors of the arts profit by this sort of communication with each other. They exchange, as it were, their experiences. There is no necessity for the Ghost to make a noise. He is not a pretender, and therefore he need not resort to the arts of human ones; and all power is great, and commanding, and awful, in proportions to its ease. The loudness, the crashing, the slamming thumps, are all comparatively vulgar. We rouse ourselves instinctively against them: we seem to say—"Oh, is that your mode of proceeding?—Well, I can be as noisy as you." There is a feeling of equality in it, as well as a reference to common human terrors, extremely hurtful to the ideas of the supernatural and the potent.

It is on these principles of our nature that the great poets, ancient and modern, have always represented power as quiet in proportion to its strength; and to ghosts they have given an especial dimness and obscurity, as beings that least of all require ordinary appearances in order to affect us.

With regard to mere power, for instance, look at the noble difference made by the ancients between Mars and Jupiter, the former a much inferior god to the other, and extremely given to noise. His shout in Homer makes the two armies start, a very sublime fancy, no doubt; but yet nothing compared with the solitary nod of Jupiter, at which the whole universe trembles. And there was something still greater and more powerful than Jupiter himself, which was Fate, a thing, or being, or whatever it was, that lay hidden in the silence and darkness of infinitude. The sublime thought of Moses is well known: "And GOD said, let there be light; and there was light." He does not say, "And a grand and mighty noise ensued, with shouts of cherubim and seraphim, &c." but we are to imagine the calm utterance of power issuing from the darkness; and light *is*. In the Psalms of David, it is observable that wherever the author gives way to the more violent and warlike part of his character, and makes the characteristics of the Deity loud and shewy, or the effects of his appearance tumultuous, his taste is by no means at its best—his effect is not greatest. When he says, for instance, that the Divine Being breaks people in pieces "like a potter's vessel," that he consumes them in fire "like the fat of lambs," that he breaks Rahab in bits, "like one that is slain," that he will cause "the righteous to bathe their legs in the blood of their enemies," and that he will "dash the heads of little children against the stones," we are only shocked; but when he talks of the "pestilence that walketh in darkness," and of fear and terror coming upon men, and when he says, that God sits with "darkness under his feet," that "his pavilion round about him is dark waters and thick clouds of the skies," that his lightnings enlighten the world, which sees and trembles, that he gives out his voice, that he stills the seas with it, that his eye is upon his creatures, and that if David could take "the wings of the morning and remain in the uttermost part of the sea, even there also his hand would *be*"—we acknowledged that these indeed however faint in the comparison, are something like ideas of the great and wonderful Spirit of Nature.

There is a very fine passage in the 1st book of *Kings* (chap. xix) where the union of power with quietness is remarkably expressed, being contrasted, as if it were on purpose, with various striking pieces of violence, so that it has an air of complete climax. Not that we mean to say it was at all written critically; but such are the instinctive feelings of our nature in all ages. The passage is as follows: "And he said, Go forth, and stand upon the mount before the Lord. And behold, the Lord passed by, and a great and strong wind rent the mountains, and broke in pieces the rocks before the Lord: but the Lord was *not* in the wind; and after the wind an earthquake, but the Lord was not in the earthquake; and after the earthquake a fire, but the Lord was not in the fire: and after the fire a *still small voice.*" The voice was the mighty Being. This is very magnificent, and appears to have given rise to a fine passage in the Koran, where there is a succession of similar agitations, after which comes a small voice, saying, "Peace be to the righteous!"

And this brings us more particularly to the idea of power as connected with apparitions. And first observe the very word *apparition;* it is a something noiseless, and only visible, an appearance. All the other words are of similar import, or still more shadowy. Thus the word *Ghost* is the same as *Spirit,* which is nothing but *Breath;* there is also a vision, a visitation, a spectre, a sight, a goblin, a shape, a phantom, a phantasma. Milton has used the force of this indistinctness to wonderful advantage in his introduction of Death, whom he calls the shadow, the monster, the goblin, the grisly terror, the hellish pest, the execrable shape, the "shape, if shape it might be called": he defines nothing:

> What *seemed his head*
> The *likeness* of a kingly crown had on;—

and yet this indescribable something was "fierce as ten furies," who are the most raging and violent of all supernatural beings"; and the phrase "fierce as ten furies" is not a tenth part so dreadful as that other one, "Black *it* stood as night." There is another passage in Milton which instantly came into our minds when we were thinking of that speaking, as it were, in *hyphens,* which we have mentioned

above, and with which Mozart makes his spectre dole out his terrible
words. It is in the same awful and shadowy style. It is where the *Lady*
speaks in *Comus,* when she is benighted in the forest:—

> A thousand fantasies
> Begin to throng into my memory,
> Of *calling shapes,* and *beckoning shadows* dire,
> And aery *tongues* that *syllable* men's names,
> On sands, and shores, and desert wildernesses.

It is gratifying to notice this point of contact between Mozart and
Milton, the latter of whom was more than fond of music, which he
both played and composed. But we must not indulge ourselves with
all the poetical passages that present themselves to our recollection.
Suffice it to say, that the greatest Greek and Latin Poets, that Dante,
Camoens, Spenser, and Shakspeare, and all other writers whose
imaginations have been of the loftiest and whose feelings of the
intensest order, have agreed to place the height of the terrible or the
powerful in the indistinct, the solemn, and the quiet. The Ghost in
*Hamlet,* who "revisits the glimpses of the moon, making night hideous," and who walks "slow and stately" by his dumb-stricken beholders, who are

> Distilled
> Almost to jelly with the act of fear,—

is alone a complete specimen of the overpowering nature of the quiet
supernatural. When it moves, it is slowly; when it speaks, it is slowly
also, and with a hollow voice; when it goes away, it *fades.*

We cannot however help concluding our observations on this
subject with an extract from the sublimest book in the Scripture, the
Arabian story of *Job.* It is another curious proof of what has been felt
on these points in ages when the feelings of mankind were in all their
ruder freshness, and when they were prepared to resist the ordinary
appearances of terror and violence, as things within everybody's
power to inflict or to resent. It is Eliphaz, Job's friend, who is speaking. "In thoughts from the visions of the night, when deep sleep
falleth on men, fear came upon me, and trembling, which made all
my bones to shake. Then a spirit passed before my face; the hair of
my flesh stood up:—it stood still, but I could not discern the form

thereof: an image was before mine eyes—*there was silence*—and I heard a voice, saying, 'Shall mortal man be more just than God? Shall a man be more pure than his maker?' "

Now from all this we infer that however fine Mozart's Ghost is in one scene, it is very inferior in another, and, as far as the loudness and clatter are concerned, is a mistake. Doubtless, something of a more distinct nature than in general, as far as *form* is concerned, may be allowed a *marble* ghost: and the idea of "the man of stone," the "white man," as *Leporello* in great horror announces the Statue when it comes to supper, is very fearful; but the noise—the noise—it is the noise only with which we quarrel; and we cannot help thinking that had the music in the orchestra been all in an undertone, the Ghost undertoned also, and the whole house comparatively silent, leaving at the same time all the chords as they are, the effect would have been twenty times finer, not to mention the double force that would have thus been given to the subsequent despair and outcries of *Don Giovanni*.

(*Examiner*, August 17, 1817.)

# The Erotic Mozart

## CHARLES ROSEN

*Charles Rosen falls into a rather exotic category that extends from Franz Liszt to Glenn Gould: the renowned pianist who is also a visionary writer and thinker. Rosen's ability to illuminate inner structures in his performances of Beethoven, Debussy, and Boulez is also exhibited in his contributions to the* New York Review of Books, The New Grove Dictionary of Music and Musicians, *and other publications. His 1972 National Book Award winner,* The Classical Style, *a work which demonstrates how the architecture of eighteenth-century music mirrors its age, is one of the most intelligent books of its kind ever written. The section on Mozart's eroticism, here excerpted, is especially provocative—a sharp challenge to those who think of Mozart as only a safe, pleasant tunesmith.*

The mixed genre in the eighteenth century is a sign of indecorum, and *Don Giovanni*, in more ways than one, is decidedly indecorous. In acknowledgement of this, da Ponte and Mozart called it not an *opera buffa*, but a *dramma giocoso*. Like *Così fan tutte* it was attacked from the beginning: it was immoral, shocking, out-of-date, and childish. The artistry of the music was naturally recognized, if its complexity was often bitterly resented. (The first Italian production had to be given up in despair after many rehearsals because of the difficulty of the score.) It was a frequent complaint of the time that Mozart's style was too learned to speak directly to the heart, but his enormous skill was never questioned. The dramatic conception, however, by no means always found favor. A critic of the first Berlin production wrote that the ear was enchanted while virtue was trampled underfoot.

The scandalous side of *Don Giovanni* had political, as well as artistic, overtones. It will not do to overstate this, but an element of liberal revolutionary aspiration is decidedly, if unsystematically, present in the work. No one in 1787 (the year when the meeting of the Estates-General echoed over all of Europe) could have missed the significance of Mozart's triumphantly overemphatic setting of 'Viva la libertà', or of the wicked exploitation of peasant innocence for dissolute aristocratic vice. The novels and political pamphlets of the time were filled with references to such matters. Mozart's ideological bias is clear in all the late operas, except for *La Clemenza di Tito* and *Così fan tutte*, which exist in abstract worlds of their own. The cartoon-like attack on the Catholic Establishment of Austria is not a negligible part of *Die Zauberflöte;* it has been denied that the identification of Maria Theresa with the Queen of the Night was intended, but it was made from the beginning, and Schikaneder and Mozart would have had to be astonishingly obtuse not to have foreseen this in a work so heavily charged with Masonic doctrine and ritual (freemasonry was the principal outlet in Austria at that time for bourgeois revolutionary ideals). In *Figaro,* too, the omission of the more overtly political passages of Beaumarchais' play can have made little difference to a public which, for the most part, knew quite clearly what was being left out; and in any case the call for the renunciation of unjust aristocratic privilege is sufficiently underlined in the opera as it stands. *Don Giovanni,* however, goes beyond all of this in its deliberate picture of a complete world disrupted by aristocratic immorality. The great ball scene in the first act is not mere musical virtuosity with all its three separate orchestras on the stage, and the complicated cross-rhythms of the dances. Each of the social classes—peasantry, bourgeoisie, and aristocracy—has its own dance, and the total independence of every rhythm is a reflection of the social hierarchy; it is this order and harmony that is destroyed by the attempted rape of Zerlina offstage.*

The political ambiance of *Don Giovanni* is given greater weight by the close relation in the eighteenth century between revolutionary thought and eroticism. I have no wish to draw a consistent doctrine from the work, but only to set in relief the significance of some of its aspects. Political and sexual liberalism were intimately connected in

---

*Don Giovanni lowers himself and raises Zerlina as he dances with her to the music for the bourgeoisie, meeting her halfway, as it were.

the 1780s; even for the most respectable citizens the idea took the shape of a governing fear that republicanism implied complete sexual license. The Marquis de Sade, in his pamphlet *One More Step* did, indeed, claim the most extravagant sexual freedom as a logical corollary of political liberty; his ideas were current everywhere in a milder form, and were the end of an already considerable amount of eighteenth-century speculation. Mozart's early and devoutly Catholic horror at French liberal thought must surely have abated considerably when he became a Freemason, but in any case his personal beliefs have little importance in this connection. The political connotations of sexual liberty were very much alive at the première of *Don Giovanni*, and they would have been inescapable. Part of the outrage and the attraction that this work inspired for years to come must be understood in this context. After 1790, the repudiation of sexual liberty and the extreme puritanism of the revolutionary government of France (and of the counter-revolutionary governments elsewhere as well) are a reaction to the intellectual climate that produced *Don Giovanni*, and are reflected in Beethoven's rejection of Mozart's libretti as unworthy of being set to music.

This sense of outrage connected with the opera—and it is implicit in Kierkegaard's view of *Don Giovanni* as the only work that perfectly embodies the essentially erotic nature of music, and in E. T. A. Hoffmann's stressing of what he called its 'romanticism'—this sense of *Don Giovanni* as an attack, at once frontal and oblique, upon aesthetic and moral values is more useful for understanding the opera, and Mozart's music in general, than the common-sense view which shrugs off this aspect impatiently. Music is the most abstract of all the arts only in the sense that it is the least representational: it is, however, the least abstract in its direct physical assault on the listeners' nerves, in the immediacy of effect that its patterns gain from the apparently almost total reduction of mediating symbolism, of all ideas that seem to call for decoding and interpretation, and so to stand between music and listener. (If, as a matter of fact, the reduction is very far from total, and the listener must expend considerable labor decoding the symbolic relationships set before him, his activity is less conscious, less verbalized, than in any other art.) When this physical immediacy of music is stressed, then its erotic aspect stands well to the fore. Perhaps no composer used the seductive physical power of music with the intensity and the range of Mozart. The flesh is corrupt and corrupting. Behind Kierkegaard's essay on *Don Giovanni* stands the idea that music is a sin: it seems fundamentally sound that he should have chosen Mozart as the most sinful composer of all. What is most extraordinary about Mozart's style is the combination of physical delight—a sensuous play of sonority, an indulgence in the most luscious harmonic sequences—with a purity and economy of line and form that render the seduction all the more efficient.

A more prosaic and more conventionally respectable view of Mozart comes not from the sober perspective of the twentieth century but from the height of Romantic enthusiasm: in the G minor Symphony, a work of passion, violence, and grief for those who love Mozart most, Schumann saw nothing but lightness, grace, and charm. It should be said at once that to reduce a work to the expression of sentiments, however powerful, is to trivialize it in any case: the G minor Symphony is not much more profound conceived as a tragic cry from the heart than as a work of exquisite charm. Nevertheless, Schumann's attitude to Mozart ends by destroying his vitality as it canonizes him. It is only through recognizing the violence and the sensuality at the center of Mozart's work that we can make a start towards a comprehension of his structures and an insight into his magnificence. In a paradoxical way, however, Schumann's superficial characterization of the G minor Symphony can help us to see Mozart's daemon more steadily. In all of Mozart's supreme expressions of suffering and terror—the G minor Symphony, *Don Giovanni,* the G minor Quintet, Pamina's aria in *Die Zauberflöte*—there is something shockingly voluptuous. Nor does this detract from its power or effectiveness: the grief and the sensuality strengthen each other, and end by becoming indivisible, indistinguishable one from the other. (Tchaikovsky's grief, for example, has an equal lubricity, but his diffuse and wasteful technique of composition makes him far less dangerous.) In his corruption of sentimental values, Mozart is a subversive artist.

Almost all art is subversive: it attacks established values, and replaces them with those of its own creation; it substitutes its own order for that of society. The disconcertingly suggestive aspects—moral and political—of Mozart's operas are only a surface appearance of this aggression. His works are in many ways an assault upon the musical language that he helped to create: the powerful chromaticism that he could employ with such ease comes near at moments to destroying the tonal clarity that was essential to the significance of his own forms, and it was this chromaticism that had a real influence upon the Romantic style, on Chopin and Wagner in particular. The artistic personality that Haydn created for himself (related to, but not to be confused with, the face he wore for everyday purposes) prevented, by its assumption of an easy-going geniality, the full development of the subversive and revolutionary aspect of his art: his music, as E. T. A. Hoffmann wrote, appears to have been composed before original sin. Beethoven's attack was naked, no art was less accommodating in its refusal to accept any other conditions than its own. Mozart was as unaccommodating as Beethoven, and the sheer physical beauty, prettiness, even, of so much of what he composed masks the uncompromising character of his art. It cannot be fully appreciated without recalling the uneasiness and even dismay that it so often evoked in its time, and without recreating in our own minds the conditions in which it could still seem dangerous.

(*The Classical Style*, 1972.)

# Mozart's Operas
# Beethoven's *Fidelio*

## THOMAS LOVE PEACOCK

*Like his contemporary Leigh Hunt, Thomas Love Peacock was a literary critic and man of letters who had a passion for opera. His love of Mozart was most succinctly expressed in an 1833 Examiner article in which he declared, "There never has been anything perfect under the sun except the compositions of Mozart." His admiration for Beethoven's dramatic music, which he judged to be "of intrinsic and indestructible beauty," was no less keen. Reprinted here are two short notes which make both cases with a minimum of fuss and words.*

There is nothing perfect in this world except Mozart's music. Criticism has nothing to do with it, but to admire. Whatever is is right. Mozart cannot even be disparaged by comparison with himself—the detractor cannot say, "How inferior this thing is to that!" for every composition seems to have a peculiar appropriateness to the occasion, and it is impossible to conceive any thing more suitable. There is nothing of mannerism in Mozart's music, and yet it cannot be mistaken for any other, or any other for it—it is peculiar in its excellence. The signature of the master is in an exalted sweetness of turns. In Mozart's operas there is every variety of style and expression, each having a marked style to which the varieties within it are subordinate and tributary. *Don Giovanni* and the *Zauberflöte* are both romantic operas, but of what different characters! In each the grandeur is relieved with gaiety; and here again how different the gaiety! In *Giovanni* it is touched with riot, in the *Zauberflöte* it is all fanciful and cheery. As wide a distinction is to be marked between the gaiety of *Figaro* and of *Cosi fan tutte;* the first is of enjoyment, the other the light laugh of the world coming more from the brain than the blood.

The expression of the serious passions has as much variety in the works of Mozart as the comic. The simple sustained style of the *Clemenza* has no likeness in any of the solemn passages of his romantic operas, and the grandeur of the *Zauberflote* is as distinguishable from the grandeur of *Giovanni*, as the devotional from the terrible. In the expression of tenderness there is most sameness in Mozart's compositions; and how could it be other than same while true to nature, which, in all states, shows herself much alike in the melting mood?

The *Zauberflote*, which has not for many years been performed in this country, was produced on Monday at Covent Garden by the German Company. Most of the beauties of this opera are, however, already familiar to the English public; and we heard several persons expressing their surprise at meeting with their old acquaintance, the *Manly Heart*, in the German guise. To many a known song in a fine opera is as acceptable as a known face in a strange land. They are glad of something to recognise when their faculties have been on the stretch to admire what they cannot understand. As a drama, the *Zauberflote* is extremely heavy and stupid. The actors, however, do all that can be done to carry it off. . . . So far as the cast is concerned the opera is well performed; and having said that, those who have any relish for the exquisite music of it, will understand the gratification which is in store for them.

(*The German Opera*, June 2, 1833.)

## Beethoven's *Fidelio*

**B**eethoven's *Fidelio* is the absolute perfection of dramatic music. It combines the profoundest harmony with melody that speaks to the soul. It carries to a pitch scarcely conceivable the true musical expression of the strongest passions, and the gentlest emotions, in all their shades and contrasts. The playfulness of youthful hope, the heroism of devoted love, the rage of the tyrant, the despair of the captive, the bursting of the sunshine of liberty upon the gloom of the dungeon, which are the great outlines of the feelings successively developed in this opera, are pourtrayed in music, not merely with truth of expression, as that term might be applied to other works, but with a force and reality that make music an intelligible language, possessing an illimitable power of pouring forth thought in sound. *Fidelio* is, we believe, Beethoven's only opera. It is the sun among the stars. It is not a step in the progress of dramatic music. It is a clear projection of it, a century in advance of its march.

(*King's Theatre*, May 27, 1832.)

# Haydn, Beethoven, and Mozart

## VIRGIL THOMSON

*One of the few undisputed verities in our musical culture is the quality of Virgil Thomson's essays on music. Unlike most composer-critics, Thomson did not treat writing as a minor adjunct to composing but as a major creative activity. For some fifty years—as an expatriate in Paris between the wars, columnist for the* New York Herald Tribune, *and regular contributor to the* New York Review of Books *and other publications—Thomson graced the world of letters with a prose style of unfailing intelligence and pungency. Although firmly "American" in his advocacy of American music and his vigorous, uninhibited literary voice, Thomson was a genuinely international figure, and like all good music essayists, a writer with broad cultural interests. As John Rockwell of the* New York Times *recently put it, "With Thomson everything, new and old, was seen with a fresh, contemporary spirit, and one not limited to music." As this 1941 piece from the* Herald Tribune *illustrates, Thomson could make even the standard and the established seem fresh. No one has summarized Haydn, Beethoven, and Mozart with more precision and wit, or tied their humanity more touchingly to their music. Yet this daunting undertaking is accomplished with the simplest metaphors. Reading Thomson is like being with a good conversationalist, someone who has impeccable phraseology but who is speaking to communicate rather than to impress.*

Lately I have been reading and rereading the Haydn piano sonatas. Like all of Haydn's music they represent a gold mine of melody and of instrumental imagination. There is scarcely one that does not contain some passage familiar to us all, familiar, I may add, more often than not because of Beethoven's unacknowledged quotation of it in sonata or symphony. They also represent, as do equally the piano sonatas of Mozart and of Beethoven, the counterpart to the symphonies of these masters. If one wants to understand the latter, one must study the former; and vice versa.

What strikes me most about Haydn is that of the three great Viennese masters he is by far the most melodious. His thematic invention is the most varied of them all and his thematic development the most tuneful. His whole musical concept is lyrical. For this reason he is at his best in the non-lyrical movements. The first movement and the minuet are commonly his richest. The development of his first-movement themes through a cycle of sonata-form modulations gives symmetry and weight to what might be merely graceful if no such formal layout were employed. Similarly, the minuet's quality of dance music enforces a certain objectivity upon his process of composition that adds to Haydn's abundance of personal fancy the welcome solidity of a straightforward and easily understood human significance. The rondo, Haydn's most frequently observed last-movement scheme, gives too much play to his musical imagination, obliges him too little to expression. The same is true of his slow movements, which are melodious and full of incidental invention, but which do not say much.

The truth is that Haydn wrote music like an old bachelor (which, for all practical purposes, he was). A self-contained and self-sufficient lyricism is its dominant characteristic, an avuncular generosity its chief means of contact with the listener. Of humane objectivity it has virtually none save in the jolly and waltz-like dance movements, where he remembers his peasant upbringing. The encounter of his native lyrical abundance with sonata-form formalities, however, as that takes place in his first movements, produces a kind of three-dimensional grandeur that is acceptable in terms of its sheer musical magnificence, without regard to what its expressive intention may be. In this respect Haydn's instrumental music looks backward to that of Domenico Scarlatti and the Bach family, just as his oratorios resemble strongly those of Handel. His technical procedures are those of Romanticism; but his thought is neither expansive, like Beethoven's, nor dramatic, like that of Mozart. It is a lyrical fountain forever overflowing and constantly inundating everybody with melody.

Beethoven really was an old bachelor. But he never liked it. All his music is cataclysmic, as if he were constantly trying to break out of his solitude. His first movements state the problem squarely. His slow movements are less interesting, because they try unsuccessfully to avoid it; they tread water. His minuets and scherzos reopen the problem and announce the hope of a solution. The finales, almost always the finest and certainly the most characteristic movements in Beethoven, are the solution that the whole piece has been working up to. That solution is usually of a religious nature. It represents redemption, the victory of soul over flesh. It varies from calm serenity to active triumph, but joy is its thesis. In the Ninth Symphony a German ode on that subject is inserted to clinch the matter. The bonds of solitude are broken because they are imagined as being broken. That breaking is of a purely mystical nature, a temporary identification of the self with God or with all humanity. The form of the musical expression is free and infinitely varied. The finales show Beethoven at his most personal and most masterful. They are grand, terribly serious, and, for the most part, inspiring.

Solitude was unknown to Mozart. Except for a short time in Paris, just after his mother died there, he was probably never in all his life alone for so much as half a day. His music, likewise, is full of dramatic animation. His themes are like people, his developments a working out of their contrasting natures. His first movements, in spite of the beauty of their material, are little more than a first act or prelude to the drama of the rest. The slow movements are always the crux of the matter, the freest, grandest, and most fanciful part of any Mozart sonata or symphony. They are impossible to interpret unless one considers them as theater, as a dramatization of real characters, a conflict among other people's emotions. The minuet which follows (in the quartets it more commonly precedes) is pure ballet. It has nothing to do with Haydn's peasant gambols. It is slow and stately and complex. It, too, shows a conflict of sentiments, as if the dramatic struggles of the preceding movement were here resolved, or at least appeased, through observance of the social amenities. It is a tense and static little affair.

The finales are not dramatic at all. They are mostly fast and always furious. Nothing in music, excepting maybe five or six of the Bach organ fugues, have that kind of power and insistence, as of an element unchained. They do not have to be played at breakneck speed. Those for piano solo definitely profit by moderation in this regard. But rhythmic tension they must have and dynamic contrast. They are the moral of the piece. They show, as Mozart was always trying to show in his operas, how marvelously vigorous life can be when people make up their minds to put their petty differences on the shelf and to collaborate in full good will at being human beings together. Their whole effect can be spoiled unless the preceding movement, whether that is an adagio or the more usual minuet, is presented at a contrasting tempo. Any speed that suggests the scherzo in rendering a Mozart minuet not only falsifies the significance of the minuet itself but steals, as well, the fire of the movement that follows.

(*New York Herald Tribune*, December 21, 1941.)

# Weber and the Fantastic
# Beethoven's Despair

## HECTOR BERLIOZ

*Hector Berlioz was the greatest of the Romantic composer-critics. He had the ardor of Schumann, Liszt, and Wagner, but he was also a meticulously careful writer, a master of irony, wit, and the most delicate shades of color and imagery. His prose is like his music: romantic in content and intensity, classically refined in color and design. Writing, in fact, was Berlioz's main source of income. In Paris, his music brought notoriety but little financial reward, nor could he secure a post as a conductor or academic. Beginning in 1823, Berlioz contributed nearly 700 pieces to various periodicals, only a small portion of which (including* Les soires de l'orchestre *[1852],* Les grotesques de la musique *[1859], and* A travers chants *[1862]) were collected. Berlioz's masterpiece, the* Memoirs *(1870), is generously sprinkled with some of the best music criticism of the century, including the prophetic assessment of Weber reprinted here. But the composer Berlioz admired above all others—his God, next to Shakespeare—was Beethoven, whose Fifth Symphony was the inspiration for more than a few Romantic composers. The following excerpt from his extensive analysis of the Fifth has been newly translated for this book by Jacques Barzun.*

In my exclusive worship of classical opera I had been intolerantly prepared to reject [Weber's] new style; but to my surprise it delighted me, garbled though it was by crude and incomplete performance. Even in this ravaged form there was a wild sweetness in the music that I found intoxicating. I must admit I was getting a little tired of the tragic muse and her high solemnities. Here, in complete contrast, was a woodnymph of ravishing freshness and charm, a creature of instinct and mercurial fancy, naïve, gay, pensive, passionate, melancholy, whose beauty overwhelmed me with a flood of undiscovered sensations.

I began to forsake the Opéra for the Odéon, where I had a pass to the pit. I never missed a performance, and soon knew the *Freischütz*, or all of it that was given there, by heart.

Weber himself came to France about that time. It is twenty-one years now since he paid his first and last visit to Paris, on the way to London, to the near-failure of one of his masterpieces, *Oberon*, and his own death. How I longed to see him! How pantingly I pursued him that evening when, already a sick man, he went to hear the revival of Spontini's *Olympie* a few days before he left for England! But it was hopeless. The same morning Lesueur had greeted me with: "Weber has just been here. If you had come five minutes earlier you would have heard him play me whole scenes from our operas; he knows them all." A few hours later, in a music shop: "Who do you think was sitting here a moment ago?"

"Who?"

"Weber!"

At the Opéra, when I arrived, everybody was talking about him. "Weber's just walked through the foyer." "He's gone in." "He's in a box on the first tier." I was in despair at never being able to catch up with him. But it was no use; no one there seemed able to point him out to me. He was like Shakespeare's apparitions in reverse—visible to all but one. Unknown as I was, I could not bring myself to write him a note, nor had I any friends there who were in a position to introduce me. So I never set eyes on him.

If great creative artists could only divine the grand passions their works inspire! If it were only given to them to perceive the enthusiasm of a hundred thousand hearts concentrated in a single heart, how they would grapple such secret devotion to their souls as a powerful consolation in adversity—against the envy and hatred of some, the dull, shallow indifference of others, the half-heartedness of all!

Despite his popularity, despite the glamour of *Freischütz* and the vogue it enjoyed, and conscious as he must have been of his own genius, Weber more than most might have been glad of such humble but devoted admiration. He had written exquisite things only to see them derided by performers and critics. His most recent opera,

*Euryanthe,* had had only a limited success, and he had good reason to be anxious for *Oberon,* realizing that such a work, to be fully appreciated, requires an audience of poets and a pit full of intellectual aristocrats. Even Beethoven, the noblest mind of all, had for long underrated him. One can see how at times (as he himself has written) he lost faith in what he was doing, and how it was that the failure of *Oberon* killed him.

If the fate of this marvellous score has been quite different from that of its elder brother, *Freischütz,* which the public has seen fit to acclaim, this is not due to any vulgarity in the character of *Freischütz,* anything shoddy in its construction, anything sham in its brilliance or blatantly sensational in its style. In neither work has the composer made the least concession to passing fashion or to the even grosser demands of singers and their vanity. He was as proudly himself, as true, as original, as hostile to formula, as resolute in integrity, as incapable of compromise for the sake of applause, as great, in *Freischütz* as in *Oberon.* The poetic invention of the former, however, is full of energy, passion and contrast; the supernatural element in it gives rise to strange and startling effects. Melody, harmony and rhythm alike are tremendously vivid and powerful; everything combines to arouse the listener. In addition the characters, being drawn from life, are more obviously appealing; the representation of their feelings and the world they live in has naturally prompted a less rarefied, more accessible style; yet it is treated with such exquisite skill that the most austere spirit cannot resist its charm, while for this same quality the mass of the people deem it the very perfection of art and a miracle of invention.

In *Oberon,* on the other hand, though human emotion plays an important part, the fantastic is predominant—but the fantastic in a cool, serene, unassertive form. In place of monsters and fearful apparitions there are choirs of aerial spirits, sylphs, fairies, waternymphs; and the musical idiom of these gentle, mild-eyed creatures—an idiom unlike any other—derives its chief attraction from the harmony. Melodically wayward and ambiguous, rhythmically fluid, unpredictable and often difficult to grasp, it is hardly likely to be understood by the general public when not even musicians can appreciate its subtleties without the most concentrated attention combined with the liveliest imagination. The romantic German temperament is presumably better attuned to this exquisite poetry. For the French, I fear, it could never be more than an object of curiosity; and we would very soon find ourselves getting bored with it.[1]

(*Memoirs*, 1870; translated by David Cairns.)

## Beethoven's Despair

Unquestionably, the most famous of his symphonies is also the first in which Beethoven gave free scope to his vast imagination without taking as guide or support an extraneous idea. In the first, second and fourth symphonies, he more or less extended forms previously known; invested them with all the poetry that his vigorous youth could bestow—brilliant, passionate, and inspired. In the third (the "Eroica") the form tends toward greater breadth, it is true, and the idea also reaches a greater height. But we cannot fail to recognize in it the influence of one or other of those divine poets to whom, from early days, the great artist had erected a temple in his heart. Beethoven, faithful to Horace's precept,

*Nocturnâ versate manu, versate diurná,*

used to read Homer habitually; and in his magnificent musical epic which, rightly or wrongly, is said to have been inspired by a modern hero, recollections of the antique *Iliad* play a part as admirable and beautiful as it is unmistakable.

The Symphony in C Minor, on the contrary, seems to me to emanate directly and solely from the genius of Beethoven. It is his own intimate thought which is there developed. His secret sorrows, his pent-up rage, his reveries full of melancholy languor, his nighttime visions and his spurts of enthusiasm furnish its entire subject; while the melodic, harmonic, rhythmic, and orchestral forms exhibit a fundamental originality, and individuality, the whole endowed with great power and nobility.

The first movement is devoted to the expression of the disordered feelings that overwhelm a great soul when a prey to despair. It is not that calm and concentrated despair which gives the appearance

[1]Since this was written, the production of *Oberon* at the Théâtre-Lyrique [1857] has proved me wrong. The work created a sensation and had an enormous success. The Parisian public must have made remarkable progress.

of resignation; not the sombre, silent grief of Romeo hearing of the death of Juliet. Rather, is it the dread fury of Othello, when told by Iago the envenomed lies that persuade him of Desdemona's crime. It is now a frenzied delirium, bursting forth in fearful cries, now an extreme lassitude, expressed only in accents of regret and seeming to turn upon itself in pity. Listen to those orchestral gasps; those chords in dialogue between winds and strings, which alternate and grow weaker, like the painful breathing of a dying man, then give way to a phrase full of violence in which the orchestra seems to recover strength, animated by a bolt of fury. Note that shuddering mass, which hesitates for an instant and then hurls itself, divided, into two ardent unisons like two streams of lava. Note all this, then say whether this passionate style is not above and beyond anything yet produced in instrumental music.

(*A Travers Chant*, 1862; translated by Jacques Barzun.)

# Beethoven and the Sublime

## E. T. A. HOFFMANN

*A master of the supernatural tale, E. T. A. Hoffmann is perhaps the ideal writer to remind us that Beethoven was considered by his contemporaries to be a source of sublime terror and anxiety rather than the safe, bland composer that overexposure in our culture has made him seem. Hoffmann is one of several examples in this book of a literary artist who was also a prodigious writer on music. He was also one of the first great composer-critics, a forerunner of Berlioz and Schumann, whose creativity and passion flowed with equal freedom through music and language. The composer of the fantasy opera* Undine, *Hoffmann was also the creator of fantasies that inspired other composers' music, including Schumann's* Kreisleriana, *Tchaikovsky's the* Nutcracker, *and Offenbach's* Tales of Hoffmann. *As a polemicist for Romanticism, he naturally emphasized the stormy side of Beethoven. Written during Beethoven's lifetime, Hoffmann's essay on that composer is the inversion of Wagner's "Beethoven: A Revelation from Another World," below. To Wagner, a creator of music drama, "the Word" in the choral section of the Ninth Symphony was the clearest and most satisfying Beethoven expression. To Hoffmann, Beethoven's wordless instrumental music was the ultimate Romanticism precisely because of the teasing indefiniteness Wagner longed to resolve.*

When we speak of music as an independent art, should we not always restrict our meaning to instrumental music, which, scorning every aid, every admixture of another art (the art of poetry), gives pure expression to music's specific nature, recognizable in this form alone? It is the most romantic of all the arts—one might almost say, the only genuinely romantic one—for its sole subject is the infinite. The lyre of Orpheus opened the portals of Orcus—music discloses to man an unknown realm, a world that has nothing in common with the external sensual world that surrounds him, a world in which he leaves behind him all definite feelings to surrender himself to an inexpressible longing.

Have you even so much as suspected this specific nature, you miserable composers of instrumental music, you who have laboriously strained yourselves to represent definite emotions, even definite events? How can it ever have occurred to you to treat after the fashion of the plastic arts the art diametrically opposed to plastic? Your sunrises, your tempests, your *Batailles des trois Empereurs*, and the rest, these, after all, were surely quite laughable aberrations, and they have been punished as they well deserved by being wholly forgotten.

In song, where poetry, by means of words, suggests definite emotions, the magic power of music acts as does the wondrous elixir of the wise, a few drops of which make any drink more palatable and more lordly. Every passion—love, hatred, anger, despair, and so forth, just as the opera gives them to us—is clothed by music with the purple luster of romanticism, and even what we have undergone in life guides us out of life into the realm of the infinite.

As strong as this is music's magic, and, growing stronger and stronger, it had to break each chain that bound it to another art.

That gifted composers have raised instrumental music to its present high estate is due, we may be sure, less to the more readily handled means of expression (the greater perfection of the instruments, the greater virtuosity of the players) than to the more profound, more intimate recognition of music's specific nature.

Mozart and Haydn, the creators of our present instrumental music, were the first to show us the art in its full glory; the man who then looked on it with all his love and penetrated its innermost being is—Beethoven! The instrumental compositions of these three masters breathe a similar romantic spirit—this is due to their similar intimate understanding of the specific nature of the art; in the character of their compositions there is none the less a marked difference.

In Haydn's writing there prevails the expression of a serene and childlike personality. His symphonies lead us into vast green woodlands, into a merry, gaily colored throng of happy mortals. Youths and maidens float past in a circling dance; laughing children, peering out from behind the trees, from behind the rose bushes, pelt one another playfully with flowers. A life of love, of bliss like that before the Fall, of eternal youth; no sorrow, no suffering, only a sweet melancholy yearning for the beloved object that floats along, far away, in the glow of the sunset and comes no nearer and does not disappear—nor does night fall while it is there, for it is itself the sunset in which hill and valley are aglow.

Mozart leads us into the heart of the spirit realm. Fear takes us in its grasp, but without torturing us, so that it is more an intimation of the infinite. Love and melancholy call to us with lovely spirit voices; night comes on with a bright purple luster, and with inexpressible longing we follow those figures which, waving us familiarly into their train, soar through the clouds in eternal dances of the spheres.

Thus Beethoven's instrumental music opens up to us also the realm of the monstrous and the immeasurable. Burning flashes of light shoot through the deep night of this realm, and we become aware of giant shadows that surge back and forth, driving us into narrower and narrower confines until they destroy *us*—but not the pain of that endless longing in which each joy that has climbed aloft in jubilant song sinks back and is swallowed up, and it is only in this pain, which consumes love, hope, and happiness but does not destroy them, which seeks to burst our breasts with a many-voiced consonance of all the passions, that we live on, enchanted beholders of the supernatural!

Romantic taste is rare, romantic talent still rarer, and this is doubtless why there are so few to strike that lyre whose sound discloses the wondrous realm of the romantic.

Haydn grasps romantically what is human in human life; he is more commensurable, more comprehensible for the majority.

Mozart calls rather for the superhuman, the wondrous element that abides in inner being.

Beethoven's music sets in motion the lever of fear, of awe, of horror, of suffering, and wakens just that infinite longing which is the essence of romanticism. He is accordingly a completely romantic composer, and is not this perhaps the reason why he has less success with vocal music, which excludes the character of indefinite longing, merely representing emotions defined by words as emotions experienced in the realm of the infinite?

The musical rabble is oppressed by Beethoven's powerful genius; it seeks in vain to oppose it. But knowing critics, looking about them with a superior air, assure us that we may take their word for it as men of great intellect and deep insight that, while the excellent Beethoven can scarcely be denied a very fertile and lively imagination, he does not know how to bridle it! Thus, they say, he no longer bothers at all to select or to shape his ideas, but, following the so-called daemonic method, he dashes everything off exactly as his ardently active imagination dictates it to him. Yet how does the matter stand if it is *your* feeble observation alone that the deep inner continuity of Beethoven's every composition eludes? If it is *your* fault alone that you do not understand the master's language as the initiated understand it, that the portals of the innermost sanctuary remain closed to you? The truth is that, as regards self-possession, Beethoven stands quite on a par with Haydn and Mozart and that, separating his ego from the inner realm of harmony, he rules over it as an absolute monarch. In Shakespeare, our knights of the aesthetic measuring-rod have often bewailed the utter lack of inner unity and inner continuity, although for those who look more deeply there springs forth, issuing from a single bud, a beautiful tree, with leaves, flowers, and fruit; thus, with Beethoven, it is only after a searching investigation of his instrumental music that the high self-possession inseparable from true genius and nourished by the study of the art stands revealed.

Can there be any work of Beethoven's that confirms all this to a higher degree than his indescribably profound, magnificent symphony in C minor? How this wonderful composition, in a climax that climbs on and on, leads the listener imperiously forward into the spirit world of the infinite! ... No doubt the whole rushes like an ingenious rhapsody past many a man, but the soul of each thoughtful listener is assuredly stirred, deeply and intimately, by a feeling that is none other than that unutterable portentous longing, and until the final chord—indeed, even in the moments that follow it— he will be powerless to step out of that wondrous spirit realm where grief and joy embrace him in the form of sound. The internal structure of the movements, their execution, their instrumentation, the way in which they follow one another—everything contributes to a single end; above all, it is the intimate interrelationship among the themes that engenders that unity which alone has the power to hold the listener firmly in a single mood. This relationship is sometimes clear to the listener when he overhears it in the connecting of two movements or discovers it in the fundamental bass they have in common; a deeper relationship which does not reveal itself in this way speaks at other times only from mind to mind, and it is precisely this relationship that prevails between sections of the two Allegros and the Minuet and which imperiously proclaims the self-possession of the master's genius.

How deeply thy magnificent compositions for the piano have impressed themselves upon my soul, thou sublime master; how shallow and insignificant now all seems to me that is not thine, or by the gifted Mozart or that mighty genius, Sebastian Bach! With what joy I received thy seventieth work, the two glorious trios, for I knew full well that after a little practice I should soon hear them in truly splendid style. And in truth, this evening things went so well with me that even now, like a man who wanders in the mazes of a fantastic park, woven about with all manner of exotic trees and plants and marvelous flowers, and who is drawn further and further in, I am powerless to find my way out of the marvelous turns and windings of thy trios. The lovely siren voices of these movements of thine, resplendent in their many-hued variety, lure me on and on. The gifted lady who indeed honored me, Capellmeister Kreisler, by playing today the first trio in such splendid style, the gifted lady before whose piano I still sit and write, has made me realize quite clearly that only what the mind produces calls for respect and that all else is out of place.

Just now I have repeated at the piano from memory certain striking transitions from the two trios.

How well the master has understood the specific character of the instrument and fostered it in the way best suited to it!

A simple but fruitful theme, songlike, susceptible to the most varied contrapuntal treatments, curtailments, and so forth, forms the basis of each movement; all remaining subsidiary themes and figures are intimately related to the main idea in such a way that the details all interweave, arranging themselves among the instruments in highest unity. Such is the structure of the whole, yet in this artful structure there alternate in restless flight the most marvelous pictures in which joy and grief, melancholy and ecstasy, come side by side or intermingled to the fore. Strange figures begin a merry dance, now floating off into a point of light, now splitting apart, flashing and sparkling, evading and pursuing one another in various combinations, and at the center of the spirit realm thus disclosed the intoxicated soul gives ear to the unfamiliar language and understands the most mysterious premonitions that have stirred it.

That composer alone has truly mastered the secrets of harmony who knows how, by their means, to work upon the human soul; for him, numerical proportions, which to the dull grammarian are no more than cold, lifeless problems in arithmetic, become magical compounds from which to conjure up a magic world.

Despite the good nature that prevails, especially in the first trio, not even excepting the melancholy Largo, Beethoven's genius is in the last analysis serious and solemn. It is as though the master thought that, in speaking of deep mysterious things—even when the spirit, intimately familiar with them, feels itself joyously and gladly uplifted—one may not use an ordinary language, only a sublime and glorious one; the dance of the priests of Isis can be only an exultant hymn. Where instrumental music is to produce its effect simply through itself as music and is by no means to serve a definite dramatic purpose, it must avoid all trivial facetiousness, all frivolous *lazzi*. A deep temperament seeks, for the intimations of that joy which, an import from an unknown land, more glorious and more beautiful than here in our constricted world, enkindles an inner, blissful life within our breasts, a higher expression than can be given to it by mere words, proper only to our circumscribed earthly air. This seriousness, in all of Beethoven's works for instruments and for the piano, is in itself enough to forbid all those breakneck passages up and down for the two hands which fill our piano music in the latest style, all the queer leaps, the farcical capriccios, the notes towering high above the staff on their five- and six-line scaffolds.

On the side of mere digital dexterity, Beethoven's compositions for the piano really present no special difficulty, for every player must be presumed to have in his fingers the few runs, triplet figures, and whatever else is called for; nevertheless, their performance is on the whole quite difficult. Many a so-called virtuoso condemns this music, objecting that it is "very difficult" and into the bargain "very ungrateful."

Now, as regards difficulty, the correct and fitting performance of a work of Beethoven's asks nothing more than that one should understand him, that one should enter deeply into his being, that—conscious of one's own consecration—one should boldly dare to step into the circle of the magical phenomena that his powerful spell has evoked. He who is not conscious of this consecration, who regards sacred Music as a mere game, as a mere entertainment for an idle hour, as a momentary stimulus for dull ears, or as a means of self-ostentation—let him leave Beethoven's music alone. Only to such a man, moreover, does the objection "most ungrateful" apply. The true artist lives only in the work that he has understood as the composer meant it and that he then performs. He is above putting his own personality forward in any way, and all his endeavors are directed toward a single end—that all the wonderful enchanting pictures and apparitions that the composer has sealed into his work with magic power may be called into active life, shining in a thousand colors, and that they may surround mankind in luminous sparkling circles and, enkindling its imagination, its innermost soul, may bear it in rapid flight into the faraway spirit realm of sound.

(*Zeitung für die elegante Welt,* December 1813; translated by Oliver Strunk.)

# Beethoven: A Revelation from Another World

## RICHARD WAGNER

*Grandiose, blazingly colorful, often overwrought, Richard Wagner's essays were the verbal equivalent of his music dramas, an attempt to combine philosophy, religion, and the history of the human race in passages often organized with associative motifs rather than traditional patterns of logic and rhetoric. In Wagner's multivolumed prose works, the most obsessive* leitmotif *was Beethoven, whom Wagner regarded as the master and even "saint" of music. In his controversial "The Art Work of the Future" (1850), Wagner found in the choral section of the Ninth Symphony a necessary emancipation of instrumental music from its limitations. Although many critics (including Donald Francis Tovey in the following "On the Beethoven Ninth") have denounced this argument as a self-serving justification of Wagner's own theories, it should not be forgotten that Wagner also gives Beethoven's instrumental music its full, heroic due, both in this piece and in two later ones excerpted below. Also excerpted is Wagner's wildly metaphorical passage on the C-Sharp Minor Quartet, an essay cited by Paul Rosenfeld as a classic example of what one composer* really hears—*as opposed to the technical jargon offered up in standard music criticism—when contemplating* another.*

I t was *Beethoven* who opened up the boundless faculty of Instrumental Music for expressing elemental storm and stress. His power it was, that took the basic essence of the Christian's Harmony, that bottomless sea of unhedged fulness and unceasing motion, and clove in twain the fetters of its freedom. *Harmonic Melody*—for so must we designate this melody divorced from speech, in distinction from the Rhythmic Melody of dance—was capable, though merely borne by instruments, of the most limitless expression together with the most unfettered treatment. In long, connected tracts of sound, as in larger, smaller, or even smallest fragments, it turned beneath the Master's poet hand to vowels, syllables, and words and phrases of a speech in which a message hitherto unheard, and never spoken yet, could promulgate itself. Each letter of this speech was an infinitely soul-full element; and the measure of the joinery of these elements was utmost free commensuration, such as could be exercised by none but a tone-poet who longed for the unmeasured utterance of this unfathomed yearning.

("The Art-Work of the Future," 1850.)

I t is impossible to keep Beethoven the man before us for an instant, without at once re-calling Beethoven the wonderful musician to explain him.

We have seen how the instinctive tendence of his life ran parallel with the tendence to emancipate his art; as he himself could be no lackey in the pay of Luxury, so should his music, too, be freed from every token of subjection to a frivolous taste. And of how his optimistic creed went hand-in-hand with an instinctive tendency to enlarge the province of his art we have evidence, of the sublimest naïvety, in his *Ninth Symphony with Choruses;* into whose genesis we now must look, to make clear the marvellous connection of these two root-tendencies. . . .

The same bent that led Beethoven's reasoning faculty to frame for itself the *good* human being, guided him in the construction of this "good man's" *melody.* Melody having lost its innocence at the hand of our art-musicians, he wished to restore to it this purest innocence. One has only to recall the Italian Opera-melody of last century, to recognise in that singular scarecrow the abject servant of the Mode and its ends: through Fashion and its uses Music had been brought so low that wanton taste demanded of it only something new, and new again, because the melody of yesterday was past all listening-to to-day. But Melody was also the sheet-anchor of our Instrumental-music, whose employment for the ends of a by no means noble social life we have already mooted above.

Here *Haydn* had soon laid hands on the blunt but cheery folk-dance, whose strains he often quite recognisably borrowed from the dances of Hungarian peasants in his immediate neighbourhood; but he thus remained in a lower sphere with a strong impress of narrow provincialism. From what sphere, then, was this Nature-melody to be derived, to bear a nobler, an eternal character? For even that peasant-dance-tune of Haydn's had its chief attraction as a piquant curiosity, in nowise as a purely-human type of art for every age. Yet it was impossible to find that type in the higher spheres of our society, for that was just where reigned the patched and powdered melody of the opera-singer and ballet-dancer, a nest of every vice. So Beethoven went Haydn's way; only, he no longer served up the folk-dance tune at a prince's banquet, but, in an ideal sense, he played it for the Folk itself to dance to. Now it is a Scotch, now a Russian, now an old-French folk-tune, in which he recognised the dreamt nobility of innocence, and at whose feet he laid his whole art in homage. But one Hungarian peasant-dance (in the final movement of his Symphony in A) he played for the whole of Nature, so played that who could see her dancing to it in orbital gyrations must deem he saw a planet brought to birth before his very eyes.

But his aim was to find the archetype of innocence, the ideal "good man" of his belief, to wed him with his "God is love." One might almost think the master had already seized the clue in his "*Sinfonia eroica*": the unusually simple theme of its last movement, a theme he worked again elsewhere, seems meant as a scaffold for this purpose; but the wealth of exquisite melos he built upon it still pertains too much to the sentimental Mozartian cantabile, so characteristically developed and expanded by himself, to rank as attainment of the aforesaid aim.—The clue is plainer in the jubilant closing section of the C-minor Symphony, where the naïvety of the simple march-tune, moving almost exclusively on tonic and dominant in the nature-scale of horns and trumpets, appeals to us the more as the whole symphony now seems to have been nothing but a straining of our attention for it; like the bank of clouds, now torn by storm, now stirred by gentlest breezes, from whence the sun at last breaks forth in splendour.

[T]he C-minor Symphony appeals to us as one of those rarer conceptions of the master's in which a stress of bitter passion, the fundamental note of the commencement, mounts rung by rung through consolation, exaltation, till it breaks into the joy of conscious victory. Here lyric pathos already verges on the definitely dramatic, in an ideal sense; and though it might be doubted whether the purity of Musical Conception would not ultimately suffer by the pursuance of this path, through its leading to the dragging-in of fancies altogether foreign to the spirit of Music, yet it cannot be denied that the master was in nowise prompted by a truant fit of aesthetic speculation, but simply and solely by an ideal instinct sprung from Music's ownest realm. As shewn when we started on this last inquiry, that instinct coincided with the struggle to rescue from every plausible objection raised by his experience of life the conscious belief in human nature's original goodness, or haply to regain it. Those conceptions of the master's which breathe wellnigh throughout the spirit of sublimest gladness (*Heiterkeit*) belong pre-eminently, as we have seen, to the period of that blessed seclusion which seems upon arrival of his total deafness to have wholly rapt him from this world of pain. From the sadder mood that reappears in certain of his most important works we perhaps have no need to infer a downfall of that inner gladness, since we undoubtedly should make a grave mistake if we thought the Artist could ever conceive save in a state of profound cheerfulness of soul. The mood expressed in the conception must therefore belong to that world's-Idea itself which the artist seizes and interprets in his artwork. But, as we have taken for granted that in Music the Idea of the whole World reveals itself, the inspired musician must necessarily be included in that Idea, and what he utters is therefore not his personal opinion of the world, but the World itself with all its changing moods of grief and joy, of weal and woe. The conscious doubt of *Beethoven the man* was included in this World, as well; and thus his doubt is speaking for itself, in nowise as an object of his reflection, when he brings the world to such expression as in his Ninth Symphony, for instance, whose first movement certainly shews us the Idea of the world in its most terrible of lights. Elsewhere, however, this very work affords us unmistakable evidence of the purposely ordaining will of its creator; we are brought face to face with it when he stops the frenzy of despair that overwhelms each fresh appeasement, and, with the anguished cry of one awaking from a nightmare, he speaks that actual Word whose ideal sense is none other than: "Man, despite all, *is* good!"

It has always been a stumbling-block, not only to Criticism, but to the ingenuous Feeling, to see the master here falling of a sudden out of Music, in a manner, as if stepping outside the magic circle he himself had drawn, and appealing to a mental faculty entirely distinct from that of musical conception. In truth this unprecedented stroke of art resembles nothing but the sudden waking from a dream, and we feel its comforting effect upon the tortured dreamer; for never had a musician led us through the torment of the world so relentlessly and without end. So it was with a veritable leap of despair that the divinely naïve master, inspired by nothing save his magic, set foot on that new world of Light. . . .

Thus with even what we have styled the ordaining will that led him to this melody, we find the master still abiding in the realm of Music, the world's Idea; for it is not the meaning of the Word, that really takes us with this entry of the human voice, but the human character of that voice. Neither is it the thought expressed in Schiller's verses, that occupies our minds thereafter, but the familiar sound of the choral chant; in which we ourselves feel bidden to join and thus take part in an ideal Divine Service, as the congregation really did at entry of the Chorale in S. Bach's great Passions. In fact it is obvious, especially with the chief-melody proper, that Schiller's words have been built in perforce and with no great skill; for this melody had first unrolled its breadth before us as an entity *per se,* entrusted to the instruments alone, and there had thrilled us with the nameless joy of a paradise regained.

Never has the highest art produced a thing more artistically simple than this strain, whose childlike innocence breathes into us a holy awe when first we hear the theme in unaccented whispers from the bass instruments of the string-orchestra in unison. It then becomes the *cantus firmus,* the Chorale of the new communion, round which, as round S. Bach's own church-chorales, the harmonic voices group themselves in counterpoint. There is nothing to equal the sweet intensity of life this primal strain of spotless innocence acquires from every new-arising voice; till each adornment, every added gem of passion, unites with it and in it, like the breathing world around a final proclamation of divinest love.

Surveying the historical advance which the art of Music made through Beethoven, we may define it as the winning of a faculty withheld from her before: in virtue of that acquisition she mounted far beyond the region of the aesthetically Beautiful, into the sphere of the absolutely Sublime. . . . And to the heart of every human being this gain reveals itself at once through the character conferred by Beethoven on music's chiefest Form, on *Melody*, which has now re-won the utmost natural simplicity, the fount whereat in every age, for every need, it may renew itself and thrive to richest, amplest multi-plicity.

("Beethoven," 1870.)

I draw attention to the peculiar position in which Beethoven was placed as regards the instrumentation of his orchestral works. He instrumented on exactly the same assumptions of the orchestra's capacity as his predecessors Haydn and Mozart, notwithstanding that he vastly outstripped them in the character of his musical concep-tions. What we may fitly define as *plastique*, in the grouping and distribution of the various instrumental families, with Mozart and Haydn had crystallised into a firm agreement between the character of their conceptions and the technique of the orchestra as formed and practised until then. There can be nothing more adequate, than a Symphony of Mozart's and the Mozartian Orchestra: one may pre-sume that to neither Haydn nor Mozart there ever occurred a musical thought which could not have promptly found expression in their Orchestra. Here was thorough congruence: the *tutti* with trumpets and drums (only truly effective in the tonic), the quartet passage for the strings, the harmony or *solo* of the wind, with the inevitable *duo* for French horns,—these formed the solid groundwork, not only of the orchestra, but of the draft for all orchestral compositions. Strange to relate, Beethoven also knew no other orchestra than this, and he never went beyond its employment on what then appeared quite natural lines.

It is astonishing, what distinctness the master manages to give to conceptions of a wealth and variety unapproached by Haydn or Mozart, with identically the same orchestra. In this regard his *"Sin-fonia eroica"* remains a marvel not only of conception, but also, and no less, of orchestration. Only, he already here exacted of his band a mode-of-rendering which it has been unable to acquire to this day: for the execution would have to be as much a stroke of genius, on the orchestra's part, as the master's own conception of the score. From this point then, from the first performance of the *"Eroica,"* begin the difficulties of judging these symphonies, ay, the hindrances to pleasure in them—a pleasure never really arrived at by the musicians of an older epoch. These works fell short of full *distinctness* in achievement for the simple reason that it no longer lay ensured in the use to which the orchestral organism was put, as in the case of Haydn and Mozart, but could be brought out by nothing save a positively virtuosic exploit of the individual instrumentists and their chief. . . .

Beethoven . . . was obliged to count on the same virtuosity in his band as he himself had before acquired at the pianoforte, where the greatest expertness of technique was simply meant to free the player from all mechanical fetters, and thus enable him to bring the most varied nuances of expression to that drastic distinctness without which they often would only make the melody appear an unintelligible chaos. The master's last piano-compositions, conceived on these lines, have first been made accessible to us by *Liszt*, and till then were scarcely understood at all. Exactly the same remark applies to his last Quartets. Here, in certain points of technique, the single player has often to do the work of many, so that a perfect performance of a Quartet from this period may frequently delude the hearer into believing he listens to more musicians than are really playing. Only at quite a recent date, in Germany, do our quartettists appear to have turned their virtuosity to the correct rendering of these wondrous works, whereas I remember hearing these same Quartets performed by eminent virtuosi of the Dresden Kapelle, Lipinski at their head, so indistinctly that my quondam colleague Reissiger might hold himself justified in calling them pure nonsense.

("Musikalisches Wochenblatt," April 1873.)

I f we would set before ourselves the picture of a day from our "holy one's" life, we scarce could gain a better than from one of those marvellous tone-pieces themselves; though, not to deceive ourselves, we must follow the course we adopted when referring the genesis of Music as an art to the phenomenon of the Dream, that is to say, employing it as a mere analogy, and not identifying one thing with the other. In illustration of such a veritable day from Beethoven's inmost life I will choose the great *C-sharp Minor Quartet:* and what we scarce could do while listening to it, as we then are forced to leave behind all cut-and-dry comparisons and give ourselves entirely to the direct revelation from another world, we may find attainable in a measure when conjuring up this tone-poem in our memory. Even thus, however, I must leave the reader's phantasy to supply the living details of the picture, and therefore simply offer the assistance of a skeleton outline.

The lengthy opening Adagio, surely the saddest thing ever said in notes, I would term the awaking on the dawn of a day "that in its whole long course shall ne'er fulfil one wish, not *one* wish!"* Yet it is alike a penitential prayer, a communing with God in firm belief of the Eternal Goodness.—The inward eye then traces the consoling vision (*Allegro* 6/8), perceptible by it alone, in which that longing becomes a sweet but plaintive playing with itself: the image of the inmost dream takes waking form as a loveliest remembrance. And now (with the short transitional *Allegro moderato*) 'tis as if the master, grown conscious of his art, were settling to work at his magic; its re-summoned force he practises (*Andante* 2/4) on the raising of one graceful figure, the blessed witness of inherent innocence, to find a ceaseless rapture in that figure's never-ending, never-heard-of transformation by the prismatic changes of the everlasting light he casts thereon.—Then we seem to see him, profoundly gladdened by himself, direct his radiant glances to the outer world (*Presto* 2/2): once more it stands before him as in the Pastoral Symphony, all shining with his inner joy; 'tis as though he heard the native accents of the appearances that move before him in a rhythmic dance, now blithe, now blunt (*derb*). He looks on Life, and seems to ponder (short *Adagio* 3/4) how to set about the tune for Life itself to dance to: a brief but gloomy brooding, as if the master were plunged in his soul's profoundest dream. One glance has shewn him the inner essence of the world again: he wakes, and strikes the strings into a dance the like whereof the world had never heard (*Allegro finale*). 'Tis the dance of the whole world itself: wild joy, the wail of pain, love's transport, utmost bliss, grief, frenzy, riot, suffering; the lightning flickers, thunders growl: and above it the stupendous fiddler who bans and bends it all, who leads it haughtily from whirlwind into whirlpool, to the brink of the abyss;— he smiles at himself, for to him this sorcery was the merest play.— And night beckons him. His day is done.—

("Beethoven, 1870; translated by William Ashton Ellis.)

---

*Goethe's *Faust*.—Tr.

# On the Beethoven Ninth

## DONALD FRANCIS TOVEY
## GEORGE BERNARD SHAW

*The Beethoven Ninth is one of the most written-about of all symphonies. Schumann, Wagner, and many other Romantics have used it as the occasion for rhapsodic musings. But as these two samples from English writers illustrate, the Ninth has also inspired witty, even sardonic commentary. In the case of Donald Francis Tovey, one of the twentieth century's most distinguished Beethoven scholars, the Ninth evoked a sharp example of his style at its best, a typically British approach to musical commentary that is leisurely yet sure of its destination. As for the Shaw piece, it is a classic tirade not only on misconceptions of the Ninth Symphony but on the vindictiveness of music criticism, the folly (even in Beethoven) of music as moral "improvement," the noisiness of audiences, and much else.*

If a great work of art could be made responsible for all subsequent failures to imitate it, then Beethoven might have had cause for doubting whether the opening of his Ninth Symphony was worth the risk. It is a privilege of the greatest works of art that they can, if they will, reveal something gigantic in their scale, their range, and their proportions at the very first glimpse or moment. This power is quite independent of the possibility that other works may be larger; it is primarily a matter of proportion, and the actual size enters into the question only when the work of art is brought by some unavoidable accident into relation with the actual size of the spectator. Thus Macaulay once shrewdly observed that the size of the Great Pyramid was essential to its sublimity, 'for what could be more vile than a pyramid thirty feet high?' And thus the faithful reproduction of the noblest proportions will not give sublimity to an architectural model that you can put under a glass case. The truth is that in architecture the size of the human frame is one of the terms, perhaps the principal term, of the art. In pictures this is not so, or rather it is so with a more elastic relativity: you can give any proportions you like to your pictures by introducing human figures or other known objects on whatever scale you please. Music has, like architecture, a fixed element to deal with, the subtlest and most implacable of all. It is no use comparing the dimensions of music for a few instruments with those of music for vast masses: the string quartets of Beethoven are in the most important of all their dimensions fully as large as the symphonies. It is no use saying that the string quartet is a pencil drawing, and the symphony an oil painting or a fresco: pencil drawings are not executed on the scale of frescoes. It is no use saying that the string quartet is monochrome, while the symphony has all the tone colours of the orchestra: people who seriously talk of string-quartet style as monochromatic are probably tone-deaf, and certainly incapable of recognizing anything short of the grossest contrasts in orchestral music. Yet there is what you may call a dimensional difference between a string quartet and an orchestra; and the difference is hardly greater in volume of tone than in range of tone colour. These differences, again, cannot fail to have some effect on the architecture of the works designed for few or for many instruments, but such effects on the designs are not less subtle than profound; and the composer himself is so far from recognizing them until his plans are matured that, as we have already seen, Beethoven for a long time thought that what eventually became the finale of his A minor Quartet was to be the finale of the Ninth Symphony.

The all-pervading, constant element in musical designs is time. Beethoven's chamber music (extending the term so as to include everything from one to eight instruments) is for the most part on the same time-scale as his symphonies. That scale was from the outset so large that his First Symphony, a masterly little comedy, shows him taking the precaution to design his first independent orchestral work on a smaller scale than much that he had already written for solo instruments. But while it was obvious from the outset that his compositions were on the largest known scale, it only gradually became evident that that scale was growing beyond all precedent. Beethoven himself did not avow this fact until he recommended that the Eroica Symphony, being longer than usual, should be placed nearer the beginning than the end of the concert.* And the Eroica does not from the outset promise to be larger than the Second Symphony, nor indeed in its first sketches did it show any signs of being so large. Contemporary critics throughout Beethoven's career were continually deceived about the scale of his designs, or they would not so constantly have considered Beethoven inferior to Mozart in power of construction. With the rarest exceptions they always listened to a work of Beethoven in the expectation that its proportions would be those of a work of Mozart; and the mere measurement of the actual length of the work as a whole would not suffice to correct that assumption, for several very perfect works of Mozart may be found which are considerably longer than some characteristic great works of Beethoven. The enlargement of the time-scale is not a matter of total length; it is a matter of contrasts in movement. Mozart's aesthetic system does not admit of such broad expanses side by side with such abrupt and explosive actions as are perfectly natural in Beethoven's art. The first signs of intelligence in this matter came from those contemporary critics of Beethoven who had the sense to be bewildered by many things which are now accepted inattentively. Two of Weber's notorious gibes will clear up the matter once for all. He regarded the introduction to the Fourth Symphony as a monstrous and empty attempt to spread some four or five notes over a quarter of an hour. This shows that he had a sense of something new in Beethoven's time-scale. The other case was that of the sustained note five octaves deep towards the end of the first movement of the Seventh Symphony; a feature which he declared showed that Beethoven was now ripe for the madhouse. This shows that he perceived something unprecedented in Beethoven's scale of tone. Now the scale of tone is a very much more difficult matter to discuss than the scale of time, and I must be content, for the present, to leave all statements about it in the form of dogmatic assertion. It naturally is more easily measured in orchestral works than in works where there is less volume of tone to deal with; but again, as with the time elements, it is not a question of the actual volume, but of the range of

*His notion of 'nearer the beginning than the end' was 'after, perhaps, an overture, an aria, and a concerto'. When he produced his next symphony, the Fourth, he preceded it with the First, the Second, and the Eroica. Four hours was short for a concert in those days.

contrast. In Beethoven's string quartets it is not less manifest than in his orchestra. In short, just as it is possible in the very first notes of a work to convey to the listener the conviction that this is going to be something on a large scale of time, so is it possible, however small the instrumental means employed, to arouse in the listener a confident expectation of an extraordinary depth and range of tone.

The opening of the Ninth Symphony is an immediate revelation of Beethoven's full power in both of these ways. Of all passages in a work of art, the first subject of the first movement of Beethoven's Ninth Symphony has had the deepest and widest influence on later music. Even with an ordinary instrumental finale, the Ninth Symphony would have remained the most gigantic instrumental work extant; its gigantic proportions are only the more wonderful from the fact that the forms are still the purest outcome of the sonata style. The choral finale itself is perfect in form. We must insist on this, because vast masses of idle criticism are still nowadays directed against the Ninth Symphony and others of Beethoven's later works in point of form; and these criticisms rest upon uncultured and unclassical text-book criteria as to musical form; mere statements of the average procedure warranted to produce tolerable effect if carefully carried out. We shall never make head or tail of the Ninth Symphony until we treat it as a law unto itself. That is the very treatment under which Berlioz and Bruckner break down; and it is also the treatment under which a Mozart symphony proves itself to be a living individual, though he wrote so many other symphonies externally similar in form.

The opening of the Ninth Symphony is, then, obviously gigantic. It is gigantic in relation to the sonata style of which it is still a perfect specimen. But its gigantic quality is so obvious in itself that it has been the actual and individual inspiring source of almost all the vast stream of modern music that has departed from the sonata style altogether. The normal opening for a sonata movement is a good, clear, pregnant theme. Whatever happens before the statement of such a theme is evidently introductory, and the introduction is generally so separable that it is in an obviously different tempo, whether or not it does itself consist largely of something broadly melodious. But it would hardly do to call the opening of the Ninth Symphony an introduction: it is impossible to imagine anything that more definitely plunges us into the midst of things. No later composer has escaped its influence. Nearly all modern music not on sonata lines, and a great deal that is on sonata lines, assumes that the best way to indicate a large scale of design is to begin with some mysteriously attractive humming sounds, from which rhythmic fragments gradually detach themselves and combine to build up a climax. When the climax is a mighty theme in unison for the whole orchestra, and the key is D minor, the resemblance to Beethoven's Ninth Symphony becomes almost absurd. And this is actually the case in Bruckner's third and ninth symphonies; while he hardly knows how to begin a first movement or finale without a long tremolo. It is no exaggeration to say that the typical opening of a modern orchestral work has become as thoroughly conventionalized on these lines as any tonic-and-dominant sonata formula of the eighteenth century. . . .

This opening of the Ninth Symphony has, then, been a radiating point for all subsequent experiments for enlarging the time-scale of music; and the simplest way to learn its lessons is to set our mind free to expect to find in the Ninth Symphony the broadest and most spacious processes side by side with the tersest and most sharply contrasted statements and actions. There are listeners (indeed their complaint is one of the intellectual fashions of the day) to whom it is a cause of nervous irritability that the Ninth Symphony is recognized by orthodoxy as the most sublime musical composition known. Orthodoxy happens to be perfectly right here, and for the same reason that it is right about Handel's *Messiah,* and Bach's *Matthew Passion* and Mass in B minor. These things do not rest upon fashion: they rest upon the solid fact that these works deal truthfully with sublime subjects. As a modern poet has remarked, "All is not false that's taught at public schools"; and if there are large numbers of contemporary music lovers who are in heated revolt against the aesthetics of Beethoven's music, that is a nervous condition which concerns nobody but themselves.*

(Tovey, *Essays in Musical Analysis,* 1935.)

*The quaintest manifestations of the revolt were those of the writers who at the centenary of Beethoven's death told us that the "humanism" of Beethoven's slow movements was antiquated. From time to time the Superman *may* seem to be as fashionable as all that: but nevertheless he does not exist as yet.

Aperformance of the Ninth Symphony always brings a special audience to St James's Hall; for it is known to be the master-piece of modern tone poetry, and the literary man comes to complete his culture by listening to it. I always pity him as he sits there, bothered and exhausted, wondering how soon the choir will begin to sing those verses which are the only part of the analytic program of which he can make head or tail, and hardly able to believe that the conductor can be serious in keeping the band nood-ling on for forty-five mortal minutes before the singers get to busi-ness. Time was when the conductor himself was often still more astray than the literary man as to the intention of Beethoven, and when those who knew the work by heart sat snorting in contemptu-ous rage, or enduring with the habitual resignation of tamed despair, whilst the dreary ceremony of reading through the band parts was proceeding.

When I say 'time *was*', I do not for a moment question the ability of London to reproduce the same discouraging results still: no doubt anyone who may be curious to know exactly what I mean will find sufficient opportunity before we have lost all the traditions of the time when the Ninth Symphony was treated exactly as if it were a quintet for pianoforte, flute, etc., by Hummel, re-scored for full orchestra by Beethoven. But it has now become a matter of tolerably common knowledge that this sort of handling stamps a conductor, not as a leading authority on Beethoven, but as a nincompoop. How far the work has become really popular it would be hard to deter-mine, because, as I have said, so many people come whenever it is in the bills, not to enjoy themselves, but to improve themselves. To them the culmination of its boredom in an Ode to Joy must seem a wanton mockery, since they always hear it for the first time; for a man does not sacrifice himself in that way twice, just as he does not read *Daniel Deronda* twice; and consequently, since it is pre-eminently true of the Ninth Symphony as of the hero of the music-hall song, that it is all right when you know it but you've got to know it first, he never becomes sufficiently familiar with the work to delight in it.

On the other hand, there must be a growing number of persons who, like myself, would rather have the Ninth Symphony, even from the purely musical point of view, than all the other eight put together, and to whom, besides, it is religious music, and its performance a celebration rather than an entertainment. I am highly susceptible to the force of all truly religious music, no matter to what Church it belongs; but the music of my own Church—for which I may be allowed, like other people, to have a partiality—is to be found in the *Die Zauberflöte* and the Ninth Symphony. I was born into evil days, when Les Huguenots was considered a sublime creation, and *Die Zauberflöte* 'a damned pantomime' (as they say nowadays of its legitimate successor, *Das Rheingold*), and when the Ninth Symphony was regarded as a too long and perversely ugly and difficult concert-piece, much inferior to such august neo-classics as Spohr's *Consecration of Sound* and Mendelssohn's Italian Symphony; and if I had won all my knowledge of the great Singspiel and the great Symphony from their interpreters, instead of from Mozart and Beethoven themselves, small and darkened would that knowledge have been.

In bygone days I have often sat at performances, and said, under my breath, to the conductor or the artists, 'Ah! if I were only a musical critic, how I would pay you out for this, you impostor, you pedant, you miserable artistic deaf-mute, you bawling upstart, you conceited minx,' etc., etc., etc. That was in the day of my hot youth. Fortunately, I never became a professed critic—to my own great surprise—until age and experience had softened me to my present indulgent mellowness; but I am by nature vindictive, and find myself not always proof against the temptation to pay off old scores against hardened sinners; so that sometimes, when a fellow-creature is catching it in this column ostensibly for some shortcoming in the previous week, he (or she) is really expiating some murderous art-outrage perpetrated on a defenceless child a quarter of a century ago— perhaps even—and this, I admit, is the climax of injustice—by somebody else of whom the performance has too vividly reminded me.

Therefore I implore all young artists to do their best under all circumstances; for they can never know who is listening to them, or how soon some insignificant brat in the cheap seats in a provincial Town Hall or Athenaeum may rise up, an avenging fury, armed with all the terrors of the London Press.

As to Mr. Henschel and his performance of the Ninth Symphony last Thursday, when I say that he quite understood the nature of the work, and was not for a moment in danger of the old fundamental error of treating it as mere musical arabesque, I imply that the performance was a success; for, with a good band and a right understanding, the obscurities and difficulties of the Ninth Symphony vanish, and a child may lead it. The concert began with Schubert's unfinished symphony, which on this occasion ought to have been his uncommenced symphony. The Ninth Symphony is quite enough for one evening. . . .

My enjoyment of the symphony was considerably interfered with by the background of young women, beauteous in their virgin robes, but visibly stifling, and agitating fans and sheets of music in all sorts of contradictory rhythms. At last, just as the exquisite coda of the adagio was stealing on me, I happened to catch sight of a face which had gone perfectly white; and then, of course, I gave up the adagio with a sigh, and resigned myself to watch the progress of the struggle not to faint and disturb the performance, the conviction that fresh air was the only salvation, the dreadful sense of the impossibility of climbing to the door over those giddy seats with the lights whirling round and the ground reeling, the alarm spreading to the neighbors, the proffering of fans and smelling-bottles, the commotion among gallant tenors and basses at the back, and the final desperate rally of the patient, and her triumphant postponement of her collapse to the top of the steep ladder at the other side of the door. During all which the band might have been playing Pop Goes the Weasel with no more fear of detection than if we had all been a St John's Ambulance class.

(Shaw, *World*, March 8, 1893.)

# Rossini and Meyerbeer
___

## HEINRICH HEINE
___

*The most entertaining chronicler of the cultural and political bombshell that constituted Paris in the 1830s and 1840s was German poet Heinrich Heine, whose musical journalism enlivened the pages of* Allgemeine Zeitung *and other periodicals. Although Heine did not quite, as his partisans insist, invent the easy, conversational mode of music criticism that influenced Shaw (who revived his music writing) and others, he served as a happy influence. His predecessors include Addison and Hunt, with whom he shared wit and metaphorical precision, respectively, though he had a looser and freer sensibility than either. All of these qualities are delightfully evident in the following comparison piece, which paints not only two composers but an era.*

What is music? This question occupied my mind for hours last night before I fell asleep. The very existence of music is wonderful; I might even say miraculous. Its domain is between thought and phenomena. Like a twilight mediator it hovers between spirit and matter, related to both, yet differing from each; it is spirit, but spirit subject to the measurement of time; it is matter, but matter that can dispense with space.

We do not know what music is. But we know what is good music, and still better do we know what is bad music; for our ears are greeted by the latter with greater frequency. Musical criticism can base itself upon experience alone, and not upon synthesis; it should classify musical works only by their analogies, and should take as criterion the collective impression produced.

Nothing is more inadequate than the theory of Music. Undeniably it has laws, laws mathematically determined. These laws, how-

ever, are not music, but the conditions thereof; just as the art of
design and the theory of colours, or even the palette and the pencil,
are not painting but the means necessary thereto. The essence of
music is revelation; it permits of no analysis, and true musical criticism is an experimental science.

I know nothing less edifying than a criticism by Mr. Fetis or by
his son Mr. Foetus, wherein the merits and demerits of a musical
work are demonstrated *à priori*. Such criticism, written in a certain
*argot*, interlarded with technical expressions familiar only to the
executant artist and not at all to the general educated world, gives to
empty verbiage a certain authority in the eyes of the mass of people.
Just as my friend Detmold has written a handbook upon painting,
which enables one to acquire a knowledge of the art in two hours, so
ought some one to write a handbook upon music, and, by means of
an ironical vocabulary, of critical phrases and of orchestral jargon,
put an end to the feeble handiwork of a Fetis and a Foetus. The best
musical criticism I ever listened to, and perhaps the most convincing
criticism possible, I overheard at Marseilles last year, during a *table
d'hôte*. Two commercial travellers were discussing the topic of the day,
whether Rossini or Meyerbeer be the greater master. As soon as one
had attributed the higher excellence to the Italian master, the other
demurred; not with dry words, however, for he trilled some of the
especially beautiful melodies from *Robert le Diable*. Thereupon the
first could find no more convincing repartee than zealously to sing
counter passages from *Le Barbier de Séville*, and thus did they both
continue throughout the repast. Instead of a noisy exchange of
insignificant phrases, they gave us most exquisite table music, and
finally I had to admit that people either should not dispute at all
concerning music, or should do so in this charmingly realistic fashion.

Take note, dear friend, that I have no intent to weary you with
any conventional tirade upon the Opera. Neither have you to fear a
discussion of comparisons, such as are usually made between Rossini
and Meyerbeer. I content myself with loving both, not the one at the
expense of the other. Even if I perhaps sympathise more with the
first than with the second, that is merely from a personal sentiment,
and in no sense involves an attribution to him of superior merit.
Perhaps there are imperfections in him that have a close affinity to
corresponding imperfections in me. I incline by nature to a certain

*dolce far niente;* willingly I stretch my length on a flowering mead, thus to contemplate the quiet procession of the clouds and revel in their lights and shadows. Chance has often willed that I should be roused from this delightful dreamland by a hard dig in the ribs from Fate. I have been constrained to take part in the sufferings and struggles of my time: my participation therein was honourable; I fought with the bravest . . . but—I don't know how to explain myself—my sensations always retained a certain dissimilarity from those of other people; I knew what my neighbours were feeling, but I experienced emotions remote from theirs. Although I urged my battle charger not less impetuously, and fell on the enemy as mercilessly with my sword, neither the fever, nor the lust, nor the agony of war took possession of me. My mind was oftentimes disturbed because of this inner serenity; I found that my thoughts often tarried elsewhere while I threw myself into the thickest press of the party fight. Thus to myself I seemed like Ogier the Dane, who fought against the Saracens in his dream wanderings. Such a one as myself would naturally prefer Rossini to Meyerbeer, though at certain times he would render enthusiastic homage to the music of the latter without yielding undivided allegiance to it. For it is on the waves of Rossini's music that the distinctive joys and sorrows of individual man are rocked most gently: love and hatred, tenderness and longing, jealousy and poutings, all the isolated emotions of the solitary soul. Rossini's music is characterised by a predominance of melody, always the direct expression of an isolated sentiment. With Meyerbeer, on the contrary, harmony preponderates. In the stream of harmonic measures the melodies are engulfed, just as the particular impressions of the individual are lost in the collective sentiment of a whole people. On this harmonious stream our soul launches itself joyfully, when absorbed in the sufferings and joys of the whole human race, and in touch with the great social questions. Meyerbeer's music is social rather than personal. The grateful Present finds its internal and external struggles revealed in this music, its soul's dissensions, the warring of its will, its agonies, and its hopes; in applauding the great *maestro* it celebrates its own sorrows and ecstasies. Rossini's music was better adapted to the spirit of the Restoration; when, after terrible struggles and manifold disillusionments, the idea of their great collective interests had dwindled into the background in the *blasé* minds of men, and the *ego* was enabled once again to assert its legitimate claims. Rossini would never have gained his great popularity during the Revolution: Robespierre would perhaps have accused him of antipatriotic melodies, and Napoleon would not have appointed him bandmaster to the grand army, a post for which communal enthusiasm was a first necessity. . . . The Restoration was Rossini's time of triumph. Even the stars in the heavens, then doubtless celebrating those reposeful hours, and no longer preoccupied with the condition of the people, they too listened with delight. The July Revolution had produced a great commotion in heaven and on earth; stars and men, angels and kings—yes, even the good God himself—were roused from their wonted tranquillity and had a host of matters to attend to, so that they had neither the leisure nor the repose of mind necessary to enjoy the melodies of private sentiment. It was only when the grand choruses of *Robert le Diable,* and even of *Les Huguenots* burst forth in harmonies of anger, of jubilation, of sobs, that their hearts listened and wept, rejoiced and groaned in enthusiastic accord.

This is perhaps the real reason of the unprecedented, colossal success which has everywhere followed these two great operas of Meyerbeer. He is the man of his time; and time, who always knows how to choose its own, raised him amid tumultuous sound upon the shield, proclaimed his reign and celebrated his triumphal entry. It is not a wholly comfortable position thus to be carried in triumph. For, by the misfortune or awkwardness of a single shield-bearer, one may find oneself perilously balanced if not seriously injured; the crowns of flowers that fly at one's head may sometimes hurt more than gratify, if indeed they do not soil when they come from dirty hands; the surcharge of laurels may produce a sweat of agony. . . . Rossini, when he meets such a procession, smiles ironically with his fine Italian lips; then he complains about his stomach, whose condition grows daily worse, so that he really can eat nothing. . . .

Meyerbeer is now writing a new opera, which I await with great curiosity. The development of this genius is, for me, a most remarkable spectacle. I follow with interest the phases of his musical and of his personal life, and watch the reciprocal attitude between him and his European public. It is now ten years since I first met him in Berlin, between the University buildings and the Watch-house, between science and the drum, and he seemed to feel himself ill at ease in that spot. . . .

Rossinism was . . . Meyerbeer's great crime; he had not attained to the honour of being attacked on his own account. He prudently refrained from all pretension, and when I related to him with what enthusiasm I had recently seen his *Crociato* performed in Italy, he said with a mournful smile: "You compromise yourself when you praise me, a poor Italian, here in Berlin, in the capital of Sebastian Bach."

Meyerbeer was at that period a devoted follower of the Italian school. Discontent against the humidly cold, intellectually spiritual, colourless Berlinism had early brought about a natural reaction in him. He escaped to Italy, rejoiced gaily in the sunny life, gave himself up entirely to his personal inclinations, and composed those exquisite operas wherein Rossinism is pushed to its sweetest exaggeration, wherein gold is gilded over anew, and flowers are perfumed with stronger scents. This was Meyerbeer's happiest time. He wrote in the gentle intoxication of Italian sensuousness; in life as in art he culled the lightest flowers.

But all this could not long suffice a German nature. A sort of home-sickness awoke in him for the earnestness of his country. While he lay under Italian myrtles, the memory of the mysterious rustle of the oak forests stole over him; while the zephyrs of the south wafted about him, he thought of the dark chorale of the north wind. It happened with him perhaps as with Madame de Sévigné, who while she lived by the side of an orangery and breathed only the scent of the orange blossoms, ended by longing for the rank but wholesome smell of a manure cart. . . .

Shortly after the July Revolution Meyerbeer appeared before the public with a new work, which had germinated in his mind during the horrors of that period. *Robert le Diable*, the hero who does not exactly know what he wants and is perpetually at strife with himself, is a faithful picture of the moral fluctuations of that time, a time wherein virtue and vice oscillated painfully, an era which fretted itself with endeavours and obstacles, and had not always sufficient strength to withstand the attacks of Satan! I do not at all like this opera, this masterpiece of cowardice. I say cowardice, not only from the point of view of the subject-matter, but also that of the execution. For the composer does not trust fully to his genius, dares not give free rein to his impulses, and is the trembling servitor of the masses, instead of the dominating master. It was with good reason that Meyerbeer was formerly called a timid genius. He lacked the compulsion of belief in himself, he bowed to public opinion. The slightest censure frightened him. He flattered every caprice of the people, gave the heartiest hand-shakes indiscriminately right and left, as though he recognised the sovereignty of the people in music, and based his rule upon the majority of votes: all this in contradistinction to Rossini, who reigned as king absolute in the empire of music by the grace of God. He has not wholly freed himself from anxiety in the affairs of private life; but the success of *Robert le Diable* has at least had this salutary result, that he is no longer hampered by those cares while he is at work, that he composes with much greater confidence, that he allows the strong bent of his soul to find expression in his creations. And it was in this freer condition of mind that he composed *Les Huguenots*, wherein all uncertainty has vanished, and the inner self combat has ceased, wherein the exterior duel has commenced which astounds us by its colossal dimensions. By this work Meyerbeer has won, never again to lose, his citizenship in the eternal city of fine minds, in the Jerusalem of celestial art. For in *Les Huguenots* he at last manifests himself fearlessly; he has drawn all his thoughts in firm, bold outlines; has dared to express the agitation of his heart in unrestrained tones.

The distinguishing mark of this work is its equilibrium, the balance between enthusiasm and artistic perfection, or, to express it better, the equal height to which art and passion rise. The man and the artist are in close rivalry; when the one peals the tocsin of wildest passion, the other knows how to tune these rude accents of nature to sweetest, most penetrating harmonies. While the mass of the audience is struck by the interior power, by the passion of *Les Huguenots*, the art lover admires the masterly handling of which the whole form is witness. This work is like a Gothic cathedral whose heaven-soaring spire and colossal cupolas seems to have been planted there by the sure hand of a giant; whereas the innumerable festoons, the rosettes, and arabesques that are spread there over it everywhere like a lace-work of stone, witness to the indefatigable patience of a dwarf. A giant in the conception and design of the whole, a dwarf in the fatiguing execution of details, the architect of *Les Huguenots* is as incomprehensible to us as the builders of the old cathedrals.

When, recently, I stood before the Cathedral at Amiens with a friend, and my friend contemplated with amazement this monument whose rock-like towers were the expression of gigantic strength, and the little carved stone figures of dwarf-like endless patience, he asked me at last why it is that we to-day, are incapable of building such edifices; I answered him, "Dear Alphonse, the men of olden times had convictions; we modern men have only opinions, and more than these are needed to raise cathedrals."

That is it. Meyerbeer is a man of convictions. Properly speaking, however, these do not embrace the social questions of the day, although with regard to these questions the ideas of Meyerbeer are more firmly grounded than those of other artists.

Meyerbeer, upon whom the united praises of the earth shower all possible marks of honour, and who, moreover, relishes these distinctions greatly,—Meyerbeer, nevertheless, carries in his breast a heart which beats in the sacred interests of humanity, and he unswervingly confesses his devotion to the heroes of the Revolution.

It is lucky for him that so many of the governments of the north do not understand music, otherwise they would discern more than a party struggle between Protestants and Catholics in *Les Huguenots*. However, these artistic convictions are not precisely political, still less religious convictions. His religion is merely negative. Unlike other artists, perhaps out of pride, he will never soil his lips with a lie; he declines certain importunate benedictions which could not be accepted without committing an equivocal action, or one certainly the reverse of magnanimous. Meyerbeer's real religion is that of Mozart, Gluck, Beethoven,—music; in this alone he believes, in this faith only does he find happiness, and he lives in a conviction not inferior to that of antecedent centuries in its depth, passion, and duration. Yes, I might truthfully say that he is the apostle of this religion. He treats everything that concerns his music with truly apostolic zeal and ardour. Whereas other artists are content when they have created something beautiful and not unfrequently lose all interest in their work as soon as it is completed, Meyerbeer, on the contrary, gives the greatest care to his children after their birth. He gives himself no rest till the creation of his mind reveals itself with equal clearness to the rest of mankind, till the whole public is edified by his music, till his operas have poured into every heart the sentiments which he wishes to preach to the whole world; in short, till he has put himself in touch with the whole of humanity. . . .

*Les Huguenots*, still more than *Robert le Diable*, is a work of conviction, with regard to subject-matter, and also form. As I have already remarked, while the mass of his audiences is enchanted by the subject-matter, the attentive observer admires the immense art progress, the new forms which herein appear. In the opinion of the most competent judges, all musicians who intend to write for the opera must henceforth first of all study *Les Huguenots*. It is in instrumentation that Meyerbeer has gone furthest. The choruses are written in an unprecedented manner, they express themselves like individuals, and have overstepped all previous traditions of the opera. Since *Don Giovanni* there has certainly been no phenomenon in music so great as the fourth act of *Les Huguenots,* where the terrible and moving scene of the blessing of the swords—the consecration of murder—is followed by a duet which surpasses the first effect; a colossal stroke which was hardly to be expected of this anxious genius, whose success excites our surprise as much as our delight. For my own part, I believe that Meyerbeer accomplished this last not by artistic means but by natural means, inasmuch as that famous duet expresses a series of sentiments which perhaps have never been reproduced, certainly never with such verisimilitude, in an opera, but with which, nevertheless, the most ardent and turbulent spirits of our time are in sympathy. For myself, I confess that never before has music made my heart beat as impetuously as during the fourth act of *Les Huguenots,* yet I can turn away from this act and its emotions to listen with infinitely greater pleasure to the second act. This is an idyll whose grace and charm recall the romantic comedies of Shakespeare, and still more perhaps the *Aminta* of Tasso. Indeed, under the roses of joy there smiles a gentle sadness akin to that of the unfortunate poet of the court of Ferrara. It is more the desire for joy itself; it is no wholehearted laughter, but a smile from the heart, from a heart that is secretly ill, and can dream only of health. How comes it that an artist, who from his cradle has been spared all the blood-sucking cares of life, born in the lap of riches, tended by his whole family—that readily, nay with enthusiasm, gratified all his longings,—who seems prepared for happiness as no other mortal artist has been—how comes it that this man has nevertheless experienced these terrible sufferings which sob and sigh through his music? For what he has not himself experienced, the musician could not reproduce with so much power and emotion. It is strange that this artist, whose material needs are satisfied, should be preyed upon by such unbearable mortal agonies! But it is good fortune for the public, which owes its most ideal joys to the sorrows of the artist. The artist is that child of whom fairy tales relate that his falling tears were pearls. Alas! the wicked stepmother, the world, beats the poor child most pitilessly, in order that he may weep as many pearls as possible.

*Les Huguenots*, still more than *Robert le Diable*, has been censured for lack of melody. This reproach proceeds from an error. The trees are not seen on account of the forest. Melody is here subordinate to the harmony. When compared with Rossini's music, in which the reverse is the case, I have already pointed out that it is this predominance of harmony which characterises Meyerbeer's music as the emotional music of humanity, of modern society. As a matter of fact there is no lack of melodies; only they are not allowed to stand out crudely, I might even say egotistically; they must subserve the whole. They are disciplined; whereas with the Italians they appear isolated, I might almost say outside the pale of the law, and they impose themselves somewhat after the manner of their illustrious bandits. How many soldiers, in a great battle, fight unnoticed but just as well as Kalabrais, the solitary bandit whose personal bravery would have impressed us less had he fought in the rank of regular troops. I will not contest the value of a certain predominance of melody. But I must observe that one of the results of it in Italy is the indifference shown for the opera as an *ensemble,* for the opera as a complete work of art; an indifference which manifests itself so naïvely, that, when no *aria* is being sung, the occupants of the boxes hold receptions and talk, if they do not even play at cards.

The predominance of harmony in the creations of Meyerbeer is perhaps a necessary consequence of a wide culture that embraces the world of thought and of phenomena. Whole treasures were disbursed upon his education, and he had a very susceptible mind. He was initiated into all the sciences at an early age, and is distinguished in this respect from most masters of music, whose brilliant ignorance is to a certain extent pardonable, since usually they have lacked time and opportunity wherein to acquire much knowledge apart from their art. Whatever he learn[ed] became a part of his nature, and the school of the world gave him the highest development. He belonged to that small number of Germans whom even France has recognised as models of urbanity. So high a culture was perhaps necessary in order to gather together the material and shape it with the sure hand that a creation such as *Les Huguenots* required. But it is a question whether or not the gain in breadth of conception and clearness of vision did not involve the loss of other points of view.

Culture destroys in the artist that fresh accentuation, that vivid colouring, that impulsiveness of thought, that directness of feeling, so often to be admired in circumscribed and uncultured natures.

("Letters on the French Stage," 1837; translated by Elizabeth A. Sharp.)

# Schubert: Music's Great Heart

## H. L. MENCKEN

*This article is one of two Mencken wrote in 1928, the centenary of Schubert's death. Mencken admired Wagner, Beethoven, and Haydn (see "The Clarity of Haydn"), but he loved Schubert most of all, as this piece makes glowingly clear.*

Franz Schubert, at least in Anglo-Saxondom, has evaded the indignity of too much popularity. Even his lovely "Serenade," perhaps the most moving love-song ever written, has escaped being mauled at weddings in the manner of Mendelssohn's march from "A Midsummer Night's Dream" and Wagner's from "Lohengrin." It is familiar, but not thread-bare; I have listened to it within the past week with new delight in its noble and poignant melody, its rhythmic and harmonic ingenuity, its indescribable Schubertian flavor. Nor is there anything stale about nine-tenths of his piano music, or the songs. The former is played very little—far, far too little. The latter are yowled in all the music studios of the world, but the populace remains unaware of them, and so they manage to hold their dignity and charm. "The Erl King" and "Who is Sylvia?" have become familiar on the air, but surely not many of the remaining six hundred.

Schubert, indeed, was far too fine an artist to write for the mob. When he tried to do it in the theater he failed miserably, and more than once he even failed in the concert-hall.

Great stretches of Schubert's music, indeed, remain almost unknown, even to musicians. Perhaps a hundred of his songs are heard regularly in the concert-hall; the rest get upon programmes only rarely. Of his chamber music little is heard at all, not even the two superb piano trios, the octet, and the quintet with the two 'cellos. Of his symphonies the orchestras play the Unfinished incessantly—but never too often!—and the huge C Major now and then, but the Tragic only once in a blue moon. Yet the Tragic remains one of Schubert's masterworks, and in its slow movement, at least, it rises to the full height of the Unfinished. There are not six such slow movements in the whole range of music. It has an eloquence that has never been surpassed, not even by Beethoven, but there is no rhetoric in it, no heroics, no exhibitionism. It begins quietly and simply and it passes out in a whisper, but its beauty remains overwhelming. I defy anyone with ears to listen to it without being moved profoundly, as by the spectacle of great grief.

We know little directly about what Schubert thought of his compositions. He was, for a musician, strangely reserved. But indirectly there is the legend that, in his last days, he thought of taking lessons in counterpoint from Simon Sechter. The story has always appealed pleasantly to the musical biographers; mainly ninth-rate men, they delight in discovering imbecilities in artists. My guess is that Schubert, if he actually proposed to seek the den of Sechter, did it in a sportive spirit. Going to school to a pedant would have appealed charmingly to his sardonic humor. What Sechter had to teach him was precisely what a Hugh Walpole might have taught Joseph Conrad, no less and no more.

It is astonishing how voluptuously criticism cherishes nonsense. This notion that Schubert lacked skill at counterpoint seems destined to go on afflicting his fame forever, despite the plain evidence to the contrary in his most familiar works. How can anyone believe it who has so much as glanced at the score of the Unfinished? That score is quite as remarkable for its adroit and lovely combinations of melodies as it is for its magnificent modulations. It is seldom that one is heard alone. They come in two by two, and they are woven into a fabric that is at once simple and complicated, and always beautiful. Here is contrapuntal writing at its very best, for the means are concealed by a perfect effect. Here is the complete antithesis of the sort of counterpoint that is taught by the Sechters.

No doubt the superstition that Schubert had no skill at polyphony gets some support from the plain fact that he seldom wrote a formal fugue. There is one at the end of his cantata, "Miriam's Siegesgesang," and in his last year he wrote another for piano duet. The strict form however, was out of accord with the natural bent of his invention; he did not think of terse, epigrammatic subjects, as Bach did and Beethoven afterward; he thought of complete melodies, the most ravishing ever heard in this world. It would be hard to imagine his making anything of the four austere notes which Beethoven turned into the first movement of the C minor symphony. He would have gone on to develop them melodically before ever he set himself to manipulating them contrapuntally. But that was not a sign of his inferiority to Beethoven; it was, in its way, a sign of his superiority. He was infinitely below old Ludwig as a technician; he lacked the sheer brain-power that went into such masterpieces as the first movement of the Eroica and the *allegretto* of the Seventh. Such dizzy feats of pure craftsmanship were beyond him. But where he fell short as an artisan he was unsurpassed as an artist. He invented more beautiful musical ideas in his thirty-one years than even Mozart or Haydn, and he proclaimed them with an instinctive skill that was certainly not inferior to any mere virtuosity, however dazzling and however profound.

This instinctive skill is visible quite as clearly in his counterpoint as it is in his harmony. Throwing off the pedantic fetters that bound even Bach, he got into polyphony all the ease and naturalness of simple melody. His subjects and counter-subjects are never tortured to meet the rules; they flow on with a grace like that of wheat rippled by the wind. The defect of prettiness is not in them. They show, at their most trivial, all the fine dignity of Schubert the man. Beautiful always in their simple statement, they take on fresh and even more enchanting beauties when one supports another. There are passages in the Unfinished, especially in the first movement, that are almost unparalleled in music, and there are passages equally fine in compositions that are seldom heard, notably the aforesaid quintet. When Schubert died the art of writing so magnificently seemed to pass out of the world. It was not until the colossal figure of Brahms arose that it found another master.

He was, to music, its great heart, as Beethoven was its great mind. All the rest begin to seem a bit archaic, but he continues to be a contemporary. He was essentially a modern, though he was born in the Eighteenth Century. In his earliest compositions there was something far beyond the naïve idiom of Mozart and Haydn. Already in "The Erl King" there was an echo of Beethoven's fury; later on it was to be transformed into a quieter mood, but one none the less austere.

The man lived his inner life upon a high level. Outwardly a simple and unpretentious fellow, and condemned by poverty to an uneventful routine, he yet walked with the gods. His contacts with the world brought him only defeat and dismay. He failed at all the enterprises whereby the musicians of his day got fame and money. But out of every failure there flowed a masterpiece.

In all the history of music there has never been another man of such stupendous natural talents. It would be difficult, indeed, to match him in any of the other fine arts. He was the artist *par excellence*, moved by a powerful instinct to create beauty, and equipped by a prodigal nature with the precise and perfect tools. The gabble about his defective training probably comes down to us from his innocent friends and fellows in Vienna. They never estimated him at his true stature, but they at least saw that there was something extraordinary and even miraculous about him—that what he did could not be accounted for logically, but lay far beyond the common bounds of cause and effect. We know next to nothing about his mental processes. He was surrounded by inferiorities who noted with wonder how savagely he worked, how many hours a day he put in at his writing-table, and what wonders he achieved, but were too dull to be interested in what went on inside his head. Schubert himself was silent on that subject. From him there issued not even the fragmentary revelations that came from Mozart. All we know is that his ideas flowed like a cataract—that he knew nothing of Beethoven's tortured wooing of beauty—that his first thoughts, more often than not, were complete, perfect and incomparable.

No composer of the first rank has failed to surpass him in this way or that, but he stands above all of them as a contriver of sheer beauty, as a maker of music in the purest sense. There is no more smell of the lamp in his work than there is in the lyrics of Shakespeare. It is infinitely artless and spontaneous. But in its artlessness there is no sign of that intellectual poverty which so often shows itself, for example, in Haydn. Few composers, not even Beethoven and Bach, have been so seldom banal. He can be repetitious and even tedious, but it seems a sheer impossibility for him to be obvious or hollow. Such defects get into works of art when the composer's lust to create is unaccompanied by a sufficiency of sound and charming ideas. But Schubert never lacked ideas. Within the limits of his interests and curiosities he hatched more good ideas in his thirty-one years than all the rest of mankind has hatched since the beginning of time.

Music is kind to its disciples. When they bring high talents to its service they are not forgotten. They survive among the durably salient men, the really great men, the remembered men. Schubert belongs in that rare and enviable company. Life used him harshly, but time has made up for it. He is one of the great glories of the human race.

(*American Mercury*, November 1928.)

# On Discovering Schubert's Last Symphony

## ROBERT SCHUMANN

*In 1854, shortly before his final depression, Robert Schumann recalled a happier time twenty years in the past when he and his friends hit upon a noble idea: "'Let us not be mere spectators! Let us lend a hand ourselves for the glory of things! Let us bring the poetry of our art into honor once again!' Thus the first pages of a new musical journal saw the light." It was in this journal,* Neue Zeitschrift für Musik, *that Schumann wrote most of his essays and aphorisms on Beethoven, Berlioz, Chopin, Liszt, Mendelssohn, Wagner, and many other titans of his century, with the same exuberance and taste for the unexpected that saturate his music. Schumann's music criticism is often cast in a narrative form that typifies a movement in the Romantic period toward a grand fusion of the arts. His models tended to be literary figures, especially the novelist Jean Paul and writer-composer E. T. A. Hoffmann. Many of Schumann's essays consist of dialogues between the assertive, unpredictable Florestan and the timid, conservative Eusebius—a splitting up of conflicting parts of Schumann's psyche viewed today as providing important clues to his mental disintegration. Schumann's article on the Schubert C-Major Symphony dispenses with the dialogue format but takes an even more vibrant narrative form, evoking the magic of Vienna as well as Schubert. The giddy sense of discovery is altogether appropriate, for this piece records one of the great finds in musical history.*

The musician who visits Vienna for the first time, awhile delights in the festive life of the streets, and often stands admiringly before the door of St. Stephen's Tower; but he soon remembers how near to the city lies a cemetery, containing something more worthy—for him—of regard than all the city boasts,—the spot where two of the glorious ones of his art rest, only a few steps apart. No doubt, then, many a young musician has wandered like me (1838) to the Währinger Cemetery, after the first few days of excitement in Vienna, to lay his flowery gift on those graves, even were it but a wild rosebush, such as I found planted on Beethoven's grave. Franz Schubert's resting-place was undecorated. One warm desire of my life was fulfilled; I gazed long on those sacred graves, almost envying the one buried between them—a certain Earl O'Donnell, if I am not mistaken. The first time of gazing on a great man, of pressing his hand, is for every one an earnestly desired moment. It had never been possible for me to meet either of the two whom I venerate most highly among all modern artists; but after this visit to their graves, I wished I could have stood by the side of a man who loved either one of them most dearly—if possible, his own brother. On the way home, I remembered that Schubert's brother Ferdinand, to whom he had been much attached, was still living. I sought him out, and found that he bore a strong resemblance to the bust that stands beside Schubert's grave; shorter than Franz, but strongly built, with a face expressive of honesty as well as of musical ability. He knew me from that veneration for his brother, which I have so often publicly professed; told me and showed me many things, of which, with his permission, I have already spoken in our paper, under the heading "Reliques." Finally, he allowed me to see those treasures of Schubert's composition, which he still possesses. The sight of this hoard of riches thrilled me with joy; where to begin, where to leave off! Among other things, he directed my attention to the scores of several symphonies, many of which have never yet been heard, but are laid on the shelf and prejudged as too heavy and turgid. One must understand Vienna, its peculiar circumstances with regard to concerts, and the difficulties attendant on bringing together the necessary material for great performances, before one can forgive the city where Schubert lived and laboured, that only his songs, but his grand instrumental works seldom or never, are brought before the public. Who knows how long the symphony of which we speak to-day might not have lain buried in dust and darkness had I not at once arranged with Ferdinand Schubert to send it immediately to the direction of the Gewandhaus concerts in Leipzig, or rather, to the directing artist himself, whose fine glance perceives even the most timid of new-budding beauties,—and necessarily, therefore, the dazzling splendours of masterly perfection. My hopes were fulfilled. The symphony went to Leipzig, was listened to, understood, again heard, and received with joyous and almost universal admiration. The busy publishing house of Breitkopf and Haertel purchased the work, and now it lies before me in separate parts; for the benefit of the world, I hope it will soon appear in score also.

I must say at once, that he who is not yet acquainted with this symphony, knows very little about Schubert; and this, when we consider all that he has given to art outside of this work, will appear to many as exaggerated praise. Partly, no doubt, because composers have been so often advised, to their own injury, that it is better for them—after Beethoven—to abstain from symphonic plans; which advice, notwithstanding, with the state of feeling that has given rise to it, we can scarcely consider as unreasonable. For we have lately had few orchestral works of consequence; and those few have rather interested us as illustrations of their composers' progress, than that of art, or as creations of decided influence with the masses. Many have been absolute reflections of Beethoven; and it is scarcely necessary to mention those tiresome manufacturers of symphonies, with power enough to shadow forth the powder and perruques of Mozart and Haydn, but not indeed the heads that wore them. Berlioz is thoroughly French, and we are too much accustomed to regard him merely as an interesting foreigner and rattle pate. The hope I had always entertained—and many, no doubt, with me—that Schubert, who had shown himself, through many other kinds of composition, so firm in form, so rich in imaginativeness, so many-sided, would also treat the symphony and find that mode of treatment certain to impress the public, is here realised in the noblest manner. Assuredly he never proposed to surpass Beethoven's ninth symphony, but, an industrious artist, he continually drew forth his creations from his own resources, one symphony after another. The only thing that seems to us objectionable in the publication of this seventh symphony, or that may lead even to a misunderstanding of the work, is the fact that the world now receives it without having followed its creator's development of this form through its forerunners. Perhaps, however, the bolts may now be drawn from the others; the least of them must possess Schubertian significance; Viennese symphony writers did not need to wander very far in search of the laurel they are so much in need of, for in a suburb of Vienna, in Ferdinand Schubert's study, they might have found sevenfold richer booty, leaf heaped on leaf. And here, too, was the place of all others which they should have crowned with laurel! But it often happens in the world that such opportunities are neglected! Should the conversation turn upon ———, the Viennese never know how to finish with their praise of their own Franz Schubert; when they are only among themselves, it does not seem as if they thought much of one or the other. But let us leave these things, and refresh ourselves with the wealth of mind that in its fulness overflows this glorious work! Vienna, with its tower of St. Stephen, its lovely women, its public pageantry, its Danube that garlands it with countless watery ribbons; this Vienna, spreading over the blooming plain, and reaching towards the higher mountains; Vienna, with its reminiscences of the great German masters, must be a fertile domain for the musician's fancy to revel in. Often when gazing on the city from the heights above, I have thought how frequently Beethoven's eyes may have glanced restlessly over the distant line of the Alps; how Mozart may have dreamily followed the course of the Danube, as it seems to vanish amid bush and wood; and how Haydn may have looked up to the tower, shaking his head at its dizzy height. If we draw together the tower, the Danube, and the distant Alps, casting over the whole a soft Catholic incense-vapour, we shall have a fair picture of Vienna; and when the charming, living landscape stands before us, chords will vibrate that never resounded within us before. On leaving Schubert's symphony, the bright, blooming, romantic life of Vienna appears to me clearer than ever; such works ought to be born amid precisely such surroundings. But I shall not attempt to set the symphony in its fitting soil; different ages select different bases for their texts and pictures; where the youth of eighteen hears a world-famous occurrence in a musical work, a man only perceives some rustic event, while the musician probably never thought of either, but simply gave the best music that he happened to feel within him just then. But every one must acknowledge that the outer world, sparkling to-day, gloomy to-morrow, often deeply impresses the inward feeling of the poet or the musician; and all must recognise, while listening to this symphony, that it reveals to us something more than mere fine melody, mere ordinary joy and sorrow, such as music has already expressed in a hundred ways,—that it leads us into a region which we never before explored, and consequently can have no recollection of. Here we find, besides the most masterly technicalities of musical composition, life in every vein, colouring down to the finest grade of possibility, sharp expression in detail, meaning throughout, while over the whole is thrown that glow of romanticism that everywhere accompanies Franz Schubert. And then the heavenly length of the symphony, like that of one of Jean Paul's romances in four thick volumes, never able to come to an end, for the very best reasons—in order to leave the reader able to go on romancing for himself. How refreshing is this feeling of overflowing wealth! With others we always tremble for the conclusion, troubled lest we find ourselves disappointed. It would be incomprehensible whence Schubert had all at once acquired this sparkling, sportive mastery of the orchestra, did we not know that this symphony had been preceded by six others, and that it was written in the ripest years of manly power (on the score is the date, "March, 1828"; Schubert died in November). We must grant that he possessed an extraordinary talent, in attaining to such peculiar treatment of separate instruments, such mastery of orchestral masses—they often seem to converse like human voices and chorusses—although he scarcely heard any of his own instrumental works performed during his life. Save in some of Beethoven's works, I have not elsewhere observed so striking and deceptive a resemblance to the voice, in the treatment of instruments; Meyerbeer, in his treatment of the human voice, attains precisely the opposite effect. Another proof of the genuine, manly inspiration of this symphony, is its complete independence of the Beethoven symphonies. And how correct, how prudent in judgment, Schubert's genius displays itself here! As if conscious of his own more modest powers, he avoids imitating the grotesque forms, the bold proportions that meet us in Beethoven's later works; he gives us a creation of the most graceful form possible, which, in spite of its novel intricacies, never strays far from the happy medium, but always returns again to the central point. Every one who closely studies this symphony, must agree with me. At first, every one will feel a little embarrassed by the brilliance and novelty of the instrumentation, the length and breadth of form, the charming variety of vital feeling, the entirely new world that opens to us—just as the first glance at anything to which we are unaccustomed, embarrasses us; but a delightful feeling remains, as though we had been listening to a lovely tale of enchantment, we feel that the composer was master of his subject, and after a time, its intricacies and connections all become clear to us. The feeling of certainty is produced at once by the splendid, romantic introduction, over which, a mysterious veil seems to have been drawn. The passage from this into the allegro is wholly new; the tempo does not seem to change, yet we reach the port, we know not how. It would not give us or others any pleasure to analyse the separate movements; for to give an idea of the novel-like character that pervades the whole symphony, the entire work ought to be transcribed. Yet I cannot take leave of the second movement, which speaks to us with such touching voices, without a few words. There is a passage in it, where a horn calls from a distance, that seems to have descended from another sphere. And every other instrument seems to listen, as if aware that a heavenly guest had glided into the orchestra.

The symphony produced such an effect among us, as none has since Beethoven's. Artists and connaisseurs united in its praise, and I heard a few words spoken by the master who had studied it with the utmost care for its perfect success, that I should have been only too happy, had such a thing been possible, to report to the living Schubert, as the gladdest of glad tidings. Years must pass, perhaps, before the work will be thoroughly made at home in Germany; but there is no danger that it will ever be overlooked or forgotten; it bears within it the core of everlasting youth.

And thus my visit to those honoured graves, reminding me of a relation of one of the great departed, became doubly a reward to me. I received my first recompense on the day itself; for I found, on Beethoven's grave, a steel pen, which I have treasured up carefully ever since. I never use it save on festal occasions, as to-day; I trust that good things may have proceeded from it!

(*Die Neue Zeitschrift für Musik,* March 10, 1840; translated by Fanny Raymond Ritter.)

# Schubert's C-Major Quintet: Two Variations

## DESMOND SHAWE-TAYLOR

*Seldom has anyone brought to life a piece of instrumental music more vividly than Desmond Shawe-Taylor in the two pieces reprinted here on Schubert's C-Major Quintet. In the first, for the* New Statesman and Nation, *a paper for which Mr. Shawe-Taylor served as music critic, the Quintet is placed in historical and critical perspective, with a tart commentary on one of the more unpleasantly puritanical aspects of music criticism. In the second, for the* New Yorker *some twenty years later, the work is placed in what we might call a human context, with a piece of musical description that has few rivals in contemporary letters. (For further commentary on the* New Yorker *article, see the editor's introduction.)*

When we hear again, after an interval, Schubert's great String Quintet in C major, the effect is intoxicating, dumbfounding; other music is for the time being obliterated. If this were merely a personal confession, it would hardly be worth making; but the feeling seems to be widespread. Nothing else, perhaps, in music has been so passionately and intimately loved; among chamber music players, amateur and professional, the supreme beauty of the work is unquestioned. The late W. W. Cobbett, in his *Cyclopedic Survey of Chamber Music,* quotes a curious instance of the affection in which the Quintet is held. "I have known four musicians," he says, "all greatly experienced in this class of music, and none in the least inclined by disposition to sentimentality, who with strange unanimity expressed the feeling that, were they fated in their last hours to listen to some lovely strain, this would be the music of their election." Many music-lovers would assent, thinking most likely of the Adagio, though it was the second subject of the first movement which was chosen by one of Cobbett's friends as an inscription for his tombstone.

In Sir George Grove's day, the String Quintet was universally accepted as a masterpiece and the composer's finest achievement in the sphere of chamber music. But if you consult recent writers on Schubert you will be surprised to discover how its reputation has waned. The professors of today hold it in lower esteem than do the public, or than their predecessors did. J. A. Westrup, in his chapter on Chamber Music in Gerald Abraham's Schubert "Symposium," praises the first three movements, but is distressed by the popular elements in the Finale: "Only the blind," he decides, "can fail to find their enthusiasm tempered with regret when they contemplate the String Quintet and the piano trios." A. J. B. Hutchings, in the "Master Musicians" series, is troubled by the want of polyphony in the work as a whole: "The Quintet . . . makes heavy demands on the indulgence of those who are trained, and I think rightly trained, not to expect almost unbroken homophony from a work of this size and nature." Alfred Einstein, in his recent study of the composer, plainly admires the work, as a good German must; but he adds a strange rider: "This Quintet is so orchestral in conception and feeling that it scarcely comes within the scope of chamber-music. The second 'cello is treated quite differently from the first. It has essentially a 'supporting' function . . . I have always felt that with a 'single' instrumental combination the weight of tone is unbalanced, and have longed to hear the work played by a 'double' string quartet with a double-bass in place of the present second 'cello."

Of our three professors, the last, who is the most eminent, is also the most puzzling. What does he mean by that remark about the functions of the two 'cellos? They are used throughout the work with unfailing instinct for sonority and blend, and in all sorts of ways; at one moment, for example, in massive unison (when they take over the opening theme in bar 35 of the first movement), at another in warm thirds and sixths (in the famous second subject). And what of the sublime Adagio? Is that also "orchestral in conception and feeling"? Apart from the long-drawn-out beauty of its melody, the feature which instantly strikes the listener here is the fascination and originality of the texture: the three inner voices spinning the theme in close chromatic harmony, while first violin and second 'cello throw in their decorations from above and below, now *arco*, now *pizzicato*, and in the reprise still further varied and elaborated. The lay-out, though new, is in the purest chamber music tradition; the web of tone is always of exquisite delicacy; the part-writing belongs to five solo strings and to nothing else. It is horrible to imagine the parts doubled; still more so to imagine the bottom line given to a double-bass.

The English professors take their stand on grounds of structure and thematic material. They are not wholly in agreement. Mr. Hutchings, for instance, is disappointed by the development section of the first movement, while Mr. Westrup thinks that nothing in the whole realm of chamber music hangs together better than this Allegro. Mr. Hutchings is also bored by the Trio—that strange succession of grave low-pitched unison descents into the unexpected caress of a full harmonic close in D flat major. Both critics find the Finale unworthy. It contains echoes of the café, the theatre and the Hungarian band, which seem to Mr. Westrup incongruous in an elevated work of art; but he frankly admits that Brahms, as well as Schubert, "saw no reason to segregate music into compartments."

We catch in these comments a characteristic English preference for the "learned" style. To those brought up in the atmosphere of the English organ loft, counterpoint has moral significance: it is upright, muscular and Christian, whereas rich homophonic harmony is sinful, flabby and Lisztian. If music cannot be contrapuntal, let it at least be strenuous and aspiring. An idiom so easy-going and so instantly enjoyable as that of Schubert cannot, it is felt, belong to the highest order of art; tunes that ask to be whistled are out of place in an instrumental work of serious pretensions. But to make these assumptions is to reckon without the mysterious transmuting powers of genius. Very similar complaints used once to be levelled against Verdi's Requiem. Because its style is operatic, listeners with oratorio in their blood were at first shocked, then suspicious, and only quite recently converted. Indeed, it is still customary for English programme analysts to write an introductory paragraph explaining away the "theatricality" of Verdi's blazing masterpiece.

Schubert, like Verdi, was accustomed to speak his own language on all occasions; and the language of both composers (like that of Haydn) unselfconsciously incorporated many popular elements. By 1828, Schubert's last year and the year of the Quintet, he had, however, already reached and passed the level laboriously attained by Verdi in his Requiem; that is to say, without abandoning his

natural utterance—the most lyrical and spontaneous in all music—
he could meditate on the most elevated and the most sorrowful of
subjects. One of these was death. As we know from his diary and his
letters, death was often in his thoughts; in many of his works the
subject is explicitly treated, and it is difficult not to suspect its presence here and there in the Quintet. The solemn trio is the most
obvious pointer; and the Adagio reveals a mysterious affinity of
mood with Keats's *Ode to a Nightingale.* In the first and last (E major)
sections the composer seems, like the poet, "half in love with easeful
death"; while the agitated passage in F minor speaks to us in unmistakable accents of "the weariness, the fever, and the fret" of that
mortal existence which, a few months later, he was to shake off. He
was indeed the most Keatsian of all musicians; and Keatsian too is the
despised Finale, with its "Dance, and Provençal song, and sunburnt
mirth." Music need be no less divine because its melodies were
cradled in the Prater.

(*New Statesman and Nation,* January 12, 1952.)

For a hundred years, most music lovers have agreed on the
disturbing beauty of Schubert's C-Major Quintet, the one in
which a second cello is brought in to supplement the normal
string quartet. Reservations have been few. Now and again objection
is made to the tone of the finale: that it is too good-humored and
easygoing to match the profundities of the preceding movements—a
criticism with which I don't agree. For those earlier movements, at
least, no praise has been thought too high, especially for the unearthly calm of the slow D-flat-major trio section of the Scherzo, and
for the linked sweetness, long drawn out, of the Adagio. Any good
performance of the Quintet is liable to renew the listener's sense of
awe at Schubert's achievement; and that which ended the last of
three Sunday-afternoon concerts at Carnegie Hall called "Isaac Stern
and His Friends" was good enough to work the customary magic. As I
made my way home through the driving rain, I pondered again on
the mystery of that slow movement.

All music—indeed, all art—is in a sense mysterious, because its
values are incapable of the kind of proof that we recognize in other
fields. For that reason, criticism is often called useless by people who
are not at all bothered by the fact that so much in their daily lives

depends on equally unverifiable judgments—on the quality of friends and acquaintances, for example. The Schubert Adagio might be called the musical equivalent of some person (luckily, we have all met one or two such) whose sweetness and depth of character are instantly recognizable, and never fail us.

But that is mere assertion, and will not satisfy the inquirer. Is there not something, some virtue more definitely musical, to which we can point in the attempt to justify our high regard? Maybe there is; let me at any rate suggest one reason for the profound impression made on many generations of listeners and chamber-music players by the Adagio. To an uncommon degree it unites melodic distinction with richness and originality of texture. The two outer sections of the simple a-b-a form into which the movement falls employ a subtle and elaborate layout that is in itself captivating, and would remain so, we are inclined to feel, irrespective of the thematic material.

The three central instruments of the group—second violin, viola, and first cello—are here the singers; in close harmony, and to a slowly pulsating 12/8 rhythm, they pursue their grave, serene melody, while above and below them the two others fill a decorative role. The cello at first underlines the beat in soft plucked notes, while the first violin makes isolated interjections based on the dotted-note rhythm of Beethoven's "quail call" (familiar from the slow movement of the "Pastoral" Symphony), later alternating these with spreading pizzicato chords of its own. The general effect—beautiful, it seems to me, even on the printed page—is that of a richly woven tapestry, which becomes richer still at the reprise, when the second cello has rapid, upward-climbing figures and is answered by the first violin from above. Equally elaborate and imaginative, although I will not presume on the reader's patience by essaying another description, is the texture of the impassioned central section in F minor, which suggests the fever and fret of life, in contrast to the healing calm of the outer sections. In spite of the fact that throughout the long movement there is not a single measure during which any one of the five instruments remains silent, there is never (and this is surprising) the slightest sense of congestion.

So much for texture. Melodic beauty is harder to describe—and, we must all agree, impossible to prove. Yet it can be safely said that Schubert, to whom a dozen immortal tunes often occurred in the course of a morning's work, here struck, in the last year of his short life, a new vein. For the outer E-major sections of the Adagio he found a long-drawn melody, rising and falling as gently as the breath of a deep sleeper and hardly exceeding an octave in outline, which conveys an impression of limitless and seamless expansion, and at the same time, paradoxically, one of compression—as of beauty pressed down and running over and yet with no drop lost or uncared for. Nothing less concentrated or less richly harmonized than this could have sufficed, we feel, to frame and contain the wild and desperate passion of the central section.

As for the strange trio of the Scherzo, it tentatively, and with many a pause, makes repeated unison descents into the void, to be answered by soft harmonies reminiscent of the consoling reply of Death in "Der Tod und das Mädchen." The resemblance is close enough to convince us of what we had already suspected: that in these two movements, as elsewhere in the work of his last year, Schubert is contemplating the idea of death.

So there was a certain appropriateness in the fact that Mr. Stern, in a brief introductory speech, should have dedicated the concert, on behalf of himself and his companions, to the memory of the great man—their friend, colleague, and teacher of many years—who had recently died, at the ripe age of ninety-six. How often Stern and Alexander Schneider, his fellow-violinist at Sunday's concert, must have played this same work with Pablo Casals! Indeed, an excellent recording of it can still be found in which these three collaborate with Milton Katims as the violist and Paul Tortelier as the additional cellist.

(*New Yorker*, December 10, 1973.)

# Donizetti's Operas

## HENRY CHORLEY

*A novelist, playwright, poet, and literary critic who contributed regularly to the* Athenaeum *for over thirty years, Henry Chorley is now remembered for his opera criticism, some of the shrewdest of the midnineteenth century, or indeed, of any time since.* His Thirty Years' Musical Recollections, *published in two volumes in 1862, is a masterpiece of the genre, a book as enjoyable for its literary stylishness as for its musical savvy. As a book critic, Chorley wrote about and befriended some of the major figures of his time, including Dickens and the Brownings. As a music critic (aside from his celebrated accounts of prominent singers), he often specialized in composers he considered minor but nonetheless important. Indeed, in this article on Donizetti, Chorley regards his subject as "essentially a second-rate composer" who "struck out some first-rate things in a happy hour." It is a superb example of major writing on the pleasures of minor art.*

D onizetti is remarkable as an instance of freshness of fancy, brought on by incessant manufacture. Such a change is almost exclusively confined to Italian genius in its workings. It learns and grows while creating. If it be moved by no deep purpose, it avails itself of self-correction; it strengthens its force on unconscious experience. Whereas German after German has gone deeper and deeper into fog-land when aspiring to produce what music cannot give, Italian after Italian has not merely perfected his own peculiar style, but has enlarged his science and arrived at novelty at a period of his career when it might have been fancied that nothing but truism remained to be given out.

The "craft" belonging to incessant production has been too

much despised. The scholar can retire for a quarter of a century to elaborate works for scholars to come, and has his just and high reward, accordingly. Those (on the other hand) who wish to speak less learnedly to the public can hardly present themselves to the public too often. They may never make themselves scholars by retreat or reserve; but they may nerve their powers of expression by exercise, if it be accompanied by self-scrutiny. Cavillers have too pedantically assumed that, by restriction and concentration, creative genius could with all men be *forced* into becoming something far more precious than it may have originally been. In music, at least, this is a huge and untenable fallacy. Dangerous though it seem to afford encouragement to idleness, to presumption, to invention by chance, to a spirit of money-making cupidity, the perpetuation of falsehood is yet more dangerous: and there are few falsehoods more complete than the reproach conveyed in the above assertions. With few exceptions, all the great musical composers have been fertile when once educated, and capable of writing with as much rapidity as ease. Bach, Handel (whose *Israel* was completed in three weeks), Haydn (more of whose compositions are lost than live), Mozart—all men remarkable as *discoverers,* and renowned as classic authors, held the pens of ready writers. Signor Rossini's *Il Barbiere,* again, which has now kept the stage for upwards of half a century, was the work of thirteen days, the *insouciant* composer being spurred to his utmost by a disparaging letter from Paisiello, who had already set Beaumarchais' comedy. Those on whom the gift of fertility has been bestowed run some danger of becoming "nothing if not fertile,"—timid, restrained, affected. Their minds are impulsive rather than thoughtful; their fancies are strengthened by the very process and passion of pouring them forth.

In the case of Donizetti it is obvious that his invention was, year by year, becoming enlarged by incessant use and practice. There are no melodies in any of his earlier works so delicious as those of the quartet and serenade in *Don Pasquale.* His instrumentation, too, always correct, became richer and more fanciful with each successive effort. It has elsewhere been remarked that, considering Donizetti was called to write for particular singers, an unusual number of the operas thus fashioned to order have become stock pieces: thereby proved to be essentially superior to the generality of works of their class.

He was born at Bergamo in 1797; he was trained by Simone Mayr at Bologna; he was drawn for a soldier in 1816, and extricated himself by the small gains from his first opera, *Enrico di Borgogna,* produced at Venice. Then came some score of operas, all forgotten, except, perhaps, *Il Borgomastro di Saardam,* for the sake of a poor but tuneable duet. His twenty-first was *L'Esule di Roma,* of which some mention has been made; his thirty-second was *Anna Bolena.* Thirty-three more were to come ere the brain of the busy man perished, under the influences of an unbridled life of indulged appetite. Gradually—Signor Rossini remaining silent, Bellini dead, and Signor Verdi as yet partially owned—Donizetti became the man to whom Europe looked for Italian opera.

*Lucia* would generally be named as Donizetti's best opera. I am not able to share in the admiration it has excited. Never, assuredly, was a story so full of suggestion for music as Scott's *Bride of Lammermoor* tamed into such insipid nothingness, even by an Italian librettist, as this. The supernatural tone of the legend entirely taken away; the dance on the bridal night, with its ghastly interruption, replaced by a sickly scene of madness, such as occur by scores in every southern serious opera; the funeral, with its one superfluous mourner and unbidden guest, abolished to make room for the long final scene so cherished by tenors; the character of Lady Ashton, affording such admirable material for contrast, obliterated; here are so many injuries to one of the most moving tragic tales existing in any literature. It would be a good deed to arrange Scott's novel anew—and anew to set it.

For only in one scene—that of the contract, which closes the second act—is Donizetti equal to the occasion. In the first act may be noticed a slight trait, meant to be Scotch, in the opening chorus; and the slow movement for two voices in the duet by the Mermaiden's Well. The song of entrance for the heroine, like others of Donizetti's show songs, is faded, in spite of the opportunities for the vocalist which it contains. In the second act, the letter duet, so high in favour with baritones who love to rage, is a piece of sounding platitude. In the concerted finale to the second act, its crescendo of passion (how admirably animated when Signor Tamburini supported and spurred it!) repeats the working-out of a form already indicated in the first finale of *Anna Bolena.* The "malediction" solo of Edgardo is in the true style of operatic declamation. He who speaks ill of the third act, closed by its long-drawn death-scene (the darling scene of tenor singers), may prepare himself to be stoned for heresy. Yet throughout that scene (with the exception of the dialogue between Ravenswood and the chorus), there is to be found little beyond singer's effects, a sadly small amount of vigour or freshness in the musical treatment of the situation—nothing to be compared with analogous passages in *Lucrezia Borgia,* or even in that less popular work (a very fine specimen of the master, nevertheless), *Marino Faliero.*

Donizetti's best serious music . . . is to be found in *La Favorita.* In this opera—written originally to another book, for Paris, and altered and extended when transferred to the Grand Opera—there is musical and dramatic beauty enough to make a story painful to the verge of vileness, forgiven. The chorus with dance which heralds the appearance of the King's mistress, protectress of the youth whom she has allured to break his monastic vows, is delicious. The anathema scene in the second act is forcible; the romance for the baritone is one of the best romances written for the voice. There is a voluptuous tone in the heroine's grand air, in the third act, which raises it above the commonplace level of similar scenes, and there is no song more becoming to a singer who has the needful voice and warmth of conception. The fourth act, it has been said, was showered out on paper during an incredibly brief period and at the last moment. There is no church chant on the stage more solemn and affecting than the hymn in the monastery (a good example of the deep pathos which is consistent with the use of the major key). So passionate is the romance for the tenor that it is hardly possible to sing it without effect. As given by such singers as M. Duprez and Signor Mario, it is to be ranked among the most thrilling songs of the Italian stage; yet it is built on one of the simplest scale passages. The duet which closes the opera rises still higher in emotion in the ecstacy of despair, succeeded by almost delirious exaltation. The stretto is hardly possible to spoil, so resistless is the sweep of the rhythm, provided it be only sung in time. . . . On the whole, this fourth act is Donizetti's noblest serious music. The ideas pertain to the situations and are always striking; the voices are judiciously employed and displayed; the orchestral portion is treated with care. In *La Favorita* he proved himself worthy of admission to the stage which a Rossini and a Meyerbeer had studied with solicitude.

Among his comic operas, *L'Elisir* is the general favourite; but here again I fancy the popular judgment may be hardly fair. In *L'Elisir* the Italian composer had to measure himself against the brilliant Frenchman, M. Auber, who, in the prime of his vivacity, treated the selfsame subject as *Le Philtre*. The gaiety of *L'Elisir* is flat and characterless as compared with that of *La Figlia del Reggimento*— a work which, having been tepidly received with the French text to which it was written, has gained universal acceptance out of Paris, and, under translation, has established itself as among the brightest and the last of comic Italian operas. There is a careless gaiety amounting to merriment, there is a frankness, always military, never vulgar, in this music. One might fancy it to have been thrown off during some sunny period of high spirits, when the well-spring of melody was in a sparkling humour. It is slight, it is familiar, it is catching, it is everything that pedants find easy to condemn.

I happened once in London to hear it laid hold of by a party of such connoisseurs, including more than one composer who would have found it hard to write eight bars having the faintest echo of hilarity in them. Some were decrying it, too, for the poor reason of anticipating the presumed censure of the one genius of the company. This was Mendelssohn. He let them rail their fill for a while, saying nothing. Then he began to move restlessly on his chair:

"Well, I don't know," said he, at last; "I am afraid I like it. I think it very pretty—it is so merry." Then, bursting into one of those fits of hearty gaiety which lit up his beautiful countenance in a manner never to be forgotten, "Do you know," said he, "I should like to have written it myself!"

The dismay and wonderment of the classicists, who had made sure of his support, were truly droll.

The last of Donizetti's operas—the last comic opera worth having which Italy, once so gay, has yielded—*Don Pasquale,* was written in a few weeks, when that bodily exhaustion had begun which was so soon to take the form of mental imbecility, followed by death. Under such circumstances, that the sixty-fifth opera of one who had for a quarter of a century been supplying the stage should have any freshness at all, is marvellous—more marvellous that the music should prove its composer's very freshest. The entrance of the coquettish Norina; the duet betwixt herself and her brother which closes the first act; in the second act, the entire finale, during which the widow springs a mine of provocations against the foolish old uncle of the man she intends to marry, including one of Donizetti's most individual concerted pieces, the quartet; in the third, the exquisite serenade behind the scenes—bear no traces of a weary brain, of a hand in which the numbness of palsy was already working. . . . For the present it may be feared that we have taken leave of mirth in Italian music, and must look for it in the Comic Opera of Paris; and even in the home of Grétry, Boieldieu, Auber, and Adam the fountain of laughter seems to be slowly dwindling and drying up. We are becoming graver without becoming more learned; we are showing our ambition at the expense of our command over melody. Compare, for instance, the old trio, "Lei faccio," from *Il Matrimonio,* with any other modern trio for three female voices—say that from Mr. Balfe's *Falstaff,* or that from M. Halévy's *Fée aux Roses* (in which there is some finesse, as in all that M. Halévy writes), and the poverty of the time, in fancy and in power of treating the voice effectively, and the absence of real gaiety become dolefully evident. Nay, as decay inevitably engenders decay, the very art of instrumental combination and effect for which so much has been sacrificed is in course of deterioration, owing to careless treatment, under the pretext of dash and originality.

To return from this digression, a peculiarity or two remain to be pointed out. The amount of characteristic music produced by Donizetti is very small. There is not one march, or good waltz, or minuet in any of his works. There is nothing to pair off with the march in *Norma,* or with the Polacca in *I Puritani.* Some of his overtures are written with care—as, for instance, that to *Maria di Rohan,* produced to propitiate Vienna, and the one to *Linda;* but there is none which arrests the ear. He had a way of his own in grouping voices. He employed the device, so abused by Signor Verdi, of unisonal effect, with transparency and skill, and is, accordingly, oftentimes more forcible, though less noisy, than his successor. His works demand and repay real singers, showing the latter to advantage without straining them. He wrote comparatively little for that most expressive of voices, the contralto—though that he could write charmingly for it the parts of Pierrotto, in *Linda,* and of Gondi, in *Maria di Rohan,* remain to prove. Compared with the music of these, the more popular Brindisi, in *Lucrezia,* is chargeable with vulgarity. Although not enterprising in his instrumentation, he was neither meagre nor incorrect. In short, it may be said that, though there be no startling beauties in the operas of Donizetti, none of those seizing melodies which, like "Di tanti," or "Largo al factotum," or "Assisa al piè d'un salice," ring through the world, neither such intensity of sentiment as reconciles us to the very limited alphabet in which Bellini wrote, they contain so much of what is agreeable, so many happy combinations and excellent opportunities for vocal display, such frequent harmony between the sounds and the situations to be portrayed, as to justify musical annalists in giving the fertile master a high place in the records of his time.

(*Thirty Years' Musical Recollections*, 1862.)

# Berlioz the Revolutionary

## ROMAIN ROLLAND

*Romain Rolland's expansive account of Berlioz's innovations, interspersed with vivid fragments from the composer's life, is a powerful example of his narrative approach to music criticism, a method which pulls the reader into the feverish center of the music, the man, and the epoch. Also included in this eulogistic piece is an argument about program music that serves as an illuminating supplement to those of Wagner, Barzun, and other writers in this volume. That Rolland wrote with equal authority and sympathy about Berlioz, the great Romantic revolutionary, and Handel, the great "objective synthesizer," (see "The Capaciousness of Handel") indicates a rare subtlety and flexibility of mind.*

It may seem a paradox to say that no musician is so little known as Berlioz. The world thinks it knows him. A noisy fame surrounds his person and his work. Germany disputes with France the glory of having nurtured and shaped his genius. Russia, whose triumphal reception consoled him for the indifference and enmity of Paris, has said, through the voice of Balakirev, that he was "the only musician France possessed." His chief compositions are often played at concerts, and some of them have the rare quality of appealing both to the cultured and the crowd; a few have even reached great popularity. Works have been dedicated to him, and he himself has been described and criticized by many writers. He was popular even to his face; for his face, like his music, was so striking and singular that it seemed to show you his character at a glance. No clouds hide his mind and its creations, which, unlike Wagner's, need no initiation to be understood; they seem to have no hidden meaning, no subtle mystery; one is instantly their friend or their enemy, for the first impression is a lasting one.

That is the worst of it; people imagine that they understand Berlioz with so very little trouble. Obscurity of meaning may harm an artist less than a seeming transparency; to be shrouded in mist may mean remaining long misunderstood, but those who wish to understand will at least be thorough in their search for the truth. It is not always realized how depth and complexity may exist in a work of clear design and strong contrasts—in the obvious genius of some great Italian of the Renaissance as much as in the troubled heart of a Rembrandt and the twilight of the North.

That is the first pitfall; but there are many more that will beset us in the attempt to understand Berlioz. To get at the man himself one must break down a wall of prejudice and pedantry, of convention and intellectual snobbery. In short, one must shake off nearly all current ideas about his work if one wishes to extricate it from the dust that has drifted about it for half a century.

Above all, one must not make the mistake of contrasting Berlioz with Wagner either by sacrificing Berlioz to that Germanic Odin or by forcibly trying to reconcile one to the other. For there are some who condemn Berlioz in the name of Wagner's theories; and others who, not liking the sacrifice, seek to make him a forerunner of Wagner or kind of elder brother, whose mission was to clear a way and prepare a road for a genius greater than his own. Nothing is falser. To understand Berlioz one must shake off the hypnotic influence of Bayreuth. Though Wagner may have learned something from Berlioz, the two composers have nothing in common; their genius and their art are absolutely opposed; each one has ploughed his furrow in a different field.

The classical misunderstanding is quite as dangerous. By that I mean the clinging to superstitions of the past and the pedantic desire to enclose art within narrow limits, which still flourish among critics. Who has not met these censors of music? They will tell you with solid complacence how far music may go and where it must stop and what it may express and what it must not. They are not always musicians themselves. But what of that? Do they not lean on the example of the past? The past! A handful of works that they themselves hardly understand. Meanwhile, music by its unceasing growth gives the lie to their theories and breaks down these weak barriers. But they do not see it, do not wish to see it; since they cannot advance themselves, they deny progress. Critics of this kind do not think favorably of Berlioz' dramatic and descriptive symphonies. How should they appreciate the boldest musical achievement of the nineteenth century? These dreadful pedants and zealous defenders of an art that they understand only after it has ceased to live are the worst enemies of unfettered genius and may do more harm than a whole army of ignorant people. I doubt if Berlioz would have obtained any consideration at all from lovers of classical music in France if he had not found allies in that country of classical music, Germany—"the oracle of Delphi," *"Germania alma parens,"* as he called her. Some of the young German school found inspiration in Berlioz. The dramatic symphony that he created flourished in its German form under Liszt; the most eminent German composer of today, Richard Strauss, came under his influence; and Felix Weingartner, who with Charles Malherbe edited Berlioz' complete works, was bold enough to write: "In spite of Wagner and Liszt we should not be where we are if Berlioz had not lived." . . .

Everything about Berlioz was misleading, even his appearance. In legendary portraits he appears as a dark southerner with black hair and sparkling eyes. But he was really very fair and had blue eyes, and Joseph d'Ortigue tells us they were deep-set and piercing, though sometimes clouded by melancholy or languor. He had a broad forehead furrowed with wrinkles by the time he was thirty, and a thick mane of hair, or, as E. Legouvé puts it, "a large umbrella of hair, projecting like a movable awning over the beak of a bird of prey." His mouth was well cut, with lips compressed and puckered at the corners in a severe fold, and his chin was prominent. He had a deep voice, but his speech was halting and often tremulous with emotion; he would speak passionately of what interested him, and at times be effusive in manner, but more often he was ungracious and reserved. He was of medium height, rather thin and angular in figure, and when seated he seemed much taller than he really was. He was very restless and inherited from his native land, Dauphiné, the mountaineer's passion for walking and climbing and the love of a vagabond life which remained with him nearly to his death. He had an iron constitution, but he wrecked it by privation and excess, by his walks in the rain and by sleeping out-of-doors in all weathers, even when there was snow on the ground.

But in this strong and athletic frame lived a feverish and sickly soul that was dominated and tormented by a morbid craving for love and sympathy, "that imperative need of love which is killing me. . . ." To love, to be loved—he would give up all for that. But his love was that of a youth who lives in dreams; it was never the strong, clear-eyed passion of a man who has faced the realities of life and who sees the defects as well as the charms of the woman he loves. Berlioz was in love with love and lost himself among visions and sentimental shadows. To the end of his life he remained "a poor little child worn out by a love that was beyond him." But this man who lived so wild and adventurous a life expressed his passions with delicacy; and one finds an almost girlish purity in the immortal love passages of *Les Troyens* or the *"nuit sereine"* of *Roméo et Juliette*. And compare this Virgilian affection with Wagner's sensual raptures. Does it mean that Berlioz could not love as well as Wagner? We only know that Berlioz' life was made up of love and its torments. The theme of a touching passage in the introduction of the *Symphonie fantastique* has been identified by Julien Tiersot, in his interesting book, with a romance composed by Berlioz at the age of twelve when he loved a girl of eighteen "with large eyes and pink shoes"—Estelle, *Stella montis, Stella matutina.* These words—perhaps the saddest he ever wrote—might serve as an emblem of his life, a life that was a prey to love and melancholy, doomed to wringing of the heart and awful loneliness; a life lived in a hollow world among worries that chilled the blood; a life that was distasteful and had no solace to offer him in its end. He has himself described this terrible *"mal de l'isolement"* which pursued him all his life, vividly and minutely. . . .

What did his compeers think of him—at least those who called themselves such? He knew that Mendelssohn, whom he loved and esteemed and who styled himself his "good friend," despised him and did not recognize his genius. The large-hearted Schumann, who was, with the exception of Liszt, the only person who intuitively felt his greatness, admitted that he used sometimes to wonder if he ought to be looked upon as "a genius or a musical adventurer." Wagner, who treated his symphonies with scorn before he had even read them, who certainly understood his genius, and who deliberately ignored him, threw himself into Berlioz' arms when he met him in London in 1855. "He embraced him with fervor and wept; and hardly had he left him when *The Musical World* published passages from his book, *Oper und Drama,* where he pulls Berlioz to pieces mercilessly." In France the young Gounod, *doli fabricator Epeus,* as Berlioz called him, lavished flattering words upon him but spent his time in finding fault with his compositions or in trying to supplant him at the theater. At the Opéra he was passed over in favor of a Prince Poniatowski. He presented himself three times at the Academy and was beaten the first time by Onslow, the second time by Clapisson, and the third time he conquered by a majority of one vote against Panseron, Vogel, Leborne, and others, including, as always Gounod. He died before the *Damnation of Faust* was appreciated in France although it was the most remarkable musical composition France had produced. They hissed its performance? Not at all; "they were merely indifferent"—it is Berlioz who tells us this. It passed unnoticed. He died before he had seen *Les Troyens* played in its entirety though it was one of the noblest works of the French lyric theater that had been composed since the death of Gluck.

But this is not all. What was the bitterness of failure compared with the great anguish of death? Berlioz saw all those he loved die one after the other: his father, his mother, Henrietta Smithson, Marie Recio. Then only his son Louis remained. He was the captain of a merchant vessel; a clever, good-hearted boy, but restless and nervous, irresolute and unhappy, like his father. "He has the misfortune to resemble me in everything," said Berlioz; "and we love each other like a couple of twins." "Ah, my poor Louis," he wrote to him, "what should I do without you?" A few months afterward he learned that Louis had died in faraway seas.

He was now alone. There were no more friendly voices; all that he heard was a hideous duet between loneliness and weariness, sung in his ear during the bustle of the day and in the silence of the night. He was wasted with disease. In 1856 at Weimar following great fatigue, he was seized with an internal malady. It began with great mental distress; he used to sleep in the streets. He suffered constantly; he was like "a tree without leaves, streaming with rain." At the end of 1861 the disease was in an acute stage. He had attacks of pain sometimes lasting thirty hours, during which he would writhe in agony in his bed. "I live in the midst of my physical pain, overwhelmed with weariness. Death is very slow."

Worst of all, in the heart of his misery there was nothing that comforted him. He believed in nothing—neither in God nor immortality. . . .

"I am in my sixty-first year, and I have no more hopes or illusions or aspirations. I am alone, and my contempt for the stupidity and dishonesty of men and my hatred for their wicked cruelty are at their height. Every hour I say to Death, 'When you like!' What is he waiting for?"

And yet he fears the death he invites. It is the strongest, the bitterest, the truest feeling he has. No musician since old Roland de Lassus has feared it with that intensity. Do you remember Herod's sleepless nights in *L'Enfance du Christ,* or Faust's soliloquy, or the anguish of Cassandra, or the burial of Juliette? Through all this you will find the whispered fear of annihilation. The wretched man was haunted by this fear, as a letter published by Julien Tiersot shows:

"My favorite walk, especially when it is raining, really raining in torrents, is the cemetery of Montmartre, which is near my house. I often go there; there is much that draws me to it. The day before yesterday I passed two hours in the cemetery; I found a comfortable seat on a costly tomb, and I went to sleep. . . . Paris is to me a cemetery and her pavements are tombstones. Everywhere are memories of friends or enemies that are dead. . . . I do nothing but suffer unceasing pain and unspeakable weariness. I wonder night and day if I shall die in great pain or with little of it—I am not foolish enough to hope to die without any pain at all. Why are we not dead?"

His music is like these mournful words; it is perhaps even more terrible, more gloomy, for it breathes death. What a contrast: a soul greedy of life and preyed upon by death. It is this that makes his life such an awful tragedy. When Wagner met Berlioz he heaved a sigh of relief—he had at last found a man more unhappy than himself.

On the threshold of death he turned in despair to the one ray of light left him: *Stella montis,* the inspiration of his childish love— Estelle, now old, a grandmother, withered by age and grief. He made a pilgrimage to Meylan, near Grenoble, to see her. He was then sixty-one years old and she was nearly seventy. . . .

Wagner, at the same age, a victor, worshiped, flattered, and—if we are to believe the Bayreuth legend—crowned with prosperity; Wagner, sad and suffering, doubting his achievements, feeling the inanity of his bitter fight against the mediocrity of the world, had "fled far from the world" and thrown himself into religion; and when a friend looked at him in surprise as he was saying grace at table, he answered: "Yes, I believe in my Savior."

Poor beings! Conquerors of the world, conquered and broken!

But of the two deaths, how much sadder is that of the artist who was without a faith and who had neither strength nor stoicism enough to be happy without one, who slowly died in that little room in the Rue de Calais amid the distracting noise of an indifferent and even hostile Paris, who shut himself up in savage silence, who saw no loved face bending over him in his last moments, who had not the comfort of belief in his work, who could not think calmly of what he had done, nor look proudly back over the road he had trodden, nor rest content in the thought of a life well lived, and who began and closed his *Mémoires* with Shakespeare's gloomy words, and repeated them when dying:

> "Life's but a walking shadow, a poor player
> That struts and frets his hour upon the stage
> And then is heard no more: it is a tale
> Told by an idiot, full of sound and fury,
> Signifying nothing."

Such was the unhappy and irresolute heart that found itself united to one of the most daring geniuses in the world. It is a striking example of the difference that may exist between genius and greatness—for the two words are not synonymous. When one speaks of greatness, one speaks of greatness of soul, nobility of character, firmness of will, and, above all, balance of mind. I can understand how people deny the existence of these qualities in Berlioz, but to deny his musical genius, or to cavil about his wonderful power is lamentable and ridiculous. Whether he attracts one or not, a thimbleful of some of his work, a single part in one of his works, a little bit of the *Fantastique* or the overture of *Benvenuto*, reveal more genius—I am not afraid to say it—than all the French music of his century. I can understand people arguing about him in a country that produced Beethoven and Bach; but with us in France, whom can we set up against him? Gluck and César Franck were much greater men, but they were never geniuses of his stature. If genius is a creative force, I cannot find more than four or five geniuses in the world who rank above him. When I have named Beethoven, Mozart, Bach, Handel, and Wagner, I do not know who else is superior to Berlioz; I do not even know who is his equal.

He is not only a musician, he is music itself. He does not command his familiar spirit, he is its slave. Those who know his writings know how he was simply possessed and exhausted by his musical emotions. They were really fits of ecstasy or convulsions. At first "there was feverish excitement; the veins beat violently and tears flowed freely." "Then came spasmodic contractions of the muscles, total numbness of the feet and hands, and partial paralysis of the nerves of sight and hearing; he saw nothing, heard nothing; he was giddy and half faint." And in the case of music that displeased him, he suffered, on the contrary, from "a painful sense of bodily disquiet and even from nausea."

The possession that music held over his nature shows itself clearly in the sudden outbreak of his genius. His family opposed the idea of his becoming a musician; and until he was twenty-two or twenty-three years old his weak will sulkily gave way to their wishes. In obedience to his father he began his studies in medicine at Paris. One evening he heard *Les Danaïdes* of Salieri. It came upon him like a thunderclap. He ran to the Conservatory library and read Gluck's scores. He forgot to eat and drink; he was like a man in a frenzy. A performance of *Iphigénie en Tauride* finished him. He studied under Lesueur and then at the Conservatory. The following year, 1827, he composed *Les Francs-Juges;* two years afterward the *Huit scènes de Faust,* which was the nucleus of the future *Damnation;* three years afterward, the *Symphonie fantastique* (commenced in 1830). And he had not yet got the Prix de Rome! Add to this that in 1828 he had already ideas for *Roméo et Juliette* and that he had written a part of *Lélio* in 1829. Can one find elsewhere a more dazzling musical debut? Compare that of Wagner who, at the same age, was shyly writing *Die Feen, Das Liebesverbot,* and *Rienzi.* He wrote them at the same age, but ten years later; for *Die Feen* appeared in 1833 when Berlioz had already written the *Fantastique,* the *Huit scènes de Faust, Lélio,* and *Harold; Rienzi* was first played in 1842, after *Le Requiem* (1837), *Benvenuto* (1838), *Roméo* (1839), *La Symphonie funèbre et triomphale* (1840)—that is to say, when Berlioz had finished all his great works and after he had achieved his musical revolution. And that revolution was effected alone, without a model, without a guide. What could he have heard beyond the operas of Gluck and Spontini while he was at the Conservatory? At the time he composed the Overture to *Les Francs-Juges* even the name of Weber was unknown to him, and of Beethoven's compositions he had heard only an Andante.

Truly he is a miracle and the most startling phenomenon in the history of nineteenth-century music. His audacious power dominates all his age; and in the face of such a genius who would not follow Paganini's example and hail him as Beethoven's only successor? Who does not see what a poor figure the young Wagner cut at that time, working away in laborious and self-satisfied mediocrity? But Wagner soon made up for lost ground; for he knew what he wanted, and he wanted it obstinately.

The zenith of Berlioz' genius was reached when he was thirty-five years old with the Requiem and *Roméo*. They are his two most important works and are two works about which one may feel very differently. For my part, I am very fond of the one, and I dislike the other; but both of them open up two great new roads in art, and both are placed like two gigantic arches on the triumphal way of the revolution that Berlioz started. I will return to the subject of these works later.

But Berlioz was already getting old. His daily cares and stormy domestic life, his disappointments and passions, his commonplace and often degrading work soon wore him out and, finally, exhausted his power. "Would you believe it?" he wrote to his friend Ferrand, "that which used to stir me to transports of musical passion now fills me with indifference or even disdain. I feel as if I were descending a mountain at a great rate. Life is so short; I notice that thoughts of the end have been with me for some time past." In 1848, at forty-five years old, he wrote in his *Mémoires:* "I find myself so old and tired and lacking inspiration." At forty-five years old Wagner had patiently worked out his theories and was feeling his power; at forty-five he was writing *Tristan* and *The Music of the Future.* . . .

Berlioz' work did not spread itself evenly over his life; it was accomplished in a few years. It was not like the course of a great river as with Wagner and Beethoven; it was a burst of genius whose flames lit up the whole sky for a little while and then died gradually down. Let me try to tell you about this wonderful blaze.

Some of Berlioz' musical qualities are so striking that it is unnecessary to dwell upon them here. His instrumental coloring, so intoxicating and exciting, his extraordinary discoveries concerning timbre, his inventions of new nuances (as in the famous combining of flutes and trombones in the *"Hostias et preces"* of the Requiem, and the curious use of the harmonics of violins and harps), and his huge and nebulous orchestra—all this lends itself to the most subtle expression of thought. Think of the effect that such works must have produced at that period. Berlioz was the first to be astonished when he heard them for the first time. At the Overture to *Les Francs-Juges* he wept and tore his hair and fell sobbing on the kettledrums. At the performance of his *Tuba mirum* in Berlin he nearly fainted. The composer who most nearly approached him was Weber, and, as we have already seen, Berlioz knew him only late in life. But how much less rich and complex is Weber's music, in spite of its nervous brilliance and dreaming poetry. Above all, Weber is much more mundane and more of a classicist; he lacks Berlioz' revolutionary passion and plebeian force; he is less expressive and less grand.*

How did Berlioz come to have this genius for orchestration almost from the very first? He himself says that his two masters at the Conservatory taught him nothing in point of instrumentation:

"Lesueur had only limited ideas about the art. Reicha knew the particular resources of most of the wind instruments, but I think that he had not very advanced ideas on the subject of grouping them."

Berlioz taught himself. He used to read the score of an opera while it was being performed. . . .

That he was an originator in this direction no one doubts. And no one disputes, as a rule, "his devilish cleverness," as Wagner scornfully called it, or remains insensible to his skill and mastery in the mechanism of expression and his power over sonorous matter, which make him, apart from his creative power, a sort of magician of music, a king of tone and rhythm. This gift is recognized even by his enemies—by Wagner, who seeks with some unfairness to restrict his genius within narrow limits and to reduce it to "a structure with wheels of infinite ingenuity and extreme cunning . . . a marvel of mechanism."

But though there is hardly anyone that Berlioz does not irritate or attract, he always strikes people by his impetuous ardor, his glowing romance, and his seething imagination, all of which makes and

*Nevertheless, Berlioz was one of Weber's most fervid champions: see "Weber and the Fantastic."—ED.

will continue to make his work one of the most picturesque mirrors of his age. His frenzied force of ecstasy and despair, his fullness of love and hatred, his perpetual thirst for life, which "in the heart of the deepest sorrow lights the Catherine wheels and crackers of the wildest joy"—these are the qualities that stir up the crowds in *Benvenuto* and the armies in the *Damnation*, that shake earth, heaven, and hell and are never quenched but remain devouring and "passionate even when the subject is far removed from passion, and yet also express sweet and tender sentiments and the deepest calm."

Whatever one may think of this volcanic force, of this torrential stream of youth and passion, it is impossible to deny them; one might as well deny the sun.

And I shall not dwell on Berlioz' love of Nature which, as Prudhomme shows us, is the soul of a composition like the *Damnation* and, one might say, of all great compositions. No musician with the exception of Beethoven has loved Nature so profoundly. Wagner himself did not realize the intensity of emotion which she roused in Berlioz and how this feeling impregnated the music of the *Damnation*, of *Roméo*, and of *Les Troyens*.

But this genius had other characteristics which are less well known though they are not less unusual. The first is his sense of pure beauty. Berlioz' exterior romanticism must not make us blind to this. He had a Virgilian soul; and if his coloring recalls that of Weber, his design has often an Italian suavity. Wagner never had this love of beauty in the Latin sense of the word. Who has understood the southern nature, beautiful form, and harmonious movement like Berlioz? Who since Gluck has recognized so well the secret of classical beauty? Since *Orfeo* was composed, no one has carved in music a bas-relief so perfect as the entrance of Andromache in the second act of *Les Troyens à Troie*. In *Les Troyens à Carthage* the fragrance of the *Aeneid* is shed over the night of love, and we see the luminous sky and hear the murmur of the sea. Some of his melodies are like statues, or the pure lines of Athenian friezes, or the noble gesture of beautiful Italian girls, or the undulating profile of the Albanian hills filled with divine laughter. He has done more than felt and translated into music the beauty of the Mediterranean—he has created beings worthy of a Greek tragedy. His Cassandra alone would suffice to rank him among the greatest tragic poets that music has ever known. And Cassandra is a worthy sister of Wagner's Brünnhilde, but she has the advantage of coming of a nobler race and of having a lofty restraint of spirit and action that Sophocles himself would have loved.

Not enough attention has been drawn to the classical nobility from which Berlioz' art so spontaneously springs. It is not fully acknowledged that he was of all nineteenth-century musicians the one who had in the highest degree the sense of plastic beauty. Nor do people always recognize that he was a writer of sweet and flowing melodies. [Conductor Felix] Weingartner expressed the surprise he felt when, imbued with current prejudice against Berlioz' lack of melodic invention, he opened by chance the score of the overture of *Benvenuto* and found in that short composition, which barely takes ten minutes to play, not one or two but four or five melodies of admirable richness and originality. . . .

And what a splendid variety there is in these melodies: there is the song of Gluck's style (Cassandra's airs), the pure German lied (Marguerite's song, *"D'amour l'ardente flamme"*), the Italian melody, after Bellini, in its most limpid and happy form (arietta of Arlequin in *Benvenuto*), the broad Wagnerian phrase (finale of *Roméo*), the folk song (chorus of shepherds in *L'Enfance du Christ*), and the freest and most modern recitative (the monologues of Faust), which was Berlioz' own invention, with its full development, its pliant outline, and its intricate nuances.

I have said that Berlioz had a matchless gift for expressing tragic melancholy, weariness of life, and the pangs of death. In a general way, one may say that he was a great elegist in music. . . . Heinrich Heine had a keen perception of Berlioz' originality when he called him "a colossal nightingale, a lark the size of an eagle." The simile is not only picturesque but of remarkable aptness. For Berlioz' colossal force is at the service of a forlorn and tender heart; he has nothing of the heroism of Beethoven or Handel or Gluck, or even Schubert. He has all the charm of an Umbrian painter, as is shown in *L'Enfance du Christ*, as well as sweetness and inward sadness, the gift of tears, and an elegiac passion.

Now I come to Berlioz' great originality, an originality which is rarely spoken of though it makes him more than a great musician, more than the successor of Beethoven or, as some call him, the forerunner of Wagner. It is an originality that entitles him to be known, even more fitly than Wagner himself, as the creator of "an art of the future," the apostle of a new music which even today has hardly made itself felt.

Berlioz is original in a double sense. By the extraordinary complexity of his genius he touched the two opposite poles of his art and showed us two entirely different aspects of music—that of a great popular art and that of music made free.

We are all enslaved by the musical tradition of the past. For generations we have been so accustomed to carry this yoke that we scarcely notice it. And in consequence of Germany's monopoly of music since the end of the eighteenth century, musical traditions— which had been chiefly Italian in the two preceding centuries—now became almost entirely German. We think in German forms: the plan of phrases, their development, their balance, and all the rhetoric of music and the grammar of composition comes to us from foreign thought, slowly elaborated by German masters. That domination has never been more complete or heavier since Wagner's victory. Then reigned over the world this great German period—a scaly monster with a thousand arms, whose grasp was so extensive that it included pages, scenes, acts, and whole dramas in its embrace. We cannot say that French writers have ever tried to write in the style of Goethe or Schiller, but French composers have tried and are still trying to write music after the manner of German musicians. . . .

Before Berlioz' time there was really only one master of the first rank who made a great effort to liberate French music: it was Rameau, and despite his genius, he was conquered by Italian art.

By force of circumstance, therefore, French music found itself molded in foreign musical forms. And in the same way that Germany in the eighteenth century tried to imitate French architecture and literature, so France in the nineteenth century acquired the habit of speaking German in music. As most men speak more than they think, even thought itself became Germanized; and it was difficult then to discover through this traditional insincerity the true and spontaneous form of French musical thought.

But Berlioz' genius found it by instinct. From the first he strove to free French music from the oppression of the foreign tradition that was suffocating it.

He was fitted in every way for the part, even by his deficiencies and his ignorance. His classical education in music was incomplete.

Saint-Saëns tells us that "the past did not exist for him; he did not understand the old composers as his knowledge of them was limited to what he had read about them." He did not know Bach. Happy ignorance! He was able to write oratorios like *L'Enfance du Christ* without being worried by memories and traditions of the German masters of oratorio. There are men like Brahms who have been nearly all their life but reflections of the past. Berlioz never sought to be anything but himself. It was thus that he created that masterpiece, *La Fuite en Égypte*, which sprang from his keen sympathy with the people.

He had one of the most untrammeled spirits that ever breathed. Liberty was for him a desperate necessity. "Liberty of heart, of mind, of soul—of everything. . . . Real liberty, absolute and immense!" And this passionate love of liberty, which was his misfortune in life since it deprived him of the comfort of any faith, refused him any refuge for his thoughts, robbed him of peace, and even of the soft pillow of skepticism—this "real liberty" formed the unique originality and grandeur of his musical conceptions.

"Music," wrote Berlioz to Lobe in 1852, "is the most poetic, the most powerful, the most living of all arts. She ought to be the freest, but she is not yet. . . . Modern music is like the classic Andromeda, naked and divinely beautiful. She is chained to a rock on the shores of a vast sea and awaits the victorious Perseus who shall loose her bonds and break in pieces the chimera called Routine."

The business was to free music from its limited rhythms and from the traditional forms and rules that enclosed it; and above all, it needed to be free from the domination of speech and to be released from its humiliating bondage to poetry. Berlioz wrote to the Princess of Wittgenstein in 1856:

"I am for free music. Yes, I want music to be proudly free, to be victorious, to be supreme. I want her to take all she can, so that there may be no more Alps or Pyrenees for her. But she must achieve her victories by fighting in person and not rely upon her lieutenants. I should like to have, if possible, good verse drawn up in order of battle; but, like Napoleon, she must face the fire herself and, like Alexander, march in the front ranks of the phalanx. She is so powerful that in some cases she would conquer unaided; for she has the right to say with Medea: 'I, myself, am enough.'"

Berlioz protested vigorously against Gluck's impious theory and

Wagner's "crime" in making music the slave of speech. Music is the highest poetry and knows no master. It was for Berlioz, therefore, continually to increase the power of expression in pure music. And while Wagner, who was more moderate and a closer follower of tradition, sought to establish a compromise (perhaps an impossible one) between music and speech and to create the new lyric drama, Berlioz, who was more revolutionary, achieved the dramatic symphony, of which the unequaled model today is still *Roméo et Juliette*.

The dramatic symphony naturally fell foul of all formal theories. Two arguments were set up against it: one derived from Bayreuth, and by now an act of faith; the other, current opinion, upheld by the crowd that speaks of music without understanding it.

The first argument, maintained by Wagner, is that music cannot really express action without the help of speech and gesture. It is in the name of this opinion that so many people condemn *a priori* Berlioz' *Roméo*. They think it childish to try to *translate* action into music. I suppose they think it less childish to *illustrate* an action by music. Do they think that gesture associates itself very happily with music? . . . In the music of *Rheingold* one pictures the stature and gait of the giants, and one sees the lightning gleam and the rainbow reflected on the clouds. In the theater it is like a game of marionettes; and one feels the impassable gulf between music and gesture. Music is a world apart. When music wishes to depict the drama, it is not real action which is reflected in it; it is the ideal action transfigured by the spirit and perceptible only to the inner vision. The worst foolishness is to present two visions—one for the eyes and one for the spirit. Nearly always they kill each other.

The other argument urged against the symphony with a program is the pretended classical argument (it is not really classical at all). "Music," they say, "is not meant to express definite subjects; it is only fitted for vague ideas. The more indefinite it is, the greater its power, and the more it suggests." I ask, what is an indefinite art? What is a vague art? Do not the two words contradict each other? Can this strange combination exist at all? Can an artist write anything that he does not clearly conceive? Do people think he composes at random as his genius whispers to him? One must at least say this: A symphony of Beethoven's is a "definite" work down to its innermost folds; and Beethoven had, if not an exact knowledge, at least a clear intuition of what he was about. His last quartets are descriptive symphonies of his soul and very differently carried out from Berlioz' symphonies. Wagner was able to analyze one of the former under the name of "A Day with Beethoven."* Beethoven was always trying to translate into music the depths of his heart, the subleties of his spirit, which are not to be explained clearly by words but which are as definite as words—in fact, more definite; for a word, being an abstract thing, sums up many experiences and comprehends many different meanings. Music is a hundred times more expressive and exact than speech; and it is not only her right to express particular emotions and subjects, it is her duty. If that duty is not fulfilled, the result is not music—it is nothing at all.

Berlioz is thus the true inheritor of Beethoven's thought. The difference between a work like *Roméo* and one of Beethoven's symphonies is that the former, it would seem, endeavors to express objective emotions and subjects in music. I do not see why music should not follow poetry in getting away from introspection and trying to paint the drama of the universe. Shakespeare is as good as Dante. Besides, one may add, it is always Berlioz himself that is discovered in his music; it is his soul starving for love and mocked at by shadows which is revealed through all the scenes of *Roméo*.

I will not prolong a discussion where so many things must be left unsaid. But I would suggest that, once and for all, we get rid of these absurd endeavors to fence in art. Do not let us say: Music can . . . music cannot express such-and-such a thing. Let us say rather, if genius pleases, everything is possible; and if music so wishes, she may be painting and poetry tomorrow. Berlioz has proved it well in his *Roméo*.

This *Roméo* is an extraordinary work: "a wonderful isle, where a temple of pure art is set up." For my part, not only do I consider it equal to the most powerful of Wagner's creations, but I believe it to be richer in its teaching and in its resources for art—resources and teaching which contemporary French art has not yet fully turned to account. . . . Study not only the most celebrated pages of his work, such as the *"Scène d'amour"* (the one of all his compositions that Berlioz himself liked best), *"La Tristesse de Roméo,"* or *"La Fête des Capulets"* (where a spirit like Wagner's own unlooses and subdues again tempests of passion and joy), but take less well-known pages,

*Reprinted in this volume.—ED.

such as the "*Scherzetto chanté de la reine Mab*," or the "*Réveil de Juliette*" and the music describing the death of the two lovers. In the one what light grace there is, in the other what vibrating passion, and in both of them what freedom and apt expression of ideas. The language is magnificent, of wonderful clearness and simplicity; not a word too much and not a word that does not reveal an unerring pen. In nearly all the big works of Berlioz before 1845 (that is up to the *Damnation*) you will find this nervous precision and sweeping liberty.

Then there is the freedom of his rhythms. Schumann, who was nearest to Berlioz of all musicians of that time and therefore best able to understand him, had been struck by this since the composition of the *Symphonie fantastique*. He wrote:
"The present age has certainly not produced a work in which similar times and rhythms combined with dissimilar times and rhythms have been more freely used. . . ."

Remark also Berlioz' freedom of melody. His musical phrases pulse and flow like life itself. "Some phrases taken separately," says Schumann, "have such an intensity that they will not bear harmonizing—as in many ancient folk songs—and often even an accompaniment spoils their fullness." These melodies so correspond with the emotions that they reproduce the least thrills of body and mind by their vigorous workings-up and delicate reliefs, by splendid barbarities of modulation and strong and glowing color, by gentle gradations of light and shade or imperceptible ripples of thought which flow over the body like a steady tide. . . .

Berlioz' other great originality lay in his talent for music that was suited to the spirit of the common people recently raised to sovereignty and the young democracy. In spite of his aristocratic disdain, his soul was with the masses. . . . Whether he was conscious of it or not, he was the musician of revolutions; his sympathies were with the people. Not only did he fill his scenes in the theatre with swarming and riotous crowds, like those of the Roman Carnival in the second act of *Benvenuto* (anticipating by thirty years the crowds of *Die Meistersinger*), but he created a music of the masses and a colossal style.

His model here was Beethoven; Beethoven of the *Eroica*, of the C minor, of the A major, and, above all, of the Ninth Symphony. He was Beethoven's follower in this as well as other things and the apostle who carried on his work. And with his understanding of material effects and sonorous matter, he built edifices, as he says, that were "Babylonian and Ninevitish," "music after Michelangelo," "on an immense scale." It was the *Symphonie funèbre et triomphale* for two orchestras and a choir, and the Te Deum for orchestra, organ, and three choirs which Berlioz loved (whose finale *Judex crederis* seemed to him the most effective thing he had ever written), as well as the *Impériale,* for two orchestras and two choirs, and the famous Requiem, with its "four orchestras of brass instruments, placed round the main orchestra and the mass of voices, but separated and answering one another at a distance." Like the Requiem, these compositions are often crude in style and of rather commonplace sentiment, but their grandeur is overwhelming. . . .

If Berlioz had had Wagner's reasoning power and had made the utmost use of his intuitions, if he had had Wagner's will and had shaped the inspirations of his genius and welded them into a solid whole, I venture to say that he would have made a revolution in music greater than Wagner's own; for Wagner, though stronger and more master of himself, was less original and, at bottom, but the close of a glorious past.

Will that revolution still be accomplished? Perhaps; but it has suffered half a century's delay. Berlioz bitterly calculated that people would begin to understand him about the year 1940.

After all, why be astonished that his mighty mission was too much for him? He was so alone. As people forsook him, his loneliness stood out in greater relief. He was alone in the age of Wagner, Liszt, Schumann, and Franck; alone, yet containing a whole world in himself, of which his enemies, his friends, his admirers, and he himself were not quite conscious; alone and tortured by his loneliness. Alone—the word is repeated by the music of his youth and his old age, by the *Symphonie fantastique* and *Les Troyens.* It is the word I read in the portrait before me as I write these lines—the beautiful portrait of the *Mémoires,* where his face looks out in sad and stern reproach on the age that so misunderstood him.

(*Musiciens d'aujourd'hui,* 1908; translated by Mary Blaiklock.)

# Schumann the Lyricist

## PHILIP HALE

*It is curious that Schumann, who wrote so much wonderful music criticism, inspired so little himself as a composer. The reasons for this strange lack are suggested in this program note by Philip Hale, who wrote annotations for the Boston Symphony from 1901 to 1933, while contributing to the Boston* Home Journal, Journal, *and* Herald. *Hale's style was highly literate and literary but also clear and crisp. In the words of Lawrence Gilman, another past master of the waning art of the program note, Hale was "almost indecently readable."*

It has been urged against Schumann that his symphonies were thought for the pianoforte and then orchestrated crudely, as by an amateur. This, however, is not the fatal objection. He had his own orchestral speech. Good, bad, or indifferent, it was his own. He could not have otherwise expressed himself through the orchestral instruments. His speech is to be accepted or rejected as the hearer is impressed chiefly by ideas, or by the manner of expression.

A more serious objection is this: the genius of Schumann was purely lyrical, although occasionally there is the impressive expression of a wild or melancholy mood, as in the chords of unearthly beauty soon after the beginning of the overture to *Manfred.* Whether the music be symphonic, chamber, a pianoforte piece or a song, the beauty, the expressive force lies in the lyric passages. When Schumann endeavored to build a musical monument, to quote Vincent d'Indy's phrase, he failed; for he had not architectonic imagination or skill.

His themes in symphonies, charming as they often are, give one the impression of fragments, of music heard in sleep-chasings. Never a master of contrapuntal technique, he repeated these phrases over and over again instead of broadly developing them, and his filling in is generally amateurish and perfunctory.

The best of Schumann's music is an expression of states and conditions of soul. This music is never spectacular; it is never objective. Take, for instance, his music to Goethe's *Faust*. The episodes that attracted the attention of Berlioz, Liszt, Gounod, were not to Schumann a source of inspiration. It was the mysticism in the poem that led him to musical interpretation. His music, whether for voice or instruments, is first of all *innig*, and this German word is not easily translated into English. Heartfelt, deep, ardent, fervent, intimate; no one of these words conveys exactly the idea contained in *innig*. There is the intimacy of personal and shy confession.

Schumann in his life was a reticent man. He dreamed dreams. He was lost in thought when others, in the beerhouse or at his home, were chattering about art. He put into his music what he would with difficulty have said aloud to his Clara. As a critic he was bold in praise and blame. As a composer he was often not assertive as one on a platform. He told his dreams, he wove his romantic fabric for a few sympathetic souls. It is true that in his days of wooing he was orchestrally jubilant, as in the first movement of the Symphony in B flat, but in this movement the anticipation aroused by the first measures is not realized. The thoughts soared above the control of the thinker; there was not the mastery over them that allowed no waste material, that gives golden expression without alloy.

In his own field, Schumann is lonely, incomparable. No composer has whispered such secrets of subtle and ravishing beauty to a receptive listener. The hearer of Schumann's music must in turn be imaginative and a dreamer. He must often anticipate the composer's thought. This music is not for a garish concert hall; it shrinks from boisterous applause.

(Boston Symphony Program Note, from *Great Concert Music*, 1935.)

# On Chopin's Piano Music

## ROBERT SCHUMANN
## FRANZ LISZT

*The piano music of Chopin inspired some of the most vivid nonfiction writing of the Romantic period. Chopin was the perfect exemplar of Romantic art, the creator of a new sound, structure, and sensibility, of music capable of being played only by the most heroically virtuosic performer, on an instrument that, in its development since the piano of Beethoven, was itself essentially new. And Chopin certainly looked the part, especially when he himself was that performer: with his combination of swooning sickliness and charismatic brilliance, he was the ideal Romantic personality. It is not surprising, therefore, that writers made little effort to separate Chopin the composer from Chopin the pianist. Schumann and Liszt, themselves great pianists as well as piano composers, led the way. Schumann, a major critic (see headnote to "On Discovering Schubert's Last Symphony"), expended some of his most imaginative metaphors on Chopin, whose Preludes he described as "ruins" and whose B-Flat Minor Sonata he called a "sphinx." Liszt is not as well known as a writer, but his formidable literary knowledge (see Jacques Barzun's "Literature in Liszt's Mind and Work") resulted in precise, if partisan, monographs on Wagner, Berlioz, and Liszt. (That Liszt wrote some of these in collaboration with Princess Caroline von Wittgenstein and Countess Marie d'Agoult does not lessen their interest.) Liszt was the more radical Romantic, at least in his rhetoric, as is indicated by his impatience with Chopin's use of classical form in the B-Flat Minor Sonata. To Schumann, as the following excerpt shows, the Sonata had a disturbing originality in no way compromised by Chopin's bow to sonata structure; to Liszt, only the Funeral March was worthy of commentary. Also revealing is the emphasis of both writers on Chopin's expressive range: far from the "easy listening" composer he is often reduced to today, Chopin was once regarded as a difficult, ugly, "intellectual" innovator who explored the blackest reaches of bitterness and despair.*

C hopin will soon be unable to write anything more without making people cry out, at the seventh or eighth bars already, "That is indeed by him!" People have called this mannerism, declaring that he makes no progress. They should be less ungrateful. Is not this the same original force that dazzled you so surprisingly in his first works, that in the first moment perplexed and then enraptured you? And now that he has given you a succession of rare creations, and you understand him more easily, do you ask something different from him? That would be like cutting down a tree because it produces the same sort of fruit every year. But his productions are not alike; the trunk is indeed the same, but its fruits vary wonderfully in growth and flavour. The above impromptu [Op. 29] so little resembles anything in the whole circle of his works, that I can scarcely compare it with any other Chopin composition; it is so refined in form, its cantilena is from beginning to end so enclosed in charming figuration; it is nothing more or less than so unique an impromptu that it cannot be placed beside any other of his compositions. The impassioned character of the scherzo [Op. 31] reminds us more of its predecessors; it is a highly attractive piece, so overflowing with tenderness, boldness, love, and contempt, that it may be compared, not inappropriately, to a Byron poem.

Any one who could glance at the first bars of the last-mentioned sonata, [Op. 35] and then remain in uncertainty as to who had written it, would not prove himself a good connoisseur. Only Chopin begins and ends so; with dissonances through dissonances into dissonances. But how many beauties this piece, too, contains! The idea of calling it a sonata is a caprice, if not a jest, for he has simply bound together four of his wildest children, to smuggle them under this name into a place to which they could not else have penetrated. Let us suppose some good country cantor visiting a musical city for the purpose of making artistic purchases; all the novelties are laid before him, but he does not care to know anything about them; finally, some rogue hands him a sonata; "Ah, yes, that is something in my way, a composition of the good old times," says he delighted, and buys it at once. Arrived at home, he takes the piece up, and I am much mistaken if he does not vow, by every musical divinity, that this is no sonata style, but rank blasphemy, before he has painfully ground out the first page. But Chopin has obtained his end; he has penetrated into the cantor's residence; and who knows whether, in years to come, in the same dwelling some romantic grandson may not brush the dust from the sonata, play it over, and think to himself, "This man was not very wrong"?

What I have just said is half an opinion. Chopin no longer writes anything that we could have equally good from others; he is true to himself, and has good reasons for remaining so.

It is a great pity that pianoforte players, even cultivated ones, are generally unable to judge, or to see beyond the limits of their own finger powers. Instead of first reading over such a difficult piece as this, they bore and hack away at it, bar by bar; and then, before they have acquired even a rough idea of its formal connections, they lay it aside, and pronounce it odd, intricate, &c. Chopin (something like Jean Paul) has his apostrophes and periods, over which it is not well to linger on a first reading, for fear of losing the principal thread. We find such passages on almost every page of this sonata, and Chopin's often wild and arbitrary chords render the disentanglement of such passages still more difficult. He is not fond of enharmonising, if I may so express it, and so we often find ten times, and oftener, sharpened keys and measures, such as none of us love except in extreme cases. He is often right, but is often entangled without any reason, and thus keeps at a distance a considerable part of the public; for people do not care to be continually quizzed (as they fancy) and driven into a corner. . . .

To [the] thoroughly Chopinean opening succeeds one of those stormy, passionate movements, of which we know several by him. . . . But even this first part of the work brings us beautiful melodies; indeed, it seems as if the national Polish flavour, which clung to most of Chopin's earlier melodies, were gradually dying out, and that he inclines more towards Italy (over Germany). It is known that Chopin and Bellini were friends, that they often showed their compositions to each other, and must necessarily have exercised an artistic influence on each other. But there is only a slight inclination to southern melody here. . . . The whole movement ends in a manner that is by no means Italian; and this reminds me of Liszt's observation. He once said, "Rossini and Co. always close with I remain your very humble servant." But it is otherwise with Chopin, whose conclusions almost express the contrary. The second movement is a continuation of this mood of feeling; it is bold intellectual, fantastic, the trio dreamy, tender, altogether in Chopin's manner; the scherzo is only such in name, like many of Beethoven's. The next is more gloomy, a *Mareia funebre*, which has some repellant points; an adagio instead, perhaps in D flat, would certainly have been more effective. The finale he has given us sounds more like a joke than a piece of music. Yet we must confess that even from this joyless, unmelodious movement, an original, a terrible mind breathes forth, the preponderance of which annihilates resistance, so that we listen, fascinated and uncomplaining, to the end, but not to praise; for, as I have said before, this is not music. The sonata commences enigmatically, and closes with an ironical smile, a sphinx.

The name to which we have so often pointed, as to a rare star at a late hour of the night, must not be wanting in our Museum. Where its course may lead, how long may last its sparkling light, who can tell? But it can always be distinguished whenever its shows itself, even by a child, for it always displays the same core of flame, the same deeply dark glow, the same brilliancy. . . . Imagine that an Aeolian harp possessed all the scales, and that an artist's hand struck these with all kinds of fantastic, elegant embellishments, ever rendering audible a deep fundamental tone, and a softly flowing upper voice—and you will have some idea of [Chopin's] playing. No wonder, then, that we were charmed with the [Études] at once, hearing them played by himself, and most of all with the first, in A flat major, rather a poem than a study. But it would be a mistake to suppose that he allowed us to hear every small note in it; it was rather an undulation of the A flat major chord, brought out more loudly here and there with the pedal, but, exquisitely entangled in the harmony; we followed a wondrous melody in the sustained tones, while, in the middle, a tenor voice broke clearly from the chords, and joined the principal melody. And when the *étude* was ended, we felt as though we had seen a lovely form in a dream, and, half awake, we strove to seize it again;—but such things cannot be described, still less can they be fitly praised.

Then he played the second in the book, in F minor, one in which his individuality displays itself in a manner never to be forgotten. How charming, how dreamy it was! Soft as the song of a sleeping child. That in F major followed; fine again, but less novel in character; here the master showed his admirable bravura powers—but what are words for all this? They are all models of bold, indwelling, creative force, truly poetic creations, though not without small blots in their details, but, on the whole, striking and powerful.

Genius creates kingdoms, the smaller states of which are again divided by a higher hand among talents, that these may organise details which the former, in its thousandfold activity, would be unable to perfect. As Hummel, for instance, followed the call of Mozart, clothing the thoughts of that master in a flowing, sparkling robe, so Chopin followed Beethoven. Or, to speak more simply, as Hummel imitated the style of Mozart in detail, rendering it enjoyable to the virtuoso on one particular instrument, so Chopin led the spirit of Beethoven into the concert-hall.

Chopin did not make his appearance accompanied by an orchestral army, as great genius is accustomed to do; he only possesses a small cohort, but every soul belongs to him. . . .

He is the pupil of the first masters—Beethoven, Schubert, Field. The first formed his mind in boldness, the second his heart in tenderness, the third his hand to its flexibility.

Thus he stood, well provided with deep knowledge in his art, armed with courage in the full consciousness of his power, when, in the year 1830, the great voice of the people arose in the West. Hundreds of youths had waited for the moment; but Chopin was the first on the summit of the wall, behind which lay a cowardly renaissance, a dwarfish Philistinism asleep. . . .

Besides this, and the favourable influence of period and condition, Fate rendered Chopin still more individual and interesting in endowing him with an original, pronounced nationality—Polish, too; and because this nationality wanders in mourning robes, in the thoughtful artist it deeply attracts us. It was well for him that neutral Germany did not receive him too warmly at first, and that his genius led him straight to one of the great capitals of the world, where he could freely poetise and grow angry. If the powerful Autocrat of the

North knew what a dangerous enemy threatens him in Chopin's works, in the simple melodies of his mazurkas, he would forbid music. Chopin's works are cannons buried in flowers.

In his origin, in the fate of his country, we find the explanation of his great qualities and of his failings. When we speak of grace, enthusiasm, presence of mind, nobility, and warmth of feeling, who does not think of him? But who does not, when the question is of eccentricity, morbid sickliness, even wildness and hatred?

Many of Chopin's earlier creations bear this impress of the sharpest nationality.

But Art requires more. The cosmopolitan must sacrifice the small interests of the soil on which he was born. Chopin's later works begin to lose something of their especial Sarmatian physiognomy, and to approach partly, and more nearly, that universal ideal which the divine Greeks cultivated, and which we find again, on another path, in Mozart.

I say "partly"; for he never can, never ought, wholly to disown his origin. But the further he removes from it, the greater will his consequence in the general world of art become.

Chopin has contributed to the general improvement of art the idea that progress in it can only be attained through the formation of an intellectual aristocracy among artists. This would not merely demand a complete knowledge of mechanism, but would also require as indispensable in its members the possession of all the qualities they might require from others, as well as active sympathy, and a lively faculty of comprehension and restoration. Such a union of productivity and reproductivity would certainly hasten the epoch of general musical cultivation, in which there would be as little doubt as to what should be regarded as correct and true, as there is regarding the manifold forms in which it appears.

Of new compositions by Chopin, we must mention a remarkable collection of preludes, besides a book of mazurkas and three waltzes. His forms seem to grow ever brighter and lighter—or are we becoming accustomed to his style? These mazurkas (Opus 33) will charm every one instantly, and seem to us more popular in character than his earlier ones; but his three waltzes (Opus 34) will delight above all things, so different in type, as they are, from the ordinary ones, and of such a kind as only Chopin dare venture on or even invent,—while gazing inspired among the dancers whom he has just called up by his preludes, and while thinking of far different things than those that are to be danced there. Such a wave of life flows through them, that they seem to have been improvised in the dancing-room. I must signalise the preludes as most remarkable (Opus 28). I will confess that I expected something quite different, carried out in the grand style, like his *études*. It is almost the contrary here; these are sketches, the beginnings of studies, or, if you will, ruins; eagles' feathers, all wildly, variegatedly intermingled. But in every piece we find, in his own refined hand, written in pearls, "This is by Frédéric Chopin"; we recognise him even in his pauses, and by his impetuous respiration. He is the boldest, the proudest poet-soul of to-day. To be sure, the book also contains some morbid, feverish, repellant traits; but let every one look in it for something that will enchant him.

    (Schumann, *Gesammelte Schriften über Musik und Musiker*, 1854; translated by Fanny Raymond Ritter.)

C hopin, so far from being solicitous for the noise of an orchestra, was content to see his thoughts integrally produced on the ivory of the keyboard, and to succeed in his effort to lose nothing in power, without claiming any pretension to orchestral effects or to the brush of the scene-painter. . . . Not yet have we studied with sufficient earnestness and attention the designs of his delicate pencil, accustomed as we are in these days to regard as worthy of a great name only those composers who have written at least half-a-dozen operas, as many oratorios, and a number of symphonies, vainly requiring every musician to do all things, or even something more than that. But however widely diffused this idea may be, the justice of it, to say the least, is highly problematical. We have no desire whatever to dispute the glory, more difficult of achievement, or the real superiority of those epic poets who display their magnificent creations upon so extended a plan, but we wish to see material proportions in music judged by the same standard as that which is applied to mere dimensions in other branches of the fine arts, as, for instance, in painting, where a canvas twenty inches square, as the "Vision of Ezekiel," or "Le Cimitière" by Ruysdael, is ranked among the *chefs-d'oeuvre*, and is more highly valued than pictures of a far greater bulk, even though they may come from the hands of a Rubens or a Tintoret. In literature, is Beranger to be reckoned a less great poet because he has chosen to condense his thoughts within the narrow sphere of his songs? Does not Petrarch owe his fame to his sonnets? And among those who most frequently recite his soothing rhymes, how many are there who know anything at all about the very existence of his long poem on Africa? We cannot doubt the ultimate disappearance of that prejudice which would deny the superiority of an artist, even though he may have produced nothing but such sonatas as those given to us by Franz Schubert, over one who has dealt out the tasteless melodies of many operas which it were useless to mention; or that in music also we shall yet come to take into account the eloquence and ability with which thoughts and feelings are expressed, whatever may be the size of the composition in which they are developed or the means which are employed for their interpretation.

In analysing the works of Chopin we meet with beauties of a high order, expressions which are quite new, and a harmonic tissue which is as original as it is erudite. In his compositions boldness is always justified; his richness, even exuberance, is never allowed to interfere with clarity; singularity is never permitted to degenerate into an uncouth fantasticality; his sculpturing never wants order; the luxury of his ornamentation is never allowed to overload the chaste eloquence of his leading outlines. His finest works abound in combinations which may be described as forming an epoch in the handling of musical style. They are daring, brilliant, always attractive; but they disguise their profundity by so much grace, and their science is concealed under so many charms, that it is a work of difficulty to free ourselves from their magical enthralment sufficiently to form in cold blood a judgment of their theoretical value. . . .

It is to Chopin that we owe extended chords played together in arpeggio or *en batterie;* those chromatic sinuosities such striking samples of which are seen in his pages; those little groups of superadded notes which drop like delicate drops of pearly dew upon the melodic figure. Hitherto this species of adornment had only been modelled on the *fioriture* of the grand old school of Italian song; embellishments for the voice, although they had become stereotyped and had grown monotonous, had been servilely copied by the pianoforte; Chopin endowed them with a charm of novelty, surprise and variety, quite unsuitable for the singer but in perfect keeping with the character of the instrument. It was he who invented those admirable harmonic progressions which have imparted a serious character to pages which, by reason of the lightness of their subjects, made no pretensions to importance. . . . [So] unassuming are the titles and the subjects of Chopin's "Studies" and "Preludes," and yet the compositions which are thus modestly named are nonetheless types of perfection in a mode which he himself created, and stamped, as he did all his other works, with the deep impress of his poetic genius. Written when his career was only just beginning, they are marked by a youthful vigour not found in some of his later works, even when they are more elaborate and finished, and richer in combinations—a vigour which we altogether miss in the subsequent works, which are marked by over-excited sensibility and morbid irritability, and which give painful indications of his own condition of suffering and exhaustion.

It is not our intention to discuss the development of pianoforte music in the language of the schools; we might dissect his magnificent pages, which furnish so fine a field for scientific observation. We should in the first instance analyse his nocturnes, ballads, impromptus, scherzos, so full of refinements of harmony never before heard, bold and startling in their originality; and we should also examine his polonaises, mazurkas, waltzes and boleros. But this is not the time or place for such an examination, which would only be of interest to adepts in counterpoint and thoroughbass.

His works have become known and popular because of the *feeling* which they contain—feeling of a kind pre-eminently romantic, individual, subjective; peculiar to the composer and yet evoking immediate response and sympathy; appealing not merely to the heart of his country, indebted to him for yet another glory, but to all who are capable of being touched by the misfortunes of exile or touched by the tenderness of love.

Not content with his success in that field where he was free to fill up with such perfect grace the outlines he had himself selected, Chopin also wished to imprison his thoughts and ideas by classical fetters. His concertos and sonatas are, indeed beautiful, but they reveal much more effort than inspiration. His creative genius was imperious, fantastic, impulsive, and the beauties of his work were only fully manifested in absolute freedom. We cannot help thinking that he did violence to the peculiar nature of his genius when he endeavoured to subject it to rules, to classifications and to regulations

not of his own making, and which he could not bend into harmony
with the requirements of his own mind. He was one of those original
souls whose graces are only fully revealed when they have cut themselves adrift from all bondage and float on at their own wild will,
controlled only by the ever-changing impulses of their own mobile
natures. . . .

And yet some of Chopin's efforts in the classic sphere are resplendent with rare dignity of style, and among them may be found
passages of wondrous interest and of astonishing grandeur. As an
example we may cite the Adagio of the Second Concerto, which he
was fond of playing frequently, and for which he always showed a
decided preference. The principal phrase is of admirable breadth,
and the accessory details are in his best style. It alternates with
a recitative in a minor key, which seems to be its antistrophe. The
whole movement is of an almost ideal perfection; its expression
is now radiant with light, and now full of tender pathos. It is as
if one had selected a happy vale of Tempé, a brilliant landscape
flooded with the glow and lustre of summer, as the background
for the rehearsal of some appalling scene of mortal anguish; even
amidst the incomparable magnificence of external nature a bitter and irreparable regret seizes on the fiercely throbbing human
heart. . . .

We cannot pass in silence the Funeral March in the First Sonata
which was arranged for the orchestra, and performed for the first
time at his own funeral. Could any other accents have been found
which would have expressed with such heartbreaking effect the emotions and tears which should accompany to his last long sleep one
who had so sublimely taught how great losses should be mourned?
We once heard a native of his own land say, "These pages could only
have been written by a Pole!" Everything that the funeral train of a
whole nation lamenting its own ruin and death can be conceived to
feel of desolating woe and majestic grief wails in the musical ring of
this passing bell, mourns in the toll of this solemn knell, as it escorts
the mighty cortège on its journey to the silent city of the dead. . . .
And yet this Mélopée, so funereal and so charged with devastating
woe, is full of such penetrating sweetness that we can scarcely believe
it had its origin upon earth. These sounds, which seem to chill by awe
and soften by distance the wild passion of human anguish, induce
most profound meditation, as if they were sung by angels and came

floating from the heavens—the cry of a nation's anguish appealing at the very throne of the Eternal! . . .

Even Weber has been outdone in this species of composition by Chopin, not merely in the number and variety of his works of this genre, but also in the more touching style of handling, and in the new and varied resources of harmony. Chopin's Polonaises in A and A flat major very much resemble, both in construction and in spirit, Weber's in E major. In others Chopin relinquished this broad style— shall we say always with more decisive success? Decision on such a point were a thorny thing. Who shall restrain the poet in his rights over the various phases of his subject? May he not be allowed, even in the midst of his joy, to be gloomy and oppressed? Having sung of the splendours of glory, may he not afterwards sing of grief? When he has rejoiced with the victor, may he not then mourn with the vanquished? We may state without fear of contradiction, that it is not Chopin's least merit that he sees consecutively all the phases of which the theme is capable; that he has been successful in bringing out of it all its brilliance and in awakening from it all its sadness. He was aided in his comprehension and reproduction of such manifold aspects by the variety of the moods of which he was himself the subject. . . .

His grand Polonaise in F sharp minor must be classed among his most energetic writings, and in it he has put a mazurka. Had he not alarmed the frivolous world of fashion by the gloomy grotesqueness with which he placed this mazurka in so fantastic an incantation, that mode might have grown into an ingenious caprice for the ball-room. The whole production is one of great originality, and excites us like the story of some broken dream told after a night of restless wakefulness in the first dull gray, cold, leaden rays of a winter sunrise. It is a dream poem in which impressions and objects follow each other with startling incoherence and with the wildest transitions, reminding us of the lines in Byron's "Dream":

> ". . . . . Dreams in their developments have breath,
> And tears and tortures and the touch of joy;
> They leave a weight upon our waking thoughts.
>  .      .      .
> And look like heralds of Eternity."

The chief *motif* is a weird air, as dark as the lurid hour before a hurricane. . . . The prolonged reiteration of the tonic at the begin-

ning of each measure reminds us of the repeated roar of cannon—
just as if we caught the sounds from some fierce contest raging afar
off. When this note has terminated a series of highly unusual chords
succeed each other bar after bar. In the works of the great masters we
know of nothing analogous to the striking effect produced by this
passage, which is suddenly interrupted by a *scène champêtre,* a mazurka in the style of an idyl, full of the scent of lavender and sweet
marjoram; but which, so far from effacing the memory of the deep
grief which has gone before, serves by its bitter irony of contrast to
augment our painful emotions, so much so that we feel almost a
sensation of comfort at the return of the original phrase. . . . This
improvisation ends like a dream, with no other conclusion than a sort
of convulsive shudder, leaving the soul the subject of the strangest,
wildest and most overpowering impressions.

The "Polonaise-Fantaisie" must be reckoned among the works
which belong to Chopin's latest period, and which are all more or less
characterised by a restless, feverish anxiety. Here we look in vain for
bold or brilliant pictures; we no longer hear the loud tramp of cavalry
accustomed to victory; those heroic chants and bold tones suited to
the audacity of men ever-victorious, songs unmuffled by visions of
defeat, no longer resound in our ears. Instead of these there reigns
everywhere a deep melancholy, forever broken by startled movements, sudden alarms, disturbed rest, stifled sighs. We are surrounded by such feelings and scenes as we may suppose to arise
among men who are surprised and surrounded by an ambuscade, for
whom the whole horizon is bereft of any vestige of hope, whose brain
is giddied by despair, as by a draught of that Cyprus wine which
imparts to all our gestures a more instructive rapidity, gives to our
words a keener point, heats our emotions with a more subtle flame,
and excites our mind to a pitch of irritability which is closely akin to
insanity. . . .

Soon after [Chopin's] arrival in Paris, in 1832, a new school both
in literature and music was started, and youthful talent came forward
to shake off with *éclat* the yoke of old-fashioned formulae. The
political effervescence of the first years of the revolution of July had
scarcely died down, when questions were raised on art and letters
which aroused attention and interest in all minds. The order of the
day was *Romanticism,* and the battle was obstinately fought both for
and against. How could there possibly be any truce between those

who on the one side would not admit the possibility of writing in any form other than that already established, and those who on the other side contended that an artist should be allowed to select such forms as he thought best suited for the expression of his ideas, and that the rule of form should be found in the fitness of the form chosen for the sentiments to be expressed, every varying shade of emotion demanding of course a different mode of expression? The former pinned their faith to a permanent form, the perfection of which represented absolute beauty. But in admitting that the greatest masters had attained to the utmost limits in art, or had, in other words, reached supreme perfection, they left succeeding artists no other glory than that of hoping to more or less closely approach these models of imitation, and thus destroyed for ever all hope of equalling them because the merit of perfecting of a process can never equal the merit of inventing it. The opposite party, on the other hand, denied that immaterial Beauty could have any fixed and absolute form; the different forms illuminated by history seemed to them to be tents strewn along the interminable road of the Ideal, mere brief halting places which genius had reached from epoch to epoch, and beyond which the heirs of the ages should ever strive to advance. The one wanted to restrict, within the lines of the same symmetrical frame, the creations of times and of natures in every way dissimilar; the other claimed that all writers should have liberty to create their own mode, obeying no rules but those which are the result of the direct relation of sentiment and form, only requiring from the form that it should be adequate for the expression of the sentiment; however great their admiration for existing models, these did not to them seem to have exhausted all the range of those sentiments which art might select, or all the forms which it might use with advantage. . . .

Those who saw the flames of Genius devouring the old worm-eaten, crumbling skeletons, attached themselves to that school of which Berlioz was the most gifted, most brilliant, and most daring representative. This school Chopin joined. He insisted most strenuously on setting himself free from the servile forms of the conventional style, and at the same time he earnestly repudiated that kind of charlatanism which sought to replace old abuses merely by the introduction of new ones.

(Liszt, *Life of Chopin*, 1852; translated by John Broadhouse.)

# Literature in Liszt's Mind and Work

## JACQUES BARZUN

*This article by cultural historian Jacques Barzun accomplishes three daunting objectives: it places in exact historical and musical perspective the achievement of Franz Liszt, one of the most misunderstood of composers; it delivers a valuable definition of Romanticism by demonstrating close connections between literature and music; and it presents a compelling case for closing the false gap—one that would have been utterly foreign to Liszt and his contemporaries—between "program" and "absolute" music. Originally a speech delivered by Professor Barzun at the Library of Congress in 1986, this piece has been recast by the author for this book. (For more on Jacques Barzun, see headnote to "Music into Words.")*

One of the curiosities of criticism as it is practiced today is that although the relation to the human mind of literature—words and ideas—is taken for granted as the most natural thing in the world, the relation of literature to music is held to be unnatural, indeed illicit. It is as if the mind had a solid partition between its faculties. The use of language to talk about music being deemed illegitimate, it follows that the voluble music lover and the voluminous music critic have no right to exist. What is said among friends leaving the concert hall and what is printed the next morning in the paper are alike nonsensical; these familiar habits are at best tolerated absurdities.

The same relation in reverse is reproved even more vehemently: subjects called literary can find no embodiment in musical sound. But since many composers seem unaware of the prohibition, they have to be dealt with somehow; they are tagged as "programmatic" and charged with lack of "purity" for making music out of "extra-musical" ideas.

To the general public these distinctions are not vivid, though it grasps the bearing of the words *program, literary,* and *pictorial* as commonly applied to certain works or particular passages within them. Some composers are notorious for their flouting of purity; they are like divorced persons 75 years ago claiming to be respectable. One such composer is Franz Liszt. He is the perfect instance to examine if the dispute over purity is ever to be shelved as one of those historical polemics that in retrospect are judged to be noise without contents.

By the very statement of the case that "some composers do and some don't" we are forced to consider types of mind and kinds of human experience. Liszt was one of the incriminated breed who advertised his heresy in prefaces and argued for it in letters and articles. How did he come to this sinful state and why did the time in which he lived at first permit and then condemn what he produced and said?

In order to answer one must take the word *literature* in its broadest possible sense. I mean by it anything that ordinarily goes by that name—tales, plays, poetry—and also whatever is or has been a topic for discourse and description. It is the whole realm of ideas, of verbalized experience and imagination, that is at issue; it is the role of ideas during Liszt's long life that explains, indeed justifies, his advocacy and practice as a composer.

The first important portion of verbalized experience that shaped Liszt's mind goes by the name of Romanticism. At that word, a host of meanings and associations rush into the mind, mostly from conventional criticism. They should be put aside in favor of different meanings and associations, untouched by the perspective and notions of the last 150 years, and thus closer to what Liszt and his contemporaries understood by Romantic.

For although some of the ideas and feelings of that past time are still with us, they no longer evoke the same judgements, their connections have changed; we do not speak the same language about them. To illustrate this difference about one such feeling which I believe still has currency, the feeling of love, Constant Lambert long ago drew a comparison: "There was nothing forced," he says, "about

Liszt's romanticism. It was the most natural thing in the world for Liszt to take his young countesses on Lake Como and read them Tasso and Victor Hugo. If anyone still thinks this spirit exists, let him visualize himself taking his young woman on the Serpentine and reading her T. S. Eliot."

And Lambert goes on to point out the inhibitions, social and individual, that would make such a modern scene impossible, or that would make it ridiculous instead of touching if it did take place.

Again, in speaking of his first love, Liszt said she was "a soul pure and chaste like the alabaster of which sacred vessels are made." We may think this is a foolish description of any human being: we know all about glands and complexes and prefer to discuss those instead of the soul. But it was a power, not a weakness, to see the beloved as Liszt did. It was the power that enabled him to compose the "Gretchen" movement of the *Faust* symphony. Our glands and complexes sing a different music.

The explanation of the difference is that Romanticism as an historical movement that swept over Europe and America in the first half of the nineteenth century did not consist merely of young love glorified; it was love fused with Tasso and Victor Hugo. Love was a more than personal concern of the body and the emotions; it had multiple connections with every new current of thought—artistic, social, political, and religious.

Twenty-five years of war—the wars of the French Revolution and Napoleon—had bred a new sensibility through repeated experiences of horror and glory, victories and massacres, betrayal and heroism, high energy and incessant anxiety. One unexpected result was that in the generations that came of age between 1790 and 1830 there appeared an amazing galaxy of geniuses in all fields. Among them, Franz Liszt, born in the exact middle year 1811, is conspicuously representative.

He was, to begin with, conspicuous as a lover; so let us look again at the scene on Lake Como, to which, in 1835, he had taken, not "young countesses" in the plural, but one, Marie d'Agoult, who was not so very young, being at thirty six years older than Liszt. They had been lovers, in Paris, where Liszt had become a celebrated virtuoso of the piano, and where she was known as a woman of remarkable character and cultivation. She left her elderly husband and young children to follow Liszt, not as an escapade of the sort we witness in twentieth-century films, but because to her and to Liszt, love was one of the high and rare powers reserved for certain chosen spirits. Love, I repeat, was not simply sexual instinct and emotional glow; it was not yet regarded as a therapeutic measure or a neurotic habit. It was a passion. As such it underlay every important and noble endeavor. It was the inner engine that drove some beings to be heroes and artists; it required a strong and beautiful soul to sustain it, and although it was Woman that enshrined love and elevated mankind (as Goethe had just said in *Faust*), the same passion could unite persons of the same sex in lifelong friendship.

This is what Constant Lambert meant when he spoke of Liszt's behavior on Lake Como as not forced. This is what Liszt took for granted when he thought about life and love.

In the village of Bellagio on the Lake, he and Marie would read to each other seated under the trees, at the foot of the Statue of Dante and Beatrice. It was by an inferior sculptor and it made Liszt indignant because (he says) Beatrice was shown as "squat and material." But he was also puzzled by Dante, who made Beatrice typify divine science—theology—instead of love. Since it is Beatrice who draws Dante upwards on the last part of his journey, Liszt thought the abstractions of theology inadequate as motive power. The Romantics had high ideals, but they believed above all in concrete realities.

At this point, one ought to speak Chinese, or rather to speak about the Chinese language, in which (as I understand) there is a word *h-s-i-n,* which means mind-and-heart, two in one. It is not a union of two things, but a single concept. This very notion is what Liszt and his fellow Romanticists discovered for themselves, without knowing Chinese. They knew that feeling and thought are the single mysterious energy we live by. They went on to say that it can be best understood by looking within and then expressing the findings in poetry, drama, music, painting—all the arts, and the sciences besides. This is the reason for their concern with the self, their egotism, if you like; the self was their research material, and the arts were the form in which the findings were expressed.

These facts should help to hold in check the tendency to think of Romantic with a capital R as the adjective that denotes romance with a small r and nothing more. The love, the passion, one might even say, in modern jargon, the libido of the Romanticists is the clue to their achievements, to what their mind and heart conceived and created. Liszt is representative because of the range of these passions in him.

In his seventeenth year, after a shattering disappointment in love, he experienced simultaneously a religious crisis and a nervous breakdown. He was reported dead and subsequently had the pleasure of reading his own obituary. From then on, he never ceased being haunted by the need for love and for God. Long before his well-known entry into the church, he had given himself heart-and-mind to several quasi-religious causes. In Paris, after the revolution of July 1830, he became what would now be called a fellow-traveler of the socialist movement inspired by Count Saint-Simon.

The Saint-Simonians could be described as Christian Technocrats. Their reform of society was to be accomplished for the good of all, and without class struggle, by industrialists and bankers, whose aim would be to establish a divine community on earth. In this task, the artist was to be the mediator between God and man; he would in fact be an artist-priest, and meanwhile a propagandist for the faith. So the cult actively recruited poets and musicians for the creation of songs and marches, and at least one unknown graphic artist must have been snared to design the pale blue troubadour costume in which the band of singing converts paraded on the boulevards.

Liszt did not compose music for them, but played at their gatherings and did compose, on the basis of their tenets, a long article on "The Situation of Artists in Society." Like his fellow artists, he thought that situation abominable. Genius starved, patronage was humiliating, and success could be bought only by charlatanism. These considerations coincided with Liszt's disenchantment about the role of virtuoso—the show-off who could play faster and louder than anybody else. He was also disenchanted with the type of composition for which virtuosos were known—fantasias and variations, always labeled "brilliant," on airs from the latest popular opera, usually Italian. He decided to compose and perform serious music.

The liberal Revolution of 1830, the socialism of Saint-Simon and other reformers, the passion for experience, the innovations emerging in every art, taken together, show that the time was bent on construction, on reconstruction, in fact, after the destruction of the Old Regime. The prerequisite of all these efforts was: new principles of organization. Socialism was one. Another was Nationalism. Liszt could not fail to feel its attraction. Here again, it is important to avoid giving a word its twentieth-century connotations. To the Romanticists, the love of nation did not mean an aggressive, self-satisfied attitude toward other peoples. On the contrary, it meant an appreciation of diversity among the national traditions. The nations of Europe were compared to a bouquet of cultures, each with its characteristic fragrance. What this conception opposed was the cosmopolitan outlook of the previous period, the idea that Man with a capital M was the same the world over.

The cultural nationalism that Liszt espoused carried with it other novel ideas. It implied that not only the elite but also the people were bearers and creators of culture. This belief started the study of the folk and its creations: collecting popular songs and dances, popular customs and myths, and making use of them in literature and the arts. These studies formed part of the new passion for history and its ruling principle—evolution: the state of society and culture was seen not as the work of pure reason by a handful of philosophers, but as the product of history, a slow development to which all individuals and all nations had contributed.

Inspired by such beliefs, Liszt set off on another intellectual adventure. He was born a Hungarian and proud of the fact; but he had not been brought up to learn the language—a lack he always regretted. He spoke German, French, and Italian, and as a traveling performer was at home in every country. This made him a cosmopolitan of a kind, but it also heightened his sense of national differences, and it is noteworthy that in composing the songs or other works. on subjects that inspired him, he made use of the musical idiom from the appropriate nation. Thus in his paraphrase of Patriarch's Sonnet 47 he opens with a clearly Italian motif; in his Historical Portraits of seven Hungarian heroes, the rhythms and intervals derive from Hungarian music.

This putting together of elements originating within national boundaries came to Liszt naturally: he did not make a point of it. But his attachment of mind-and-heart to Hungary impelled him to one highly conscious effort. He determined not only to compose on Hungarian themes, as Chopin had done on Polish, but also to study where those song and dance tunes came from. He did much reading and field work—visiting remote villages and camping out with Gypsies and finally publishing a large book. Here is a fine instance of

Romantic nationalism proving its open-minded, nonaggressive nature, for Liszt's conclusion was that the source of Hungarian music was actually Gypsy.

Liszt used local themes and rhythms both in works like the nineteen Hungarian Rhapsodies and the Rakóczy March, where they are developed by themselves, and in works such as *La Notte* (inspired by Michelangelo), where they mingle with other national or international formulas. He also worked up Italian, Polish, Russian, and Spanish folk tunes. The time of composers specializing in the music of one nation in the manner of Dvorák, Smetana, Grieg, Bartók, Ives, or Copland, had not yet come.

It is clear that Liszt was by temperament impressionable, eager, inquisitive, and supercharged with restless energy; obviously a genius, yet so receptive to every influence as to suggest the lack of a strong directing center; he was always in search of one, on earth and in heaven. After the Saint-Simonian cult, he attached himself to an eloquent priest named Lamennais, who had gathered a few disciples at his place outside Paris. Liszt lived there for weeks at a time, imbibing a different brand of Christian socialism, aimed at the working classes. And whereas the Saint-Simonians wanted to become the new church, Lamennais had no wish to break with Rome, though in the end Rome broke with him; it should have been a forewarning to Liszt.

The most curious fact about these adventures of the mind-and-heart is that, once caught, Liszt remained faithful, even though no longer in touch. To the end of his life he kept speaking with respect of these incompatible socialist pioneers and as one who still believed. He had truly given himself to them. After a severe strike of the silk workers in Lyon in 1834, he composed a piano work in their honor, and a little after went with a singer friend to that city, to give a benefit concert for the unemployed. He composed choruses on the dignity of labor and even on particular trades. Liszt's memory of his passionate encounters always led to action or creation. The story of his struggle to organize—and subsidize—the putting up of a statue to Beethoven in Bonn, with concerts (including a cantata of his own) that should bring together in celebration all the musical genius of Europe, is an epic in itself. In a word, hardly any person or place or idea of importance in Liszt's life-span is without an echo in the catalog of his musical works.

In his friendships and love affairs one finds the same pattern, modified by the failure of human beings to stay as constant to persons as to ideas. Liszt's choice of Marie d'Agoult, and later of the Princess Carolyne von Sayn-Wittgenstein, was preeminently a response to their strength of mind and character. For Marie's looks were striking rather than handsome and Carolyne was positively ill-favored. Both women were intense, learned, and humorless. Liszt's early writings in French, were in fact collaborations with Marie, who later wrote novels on her own; his writings in German were collaborations with Carolyne, who later produced a twenty-four-volume work on the salvation of Europe through a reform of the Catholic Church.

These two women did not so much inspire as direct Liszt's literary and musical energies during two important periods totaling twenty-one years—and not solely his political and social opinions. For example, Liszt, having made his mark through the piano, felt very insecure about scoring for orchestra, and until his forties he relied on two or three helpers for his instrumentation. Seeing this, the princess uttered a reproach: "Why do you use Raff to orchestrate the march?" she asked. "What painter would content himself with handing over his drawing and leaving the colouring of it to his apprentice? . . . I think that you do not put enough emphasis on giving colour to your musical thoughts. You content yourself with retouching . . . if I compare this with literary style, correction is never as good as original writing." Very sound advice, which Liszt finally accepted. He may have remembered that his Saint-Simonian comrades held that Woman should be worshipped as the Revealer of Truth.

Nor was Liszt a one-man dog in his submissiveness; having told Wagner that he was working on a symphony in three movements about Dante, he received a long letter back arguing that although a composer could readily express in music the ambience of Hell and of Purgatory, Paradise was not possible. Wagner had a way of improvising theories of this sort, which he promptly forgot or contradicted. But Liszt was earnest, pondered the arguments, and cut back poor Dante to two-thirds of his symphony.

In these and other ways, Liszt presents the unusual spectacle of a genius as it were "available" to multiple and unpredictable influences. Ordinarily, this is a sign of youth. We are not surprised when we hear the critics say that Liszt in his twenties was "profoundly influenced" by Berlioz, "profoundly influenced" by Paganin, "profoundly influenced" by Chopin, to say nothing of their contemporaries in Paris during the 1830s—Victor Hugo, George Sand, Heinrich Heine, Sainte Beuve, Vigny, and the rest. The satirical Heine wrote an article making fun of Liszt's plural enthusiasms, which upset Liszt into replying.

But there was no frivolity in his stockpiling of mentors. We find their imprint not just in early works but in late as well, and Liszt keeps adding to them. In mid-career he discovers Glinka and proceeds to call himself his disciple. He comes across the Russian Five and Russian folksongs and adopts their ways. On one occasion, he went so far as to tell a gathering of musicians that everyone in the room was a greater master than he. The remark struck some people as insincere; Liszt had a reputation for vanity which seemed incompatible with this humble acknowledgment. But Liszt's vanity was not conceit; it was a boyish pleasure in being on stage, handsome, potent, and wildly applauded; and that is a feeling quite compatible with the feeling of indecisiveness, of uncertainty about the direction to follow next. The complication of mind-and-heart was the price he paid for being so susceptible to novel ideas.

No doubt it was troublesome at times. It made Liszt loosen the ties of his friendship with Berlioz, who was a firm friend and supporter, and become a devotee of Wagner, who was an exploiter. Liszt's music and fame did not greatly matter to Wagner, who, after their quarrel, had only one thing to say: "He has served me well."

Liszt in his fifties rediscovered Catholicism and the beauties of Gregorian chant. He lived in Rome a great part of each year. But he was an embarrassment to the Vatican because of his liaison with the princess. He had made all arrangement to marry her on his fiftieth birthday and he wrote a piece for the occasion, but she had been divorced and the Church refused to sanction the marriage. He went into retreat and two years later took minor orders. He was made a door-keeper, acolyte, lector, and exorcist, but had no right to the title of abbé by which he became known. The conversion did not make him more acceptable to the Roman ecclesiastics, but one good result was his new mission—to reform church music—and that produced at least one great work in his latter years.

In those declining years, like many artists and others of his generation, Liszt suffered unhappiness and misunderstanding. The revolutions of 1848 all over Europe had affected a radical change of temper while he remained unaltered. Four years of brutal war cost many lives and the aftermath of repression broke many spirits. Art, genius, love, and the cult of the new no longer ruled the imagination; it was submerged in politics and machine industry. Reform gave way to class war; the artist turned outsider and enemy of society, or else adopted a sober classicism as a retreat. The young developed contempt for grandeur and heroism; in short, the Romanticist impulse had been killed; its fusion of the ideal and the real was reduced to an angry study of the physically actual, mistakenly called Realism.

With his great fund of passionate energy, Liszt did not succumb or submit. Indeed, in the ten years following 1848, when the Princess Wittgenstein joined him at Weimar, he had a most fruitful period of composing and of conducting the "new music," Berlioz, Liszt, and Wagner forming the avant-garde. But the hostile reaction was prompt. In 1854 Hanslick, a far from negligible critic, declared war on the new school in a best-seller called *Beauty in Music*; and in 1860 the young Brahms drafted and circulated a manifesto singling out Liszt as a nefarious influence. The year before, Liszt's only son Daniel had died; two years later his older daughter Blandine. It was in the following year that Liszt, balked in his desire to marry the princess, withdrew into religious seclusion. He did make a comeback into the secular world in 1869, dividing his time between Rome, Budapest, and Weimar, where he acquired his numerous pupils. But in those final twenty-five years he felt misjudged by his contemporaries, unrecognized as a composer, and hopeful only that posterity would make amends, as it had for his poet-hero Tasso, around whose image he composed a second orchestral work.

It was this singular combination of restlessness and fidelity that made Liszt a great disseminator. By instinct he played the busy bee going from flower to flower, and like the bee he picked up and spread pollen. What is more, in spite of his cumulative infatuations, he managed to produce music that was distinctively his. In his production of more than 1,700 songs, piano pieces, choruses, symphonies, masses, and arrangements, one finds much that is not home-grown— unassimilated elements that jangle and ideas that he could not handle satisfactorily. But from his tremendous output a remarkable body of work remains that is Liszt himself—so remarkable that it has lately been revalued and raised by some critics to the highest rank. Bartók said that Liszt was more important than Strauss or Wagner. Virgil Thomson and others in our midst consider Liszt the precursor of twentieth-century atonality and harmonic methods. I would add, for my part, the very modern habit of sudden changes of mood for no dramatic purpose.

This case made in Liszt's behalf depends on the way one gauges importance. Does greatness in music reside in showing new ways of composing, or in producing works whose hearing affords an experience of the kind called profound and unique? In other words, is it historical or aesthetic importance that matters? The professional musician is captivated by the former; the selfish music lover prefers the latter. Some may say why not have both? To satisfy these greedy ones, Liszt offers a relatively small number of works, among which a consensus has settled on at least three—the Piano Sonata in B minor, the *Faust* Symphony, and the *Gran* Mass. Many other works are fine or interesting, or both, but not unquestionable masterpieces. Still, it is not given to everybody to create fine works that are also milestones in the development of the art. Hence the need to say a word about Liszt's place in nineteenth-century music, especially since he himself wrote about his intentions at length. They were one of his literary adventures; the "new Music" was one of his passionate causes.

If in the histories of music you turn to the pages on Liszt, your eye will probably fall on the phrase "Program Music," followed by something about the symphonic poem and "the School of Berlioz and Liszt." It is assumed that everybody knows what program music is and that these two composers must be credited with establishing it as a genre. The assumption is false and the assertion mistaken. Liszt's achievement, let alone that of Berlioz, cannot be understood if this conventional opinion is accepted. Therefore, as with Romanticism, Socialism, and Nationalism, one must set aside whatever ideas one may have about program music.

To begin with, if one goes beyond the two phrases I have quoted, one finds nothing but confusion and contradiction. Take the standard scholarly work by Frederick Niecks entitled *Program Music*. It discusses six periods of such music, beginning with the sixteenth century, where Janequinn, Palestrina, Orlando di Lasso, and others are found "programming" right and left, 300 years before Liszt was born. And toward the end of the book Brahms comes in as a program composer, though over his own signature he said that he did not approve of programs.

So the very writers who believe in the existence of program music show that it cannot have been invented or established by Berlioz and Liszt. The truth is, so much bad thinking and poor verbalizing has been expended on what is really a simple matter that it would take a book to untwist it thoroughly.

Forget the word *program;* substitute the word *plan.* Obviously, any piece of music must have a plan. If one is inspired to write a four-bar theme and leaves it on one's desk, it will not rise overnight like a bowl of dough and develop itself into a piece. The composer must choose to write a fugue, a rondo, a sonata, a set of variations, or whatnot. These are recognized recipes. They supply each an outline within which freedom for invention remains. This outline is a pre-established program of work, which somebody in the past devised or developed from a still earlier formula. All formulas necessarily come from outside the material itself. So when one reads or hears that this or that work by Liszt is based on "extra-musical ideas," ideas outside music, it is useful to remember that no music is composed in any other way.

The illusion that somehow the sounds themselves generate the formulas is due to the force of tradition. We do not know who decided that a suite should have three movements and that these should be fast-slow-fast; but after ten million suites have been written the plan seems inevitable. In like manner, some may think that a sonnet of fourteen lines, with a division after the eighth, was decreed from the dawn of human speech. But we happen to know that the first sonnets varied greatly in length and that George Meredith in *Modern Love* wrote a masterly sequence of sonnets of *sixteen* lines.

Sonnet means little song and brings us back to the various plans in use for music. Undoubtedly the first plan was to fit sounds to the words of poems or to the steps of a dance. These two purposes are obviously extramusical; they are programs. A piece of dance music repeats many more times than a song, for practical, external reasons. When we get to church ritual and later to opera, the shaping of musical material by an outside requirement becomes even more obvious.

From all this it follows that the overwhelming bulk of all the music we have has been composed for purposes outside itself and shaped accordingly. These shapes are further conditioned by the physical limitations of the voice or the instruments; which does not mean, of course, that the interrelations of the sounds themselves did not suggest various devices within the plans. But even sounds themselves have been interfered with from outside by the inspired cheating called the even-tempered scale.

We come at last to the point where Liszt enters the game. He is supposed to have said: let us drop the traditional plans and substitute stories and pictures as principles of organization. He gave his pieces the names of people, of scenic spots, of famous literary works. He changed the name symphony to symphonic poem. He wrote prefaces to his scores. He even projected a history of the world jointly with a painter—twelve panels each, in paint and in music. All this is what set the angry lions roaring. Music was being destroyed, annihilated by literary and pictorial purposes.

In their outcry, these opponents of Liszt made one obvious and unanswerable point: music by itself cannot tell a story or depict a scene. That is so true that one wonders why a composer should be attacked for doing what cannot be done. Perhaps the critics would say, the crime consists in the attempt. But *did* Liszt try to do the impossible? One of his piano pieces is called "After reading Dante"; another is: "The Fountains of the Villa d'Este"; one of the symphonic poems is named after our old friend Tasso. Was Liszt so stupid as to believe that these works somehow copied or retold what he had read or seen out of his window? Let us hear what he himself said about the purpose of a title or a written-out program:

A program he writes, is "any foreword in intelligible language added to a piece of pure instrumental music." One of its purposes is "to guard the listener against an arbitrary poetical interpretation and to direct his attention in advance to the poetical idea of the whole"; another is "to indicate preparatively the spiritual moments which impelled the composer to create his work." In other words, the listener is expected to *associate* the music with the scene or character, as the composer says that he himself has done and as he sometimes records by means of a title or subtitle.

So far was Liszt from trying to blend abstractions with music that he points out the superiority of music over words: "Only in music does feeling freely dispense with the aid of reason and its means of expression, which are so inferior to intuition." What is taken from life then—not the fact or story, but their experiencing—may be intuited from the music or overlooked entirely; it does not matter, but if intuited, it is pleasant to learn what namable fragment of experience is at the root of the intuition.

Take for example Liszt's *Tasso*. What moved Liszt was not the poet's epic poem about the crusades, but his life as Byron dramatized it in the monologue called "The Lament of Tasso." Accordingly, Liszt's work is subtitled *Lamento e trionfo*—lament and triumph. From the foreword we learn further that the minuet section suggests Tasso's presence at the court of Ferrara. Incidentally, Byron says that he wrote his poem after a visit to Ferrara, where he saw the hospital cell in which Tasso had been confined as a madman. That cell is therefore the program behind the poem which is the program behind the music.

What may we conclude? First, that such titles and programs afford but very mild and vague indications—a mere orientation of one's mood; and next, that they relate to the music at very few points. They cannot possibly direct or control the course of the music to the same extent as a musical form of the kind I have called a plan. Compare the casualness of the title or a program with such rigid prescriptions as classical fugue and modern serial composition. Nor did Liszt and his followers—much less Berlioz and Mendelssohn—go in for inserting in their music messages in code, as we have recently learned that Alban Berg did in his last work.

The influence of mood, then, is indefinite and intermittent. A mood, moreover, can have many different causes. This is well illustrated by another of Liszt's symphonic poems, the one called *Les Préludes*. Here is the gist of the blurb: "What is our life but a series of preludes to that unknown song of which Death intones the first solemn note? Love is the enchanted dawn of every life. . . ." It goes on in the same generalizing way for another ten lines. For years, this program has been known as a paraphrase of a poem by Lamartine, and the music has been praised or damned as a faithful rendering of this moonshine. Well, it turns out that the music was originally composed in response to another poem by another poet—something called "The Four Elements" by Joseph Autran. When years later

Liszt prepared the work for publication the princess said in effect: "Whoever heard of Joseph Autran and his four elements? Make it Lamartine," and *she* wrote the program.

Meanwhile the music stayed put with its old mood on its head. What does the listener make of it? Neither four elements nor a series of preparations for death, but a simple contrast between a calm, pastoral piece and a bustling one that could be called warlike. How mood or atmosphere gets translated from "intuition" into music so as to awaken a similar intuition when heard is a large subject that calls for separate treatment. Rhythm, dynamics, and other contrasts, the associations of tempo and timbre, all play a part in this magic—a magic, by the way, of which the artist who writes poems, novels, or plays also has to be a master, for words in literature cannot simply tell; they must evoke, reawaken the intuition of life, in a fashion parallel to music.

To sum up, titles and programs do not make music literary or pictorial, as some affect to believe; the verbalizing merely reports an association of mood, place, or reading matter that the composer chose for his work, either before or after producing it. He reports the link as a sort of setting or occasion. The ways in which he reproduces his intuition, his successive moods, are necessarily technical ways, and in that sense "purely" musical, "intramusical" par excellence.

It may be objected that a determined programmer will distort proper musical form so as to fit some part of his program. The rejoinder is that, if so, the attempt is self-defeating: the listener and critic would detect the flaw and declare the work a bad piece of music—incoherent or ill-balanced. What then, of Liszt's crusade against the rules of classical form, which he wanted the symphonic poem to supersede? The answer is, he overstated his case. Where he himself departed from strict sonata form, he was only taking the same musical liberties as Haydn and Beethoven did. Modern students of Liszt's work have found nothing wild about his methods of composition. The latest analyst of the symphonic poems, Richard Kaplan, writes: "Rather than claim that Liszt 'invented a form,' . . . one might say at most that he invented a genre. To be even more precise . . . he really invented only the *name* of a genre." And he adds: "Liszt's sonata form makes constant reference to those of earlier composers, especially Beethoven and Berlioz. . . . The radical quality of Liszt's musical thought resides in his harmonies and melodies, his gestures and contrasts: in short, in his rhetoric rather than in his craftsmanship."

Rhetoric is the word. For every composer has preferences and habits that are distinctive and thus uniquely "extramusical" and "intramusical" at the same time. Liszt was fond of repeating long sections. He himself said that this practice was not lack of invention but a means of achieving "clarity, order, and effect." An anecdote suggests a further reason. Felix Weingartner, who was one of Liszt's last pupils and later a famous conductor, showed the master the score of an opera he had composed. Liszt studied the work and said about one passage, "Now that is very beautiful, but it comes only once; you must repeat it. Always repeat a beautiful passage." Weingartner was pleased but had to reply: "That's the entrance of the king; I can't have the king entering twice." "Never mind," said Liszt, "don't think so much."

The truth is, the whole program controversy which Liszt thought of great moment is a mare's nest. Program music itself is the Loch Ness monster—people think they have seen it and that it is a beast of a new species, but it does not exist. Yet one can understand why Liszt devoted so much time and thought to the fight. He was first of all reaffirming the Romanticist principle of freedom to innovate; but, more important, he was using his fame and strength to promote the idea that music is an art as far-ranging and as profound as the others. We now take this proposition for granted, but it was by no means self-evident in the eighteen thirties and forties. Beethoven had just died, and it was not his symphonies that enthralled the public, it was grand opera—and opera was a diversion. Instrumental music was only just coming out of the private house into the public concert hall where, aided by technology, it was exploring the possibilities of two virtually new instruments—the piano and the orchestra.

The modern piano engendered the virtuoso, a kind of audible acrobat and prestidigitator. Liszt was one of those, and he produced his own repertory in the form of dazzling, thundering variations on tunes the public had learned at the opera. But as we saw he tired of these empty feats; being the earnest youth that we know, he could not contemplate turning out pyrotechnic trivialities forever. So he ventured to make a piano version of Berlioz's *Symphonie Fantastique*—a landmark in orchestration—and played it to great applause. Moreover, Liszt had the example of Chopin's original and serious handling of the piano. The final push toward showing music as an all-encompassing art was to link it spiritually with contemporary master-pieces in the other arts.

To the Romanticists, the works of Goethe and Byron, Scott and Balzac, as well as the freshly rediscovered Dante and Shakespeare, were not just literature; they were revelations; they were secular scriptures. As such, they furnished themes to the new artists, as in the past the Bible had done. The painters no less than the musicians were inspired by Hamlet, Faust, Beatrice, and the ubiquitous Tasso. And since the general public is usually but half aware, it had to be told again and again what the new art, the new music signified. Hence, the program. Beethoven's symphonies were popularized thanks to fanciful programs that other musicians wrote. And from that day to this, we have had associative titles—not just an *Eroica,* but a *Domestic Symphony* from Strauss, *Images* and *Footsteps in the Snow* from Debussy, *The Moldau* from Smetana, portraits galore from Elgar and Mussorgsky to Copland and Virgil Thomson, and strange semi-scientific tags from Varèse and Boulez. Liszt has not been a solitary criminal.

Even for us, the listeners, printed commentary precedes every concert and surrounds every disc—notes biographical, critical, and miscellaneous, which are even less relevant to the music than Liszt's and the princess's rhetoric.

These bring us back to Romanticism as it shaped Liszt's mind-and-heart in his early youth. Looking at him again under that bright light, a rising star in the galaxy, we are reminded that there is one kind of "program" that underlies every piece of music, every work of art. I mean the continuous force of suggestion and desire that impels the artist to do one thing rather than another at each moment of composition—the program dictated from within. This unrolling stream of intent, made up of memories, feelings, ideas fused to-gether, is of course guided by technique and later reviewed by critical judgment; but unless that inner plan, half lucid and half visceral, is inherently good, no amount of acquired skill will make up for it. Its richness and freshness is what makes one fugue thrilling and another dull though it obeys all the rules.

This bubbling spring within, Liszt externalized with special bril-liance in his improvisations, and it was doubtless through these that he came to be the innovator in harmony which is now his highest claim to fame. But all his genius, all his hopes, loves, and causes, all his generosities and conversions, all his ventures in ideas would have gone for naught if he had not been also a tremendous worker; a Titan at the keyboard, he was a Hercules at the desk. On this point too he represents the Romanticist tenacity. Despite the pain of being at the last a kind of King Lear to his daughter Cosima Wagner, he affected a reconciliation and went to Bayreuth for the first rehearsals of *The Ring*. Art was the best mistress, and his proud motto prevailed: *génie oblige*.

(Extracted by the author from an address at the Library of Congress, June 27, 1986.)

# The Significance of Wagner

## GEORGE ELIOT

*In this early assessment of the Wagner revolution, excerpted from a lengthy 1855 Fraser's Magazine article called "Liszt, Wagner, and Weimar," novelist George Eliot reveals herself to be a music critic of exceptional vision and scrupulous objectivity. She is able to pinpoint, before the composition of* Tristan *or the* Ring Cycle, *exactly what Wagner was up to and where he was taking Western music— this despite her personal difficulty warming to Wagner's operas.*

Without pretending to be a musical critic, one may be allowed to give an opinion as a person with an ear and a mind susceptible to the direct and indirect influences of music. In this character I may say that, though unable to recognize Herr Wagner's compositions as the ideal of the opera, and though, with a few slight exceptions, not deeply affected by his music on a first hearing, it is difficult to me to understand how any one who finds deficiencies in the opera as it has existed hitherto, can give fair attention to Wagner's theory, and his exemplification of it in his operas, without admitting that he has pointed out the direction in which the lyric drama must develop itself, if it is to be developed at all. Moreover, the musician who writes librettos for himself, which can be read with interest as dramatic poems, must be a man of no ordinary mind and accomplishments, and such a man, even when he errs, errs with ingenuity, so that his mistakes are worth studying.

Wagner would make the opera a perfect musical drama, in which feelings and situations spring out of *character*, as in the highest order of tragedy, and in which no dramatic probability or poetic beauty is sacrificed to musical effect. The drama must not be a mere pretext for the music; but music, drama, and spectacle must be blended, like the coloured rays in the sunbeam, so as to produce one undivided impression. The controversy between him and his critics is the old controversy between Gluck and Piccini, between the declamatory and melodic schools of music, with the same difference in comprehensiveness as between the disputes of La Motte and the Daciers about the value of the classics, and the disputes of the classical and romantic schools of literature in our own day. In its first period the opera aimed simply at the expression of feeling through melody; the second period, which has its culmination in the joint productions of Meyerbeer and Scribe, added the search for effective situations and a heightening of dramatic movement, which has led more and more to the predominance of the declamatory style and the subordination of melody. But in Meyerbeer's operas the grand object is to produce a climax of spectacle, situation, and orchestral effects; there is no attempt at the evolution of these from the true workings of human character and human passions; on the contrary, the characters seem to be a second thought, and with a few exceptions, such as Alice and Marcel, are vague and uninteresting. Every opera-goer has remarked that *Robert* is a mere nose of wax; or has laughed at the pathos with which the fiend Bertram invites his son to go to the bottomless pit with him, instead of settling into respectability above ground; or has felt that *Jean, the Prophet,* is a feeble sketch, completely lost in the blaze of spectacle. Yet what a progress is there in the libretto of these operas compared with the libretto of *Der Freischütz,* which, nevertheless, was thought so good in its day that Goethe said Weber ought to divide the merit of success with [his librettist] Kind. Even Weber's enchanting music cannot overcome the sense of absurdity when, in a drinking party of two, one of whom is sunk in melancholy, a man gets up and bursts into a rolling song which seems the very topmost wave in the high tide of bacchanalian lyrism; or when Caspar climbs a tree apparently for no other reason than because the *dénouement* requires him to be shot.

Now, says Wagner, this ascent from the warbling puppets of the early opera to the dramatic effects of Meyerbeer, only serves to bring more clearly into view the unattained summit of the true musical drama. An opera must be no mosaic of melodies stuck together with no other method than is supplied by accidental contrast, no mere succession of ill-prepared crises, but an organic whole, which grows up like a palm, its earliest portion containing the germ and prevision of all the rest. He will write no *part* to suit a *primo tenore,* and interpolate no *cantata* to show off the powers of a *prima donna assoluta;* those who sing his operas must be content with the degree of prominence which falls to them in strict consonance with true dramatic development and ordonnance. Such, so far as I understand it, is Wagner's theory of the opera—surely a theory worth entertaining, and one which he has admirably exemplified so far as the libretto of his operas is concerned. . . .

Certainly Wagner has admirably fulfilled his own requisition of organic unity in the opera. In his operas there is a gradual unfolding and elaboration of that fundamental contrast of emotions, that collision of forces, which is the germ of the tragedy; just as the leaf of the plant is successively elaborated into branching stem and compact bud and radiant corolla. The artifice, however, of making certain contrasted strains of melody run like coloured threads through the woof of an opera, and also the other dramatic device of using a particular melody or musical phrase as a sort of Ahnung or prognostication of the approach or action of a particular character, are not altogether peculiar to Wagner, though he lays especial stress on them as his own. No one can forget the recurring hymn of Marcel in the *Huguenots,* or the strain of the Anabaptists in the *Prophète,* which is continually contrasted with the joyous song or dance of the rustics. Wagner, however, has carried out these devices much more completely, and, in the *Fliegender Holländer* and *Tannhäuser,* with very impressive effect. With all my inability at present to enjoy his music as I have enjoyed that of Mozart, or Beethoven, or Mendelssohn, these two operas left in me a real desire to hear them again.

(*Fraser's Magazine,* July, 1855.)

# Music and Words in Wagner

## GEORGE BERNARD SHAW

*The battle over Wagner and Wagnerism was one of the most intense and pro-*
*tracted controversies in the history of music. For much of the second half of the*
*nineteenth century, Wagnerites and anti-Wagnerites exchanged insults and in-*
*vective over whether Wagner's innovations constituted a revolutionary advance*
*or a monstrous decadence that could only destroy music as an art. Much of this*
*commentary now seems unpleasant and merely overheated, with little of the*
*inspired wit displayed in the fight over opera aesthetics in the eighteenth century*
*(see Addison's "Opera and Realism") or in the delightfully physical ruckus over*
*Stravinsky's* Le Sacre du Printemps *in the twentieth. A sparkling exception is*
*the Wagner criticism of Shaw, who managed to enter the fray solidly in the*
*Wagner camp without losing his head or sense of humor. In 1898 he published*
*The Perfect Wagnerite, and some of the most probing of his shorter music*
*criticism is on Wagner's operas. The following excerpts constitute an illuminating*
*commentary not only on Wagner but on the issue that was often uppermost in*
*Wagner's mind—the relationship between music and language.*

To be able to follow the music of *The Ring*, all that is necessary is
to become familiar enough with the brief musical phrases out
of which it is built to recognize them and attach a certain
definite significance to them, exactly as any ordinary Englishman
recognizes and attaches a definite significance to the opening bars of
God Save the Queen. There is no difficulty here: every soldier is
expected to learn and distinguish between different bugle calls and
trumpet calls; and anyone who can do this can learn and distinguish

between the representative themes or "leading motives" (Leitmotifs) of *The Ring*. They are the easier to learn because they are repeated again and again; and the main ones are so emphatically impressed on the ear whilst the spectator is looking for the first time at the objects, or witnessing the first strong dramatic expression of the ideas they denote, that the requisite association is formed unconsciously. The themes are neither long, nor complicated, nor difficult. Whoever can pick up the flourish of a coach-horn, the note of a bird, the rhythm of the postman's knock or of a horse's gallop, will be at no loss in picking up the themes of *The Ring*. No doubt, when it comes to forming the necessary mental association with the theme, it may happen that the spectator may find his ear conquering the tune more easily than his mind conquers the thought. But for the most part the themes do not denote thoughts at all, but either emotions of a quite simple universal kind, or the sights, sounds and fancies common enough to be familiar to children. Indeed some of them are as frankly childish as any of the funny little orchestral interludes which, in Haydn's *Creation*, introduce the horse, the deer, or the worm. We have both the horse and the worm in *The Ring*, treated exactly in Haydn's manner, and with an effect not a whit less ridiculous to superior people who decline to take it good-humoredly. Even the complaisance of good Wagnerites is occasionally rather overstrained by the way in which Brynhild's allusion to her charger Grani elicit from the band a little rum-ti-tum triplet which by itself is in no way suggestive of a horse, although a continuous rush of such triplets makes a very exciting musical gallop.

Other themes denote objects which cannot be imitatively suggested by music: for instance, music cannot suggest a ring, and cannot suggest gold; yet each of these has a representative theme which pervades the score in all directions. In the case of the gold the association is established by the very salient way in which the orchestra breaks into the pretty theme in the first act of *The Rhine Gold* at the moment when the sunrays strike down through the water and light up the glittering treasure, thitherto invisible. The reference of the strange little theme of the wishing cap is equally manifest from the first, since the spectator's attention is wholly taken up with the Tarnhelm and its magic when the theme is first pointedly uttered by the orchestra. The sword theme is introduced at the end of *The Rhine Gold* to express Wotan's hero inspiration; and I have already mentioned that Wagner, unable, when it came to practical stage management, to forego the appeal to the eye as well as to the thought, here made Wotan pick up a sword and brandish it, though no such instruction appears in the printed score. When this sacrifice to Wagner's scepticism as to the reality of any appeal to an audience that is not made through their bodily sense is omitted, the association of the theme with the sword is not formed until that point in the first act of *The Valkyries* at which Siegmund is left alone by Hunding's hearth, weaponless, with the assurance that he will have to fight for his life at dawn with his host. He recalls then how his father promised him a sword for his hour of need; and as he does so, a flicker from the dying fire is caught by the golden hilt of the sword in the tree, when the theme immediately begins to gleam through the quiver of sound from the orchestra, and only dies out as the fire sinks and the sword is once more hidden by the darkness. Later on, this theme, which is never silent whilst Sieglinda is dwelling on the story of the sword, leaps out into the most dazzling splendor the band can give it when Siegmund triumphantly draws the weapon from the tree. As it consists of seven notes only, with a very marked measure, and a melody like a simple flourish on a trumpet or post horn, nobody capable of catching a tune can easily miss it. . . .

The thematic system gives symphonic interest, reasonableness and unity to the music, enabling the composer to exhaust every aspect and quality of his melodic material, and, in Beethoven's manner, to work miracles of beauty, expression and significance with the briefest phrases. As a set-off against this, it has led Wagner to indulge in repetitions that would be intolerable in a purely dramatic work. Almost the first thing that a dramatist has to learn in constructing a play is that the persons must not come on the stage in the second act and tell one another at great length what the audience has already seen pass before its eyes in the first act. The extent to which Wagner has been seduced into violating this rule by his affection for his themes is startling to a practised playwright. Siegfried inherits from Wotan a mania for autobiography which leads him to inflict on everyone he meets the story of Mimmy and the dragon, although the audience have spent a whole evening witnessing the events he is narrating. Hagen tells the story to Gunther; and that same night Alberic's ghost tells it over again to Hagen, who knows it already as well as the audience. Siegfried tells the Rhine maidens as much of it

as they will listen to, and then keeps telling it to his hunting companions until they kill him. Wotan's autobiography on the second evening becomes his biography in the mouths of the Norns on the
fourth. The little that the Norns add to it is repeated an hour later by
Valtrauta. How far all this repetition is tolerable is a matter of individual taste. A good story will bear repetition; and if it has woven into it
such pretty tunes as the Rhine maiden's yodel, Mimmy's tinkling
anvil beat, the note of the forest bird, the call of Siegfried's horn, and
so on, it will bear a good deal of rehearing. Those who have but newly
learnt their way through *The Ring* will not readily admit that there is a
bar too much repetition.

 (*The Perfect Wagnerite*, 1898.)

I t is not often that one comes across a reasonable book about music,
much less an entertaining one. Still, I confess to having held out
with satisfaction to the end of M. Georges Noufflard's *Richard
Wagner d'après lui-même* (Paris, Fischbacher, 2 vols., at 3.50 fr. apiece).
Noufflard is so exceedingly French a Frenchman that he writes a
preface to explain that though he admires Wagner, still Alsace and
Lorraine must be given back; and when he records an experiment of
his hero's in teetotalism, he naïvely adds, "What is still more surprising is that this unnatural régime, instead of making Wagner ill,
operated exactly as he had expected." More Parisian than this an
author can hardly be; and yet Noufflard always understands the
Prussian composer's position, and generally agrees with him,
though, being racially out of sympathy with him, he never entirely
comprehends him. He is remarkably free from the stock vulgarities
of French operatic culture: for instance, he washes his hands of
Meyerbeer most fastidiously; and he puts Gluck, the hero of French
musical classicism, most accurately in his true place.

 And here let me give a piece of advice to readers of books about
Wagner. Whenever you come to a statement that Wagner was an
operatic reformer, and that in this capacity he was merely following
in the footsteps of Gluck, who had anticipated some of his most
important proposals, you may put your book in the waste-paper
basket, as far as Wagner is concerned, with absolute confidence.
Gluck was an opera composer who said to his contemporaries: "Gen-

tlemen, let us compose our operas more rationally. An opera is not a stage concert, as most of you seem to think. Let us give up our habit of sacrificing our common sense to the vanity of our singers, and let us compose and orchestrate our airs, our duets, our recitatives, and our sinfonias in such a way that they shall always be appropriate to the dramatic situation given to us by the librettist." And having given this excellent advice, he proceeded to shew how it could be followed. How well he did this we can judge, in spite of our scandalous ignorance of Gluck, from *Orfeo.* . . .

When Wagner came on the scene, exactly a hundred years later, he found that the reform movement begun by Gluck had been carried to the utmost limits of possibility by Spontini, who told him flatly that after La Vestale, etc., there was nothing operatic left to be done. Wagner quite agreed with him, and never had the smallest intention of beginning the reform of opera over again at the very moment when it had just been finished. On the contrary, he took the fully reformed opera, with all its improvements, and asked the nineteenth century to look calmly at it and say whether all this patchwork of stage effects on a purely musical form had really done anything for it but expose the absurd unreality of its pretence to be a form of drama, and whether, in fact, Rossini had not shewn sound common sense in virtually throwing over that pretence and, like Gluck's Italian contemporaries, treating an opera as a stage concert. The nineteenth century took a long time to make up its mind on the question, which it was at first perfectly incapable of understanding. Verdi and Gounod kept on trying to get beyond Spontini on operatic lines, without the least success, except on the purely musical side; and Gounod never gave up the attempt, though Verdi did.

Meanwhile, however, Wagner, to shew what he meant, abandoned operatic composition altogether, and took to writing dramatic poems, and using all the resources of orchestral harmony and vocal tone to give them the utmost reality and intensity of expression, thereby producing the new art form which he called "music drama," which is no more "reformed opera" than a cathedral is a reformed stone quarry. The whole secret of the amazing futility of the first attempts at Wagner criticism is the mistaking of this new form for an improved pattern of the old one. Once you conceive Wagner as the patentee of certain novel features in operas and librettos, you can demolish him point by point with impeccable logic, and without the least misgiving that you are publicly making a ludicrous exhibition of yourself.

The process is fatally easy, and consists mainly in shewing that the pretended novelties of reformed opera are no novelties at all. The "leading motives," regarded as operatic melodies recurring in connection with the entry of a certain character, are as old as opera itself; the instrumentation, regarded merely as instrumentation, is no better than Mozart's and much more expensive; whereas of those features that really tax the invention of the operatic composer, the airs, the duos, the quartets, the cabalettas to display the virtuosity of the trained Italian singer, the dances, the marches, the choruses, and so on, there is a deadly dearth, their place being taken by—of all things—an interminable dull recitative.

The plain conclusion follows that Wagner was a barren rascal whose whole reputation rested on a shop-ballad, O star of eve, and a march which he accidentally squeezed out when composing his interminable *Tannhäuser*. And so you go on, wading with fatuous self-satisfaction deeper and deeper into a morass of elaborately reasoned and highly conscientious error. You need fear nothing of this sort from Noufflard. He knows perfectly well the difference between music-drama and opera; and the result is that he not only does not tumble into blind hero-worship of Wagner, but is able to criticize him—a thing the blunderers never could do. Some of his criticisms: for example, his observation that in Wagner's earlier work the melody is by no means so original as Weber's, are indisputable—indeed he might have said Meyerbeer or anybody else; for Wagner's melody was never original at all it that sense, any more than Giotto's figures are picturesque or Shakespear's lines elegant.

But I entirely—though quite respectfully—dissent from Noufflard's suggestion that in composing *Tristan* Wagner turned his back on the theoretic basis of Siegfried, and returned to "absolute music." It is true, as Noufflard points out, that in *Tristan*, and even in *Der Ring* itself, Wagner sometimes got so rapt from the objective drama that he got away from the words too, and in *Tristan* came to writing music without coherent words at all. But wordless music is not absolute music. Absolute music is the purely decorative sound pattern: tone poetry is the musical expression of poetic feeling. When Tristan gives musical expression to an excess of feeling for which he can find no coherent words, he is no more uttering absolute music than the shepherd who carries on the drama at one of its most deeply felt passages by playing on his pipe.

Wagner regarded all Beethoven's important instrumental works as tone poems; and he himself, though he wrote so much for the orchestra alone in the course of his music dramas, never wrote, or could write, a note of absolute music. The fact is, there is a great deal of feeling, highly poetic and highly dramatic, which cannot be expressed by mere words—because words are the counters of thinking, not of feeling—but which can be supremely expressed by music. The poet tries to make words serve his purpose by arranging them musically, but is hampered by the certainty of becoming absurd if he does not make his musically arranged words mean something to the intellect as well as to the feeling.

For example, the unfortunate Shakespear could not make Juliet say:

O Romeo, Romeo, Romeo, Romeo, Romeo;

and so on for twenty lines. He had to make her, in an extremity of unnaturalness, begin to argue the case in a sort of amatory legal fashion, thus:

O Romeo, Romeo, wherefore art thou Romeo?
Deny thy father and refuse thy name,
Or, if thou wilt not, etc., etc., etc.

It is verbally decorative; but it is not love. And again:

Parting is such sweet sorrow
That I shall say goodnight till it be morrow;

which is a most ingenious conceit, but one which a woman would no more utter at such a moment than she would prove the rope ladder to be the shortest way out because any two sides of a triangle are together greater than the third.

Now these difficulties do not exist for the tone poet. He can make Isolde say nothing but "Tristan, Tristan, Tristan, Tristan, Tristan," and Tristan nothing but "Isolde, Isolde, Isolde, Isolde, Isolde," to their hearts' content without creating the smallest demand for more definite explanations; and as for the number of times tenor and soprano can repeat "Addio, addio, addio," there is no limit to it.

There is a great deal of this reduction of speech to mere ejaculation in Wagner; and it is a reduction directly pointed to in those very pages of Opera and Drama which seem to make the words all-important by putting the poem in the first place as the seed of the whole music drama, and yet make a clean sweep of nine-tenths of the dictionary by insisting that it is only the language of feeling that craves for musical expression, or even is susceptible of it.

Nay, you may not only reduce the words to pure ejaculation, you may substitute mere roulade vocalization, or even balderdash, for them, provided the music sustains the feeling which is the real subject of the drama, as has been proved by many pages of genuinely dramatic music, both in opera and elsewhere, which either have no words at all, or else belie them. It is only when a thought interpenetrated with intense feeling has to be expressed, as in the Ode to Joy in the Ninth Symphony, that coherent words must come with the music. You have such words in *Tristan;* you have also ejaculations void of thought, though full of feeling; and you have plenty of instrumental music with no words at all. But you have no "absolute" music, and no "opera."

Nothing in the world convinces you more of the fact that a dramatic poem cannot possibly take the form of an opera libretto than listening to *Tristan* and comparing it with, say, Gounod's *Romeo and Juliet.* I submit, then, to Noufflard (whose two volumes I nonetheless cordially recommend to all amateurs who can appreciate a thinker) that the contradictions into which Wagner has fallen in this matter are merely such verbal ones as are inevitable from the imperfection of language as an instrument for conveying ideas; and that the progress from *Der fliegende Holländer* to *Parsifal* takes a perfectly straight line ahead in theory as well as in artistic execution.

(*World,* January 17, 1894.)

**T**ristan and Isolda comes off better than *Parsifal* by just so much as the impulse to play it is more genuine and the power to understand it more common. To enjoy *Parsifal,* either as a listener or an executant, one must be either a fanatic or a philosopher. To enjoy *Tristan* it is only necessary to have had one serious love affair; and though the number of persons possessing this qualification is popularly exaggerated, yet there are enough to keep the work alive and vigorous. In England it is not yet familiar: we contentedly lap dose after dose of such pap as the garden scene in Gounod's *Faust,* and think we are draining the cup of stage passion to the dregs. The truth is that all the merely romantic love scenes ever turned into music are pallid beside the second art of *Tristan.* It is an ocean of sentiment, immensely German, and yet universal in its appeal to human sympathy. At eight o'clock yesterday (Monday) I wondered that people fresh from such an experience did not rashly declare that all other music is leather and prunella; shrug their shoulders at the triviality of *La ci darem;* and denounce a proposal to try the effect of the fourth act of *Les Huguenots* as a direct incitement to crime.

(*Star,* August 6, 1889.)

This *Parsifal* is a wonderful experience: not a doubt of it. The impression it makes is quite independent of liking the music or understanding the poem. Hardly anybody has the slightest idea of what it all means; many people are severely fatigued by it; and there must be at least some who retain enough of the old habit of regarding the theatre as an exception to the doctrine of Omnipresence, to feel some qualms concerning the propriety of an elaborate makebelieve of Holy Communion, culminating in the descent of a stuffed dove through a flood of electric radiance. Yet *Parsifal* is the magnet that draws people to Bayreuth and disturbs their journey thence with sudden fits of desperate desire to go back again. When you leave the theatre after your first *Parsifal* you may not be conscious of having brought away more than a phrase or two of *leitmotif* mingled with your burden of weariness and disappointment. Yet before long the music begins to stir within you and haunt you with a growing urgency that in a few days makes another hearing seem a necessity of life. By that time, too, you will have been converted to the Church and Stage Guild's view that the theatre is as holy a place as the church and the function of the actor no less sacred than that of the priest.

(*Star,* August 7, 1889.)

# The Overture to *Die Meistersinger*
# Wagner Versus Bizet

## FRIEDRICH NIETZSCHE

*Nietzsche's struggle to come to terms with Wagner was a troubling, fascinating intellectual odyssey that set off sparks in the worlds of both philosophy and music. The change from early, ardent advocacy to disillusionment and strident opposition was by no means simple and linear. Nietzsche's youthful reverence for Wagner was as tempered by doubt as his later revulsion was complicated by grudging admiration. In other words, Nietzsche was a perfect mirror of his age, embodying both the pro- and contra-Wagnerian ideologies in one view. To Nietzsche, Wagner was a disease, one including euphoria as well as nausea, which reflected a larger sickness in Western culture. His magnificently tortured passage on [Die* Meistersinger] *in* Beyond Good and Evil *shows both feelings and myriad others as well. In Bizet, however, Nietzsche found the perfect antidote to Wagner: his words on that composer convey the feeling of a desperate patient who has finally hit upon the right medication.*

I heard, once again for the first time, Richard Wagner's overture to *Die Meistersinger*: it is a piece of magnificent, gorgeous, heavy, latter-day art, which has the pride to presuppose two centuries of music as still living, in order that it may be understood:—it is an honour to Germans that such a pride did not miscalculate! What flavours and forces, what seasons and climes do we not find mingled in it! It impresses us at one time as ancient, at another time as foreign, bitter, and too modern, it is as arbitrary as it is pompously traditional, it is not infrequently roguish, still oftener rough and coarse—it has fire and courage, and at the same time the loose, dun-coloured skin of fruits which ripen too late. It flows broad and full:

and suddenly there is a moment of inexplicable hesitation, like a gap that opens between cause and effect, an oppression that makes us dream, almost a nightmare; but already it broadens and widens anew, the old stream of delight—the most manifold delight,—of old and new happiness; including *especially* the joy of the artist in himself, which he refuses to conceal, his astonished, happy cognisance of his mastery of the expedients here employed, the new, newly acquired, imperfectly tested expedients of art which he apparently betrays to us. All in all, however, no beauty, no South, nothing of the delicate southern clearness of the sky, nothing of grace, no dance, hardly a will to logic; a certain clumsiness even, which is also emphasised, as though the artist wished to say to us: "It is part of my intention"; a cumbersome drapery, something arbitrarily barbaric and ceremonious, a flirring of learned and venerable conceits and witticisms; something German in the best and worst sense of the word, something in the German style, manifold, formless, and inexhaustible; a certain German potency and super-plenitude of soul, which is not afraid to hide itself under the refinements of decadence.

(*Beyond Good and Evil*, 1886; translated by Helen Zimmern.)

## Wagner Versus Bizet

I am writing this to relieve my mind. It is not malice alone which makes me praise Bizet at the expense of Wagner in this essay. Amid a good deal of jesting I wish to make one point clear which does not admit of levity. To turn my back on Wagner was for me a piece of fate; to like anything else whatever afterwards was for me a triumph. Nobody, perhaps, had ever been more dangerously involved in Wagnerism, nobody had defended himself more obstinately against it, nobody had ever been so overjoyed at ridding himself of it. A long history!—Shall I give it a name?—If I were a moralist, who knows what I might not call it! Perhaps a piece of *self-mastery.*—But the philosopher does not like the moralist, neither does he like high-falutin' words.

What is the first and last thing that a philosopher demands of himself? To overcome his age in himself, to become "timeless." With what then does the philosopher have the greatest fight? With all that in him which makes him the child of his time. Very well then! I am just as much a child of my age as Wagner—*i.e.*, I am a decadent. The only difference is that I recognised the fact, that I struggled against it. The philosopher in me struggled against it. . . .

The greatest event of my life took the form of a *recovery*. Wagner belongs only to my diseases.

Not that I wish to appear ungrateful to this disease. If in this essay I support the proposition that Wagner is *harmful*, I none the less wish to point out unto whom, in spite of all, he is indispensable—to the philosopher. Anyone else may perhaps be able to get on without Wagner: but the philosopher is not free to pass him by. The philosopher must be the evil conscience of his age,—but to this end he must be possessed of its best knowledge. And what better guide, or more thoroughly efficient revealer of the soul, could be found for the labyrinth of the modern spirit than Wagner? Through Wagner modernity speaks her most intimate language: it conceals neither its good nor its evil; it has thrown off all shame. And, conversely, one has almost calculated the whole of the value of modernity once one is clear concerning what is good and evil in Wagner. I can perfectly well understand a musician of to-day who says: "I hate Wagner but I can endure no other music." But I should also understand a philosopher who said: "Wagner is modernity in concentrated form." There is no help for it, we must first be Wagnerites.

Yesterday—would you believe it?—I heard *Bizet's* masterpiece for the twentieth time. Once more I attended with the same gentle reverence; once again I did not run away. This triumph over my impatience surprises me. How such a work completes one! Through it one almost becomes a "masterpiece" oneself.—And, as a matter of fact, each time I heard *Carmen* it seemed to me that I was more of a philosopher, a better philosopher than at other times: I became so forbearing, so happy, so Indian, so *settled*. . . . To sit for five hours: the first step to holiness!—May I be allowed to say that Bizet's orchestration is the only one that I can endure now? That other orchestration which is all the rage at present—the Wagnerian—is brutal, artificial and "unsophisticated" withal, hence its appeal to all the three senses of the modern soul at once. How terribly Wagnerian orchestration affects me! I call it the *Sirocco*. A disagreeable sweat breaks out all over me. All my fine weather vanishes.

Bizet's music seems to me perfect. It comes forward lightly, gracefully, stylishly. It is lovable, it does not sweat. "All that is good is easy, everything divine runs with light feet": this is the first principle of my aesthetics. This music is wicked, refined, fatalistic: and withal remains popular,—it possesses the refinement of a race, not of an individual. It is rich. It is definite. It builds, organises, completes: and in this sense it stands as a contrast to the polyp in music, to "endless melody." Have more painful, more tragic accents ever been heard on the stage before? And how are they obtained? Without grimaces. Without counterfeiting of any kind. Free from the *lie* of the grand style. In short: this music assumes that the listener is intelligent even as a musician—thereby it is the opposite of Wagner, who, apart from everything else, was in any case the most *ill-mannered* genius on earth. . . .

And once more: I become a better man when Bizet speaks to me. Also a better musician, a better *listener*. Is it in any way possible to listen better?—I even burrow behind this music with my ears. I hear its very cause. I seem to assist at its birth. I tremble before the dangers which this daring music runs, I am enraptured over those happy accidents for which even Bizet himself may not be responsible.— And, strange to say, at bottom I do not give it a thought, or am not aware how much thought I really do give it. For quite other ideas are running through my head the while. . . . Has any one ever observed that music *emancipates* the spirit? gives wings to thought? and that the more one becomes a musician the more one is also a philosopher? The grey sky of abstraction seems thrilled by flashes of lightning; the light is strong enough to reveal all the details of things; to enable one to grapple with problems; and the world is surveyed as if from a mountain top.—With this I have defined philosophical pathos.— And unexpectedly *answers* drop into my lap, a small hailstorm of ice and wisdom, of problems *solved*. Where am I? Bizet makes me productive. Everything that is good makes me productive. I have gratitude for nothing else, nor have I any other touchstone for testing what is good.

Bizet's work also saves; Wagner is not the only "Saviour." With it one bids farewell to the *damp* north and to all the fog of the Wagnerian ideal. Even the action in itself delivers us from these things. From Merimée it has this logic even in passion, from him it has the direct line, inexorable necessity; but what it has above all else is that which belongs to sub-tropical zones—that dryness of atmosphere, the *limpidezza* of the air. Here in every respect the climate is altered. Here another kind of sensuality, another kind of sensibility and another kind of cheerfulness make their appeal. This music is gay, but not in a French or German way. Its gaiety is African; fate hangs over it, its happiness is short, sudden, without reprieve. I envy Bizet for having had the courage of this sensibility, which hitherto in the cultured music of Europe has found no means of expression,—of this southern, tawny, sunburnt sensibility. What a joy the golden afternoon of its happiness is to us! When we look out, with this music in our minds, we wonder whether we have ever seen the sea so *calm*. And how soothing is this Moorish dancing! How, for once, even our insatiability gets sated by its lascivious melancholy!—And finally love, love translated back into *Nature!* Not the love of a "cultured girl!"—no Sentasentimentality.* But love as fate, as a fatality, cynical, innocent, cruel,—and precisely in this way *Nature!* The love whose means is war, whose very essence is the *mortal hatred* between the sexes!—I know no case in which the tragic irony, which constitutes the kernel of love, is expressed with such severity, or in so terrible a formula, as in the last cry of Don José with which the work ends:

> "Yes, it is I who have killed her,
> I—my adored Carmen!"
> (*The Case of Wagner*, 1888; translated by Anthony M. Ludovici.)

*Senta is the heroine in the "Flying Dutchman."—*Tr.*

# The Brahms "Eroica"

## EDUARD HANSLICK

*Viennese critic Eduard Hanslick was the scourge of the Wagnerians, so much so that he was savagely satirized (as Beckmesser in* Die Meistersinger) *by Wagner himself. Hanslick waged a relentless, gradually losing battle against Wagner and his disciples in the* Presse *and the* Neue Freie Presse. *What is sometimes forgotten is that Hanslick wrote extensively, often perceptively, about other music, especially Brahms, whose classicism he used as a battering ram in the fight against Wagner. (Hanslick would surely have been horrified had he known that Brahms would later be championed by Arnold Schönberg.) Hanslick's account of Brahms's First Symphony, in which he makes the curious assertion that Brahms "seems to favor too one-sidedly the great and the serious," is a bit cranky; his radiant review of the Second, a gem of musical description, is reprinted in virtually every program note and recording annotation of that work. His commentary on the Third, although less well known, represents Hanslick at his most characteristic. Elegant, fastidious, and well composed, Hanslick's piece is the work of the quintessential musical conservative, one who places tradition, simplicity, and safe "intelligibility" above all else—who ultimately narrows rather than broadens thought.*

The still unpublished Third Symphony of Brahms is a feast for the music lover and musician rather than for the critic, who must subsequently describe how it looks and what its beauties are. It is neither one of the rarest nor one of the most inexplicable of misfortunes that the eloquence of the critic declines in inverse proportion to that of the composer. The language of prose is not only poorer than that of music; as far as music is concerned, it is no language at all, since music cannot be translated into it. This may not have meant so much in former and less demanding times. But if one reads today the best of the reviews which appeared immediately following the first performances of the Beethoven symphonies, and imagines himself in the place of the first reader, one must confess that, while he has sensed the proclamation of great and beautiful music, he has been vouchsafed hardly a hint of its individual physiognomy. Only after the Beethoven symphonies had become generally known, and when critics were able to refer to what the reader himself had already heard and experienced, did we gain the substantial instruction of the better Beethoven studies of our own time. The new Brahms symphony has yet to build such a bridge between critic and reader. The former is left with no other recourse than to compare it with earlier and better known works of the same master.

[Conductor] Hans Richter, in a gracious toast, recently christened the new symphony "Eroica." Actually, if one were to call Brahms's first symphony the "Appassionata" and the second the "Pastoral," then the new symphony might well be called the "Eroica." The title is, to be sure, not fully applicable, since only the first and last movements strike us as "heroic." In his Symphony in C minor, Brahms plunged with desperate passion into a dark Faustian struggle in the very first dissonant measures. The Finale, with its reminiscences of the last movements of Beethoven's Ninth, does not, for all its ultimate achievements, change the essentially emotional, almost pathological character of the composition. It is the expression of a suffering, abnormally agitated individual. The Symphony No. 2 is a peaceful, often pastoral counterpart. While the thunder of the old Beethoven is still heard receding in the distance, we hear the voices of Mozart and Haydn as if from celestial sanctuary. The Symphony No. 3 is really something new. It repeats neither the unhappy fatalism of the first, nor the cheerful idyll of the second; its foundation is self-confident, rough and ready strength. The "heroic" element in it has nothing to do with anything military, nor does it lead to any tragic dénouement, such as the Funeral March of Beethoven's "Eroica." Its musical characteristics recall the healthy soundness of Beethoven's second period, never the eccentricities of his last. And here and there are suggestions of the romantic twilight of Schumann and Mendelssohn.

The first movement belongs among the most significant and masterly compositions Brahms has given us. Wonderful is the way in which, after two resounding chords in the winds, the belligerent theme of the violins plunges down from above and then soars proudly upward again. The whole movement gives the impression of having been created in the flush of an inspired hour. Its second theme, in A-flat, blends incomparably with the movement as a whole. The climax in the development section is of impressive dimensions but, surprisingly, gives way towards the end to a gradually calmer mood, which, in turn, fades away swiftly and beautifully. The two middle movements prepare the listener for no mighty convulsions; they are rather an invitation to peaceful repose. The slow movement does not sing of deathly depression, nor the fast movement of heavenly exhilaration. They are moderate in pace and expression, tender and gracious in sentiment. The slow movement is a very simple song dialogue between the winds and the deeper strings. It would not be out of place in a Brahms serenade. Short, and without organic development or climax, it provides surprises and effects of tone colour suggesting the musical conversation of softly sounding, tuned bells. The Scherzo is represented by an Allegretto in C minor, superficially reminiscent of Mendelssohn, which hovers easily in that hybrid, indeterminate mood which Brahms so favours in his middle movements. The piece is simply scored (without trumpets, trombones, and kettle-drums) and is rendered particularly effective by the spirited charm of a middle section in A-flat.

For all their fundamental differences, Brahms's first and third symphonies are similar in one important respect: their respective middle movements are rather too small scaled, in content as well as in extent, for the imposing movements which adjoin them. The Finale of the Symphony No. 3 is again an accomplishment of the first order, the equal of the first movement, if not its superior. It rolls upon us with a fast, sultry figure in the deep strings. The theme as such is not impressive, but it immediately experiences the most astonishing development. The eerie sultriness of the opening is discharged in a magnificent storm, exalting and refreshing. The intensity of the music increases continuously. The second theme, in C major, brilliantly and emphatically intoned by the horn, soon makes way for a third, in C minor, even more forcefully introduced. At the peak of all this imposing development, one naturally expects a brilliant, triumphal conclusion. But with Brahms, and with Brahms alone, it is well to be prepared for the unexpected. This Finale moves imperceptibly from the key of F minor to that of D major, the raging winds subside to a mysterious whisper—long sustained chords in the winds are interrupted by the light rustlings of the muted violins and violas in thirds and sixths. The movement draws to a close, strangely, inconclusively, but most beautifully.

Many music lovers may prefer the titanic force of the First, others the untroubled charm of the Second. But the Third strikes me as artistically the most perfect. It is more compactly made, more transparent in detail, more plastic in the main themes. The orchestration is richer in novel and charming combinations. In ingenious modulations it is equal to the best of Brahms's works; and in the free association of contrary rhythms, of which Brahms is so fond and in the handling of which he is such a master, it has the virtue of not seeking effects at the cost of intelligibility.

(*Neue Frei Presse*, 1883; translated by Henry Pleasants.)

# Moussorgsky's Vision of Childhood

## CLAUDE DEBUSSY

*Originally published between 1901 and 1917, the essays and reviews of Claude Debussy offer a playful sense of irony and caprice, one similar to the style of Berlioz and Shaw but rarely found in contemporary music criticism. He dismissed the Grieg Piano Concerto by asking, "Has anyone noticed how awful people from the North become when they try to be Mediterranean?" He described Stravinsky's Le Sacre du Printemps as "primitive with every modern convenience"—an ironic form of praise. Yet beneath the mask of irreverence, Debussy was a serious and prophetic music essayist. He was the first to recognize Wagner as "a beautiful sunset who has been mistaken for a sunrise"; he was certainly one of the first to call for "lucid" performances of Baroque music and to complain about how the nineteenth century had romanticized and "intruded" on Bach. His early championing of Moussorgsky—whose freedom of expression and predilection for mystery and fantasy mirrored Debussy's own art—was equally on the mark.*

The Nursery is the title of a cycle of seven songs of which each one is a scene from childhood, and it's a masterpiece. Moussorgsky is little known in France and for this we can excuse ourselves, it is true, by remarking that he is no better known in Russia. He was born in Karevo (central Russia) in 1839, and he died in 1881 in a bed in the Nicolas military hospital at Saint Petersburg. So you can see from these two dates that he had no time to lose if he was to become a genius. He did not lose a moment and he will leave an indelible imprint on the memories of those who love his music. Nobody has spoken to that which is best in us with such tenderness and depth; he is quite unique, and will be renowned for an art that suffers from no stultifying rules or artificialities. Never before has such a refined sensibility expressed itself with such simple means: it is almost as if he were an inquisitive savage discovering music for the first time, guided in each step forward by his own emotions. There is no question of any such thing as "form," or, at least, any forms there are have such complexity that they are impossible to relate to the accepted forms—the "official" ones. He composes in a series of bold strokes, but his incredible gift of foresight means that each stroke is bound to the next by a mysterious thread. Sometimes he can conjure up a disquieting impression of darkness so powerful that it wrings tears from one's heart. In the first piece, "The Nursery," we can hear the prayer of a little girl before she goes to sleep. Here the gestures themselves, the delicate, troubled soul of the child, even the wonderful way in which little girls pretend to be grown up—all these are captured with a truthfulness that is to be found nowhere else. "The Doll's Lullaby" seems to have been taken down word for word, thanks to enormous powers of assimilation and an ability to inhabit those magic landscapes so special to a child's mind. The end of this lullaby is so beautifully restful that even the little girl who is telling the story falls gently to sleep at the sound of her own voice. There is also a horrible little boy! He transforms the playroom into a battlefield by riding a toy truncheon like a horse, breaking the arms and legs of the poor defenseless chairs as he careens around, not to mention the more personal wounds he inflicts. Of course he soon hurts himself as well, and all the playful exuberance dissolves into screams and tears. But it is not too serious: a couple of minutes on his mommy's knee, a kiss to make him better, and he is off again and the battle begins once more. The chairs don't know where to hide themselves.

As I said, all these little happenings are noted with an extreme simplicity: for Moussorgsky, one chord is often sufficient (although it would have seemed poor to M. What's-his-name). Or else he uses a modulation so individual that it wouldn't even have been in the books of M. So-and so. (Need I add that they are the same monsieur?)

(*La Revue Blanche*, April 15, 1901; translated by Richard Langham Smith.)

# Tchaikovsky: A Modern Music Lord
# Richard Strauss and Nietzsche

---

## JAMES HUNEKER

---

*Colorful, ostentatious, aggressively metaphorical, the prose of James Huneker was perhaps the most vivid specimen of American musical journalism in the early twentieth century. A novelist as well as critic, Huneker wrote for the* New York Times, Sun, Recorder, *and* Morning Adviser; *the world of art was his beat, including literature, music, and painting, all of which he covered prodigiously. His specialty was drawing connections between the arts, which he did in a manner that was illuminating and full of surprise, if sometimes a bit show-offy. His effusive, post-Victorian style may seem a bit dated, now; on the other hand, it is a refreshing antidote to the frequently colorless music criticism of our own time. As the two following articles illustrate, Huneker was at his best describing his contemporaries. The piece on Tchaikovsky, written shortly after the composer's tragic death, is an agonizing, still accurate assessment; the article on Strauss, who was considered highly "modern" and controversial when Huneker was promoting his cause, is a good example of Huneker's deftness at linking literary and musical topics—a highly appropriate linkage in this case since Strauss made it himself. Readers who enjoy these articles might want to track down Huneker's books on* Chopin (Chopin: The Man and His Music, *1900) and* Liszt (Franz Liszt, *1911), composers he wrote about with vigor and sympathy.*

Tchaikovsky] was a poet as well as a musician. He preached more treason against his government than did Pushkin, or those "cannons buried in flowers" of the Pole Chopin. His culture was many sided; he could paint the desperate loves of Romeo and Juliet, could master Hamlet, the doubting thinker and man of sensibility; could feel the pathetic pain of Francesca da Rimini, and proved that Lermontov was not the only Slav who understood Byron's Manfred; he set Tolstoy's serenade to barbaric Iberian tones, and wrote with tears at his heart that most moving song, Nur wer die Sehnsucht Kennt, a song that epitomizes Goethe's poem; and then only think of the F minor, the E minor and the B minor symphonies! What a wonderful man he was! and how his noble personality tops all the little masters of the Neo-Russian school!

Tchaikovsky was one who felt many influences before he hewed for himself a clear cut, individual path. We continually see in him the ferment of the young East, rebelling, tugging against the restraining bonds of Occidental culture. But, like Turgenev, he chastened his art; he polished it, and gave us the cry, the song of the strange land in a worthy, artistic setting. His feeling for hues, as shown in his instrumentation, is wonderful. His orchestra fairly blazes at times. He is higher pitched in his color scheme than any of the moderns, with the exception of Richard Strauss; but while we get daring harmonic combinations, there are no unnatural unions of instruments; no forced marriages of reeds and brass; no artificial or high pitched voicing, nor are odd and archaic instruments employed. Indeed Tchaikovsky uses sparingly the English horn. His orchestra is normal. His possible weakness is the flute, for which he had an enormous predilection. His imagination sometimes played him sinister tricks, such as the lugubrious valse in the Fifth Symphony and the stinging shower of pizzicati in the Fourth.

He was not a great symphonist like Brahms; he had not the sense of formal beauty, preferring instead to work in free fashion within the easy and loosely flowing lines of the overture-fantaisie. The roots of the form are not difficult to discover. The Liszt symphonic poem and its congeries were for Tchaikovsky a point of departure. Dr. Dvořák was therefore in a sense correct when he declared to me that Tchaikovsky was not as great a symphonist as a variationist.

He takes small, compact themes, nugget-like motives, which he subjects to the most daring and scrutinizing treatment. He polishes, expands, varies and develops his ideas in a marvellous manner, and if the form is often wavering the decoration is always gorgeous. Tchaikovsky is seldom a landscape painter; he has not the open air naïveté of Dvořák, but his voice is a more cultivated one. He has touched many of the master minds of literature—Shakespeare, Dante, Goethe, Byron and Tolstoy, and is able to give in the most condensed, dramatic style his subjective impressions of their poems. He is first and last a dramatic poet. He delineates the human soul in the convulsions of love, hate, joy and fear; he is an unique master of rhythms and of the torrential dynamics that express primal emotions in the full flood. His music has not the babbling rivulets, the unclouded skies, the sweet and swirling shepherds and shepherdesses of Dvořák, but it is more psychologic. Give Tchaikovsky one or two large human figures, give him a stirring situation, and then hark to the man as his dramatic impulse begins to play havoc. . . .

He is eminently nervous, modern and intense; he felt deeply and suffered greatly; so his music is fibred with sorrow, and sometimes morbid and full of hectic passion. He is often feverishly unhealthy, and is never as sane as Brahms or Saint-Saëns. His gamut is not so wide as deep and troubled, and he has exquisite moments of madness. He can be heroic, tender, bizarre and hugely fierce. His music bites, and the ethical serenity of Beethoven he never attains; but of what weighty import are some of his scores; what passionate tumults, what defiance of the powers that be, what impotent titanic straining, what masses of tone he sends scurrying across his pain-riven canvases! The tragedy of a life is penned behind the bars of his music. Tchaikovsky was out of joint with his surroundings; women delighted him not, and so he solaced himself with herculean labors— labors that made him the most interesting, but not the greatest composer of his day.

He had in a rare degree the gift of musical characterization; the power of telling in the orchestra a poetic story, and without the accessories of footlights, scenery, costumes or singers. Charles Lamb most certainly would not have admired him. . . .

Since the music of the march in the "Eroica," since the mighty funeral music in *Siegfried*, there has been no such death music as this "adagio lamentoso" [in the Sixth Symphony], this astounding torso, which Michel Angelo would have understood and Dante wept over. It is the very apotheosis of mortality, and its gloomy accents, poignant melody and harmonic coloring make it one of the most impressive of contributions to mortuary music. It sings of the entombment of a nation, and is incomparably noble, dignified and unspeakably tender. It is only at the close that the rustling of the basses conveys a sinister shudder; the shudder of the Dies Irae when the heavens shall be a fiery scroll and the sublime trump sound its summons to eternity.

No Richard Strauss realism is employed to describe the halting heart beats; no gasps in the woodwind to indicate the departing breath; no imitative figure to tell us that clods of earth are falling heavily on the invisible coffin; but the atmosphere of grief, immutable, eternal, hovers about like a huge black-winged angel.

The movement is the last word in the profoundly pessimistic philosophy which comes from the East to poison and embitter the religious hopes of the West. It has not the consolations of Nirvana, for that offers us a serene non-existence, an absorption into Neánt. Tchaikovsky's music is a page torn from Ecclesiastes, it is the cosmos in crape. . . .

Whether or not the composer had a premonition of his approaching death is a question I gladly leave to sentimental psychologists.

Again we must lament the death of the master. What might his ninth symphony not have been! He was slain in the very plenitude of his powers, at a time when to his glowing temperament was added a moderation born of generous cosmopolitan culture.

Little remains to be added. All who met Tchaikovsky declare that he was a polished, charming man of the world; like all Russians, a good linguist, and many sided in his tastes. But not in his musical taste. He disliked Brahms heartily, and while Brahms appreciated his music, the Russian shrugged his shoulders, and frankly confessed that for him the Hamburg composer was a mere music-maker. In a conversation with Henry Holden Huss he praised Saint-Saëns, and then naïvely admitted that it was a pity an artist whose facture was so fine had so little original to say. He reverenced the classics, Mozart more than Beethoven, and had an enormous predilection for Berlioz, Liszt and Wagner. This was quite natural, and we find Rubinstein, with whom Tchaikovsky studied, upbraiding him for his defection from German classic standards. Curiously enough, Wagner did not play such a part in Tchaikovsky's music as one might imagine. The Russian's operas were made after old-fashioned models and, despite his lyric and dramatic talent, have never proved successful. He dramatically expressed himself best in the orchestra, and totally lacked Wagner's power of projecting dramatic images upon the stage.

As regards the suicide story, I can only repeat that while it has been officially denied, it has never been quite discredited.* Kapellmeister Wallner of St. Petersburg, a relative by marriage of Tolstoy, and an intimate of Tchaikovsky, told me that his nearest friends had the matter hushed up. He is supposed to have died of cholera after drinking a glass of unfiltered water, but his stomach was never subjected to chemical analysis. The fact that his mother died of the same malady lent color to the cholera story. It is all very sad.

---

## Richard Strauss and Nietzsche

In discussing Richard Strauss' symphonic poem, *Also Sprach Zarathustra*, its musical, technical, emotional and aesthetic significance must be considered,—if I may be allowed this rather careless grouping of categories. The work itself is fertile in arousing ideas of a widely divergent sort. It is difficult to speak of it without drifting into the dialectics of the Nietzsche school. It is an absolute music that it should be critically weighed, and that leads into the somewhat forbidding field of the nature of thematic material. Has Strauss, to put it briefly, a right, a precedent to express himself in music in a manner that sets at defiance the normal eight bar theme; that scorns euphony; that follows the curve of the poem or drama or thesis he is illustrating, just as Wagner followed the curve of his poetic text? The question is a fascinating one and a dangerous one, fascinating because of its complexity, and also because any argument that attempts to define the limits of absolute music is an argument that is dangerous.

Berlioz, Liszt and Wagner, three heroes of poetic realism, pushed realism to the verge of the ludicrous, according to their contemporaries. Liszt was especially singled out as the champion of

*According to stories recently publicized in the West, the suicide rumors are accurate: Tchaikovsky was blackmailed by an honor court of the St. Petersburg College of Law, which confronted Tchaikovsky with his homosexuality and demanded his death.—ED.

making poems in music, making pictures in music, and giving no more clue to their meaning than the title. Liszt's three great disciples, Saint-Saëns, Tchaikovsky and Richard Strauss, have dared more than their master. In Saint-Saëns we find a genial cleverness and a mastery of the decorative and more superficial side of music—all this allied to a charming fancy and great musicianship. Yet his stories deal only with the external aspects of his subject. Omphale bids Hercules spin, and the orchestra is straightway transformed into a huge wheel and hums as the giant stoops over the distaff. Death dances with rattling xylophonic bones; Phaeton circles about the Sun God, and we hear his curved chariot and fervent pace. But the psychology is absent. We learn little of the thoughts or feelings of these subjects, and indeed they have none, being mere fabled abstractions clothed in the pictorial counterpoint of the talented Frenchman.

In Tchaikovsky, the lights are turned on more fiercely; his dramatic characterization is marvellous when one considers that the human element is absent from his mechanism. He employs only the orchestra, and across its tonal tapestry there flit the impassioned figures of Romeo and Juliet, the despairing apparition of Francesca da Rimini, and the stalking of Hamlet and Manfred, gloomy, revengeful, imperious, thinking and sorrowing men.

Tchaikovsky went far, but Richard Strauss has dared to go further. He first individualized, and rather grotesquely, Don Juan, Til Eulenspiegel, Macbeth; but in *Death and Apotheosis* and in *Also Sprach Zarathustra* he has attempted almost the impossible; he has attempted the delineation of thought, not musical thought, but philosophical ideas in tone. He has disclaimed this attempt, but the fact nevertheless remains that the various divisions and subdivisions of his extraordinary work are attempts to seize not only certain elusive psychical states, but also to paint pure idea—the "Reine vernunft" of the metaphysicians. Of course he has failed, yet his failure marks a great step in the mastery over the indefiniteness of music. . . .

The object of music is neither to preach nor to philosophize, but the range of the art is vastly enlarged since the days of music of the decorative pattern type. Beethoven filled it with his overshadowing passion, and shall we say ethical philosophy? Schumann and the romanticists gave it color, glow and bizarre passion; Wagner moulded its forms into rare dramatic shapes, and Brahms has endeavored to fill the old classic bottles with the new wine of the romantics. All these men seemed to dare the impossible, according to their contemporaries, and now Strauss has shifted the string one peg higher; not only does he demand the fullest intensity of expression but he insists on the presence of pure idea, and when we consider the abstract nature of the first theme of Beethoven's fifth symphony, when we recall the passionate inflection of the opening measures of *Tristan and Isolde,* who shall dare criticise Strauss, who shall say to him, Thus far and no farther? . . .

It were madness to search for Nietzsche in Strauss—that is, in this score. It is un-Nietzsche music—Nietzsche who discarded Wagner for Bizet, Beethoven for Mozart. Schopenhauer, it may be remembered, laughed at Wagner the musician, played the flute and admired Rossini!

If Nietzsche, clothed in his most brilliant mind, had sat in the Metropolitan Opera House of New York City on the occasion of the first performance of his poem by the Boston Symphony Orchestra, December, 1897, he would probably have cried aloud: "I have pronounced laughter holy," and then laughed himself into the madhouse. Poor, unfortunate, marvellous Nietzsche! But it is Strauss mirroring his own moods after feeding full on Nietzsche, and we must be content to swallow his title, "Also Sprach Zarathustra," when in reality it is "Thus Spake Richard Strauss!" . . .

[*Also Sprach Zarathustra*] is a cathedral in architectonic and is dangerously sublime, dangerously silly, with grotesque gargoyles, hideous flying abutments, exquisite traceries, fantastic arches half gothic, half infernal, huge and resounding spaces, gorgeous façades and heaven splitting spires. A mighty structure, and no more to be understood at one, two or a dozen visits than the Kölner Dom.

It lacks only simplicity of style; it is tropical, torrential, and in it there is the note of hysteria. It is complex with the diseased complexity of the age, and its strivings are the agonized strivings of a morbid Titan. Truthful? aye, horribly so, for it shows us the brain of a great man, overwrought by the vast emotional problems of his generation. . . .

Musically it is a symphonic poem of rather loose construction and as to outline; but rigorously logical in its presentment of thematic material, and in its magnificent weaving of the contrapuntal web. There is organic unity, and the strenuousness of the composer's ideas almost blind his hearers to their tenuity, and sometimes a squat ugliness. Strauss has confessed to not following a definite scheme, a precise presentation of the bacchantic philosophy of Nietzsche. Nietzsche was a lyrical rhapsodist, a literary artist first, perhaps a philosopher afterward. It is the lyric side of him that Strauss seeks to interpret. Simply as absolute music it is astounding enough—astounding in its scope, handling and execution. It is not as realistic as you imagine, not as realistic for instance as the Don Juan and Til Eulenspiegel. Strauss is here an idealist striving after the impossible, yet compassing the hem of grandeur, and often a conscious seeker after the abnormally ugly. . . .

As a mere matter of musical politics I do not care for programme music. Wagner and, before him, Beethoven, fixed its boundaries. Liszt, in his *Faust* symphony, and Wagner, in his *Faust* overture, read into pure music as much meaning as its framework could endure without calling in the aid of the sister arts. Strauss pushed realism to a frantic degree, giving us in his *Death and Apotheosis* the most minute memoranda. But in *Also Sprach Zarathustra* he has deserted surface imitations. The laughter of the convalescent, and the slow, creeping fugue betray his old tendencies. There is an uplifting roar in the opening that is really elemental. Those tremendous chords alone proclaim Strauss a man of genius, and their naked simplicity gives him fee simple to the heritage of Beethoven. But this grandeur is not maintained throughout.

The close is enigmatic, and the juggling with the tonality is fruitful of suspense, bewilderment. Yet it does not plunge the listener into the gloomy, abysmal gulf of Tchaikovsky's last movement of the B minor symphony. It is not so simple nor yet so cosmical. Strauss has the grand manner at times, but he cannot maintain it as did Brahms in his Requiem, or Tchaikovsky in his last symphonic work.

The narrative and declamatory style is often violently interrupted by passages of great descriptive power; the development of the themes seems coincidental with some programme in Strauss' mind and the contrapuntal ingenuity displayed is just short of the miraculous. There is a groaning and a travailing spirit, a restless, uneasy aspiring which is Faust-like, and suggests a close study of Eine Faust Overture, but there is more versatility of mood, more hysteria and more febrile agitation in the Strauss score. . . .

Formalism is abandoned—Strauss moves by episodes; now furiously swift, now ponderously lethargic, and one is lost in amazement at the loftiness, the solidity and general massiveness of his structure. The man's scholarship is so profound, almost as profound as Brahms'; his genius for the orchestra so marked, his color and rhythmic sense so magnificently developed that the general effect of his rhetoric is perhaps too blazingly brilliant. He has more to say than Berlioz and says it better, is less magniloquent and more poetical than Liszt, is as clever as Saint-Saëns, but in thematic invention he is miles behind Wagner.

His melodies, it must be confessed, are not always remarkable or distinguished in quality, setting aside the question of ugliness altogether. But the melodic curve is big and passional. Strauss can be tender, dramatic, bizarre, poetic and humorous, but the noble art of simplicity he sadly lacks—for art it is. His themes in this poem are often simple; indeed the waltz is distinctly commonplace, but it is not the Doric, the bald simplicity of Beethoven. It is rather a brutal plainness of speech.

Strauss is too deadly in earnest to trifle or to condescend to ear-tickling devices. The tremendous sincerity of the work will be its saving salt for many who violently disagree with the whole scheme.

(*Mezzotints in Modern Music*, 1899.)

# Italian Opera of Today

## W. J. HENDERSON

*Like his friend and colleague James Huneker, William James Henderson was part of what has come to be dubbed the "classical age" of New York music criticism. (Other notable writers in the group included Richard Aldrich and Henry Edward Krehbiel.) In his work for the* New York Times *and* Sun *during the early twentieth century, Henderson had a style that, in contrast to Huneker's metaphorical richness, is lean and straightforward, with clipped sentences and pared-down rhetoric. Henderson's writing has a certain syntactical predictability but also an attractive momentum and clarity. His article on Italian opera has an added immediacy that comes from being contemporary with its subject matter. Readers of today may be startled to find composers such as Puccini and Mascagni characterized as modern and "acrid," or Richard Strauss held up as the most far-out representative of the avant-garde. These assessments indicate just how shocking the music of Schönberg, Stravinsky, and Varèse—which burst upon the scene only a few years later—must have been to an age which had barely assimilated the* Tristan *chord.*

Several factors have united in causing a new interest in the opera of Italy. In so far as New York is concerned the singing together of two such admirable exponents of the art of bel canto as Mme. Marcella Sembrich and Enrico Caruso has restored to life some of the older works, while a recent visit of Mascagni and the frequent performances of Puccini's *La Bohème* and *Tosca* have directed serious attention to the tendency of the younger art. The struggles of the youthful school to maintain its national characteristics in the face of its own yearnings after the flesh-pots of Wagnerism have afforded an absorbing spectacle for observers of musical progress.

The leader and master of all these young eagles was, of course, the incomparable Verdi, the most characteristic composer of opera Italy ever brought forth. But although he showed them all precisely how to mingle the fruits of the new fields opened by Wagner with those of the old Italian soil, they have not always wisely accepted his instruction. They have sought for independence in manner, and in some instances with disheartening results. But perhaps a cursory review of some of their achievements may not be in vain.

Doubtless the casual observer will be struck first by the instrumentation of these modern Italians. Puccini's scores certainly offer abundant food for study, and his clever adjustment of the leading motive scheme to the instrumental background of a thoroughly Italian vocal melody, as in *Tosca*, is an accomplishment not to be passed by with a smile. If we compare the scores of such works as those of Puccini and Mascagni with the works of the Donizetti period, we note with astonishment the immense strides made in the use of the orchestra.

But we must not be deceived. The Donizettian period was one of reaction. The Gluck-Piccini battle had not long since been fought out in Paris, and the principles of dramatic verity in opera had once more been vindicated, but at the cost of a great public weariness. The classic polish and repose of Gluck's music were intellectually satisfying, but his scores lacked the vital heat to keep warm the blood of the artistically indolent. To this day the best works of Gluck invite our admiration, but seldom awaken our feelings. The idle, pleasure-seeking public of Europe soon turned again to its strumming ditties. It threw itself at the feet of Rossini, and within forty years after the establishment of Gluck's superiority in Paris the whole Continent was beating time to "Di tanti palpiti."

Once more the Voice was the deity of the operatic stage, and woe betide the composer who so wrote for his orchestra as to interfere with its supremacy. Rossini, who had artistic aspirations in spite of all his insincerity and intellectual laziness, made many improvements in operatic writing. It was he who first omitted from an opera all use of the old-fashioned dry recitative and used throughout that which has the support of the orchestra. He enriched the manner of writing for horns and clarinets, and he introduced instrumental effects which later composers have adopted with good effect. But, nevertheless, *William Tell* was a failure, and Rossini sulked in his tent for thirty years, while Bellini and Donizetti turned out their nursery operas, in which the orchestra has been likened to a "big guitar."

The advance in orchestral writing in opera after this time is often erroneously attributed wholly to Wagner, but undoubtedly it is the king of all musical charlatans, Meyerbeer, who should have the lion's share of the honor. When Wagner was a young, struggling, and utterly unknown composer, seeking for an opening in Paris, he threw himself at the feet of Meyerbeer, who was the idol of both the French and the Prussian capitals. Meyerbeer's operas were already known throughout Europe, and to their cheap and tawdry orchestral effects the later composers no doubt owed the suggestion that with the orchestra much might be said that could not be given to the voices. Subsequently the leaven of Wagnerism permeated European musical art, but the despised Meyerbeer undoubtedly pointed out to many writers the path which led back toward the true source of Italian operatic composition.

For in the beginning of opera, Monteverde experimented with orchestral effects, chiefly descriptive, to be sure, but indicating what might be done. Lully afterward developed some ideas as to dramatic expression in the instrumental score, and these were further expanded by Gluck. The progress along this path was checked temporarily by the reaction in favor of cheap tunes for the display of voices. Verdi took up the development of the orchestral part of Italian opera where Rossini left off, and in his early works wrote in a style that bears more than a family resemblance to that of *William Tell*. But Verdi was a man of broad vision, an assimilator of universal ideas, and he was not slow to recognize the drift of operatic art. He discerned the rising importance of the orchestral score and realized the full value of the instrumental adjunct. In *Aïda* he utilized to their utmost capacity its resources in coloring and in *Otello* he placed in the orchestra some of the most important and significant passages of his music,—passages which went further than anything in the setting of the text itself toward the complete explication of the emotions working in the drama. In *Falstaff* he used the orchestra as a commentator on the humor of every situation, and even succeeded in making it aid in the interpretation of Falstaff's ridiculous philosophy.

One has only to hearken for a minute to Mascagni's use of the basses in *Cavalleria Rusticana* to recognize the source of his knowledge. *Otello,* with its wonderful bass recitative in the murder scene, was produced in 1887; *Cavalleria Rusticana* was brought out in 1890. Mascagni's dramatic treatment of the orchestral part of the lyric drama is no mere imitation, however; it is a part of the general movement in Italian opera which began with Verdi's *Aïda* and which may without difficulty be traced back through Boito's *Mefistofele* (of which the first version was produced in 1868) to Rossini's *William Tell.* The advance was akin to that made in all species of music. The first experiments were in the direction of description by means of imitative figuration. These are what we find in *Tell.* The allotment to the orchestra of the emotional background of the drama was bound to come later, in the natural order of things. Mascagni stands in the direct line of progress in this matter, and his contribution to the general results is, though small, nevertheless worthy of remark.

How much he and Leoncavallo and Puccini owe to Ponchielli would be hard to determine. The composer of *La Giaconda* was somewhat ahead of his time, and his work was not fairly understood when it was new. But in one feature of operatic composition suggested by this work all the later composers seem inclined to go too far. They are striving to follow Verdi in his earnest attempt to set every phrase of the text of *Otello* to music perfectly adapted to the expression of its meaning. But Verdi avoided the fatal error into which these young Italians are falling. He never went so far as to obliterate from his scores all trace of melodic character. . . .

Do [the young Italians] need a model? Well, there is one of whom they seemingly know not. Away back in the years before even Rossini assailed flaccid Paris with the strenuous peal of *William Tell,* a German boy of seventeen wrote in 1814 a song called "Gretchen am Spinnrade," and the following year he cast upon the waters that marvellous condensed drama "Der Erl-König." In the five minutes of that one song by Franz Peter Schubert lies the history of a human soul. It is an epitome of emotion, and the piano does quite as much as the voice—but not more—in the expression. If the young Italians would like to learn something more than they already know about the way to build condensed opera, let them study the songs of Schubert. There they will find a solution of the problem of how to combine perfect vocal melody with a dramatic accompaniment without sacrificing one iota of dramatic verity.

An additional question of high import is whether these young firebrands are not setting the torch to the roots of nationality in their art. It is useless for theoreticians to argue that there is no nationality in music. There is nationality in all art, and the "Virgin" painted by Rubens is a Flemish woman just as surely as she is Italian when limned by Michael Angelo. There never was a German who could have conceived the lilt of "Funiculi, funicula," nor an Italian who could have composed "Schwesterlein." No Russian could have penned the dainty "Pierre et sa Mie," nor could a Frenchman have imagined "Ay Ouchnem." Only an Englishman could have written "Rule Britannia," of which Wagner said that the first four measures contained the whole character of the English people. . . .

The Italians of today have not wholly forgotten the essentials of their native melody. Indeed, their composing betrays a deep self-consciousness. They see the character of their own music and try to escape it, and it is of this very act that complaint is here made. But the fundamentals of Italian melody are not entirely lost. The pages of Puccini's *Manon*, *La Bohème*, and *Tosca* are not completely devoid of song which is indisputably Italian. No one would ever mistake it for French or German. But it is no longer the melody of Donizetti and Bellini. That is well. The Italian masters of the beginning of this century wrote tunes for their own sake without thought of their dramatic expressiveness, and Donizetti did not hesitate to stop the entire action of his *Lucia* at one of the most critical points in order that the famous sextet might be sung.

The modern Italians do not fall into that sort of error. They are striving with all their power to compose dramatically. They are striving, too, to preserve Italian music, and for this all honor should be shown them. More than that, they have shown plainly the path along which Italian music should advance. They have demonstrated beyond question that the aria, which was the central sun of the old Neapolitan system of opera, is wholly unessential. They have shown that the dialogue of the lyric drama can be carried on in a musical speech which is melodious, but not dominated by musical patterns. They have illustrated to the full the possibilities of a flexible and eloquent recitative. They have carried to a high degree of excellence the art of fitting the musical accent to the word, and the contour of the phrase to the natural inflection of the speech. This they have done, too, in the full knowledge that their art in this detail is quite lost upon the general public and appeals only to a few studious critics of their music.

It is not possible in a brief essay to point out the details of the methods of these young men. It may be said, however, that what they have apparently striven to do is to rear a distorted vocal structure, composed of the elements of the older Italian singing style, upon a foundation of acrid, restless, changeful, distressful harmonies. It may perhaps be injudicious to find fault with them for this, for no thoughtful observer of musical progress can fail to see that toward something new and strange in harmonic sequences all music is advancing.

(*Modern Musical Drift*, 1904.)

# Gilbert and Sullivan

## G. K. CHESTERTON

*The magical collaboration of W. S. Gilbert and Sir Arthur Sullivan has inspired the muse of essayists ranging from T. H. White to Isaac Asimov. What has always been enticing to writers about the Gilbert and Sullivan phenomenon is that what at first seems to be simple charm is actually something complex and mysterious, a perfect melding of literature, drama, and music by two artists whose sensibilities were remarkably dissimilar. Gilbert's hard, diamond-like prose, his cynicism and misogyny, were somehow mediated by the glow of Sullivan's music, just as the latter was given a needed pungency and dissonance by Gilbert's lyrics. No one wrote of Gilbert and Sullivan with more wit and authority than G. K. Chesterton. To Chesterton, Gilbert's style was "an airy, artistic, detached and almost dehumanized thing . . . not unlike a certain almost empty radiance in some of the late lyrics of the Renaissance"—and therefore much in need of Sullivan's humanizing music. The following little-known essay manages to capture not only the essence of Gilbert and Sullivan but also the age they so gloriously lampooned.*

The best work of the Victorian age, perhaps the most Victorian work of the Victorian age, was its satire upon itself. It would be well if this were remembered more often by those who talk of nothing but its pomposity and conventionality. There was, indeed, a strain in it not only of pomposity but of hypocrisy; but like everything English, it was rather subtle. In so far as it existed it should be called rather humbug than hypocrisy, for hypocrisy implies intellectual clarity, and humbug suggests rather that convenient possession, a confused mind. The exclamation that a thing is all damned humbug is of the same sort as the exclamation that it is all damned nonsense. English humbug has had at least the comforting quality of nonsense, and something of that quality belongs even to the nonsense which made fun of the nonsense. And it will be found, I think, in the long run that this Victorian nonsense will prove more valuable than all that was considered the solid Victorian sense.

It is idle to prophesy about tastes and fashion; but to speak of the failure of the practical compromise of our great unwritten Constitution, for instance, is not to prophesy. It is merely to record. All that side of the British pomposity of the time has obviously collapsed in our time. The political balance and repose of the Victorians, the serious satisfaction of their social arrangements, is already a thing of the past; and perhaps this unbalanced absurdity may prove far more permanent in the future. But it is not only true of practical politics, which have become so exceedingly unpractical. It is true even of pure literature, which in one sense can always remain ideal. The Gilbert and Sullivan Operas can still be revived, and revived with complete popular success. I think it very doubtful whether "The Idylls of the King," if they were published now, would produce the same sort of effect as when they were published then. I doubt whether Longfellow would immediately obtain his large crowd or Browning his small one. It is not a question of the merits of the poetry or even of the truth of the criticism. People who talk thus about the appeal to posterity often seem to forget that posterity may be wrong—especially about the books that it has not read. Browning's work will always be worthy of study, just as Donne's work will always be worthy of study, but it would be rash to infer that it is always studied. Tennyson will always present certain triumphs of diction for those who are acquainted with the English language. But when Anglo-Saxon is talked all over the world, those acquainted with the English language may be comparatively few. There may be a very general neglect of the Victorian achievements, and as this will be merely an effect of time, it may be merely temporary. But as things stand, the Victorian monument which best supports and survives the change of fashion, is not the Laureate ode and office any more than the Albert Memorial: it is all that remains of the Savoy Opera.

But anyone who understands what was really to be said for and against the Victorian interlude or compromise will note with interest that the Victorian satirist did lash the age, in the old phrase; and if in a sense he lashed lightly he also lashed with precision; he touched the spot. He was an inquisitor, as waggish as his own Inquisitor in "The Gondoliers," but he did really persecute the rather hazy heresies of the hour. He did really persecute in the exact sense of pursue; he tracked an untrue or unreasonable idea back to its first principle. Gilbert's gayest songs and most farcical rhymes are full of examples which a philosopher or a logician will value as real ideas or criticisms of ideas. And it was always the criticism really demanded by the half-formed ideas of the Victorians, those half-warmed fish which the Spooners of the age had in their hearts, but not very clearly in their heads. Any number of examples of this sort of thing could be given. For instance, nothing was more subtly false in the Victorians' conception of success than a certain conception of the elect who were above temptation. There was a queer sort of cheery Calvanism in it; a sort of jovial predestination. Certain social types, the good sportsman, the English lady, the frank and fearless English school boy (provided, of course, he were a public school boy), were regarded, not as heroes who had overcome the baser passions, but as gods who could never have been touched by them. The phraseology of the time testified to the notion again and again. Such people were not innocent of a crime; they were "incapable" of it. Political corruption (which was increasing by leaps and bounds) was calmly ignored on the assumption of it being simply "impossible" in what was generally described as "a man of that position." Men who really preserved their honour under trials had no reward or recognition of their real merit, if they were of the sort in whom such things were supposed to be inconceivable. Everyone who has read the novels and newspapers of that time will recognise this formless impression, but not everybody could have put it into logical form. Yet it is pricked or stabbed with deadly precision in five or six absurd lines of a light refrain in *The Mikado:*

> We know him well,
> He cannot tell
> Untrue or groundless tales—
> He always tries
> To utter lies
> And every time he fails.

It is the same with the heresy that haunted the great Victorian virtue of patriotism. What was the matter with it was that it was a sort of unconscious shuffling of an unselfish into a selfish emotion. It was not so much that a man was proud of England, as that he was proud of being an Englishman, which is quite a different thing. Being proud of your country is only like being proud of your father or your friend; it is not, in the spiritual and evil sense, really pride at all. But being proud of yourself for being a citizen of that country is really using something else as an excuse for being proud of yourself. Now, the logical or illogical point of that process is in the matter of merit, and the satirist really hits it with the exactitude of a subtle theologian. It is a question of how much there is implied some moral superiority such as ought to be founded on the individual will, and it could not be better exposed than in the few words of that old familiar and even rowdy song:

> But in spite of all temptations
> To belong to other nations
> He remains an Englishman.

The rapier of Voltaire could not have run a thing more straight through the heart. Now the work of Gilbert, especially in his operas, but very notably also in his Bab Ballads, is full of triumphs of that intellectual and even theoretical sort. There was even something about him personally not altogether unlike the tone of the theologian and inquisitor; his wit was staccato and sometimes harsh, and he was not happy in his own age and atmosphere. It did not provide him with any positive philosophy for which to fight, but that was not his fault. He did fight for what he conceived to be common sense, and he found plenty of things that wanted fighting.

And then the odd thing happened that was like a lucky coincidence in a farce or a magic gift in a fairy tale. As it stood, his satire was really much too intelligent to be intelligible. It is doubtful whether by itself it would ever have been completely popular. Something came to his aid which is much more popular than the love of satire: the profound and popular love of song. A genius in another school of art crossed his path and co-operated in his work; giving wings to his words, and sending them soaring into the sky. Perhaps no other musician except Sullivan would have done it in exactly the right way; would have been in exactly the right degree frivolous and exactly the right degree fastidious. A certain fine unreality had to hang over all the fantasies; there was nothing rowdy, there was nothing in the special sense even rousing about such song, as there is in a serious, patriotic, or revolutionary song, or even drinking song. Everything must be seen in a magic mirror, a little more delicately distorted than the mirror of Shalott; there must be no looking out directly upon passing events. The satiric figures were typical but not topical. All that precise degree of levity and distance from reality seemed to be expressed, as nothing else could express it, in the very notes of the music; almost, one might say, in the note of the laughter that followed it. And it may be that in the remote future that laughter will still be heard, when all the voices of that age are silent.

(Introduction to A. H. Godwin's *Gilbert and Sullivan*, 1926.)

# Mahler: His Time Has Come

## LEONARD BERNSTEIN

*Leonard Bernstein writes the way he conducts. In the many essays, speeches, poems, and television tapes written between 1935 and the present, his prose is sometimes gushy in its hyperbole but always invigorating in its exuberance and absolute commitment to the subject at hand. No one has done more than he has to increase the audience for "classical" music, including much that is difficult and experimental. Bernstein's impact is perhaps most dramatically visible in the current Mahler renaissance. Now one of the most popular of all composers, Mahler went largely unheard before Bernstein popularized and recorded his "unrecordable" symphonies. Nowhere does Bernstein write with a more burning sense of mission than in this 1967 explication of Mahler's sublime "doubleness," an essay written in conjunction with the release of the historic Bernstein set of the nine Mahler symphonies.*

H as come? Had come, rather; was there all along, even as each bar of each symphony was being penned in that special psychic fluid of his. If ever there was a composer of his time it was Mahler, prophetic only in the sense that he already knew what the world would come to know and admit half a century later.

Basically, of course, all of Mahler's music is about Mahler—which means simply that it is about conflict. Think of it: Mahler the Creator vs. Mahler the Performer; the Jew vs. the Christian; the Believer vs. the Doubter; the Naïf vs. the Sophisticate; the provincial Bohemian vs. the Viennese *homme du monde;* the Faustian Philosopher vs. the Oriental Mystic; the Operatic Symphonist who never wrote an opera. But mainly the battle rages between Western Man at the turn of the century and the life of the spirit. Out of this opposition proceeds the endless list of antitheses—the whole roster of Yang and Yin—that inhabit Mahler's music.

What was this duple vision of Mahler's? A vision of his world, crumbling in corruption beneath its smug surface, fulsome, hypocritical, prosperous, sure of its terrestrial immortality, yet bereft of its faith in spiritual immortality. The music is almost cruel in its revelations: it is like a camera that has caught Western society in the moment of its incipient decay. But to Mahler's own audiences none of this was apparent: they refused (or were unable) to see themselves mirrored in these grotesque symphonies. They heard only exaggeration, extravagance, bombast, obsessive length—failing to recognize these as symptoms of their own decline and fall. They heard what seemed like the history of German-Austrian music, recapitulated in ironic or distorted terms—and they called it shameful eclecticism. They heard endless, brutal, maniacal marches—but failed to see the imperial insignia, the Swastika (make your own list) on the uniforms of the marchers. They heard mighty Chorales, overwhelming brass hymns—but failed to see them tottering at an abyss of tonal deterioration. They heard extended, romantic love songs—but failed to understand that these *Liebesträume* were nightmares, as were those mad, degenerate *Ländler.*

But what makes the heartbreaking duplicity is that all these anxiety-ridden images were set up alongside images of the life of the spirit, Mahler's anima, which surrounds, permeates, and floodlights these cruel pictures with the tantalizing radiance of how life could be. The intense longing for serenity is inevitably coupled with the sinister doubt that it can be achieved. Obversely, the innate violence of the music, the excesses of sentiment, the arrogance of establishment, the vulgarity of power-postures, the disturbing rumble of status-non-quo are all the more agonizing for being linked with memories of innocence, with the aching nostalgia of youthful dreams, with aspirations towards the Empyrean, noble proclamations of redemption, or with the bittersweet tease of some Nirvana or other, just barely out of reach. It is thus a conflict between an intense love of life and a disgust with life, between a fierce longing for *Himmel* and the fear of death.

This dual vision of Mahler's, which tore him apart all his life, is the vision we have finally come to perceive in his music. This is what Mahler meant when he said, "My time will come." It is only after fifty, sixty, seventy years of world holocausts, of the simultaneous advance of democracy with our increasing inability to stop making war, of the simultaneous magnification of national pieties with the intensification of our active resistance to social equality—only after we have experienced all this through the smoking ovens of Auschwitz, the frantically bombed jungles of Vietnam, through Hungary, Suez, the Bay of Pigs, the farce-trial of Sinyavsky and Daniel, the refueling of the Nazi machine, the murder in Dallas, the arrogance of South Africa, the Hiss-Chambers travesty, the Trotzkyite purges, Black Power, Red Guards, the Arab encirclement of Israel, the plague of McCarthyism, the Tweedledum armament race—only after all this can we finally listen to Mahler's music and understand that it foretold all. And that in the foretelling it showered a rain of beauty on this world that has not been equaled since.

Now that the world of music has begun to understand the dualistic energy-source of Mahler's music, the very key to its meaning, it is easier to understand this phenomenon in specific Mahlerian terms. For the doubleness of the music is the doubleness of the man. Mahler was split right down the middle, with the curious result that whatever quality is perceptible and definable in his music, the diametrically opposite quality is equally so. Of what other composer can this be said? Can we think of Beethoven as both roughhewn and epicene? Is Debussy both subtle and blatant? Mozart both refined and raw? Stravinsky both objective and maudlin? Unthinkable. But Mahler, uniquely, is all of these—roughhewn *and* epicene, subtle *and* blatant, refined, raw, objective, maudlin, brash, shy, grandiose, self-annihilating, confident, insecure, adjective, opposite.

The first spontaneous image that springs to my mind at the mention of the word "Mahler" is of a colossus straddling the magic dateline "1900." There he stands, his left foot (closer to the heart!) firmly planted in the rich, beloved nineteenth century, and his right, rather less firmly, seeking solid ground in the twentieth. Some say he never found this foothold; others (and I agree with them) insist that twentieth-century music could not exist as we know it if that right foot had not landed there with a commanding thud. Whichever assessment is right, the image remains: he straddled. Along with Strauss, Sibelius and, yes, Schoenberg, Mahler sang the last rueful songs of nineteenth-century [r]omanticism. But Strauss's extraordinary gifts went the route of a not very subjective virtuosity; Sibelius and Schoenberg found their own extremely different but personal routes into the new century. Mahler was left straddling; his destiny was to sum up, package, and lay to ultimate rest the fantastic treasure that was German-Austrian music from Bach to Wagner.

It was a terrible and dangerous heritage. Whether he saw himself as the last symphonist in the long line started by Mozart, or the last *Heilige Deutsche Künstler* in the line started by Bach, he was in the same rocky boat. To recapitulate the line, bring it to climax, show it all in one, soldered and smelted together by his own fires—this was a function assigned him by history and destiny, a function that meant years of ridicule, rejection, and bitterness.

But he had no choice, compulsive manic creature that he was. He took all (all!) the basic elements of German music, including the clichés, and drove them to their ultimate limits. He turned rests into shuddering silences; upbeats into volcanic preparations as for a death blow. *Luftpausen* became gasps of shock or terrified suspense; accents grew into titanic stresses to be achieved by every conceivable means, both sonic and tonic. *Ritardandi* were stretched into near-motionlessness; *accelerandi* became tornadoes; dynamics were refined and exaggerated to a point of neurasthenic sensibility. Mahler's marches are like heart attacks, his chorales like all Christendom gone mad. The old conventional four-bar phrases are delineated in steel; his most traditional cadences bless like the moment of remission from pain. Mahler is German music multiplied by $n$.

The result of all this exaggeration is, of course, that neurotic intensity which for so many years was rejected as unendurable, and in which we now find ourselves mirrored. And there are concomitant results: an irony almost too bitter to comprehend; excesses of sentimentality that still make some listeners wince; moments of utter despair, often the despair of not being able to drive all this material even further, into some kind of paramusic that might at last cleanse us. But we *are* cleansed, when all is said and done; no person of sensibility can come away from the Ninth Symphony without being exhausted and purified. And that is the triumphant result of all this purgatory, justifying all excesses: we do ultimately encounter an apocalyptic radiance, a glimmer of what peace must be like.

So much for the left foot: what of the right, tentatively scratching at the new soil of the twentieth century, testing it for solidity, fertility, roots? Yes, it was found fertile; there were roots there, but they had sprung from the other side. All of Mahler's testing, experiments, incursions were made in terms of the past. His breaking-up of rhythms, his post-Wagnerian stretching of tonality to its very snapping point (but not beyond it!), his probings into a new thinness of texture, into bare linear motion, into transparent chamber-music-like orchestral manipulation—all these adumbrated what was to become twentieth-century common practice; but they all emanated from those nineteenth-century notes he loved so well. Similarly, in his straining after new forms—a two-movement symphony (#8), a six-movement symphony (#3), symphonies with voices, not only in the Finales (#3, #8, *Das Lied*), movements which are interludes, interruptions, movements deliberately malformed through arbitrary abridgment or obsessive repetition or fragmentation—all these attempts at new formal structures abide in the shadow of Beethoven's Ninth, the last Sonatas and string quartets. Even the angular melodic motions, the unexpected intervals, the infinitely wide skips, the search for "endless" melody, the harmonic ambiguities—all of which have deeply influenced many a twentieth-century composer—are nevertheless ultimately traceable back to Beethoven and Wagner.

I think that this is probably why I doubt that I shall ever come to terms with the so-called Tenth Symphony. I have never been convinced of those rhythmic experiments in the Scherzo, of the flirtation with atonality. I often wonder what would have happened had Mahler not died so young. Would he have finished that Tenth Symphony, more or less as the current "versions" have it? Would he have scrapped it? Were there signs there that he was about to go over the hill, and encamp with Schoenberg? It is one of the more fascinating Ifs of history. Somehow I think he was unable to live through that crisis, because there was no solution for him; he had to die with that symphony unfinished. After all, a man's destiny is nothing more or less than precisely what happened to him in life. Mahler's destiny was to complete the great German symphonic line and then depart, without it being granted him to start a new one. This may be clear to us now; but for Mahler, while he lived, his destiny was anything but clear. In his own mind he was at least as much part of the new century as of the old. He was a tormented, divided man with his eyes on the future and his heart in the past.

But his destiny did permit him to bestow much beauty, and to occupy a unique place in musical history. In this position of Amensayer to symphonic music, through exaggeration and distortion, through squeezing the last drops of juice out of that glorious fruit, through his desperate and insistent reëxamination and reëvaluation of his materials, through pushing tonal music to its uttermost boundaries, Mahler was granted the honor of having the last word, uttering the final sigh, letting fall the last living tear, saying the final good-by. To what? To life as he knew it and wanted to remember it, to unspoiled nature, to faith in redemption; but also to *music* as he knew it and remembered it, to the unspoiled nature of tonal beauty, to faith in its future—good-by to all that. The last C major chord of *Das Lied von der Erde* was for him the last resolution of all Faustian history. For him?

(*High Fidelity,* September 1967.)

# Debussy and the Dawn of Modernism
# Webern's Rarified Beauty
# Stravinsky's *Sacre:* The Cornerstone
# of Modern Music

---

## PIERRE BOULEZ

*As composer, conductor, and champion of twentieth-century music, Pierre Boulez is one of the major musical figures of our time. The title of his orchestral masterpiece* Pli Selon Pli *suggests a method and vision in which layers of thought and feeling are revealed "fold upon fold," with radiant clarity. As a conductor, Boulez illuminates hidden textures and nuances in the most complex (or commonplace) scores, sometimes earning the label of "coldness" from critics who equate intelligence with lack of feeling. As a writer, he evinces a similar rigor and clarity, coupled with an underlying passion which sweeps aside tradition-bound clichés. In his article on Debussy, he cleans away the "impressionist" clouds (as he does in his revelatory recordings of that composer); in his article on Webern, he reveals this notoriously "cerebral" modernist to be a connoisseur of beauty. In the case of Stravinsky's much written-about* Le Sacre du printemps, *Boulez does the opposite of what we might expect, knocking away the score's celebrated complexity to illuminate an elemental simplicity. Boulez does nothing less than change the way we experience the music of our time.*

The Quartet is not Debussy's masterpiece, but it heralded an undeniable renewal in the spirit of chamber music, which it pried loose from the rigid structure, congealed rhetoric, and rigoristic esthetic in which Beethoven's successors had shut it up; it introduced "modernity" into one of the forms of musical literature which had been least disposed to it, probably because of the small number and the demands of a caste: the "enlightened amateurs."

That "modernity" was going to triumph easily with a less restricted audience, one above all less prejudiced, one that did not raise pretentions to the point of considering itself privileged, "specialist,"—and that in a field forbidden to most amateurs. The *Prélude à L'Aprés-midi d'un faune*, given for the first time on December 22, 1894, by the Société Nationale under the direction of Gustave Doret, won success immediately; it was so much applauded that it had to be repeated. Undeniably, the *Prélude* gave proof of much greater audacity than the String Quartet; that doubtless was owing in large part to the poem, the extensions of which incited Debussy's thought to free itself of any scholastic impediment. This masterwork of Debussy's rapidly became the most popular of his concert works; it marked the decisive advent of a music merely foreseen by Mussorgsky. It has been said often: the flute of the *Faune* brought new breath to the art of music; what was overthrown was not so much the art of development as the very concept of form itself, here freed from the impersonal constraints of the schema, giving wings to a supple, mobile expressiveness, demanding a technique of perfect instantaneous adequacy. Its use of timbres seemed essentially new, of exceptional delicacy and assurance in touch; the use of certain instruments—flute, horn, and harp—showed the characteristic principles of the manner in which Debussy would employ them in later works. The writing for woodwinds and brasses, incomparably light-handed, performed a miracle of proportion, balance, and transparency. The potential of youth possessed by that score defies exhaustion and decrepitude; and just as modern poetry surely took root in certain of Baudelaire's poems, so one is justified in saying that modern music was awakened by *L'Après-midi d'un faune*. . . .

Debussy certainly was not that *"musicien français"* dear to adepts wanting to reduce him to their own paltry dimension, although his belated patriotism willingly accepted that sobriquet. Furthermore, he was not an "impressionist," although he himself furnished pretexts for that limiting designation. The misunderstanding resulted from the titles of his works and from the fact that "Monsieur Croche talked about an orchestral score as about a picture"—a simple question of antidilettantism. On the other side stands the great force of refusal with which he opposed the Schola: he took the side of "sound-alchemy" against the "beaver-science." He rejected the heritages and followed a dream of vitrified improvisation; he refused to play that game of construction which so often transforms the composer into a child playing architect; in his eyes, form was never a given thing; his pursuit of the unanalyzable was constant, developing so as to admit the rights of surprise and imagination. He had only disdain for the architectural monument, preferring structures mixing rigor and free will; with him, the words, the keys—all the scholarly apparatus—lost their sense and pertinence. Even if one expands the extension of the usual categories of an exhausted tradition, it cannot be applied to his work. He would have suffered in the face of the debauch of "classicism" which took place after his death. There are some hints of Pre-Raphaelitism in the procedure that led him to turn back to Villon and Charles d'Orléans, but that poetic deviation is not comparable to his successors' errors. The title *Hommage à Rameau* was not justified by any considerations of style—the piece is "in the style of a sarabande, but not rigorously." *The Debussy reality* excludes all academicism. Incompatible with any stereotyped order, with all ordering not created at the instant, that reality has remained isolated in Occidental music, the latest evolution of which has remained impermeable by it. The cause of that isolation is only too clear: Debussy rejected all hierarchy outside the musical moment itself. With him, and above all in his final works, musical time often changes in significance. Wanting to create his technique, create his vocabulary, and create his form, he was led to dispense completely with ideas that had remained static up to that time. Motion, the instant, irrupt into his music, not merely an impression of the instant, of the fugitive to which it has been reduced, but really a relative and irreversible conception of musical time and, more generally, of the musical universe. In the organization of sounds, that conception rejected the harmonic hierarchies existing as unique *données* of the sound-world. The relations between object and object were established in the context, following functions that were not constant. As for the rhythmic writing, it partakes of that manifestation no less, of that will toward mobility in the metric concept. In the same way, his experiments with timbre deeply modified the writing, the instrumental combinations, the sonority of the orchestra. Debussy's courage as a voluntary autodidact obliged him to rethink all aspects of musical creation. Doing that, he brought about a radical, though not always spectacular, revolution. The two portraits of M. Croche bear witness to that: in black—"They salute you with sumptuous epithets, and you are nothing but a rogue! something between a monkey and a domestic"; in white—"One must seek discipline in liberty and not in the formulations of a philosophy that has become decrepit and good only for the feeble." In the eyes of the builders, his fatal fault was that he promulgated nothing. There, nonetheless, you have the most fascinating myths. Debussy remains one of the most isolated of all musicians. Although his epoch at times forced him to find fugitive, feline solutions, in view of his incommunicable experience and his sumptuous reserve, he is the only universal French musician, at least during the nineteenth and twentieth centuries. He preserves a power of magical, mysterious seduction. His position at the beginning of the contemporary movement is a position in flux, but solitary. Moved by that "desire always to go farther which for him took the place of bread and wine," he contradicted in advance any attempt to relate him to the old order. We should not forget that Debussy's period was also Cézanne's and Mallarmé's—a triple conjunction that may lie at the root of all modernity, although one cannot exactly find any formulated teaching there. But no doubt it is possible that Debussy wanted it known that he needed to dream his revolution no less than to construct it.

## Webern's Rarified Beauty

**B**eginning with opus 5, the genius of Webern appears as unprecedented, both for the radicalism of his points of view and for the novelty of his sensibility—a rare amalgam testified to by a series of works that still astonish us. This group includes the Five Movements for String Quartet, opus 5, the Six Pieces for Orchestra, opus 6, and the Pieces for Piano and Violin, opus 7. In these one sees made precise his predilection for the "little form," by which I do not mean a brief form, but a form so highly concentrated that it cannot support long development in time because of the richness of means involved and the poetic governing them.

The Movements, opus 5, and the Six Pieces for Orchestra, opus 6, have now become the most accessible of Webern's compositions; each time they are performed, they win their audience, however prejudiced it may have been in the beginning. In fact, Webern never had been so seductive before and perhaps never would be again. For the baroque charm—in the stylistic sense of the word—emanating from these pieces proved completely transitory in Webern's work. He was to bend his effort toward a rigor that is no less beautiful but is less directly intelligible.

One can, *grosso modo,* organize the elements of his style at that time and make their fundamental characteristics precise: the individual lines are excessively supple; their curve, their unexpectedness, their grace, and their complete lack of heaviness are captivating; the polyphony itself is rarely complex, for most of the pieces consist of a melody—if one will give a large meaning to the term—accompanied by chords that, although they no longer have any tonal function, nonetheless are in close relation (chromatically) with that melody. In another sense, the chromatic universe in which this music moves is again composed of conjunct intervals or, if they are disjunct, intervals disposed in a register sufficiently narrowed so that the ear is able to perceive the continuity at once. Finally, a sensibility extremely close to Debussy's in its refinement, its taste for ellipsis, its delicacy, creates an atmosphere almost familiar to our ears. The use of instrumental color is of so direct a beauty that the listener has no difficulty in enjoying it, although at first it may be so strange to him as to seem a rarefaction of the musical atmosphere. There is no aggressivity in the sonority; on the contrary—an exceptional instance aside—sweetness and transparency are the determining qualities of this group of works. . . .

In the period from 1910 to about 1914, he went ahead, almost to asphyxia, in exploring the microcosm toward which his temperament already had attracted him. This was the epoch of his shortest works: Six Bagatelles for String Quartet, opus 9; Five Pieces for Chamber Orchestra, opus 10; Three Pieces for Piano and Violoncello, opus 11. In these last, the parallel with the Japanese *haï-kaï* can be established easily: a phrase suffices to place a universe and impose it forcibly. The third piece of opus 11, for example, is restricted to six short measures; the fourth of opus 10 lasts twenty seconds. (It is very difficult to present such works in concert because of their brevity, but even more because of their restricted sound-dynamic, which makes use of nuances at the edge of the audible.) An elementary problem in perception sometimes is posed here: in a large hall, for example, the environing noise has a tendency in itself to cover the dynamic level of the music. The psychological relationship with an audience, what is more, cannot be established on large dimensions unless one disposes of a sufficient margin of time and of hearing; otherwise the contact, scarcely established, is broken off and the effort to re-create a "circuit of hearing" must be made with each new piece. Whence the painful impression for the interpreter that he is not "catching on": he is not given the almost material possibility of taking his public in hand; for, another face of the problem, the great difficulty of these works is to know how to listen to them. Perhaps our Occidental tradition does not predispose us in that direction as much as is necessary; the Occident always has needed a largely explicit gesture in order to understand what is being told to it. If one compares, in the theater, the style of our actors and the style of, for example, Japanese actors or our dancers' style with that of the dancers of India, one sees immediately what I mean. Webern is an innovator, one sees, not only in the esthetic of his works, but also in the physics and gestures of the concert.

Thus Webern moved in a more and more rarefied universe; he sought a way to metamorphose his experiences, never to condemn himself to the sterility of repetition. . . .

A remarkable fact: while Webern was alive, his work provoked no noisy scandals, no marked blame such as was aroused by *Le Sacre du printemps*, *Pierrot lunaire*, and *Wozzeck*. Even at the time when his compositions were played regularly in Germany (1919–33), they were looked upon as an extremist solution without future, as a closed, isolated domain that one could ignore and need not fight—in a way, a musical Kamchatka.

It was after the Second World War, in 1945, that his work was found bringing to young musicians precisely what they found lacking in the music of the generation that had preceded them. I speak not only of musical qualities but also, it can be said, of the intellectual and moral qualities that they found in it. Webern's name has emerged from the shadow: its radiance no longer needs explanation or justification.

By now, the elements of his vocabulary, properly speaking, have been assimilated by the succeeding generation; it nonetheless remains true that his intellectual rigor, his probity, his courage, his line of conduct, his perseverance remain a unique model for contemporary musical literature.

I believe more than ever what I have already said: Webern remains the threshold of the new music. Any composer who has not deeply felt and understood the ineluctable necessity of Webern is completely futile. Perhaps Webern's music, exactly like Mallarmé's poetry, will never become as "popular" as that of some of his contemporaries. Nonetheless, it will maintain its force as example, its exceptional purity, which will always oblige music to place guidelines in relation to it, and in a much sharper fashion than in relation to any other composer.

Webern has been the master thinker of a whole generation, in posthumous revenge for the obscurity that hid his existence. As of today, he can be considered one of the greatest of all musicians, an indelible man.

(*Encyclopédie de la Musique*, 1958, 1961; translated by Herbert Weinstock.)

---

## Stravinsky's *Sacre:* The Cornerstone of Modern Music

L*e Sacre du printemps* serves as a point of reference to all who seek to establish the birth certificate of what is still called "contemporary" music. A kind of manifesto-work, somewhat in the same way and probably for the same reasons as Picasso's *Demoiselles d'Avignon*, it has not ceased to engender, first, polemics, then, praise, and, finally, the necessary clarifications. In fifty years, its presence has been felt continuously. Paradoxically, until recent years, *Le Sacre* has made its career much more as a concert piece than as a ballet; even today, despite a few resoundingly successful stagings, symphonic performances far outnumber ballet productions.

In the same way that the name of Schoenberg remains identified primarily with *Pierrot lunaire*, the name of Stravinsky remains attached to *Le Sacre du printemps*, or, I should say, to the *phenomenon* of *Le Sacre* in which both the work and the context are united. This "piece" has become (of itself and by the legend quickly spread around its creation) the cornerstone of modern music.

Even if, today, the historical landscape seems more varied and the personality of Stravinsky more complex, nothing can dilute the physical excitement provoked by the tension and the rhythmic life of certain sections: It is not difficult to imagine what amazement these sections caused in a world in which a "civilized" aesthetic often exhausted itself in dying affabilities. It was the new blood of the "barbarians," a kind of electric shock applied without tact to chlorotic organisms. In algebra, the term "simplification" is applied when the terms of an equation are reduced to a more direct expression. In this sense, *Le Sacre* may be spoken of as a *basic:* It reduces the terms of a complex language and allows a new start.

This simplified language permits the decisive recapture of a long-neglected element; from the very start, and throughout the most important episodes of *Le Sacre*, this right is aggressively claimed. Harmonic relations or melodic figures are reduced to striking formulae, extremely easy to remember; they serve to support a *rhythmic invention* the like of which Western tradition had never known before. Unquestionably, the music of Western Europe already contained the seeds of rhythmic preoccupation, especially at the outset; but in the quest for solutions in the areas of polyphony, melody and form, the role of rhythm had gradually been reduced to that of a necessary substratum, sometimes refined, based on a certain number of archetypes, or "models." Nevertheless, rhythm followed the general evolution of musical writing in the direction of subtlety, flexibility and complexity.

But with Stravinsky, the preeminence of rhythm is shown by the reduction of polyphony and harmony to subordinate functions. The extreme and most characteristic example of this new state of affairs is furnished by the "Danses des adolescentes" (Dances of the Young Girls), where *one* chord contains, literally, the entire invention. Reduced to its simplest and most summary expression (because a single chord cannot imply any functional relationship), the harmony serves as material for rhythmical elaboration which is perceived by means of accents. The orchestration helps us to hear these accents more clearly, by the "barking" of the horns above the continuity of the strings. This is how we perceive music so conceived: Before worrying about what chord we are hearing, we are sensitive to the *pulse* emitted by this chord. "Glorification de l'élue" (Glorification of the Chosen Victim) or "Danse sacrale" (Sacrificial Dance), though they present us with less simplified moments, impress us initially in the same manner; for, beyond melodic fragments (which repetition allows us to grasp so quickly as to neutralize them), what we hear is the rhythmic impulse almost in its pure state.

Stravinsky changed the direction of rhythmic impulse. Musical writing until his time relied essentially on a basic meter, within which were produced "conflicts," due to overlappings, superimpositions and displacements of rhythmic formulae attached mainly to melodic invention and to harmonic functions. There was thus a kind of order and regularity momentarily disturbed by foreign elements. With Stravinsky, and more particularly in *Le Sacre*, there exists primarily a basic pulse, felt almost physically. (Not without reason, his music is always conceived exactly in relation to a given metronome marking, a phenomenon much rarer among composers than one would think.) This basic pulse, according to a given unit, is multiplied, regularly or irregularly. Naturally, the most exciting effects are provoked by the *irregular* multiplication, for this gives a certain proportion of the "unforseeable" within a "forseeable" context.

As to the composition itself, it does not *depend* on the argument of a ballet; and that is why it has no need of any modification in passing from the theater to the concert hall. One can state that the plot of the ballet blends with the musical form into a single entity: The form of the ballet *is* its argument. This quest for coincidence between form and expression was often pursued by Stravinsky in the ensuing years; here, in *Le Sacre du printemps,* he stumbled upon the solution almost unaware, and rendered null and void the distinctions (however sterile they may be) between pure and "program" music, between music that is formal and that which is expressive.

This ritual of "Pagan Russia" attains by itself a dimension quite beyond its formal point of departure: It has become the ritual—and the myth—of modern music.

(Cleveland Orchestra Program Annotation, 1971; translated by Felix Aprahamian.)

# Struggling with Schönberg
# Scriabine the Visionary

---

## ERNEST NEWMAN

---

*Ernest Newman is regarded by many as the most literate and readable music critic in England during the first half of the twentieth century. As a young man, he wrote mainly of literary and philosophical matters, being an early advocate of Ibsen and Conrad before these writers were fashionable. As a musician, he was self-taught, yet he contributed regular music criticism to the* Manchester Guardian, *the* New York Post, *and other publications. These pieces quickly gained him a reputation for fanatic musicological accuracy combined with expansiveness of thought. Newman is best known for his advocacy of Wagner, but with this composer he had a tendency to pontificate and clear his throat on the page. It is in the lesser-known pieces that he is at his best. In the following 1914 article on Schönberg, for example, he articulates a sense of challenge and struggle that to this day is relevant for listeners trying to come to terms with this music. Schönberg will perhaps never be a "comfortable" composer—nor should he be—and Newman shows us why. As for the article on Scriabin, Newman demonstrates why this odd but compelling figure was likely to be influential in our culture. The exotic mysticism in much contemporary Western music suggests that, for better or worse, he was right.*

Arnold Schönberg—one of the advanced composers of our day who make people like Richard Strauss seem quite old-fashioned—made his first appearance in London at a Queen's Hall concert on Saturday afternoon, when he conducted a performance of his *Five Orchestral Pieces*. It may be remembered that when these works were played at a Queen's Hall promenade concert in September 1912, they seemed so destitute of meaning and so full of discords that the audience laughed audibly all through the performance, and hissed vigorously at the end—which is a very unusual thing for an English audience to do, even when it is not pleased. The management was evidently apprehensive that something of the same sort might happen again on Saturday and hurt Schönberg's feelings, for in the programme there appeared the following diplomatically worded note: "Herr Arnold Schönberg has promised his co-operation at today's concert on condition that during the performance of his Orchestral Pieces perfect silence is maintained." In other words, "Don't shoot the composer; he is doing his best." It was hardly to be expected that the audience would in any case be so rude to Schönberg to his face as it had been behind his back; but as events turned out, although there was a faint hiss or titter now and then, the music was actually applauded with some warmth. The applause was evidently not merely a matter of good nature and politeness to Schönberg himself; for though he was greeted cordially when he came on the platform, smiling and looking very much alive and alert, the first of the Five Pieces was received practically in silence, the applause commencing after the second piece and increasing to the end. It was not universal, of course, and in volume was nothing like what was lavished on Tchaikovsky's Circus—and sawdust—piano concerto in B flat minor and its performer; but it was fully evident that the audience, though often puzzled, was decidedly impressed.

It was clear, indeed, that we were now really hearing the music for the first time. Perhaps it had been better rehearsed; and of course the composer knew, as no one else could know, exactly how it ought to be made to sound. Certainly I cannot imagine a greater difference between two performances of music, and the effects of them, than there was between Saturday's performance of this Schönberg work and that fifteen months ago. Only the composer, I imagine, can show them to us as they are really meant to be. They have a new orchestral feeling and technique, to which the score is only an imperfect guide. A note prefixed by Schönberg to one of the movements—to the effect that the conductor is not to concern himself with bringing out this or that voice, that seems to him important, or to soften what seems to him discords, for all this is allowed for in the orchestration, and all the conductor has to do is to see that each player employs the precise degree of force indicated in his part—I thought at first a little

284 Struggling with Schönberg

affected. But the music, when properly given, justifies what Schönberg says of it. The various timbres are blended in the most cunning
way imaginable. Discords that on paper look unendurable and meaningless are tinted in such a way that one feels only a vague and often
most alluring effect of atmosphere and distance. This is not absolutely new, of course, in orchestral music, but Schönberg's vision of
the things to be done in this line, and his skill in doing them, go
beyond those of any other composer I know. The third piece is quite
remarkable in this respect; it does not contain a single phrase that
can be called a "theme" in the ordinary significance of that term, and
is a sort of shimmering, gently heaving sea of tone. It is impressionism pure and simple, and impressionism is bound to bulk more and
more largely in the music of the future. It will be a little hard for us to
adapt ourselves to it at first, for the very vagueness of the picture in
the composer's mind, and the absence from the music of all literary
or materialistically pictorial sign-posts, often destroy all the connecting links we have been accustomed to between the composer's imagination and ours. Others of these Five Orchestral Pieces are not
impressionistic in the same way as No. 3, though what at present
seems their lack of definite thematic working and clear outline is apt
to make us sum them all up under the same term. There is thematic
repetition in the First, but here, too, the main effect comes from the
harmonic and orchestral colour and the sense of driving energy
conveyed by the rhythmic motion.

But always we come back to the harmonic problem. What distinguishes all Schönberg's music since the Three Piano Pieces of Op. II
from his earlier work is the apparently deliberate throwing over of
the century-old distinction between consonance and dissonance.
Hitherto, though we have become more tolerant each decade of
discords that our predecessors would have winced under, they have
justified themselves to us by standing in some sort of logical relation
to a central idea of consonance. Schönberg upsets all this. He treats
dissonance as a tonal language, complete and satisfying in itself,
owing no allegiance, or even lip-service to consonance, either at the
beginning, in the middle, or at the end of the work. It is amazing how
far we can already go with him, how strangely beautiful and moving
much of this music is, that, judged by the eye alone, is a mere jumble
of discordant parts. But it is frankly impossible for the most advanced
musician to see a coherent idea running through a great deal of this

music. I do not say the coherent idea is not there, but simply that at present its coherence and its veracity are not always evident. Time alone can show whether it is our harmonic sense that thinks too slowly, or Schönberg's harmonic sense that thinks a little too rapidly for the rest of the world.

(*Birmingham Post*, 1914.)

---

## Scriabine the Visionary

With the curious ignorance of everything that goes on outside London that is so characteristic of the Londoner, the device of giving Scriabine's *Prometheus* twice at the same concert last Saturday was announced as an innovation so far as England is concerned. It is not unknown to Manchester, however, and I remember that on the occasion of the first performance of Debussy's *L'Après-midi d'un Faune* in Liverpool some years ago, the work was repeated in the second half of the concert. It is a pity, indeed, that the practice of playing big new works twice at the same concert is not more prevalent. Last week at Queen's Hall we had an interesting sidelight on the relations between the critics and the public. Concert-givers and theatrical managers pretend that the disparaging articles of the critics upon new works do more than anything to kill their chances. The critic knows that his words influence the public very slightly, if at all; if the man in the street has so much faith in the critic's judgment, he ought obviously not only to stay away from things of which the critic disapproves, but fly post haste to the things the critic admires. No amount of ridicule of musical comedy for its brainlessness and unoriginality manages to keep the public away from it; and no amount of enthusiasm over a great work of a new type suffices to inspire the public with any faith in it. On Saturday the public gave itself away; probably not more than half of the people who heard the first performance of *Prometheus* remained for the second. They went out with their noses in the air and a look of outraged virtue—and this before a single critic had delivered himself of a judgment on the work!

One could foresee that *Prometheus* would be a poser to the plain music lover, whose education has stopped short at Wagner and

Strauss. But in truth it is often a difficult problem even for those of us who believe that music can no more cease its evolution with Wagner and Strauss than with Bach and Beethoven, and who keep our ear always astrain for any authentic new note that may be borne to us on the wind. It is absurd for any of us to dogmatize about a work that aims at carrying the idiom and the vision of music to a point as far beyond Strauss as Strauss is beyond Tchaikovsky; the more confidently any critic tries to sweep it off the board as the mere effusion of a musical lunatic, the more certainly he writes himself down as a superficial duffer, intrepidly denying the existence of things simply because he cannot see them. I do not contend that everything in *Prometheus* is clear even at a second hearing, or that there may not be a good deal in it to which no number of hearings would reconcile us. But I do urge that to a listener with an imagination it mostly talks in a perfectly lucid language of things that have never been expressed in music before.

The linking of Scriabine's name with that of Schönberg is a gratuitous error. Schönberg is really a better composer than his music would sometimes lead us to imagine; but his style is to some extent obviously a calculated one. It is the idiom of a man who was consciously determined from the first that however he might write, he would not write like other composers. Scriabine has developed as naturally as Beethoven or Wagner or Strauss, beginning, as they did, with his roots in the past, and gradually evolving a highly individual style of his own as his whole personality developed. Whatever may be thought of his later style, there is no affectation in it on the musical side, and there is no fumbling. What struck some of us in the *Prometheus* was the almost infallible certainty of the adaptation of the means to the end throughout; only a composer who is at once master of his ideas and of his technique can work so surely as this. Whether, however, the brain as a whole is evolving harmoniously, whether it may not be developing a strain of excessive idealism, losing itself somewhat in the void of the thought that lies in the far beyond of the other side of music, and failing to see its vision not merely with theosophical but with musical clearness, failing to find the firm enclosing line that alone can make the vision as real to us as it is to him—on these points one cannot be wholly sure.

The truth probably is that certain parts of *Prometheus*—as of still later works of Scriabine such as the recently published pianoforte sonata—will never be quite clear to us because they were never quite clear to the composer, either because he has not thought his way exactly enough through the subtleties he is envisaging, or because music's means of expression are not yet equal to the task he imposes on them. I cheerfully present these parts of *Prometheus* to the ordinary objector to the work, for him to make what capital he likes out of them. But to the rest—and that much the greater part—I firmly pin my faith. *Prometheus* is the one work I have ever heard that seems to me to approach the new territory that music will some day make its own. It is in essence the most immaterial of the arts; but circumstances have forced it to develop so far upon more or less material lines. It first of all had to win for itself, by means of rather rigid rhythms and formal designs, the faculty of coherent thinking upon a large scale. Then the purely human impulse surged up within it, and—mainly under Wagner—substituted for the set design the modelling of the tissue of music upon the forms and vicissitudes of the emotions themselves. But music of this kind needed an obvious and detailed "poetic purpose"—the plot of the opera or the story of the symphonic poem—just as much as the older music needed the material scaffolding of sonata or fugue. Clearly music will be able to dispense with even this "poetic" support in the future, and yet speak to us quite plainly of mysteries as far surpassing the operatic or symphonic-poem subject in subtlety and remoteness as music in general surpasses words in general; it is all a matter of how lucidly and logically a composer can think in this tenuous atmosphere, what body he can give to his visions, and how far we can think and see along with him. A rough analogy to this progress of music to immaterialities ever more and more refined may be had in the theories men have held upon matter. To the first philosophers, matter was solid substance; to the later ones, a bundle of atoms; to those still later, a play of electrons. Always the immaterial mystery encroaches upon the material fact, or upon the mystery a shade more material.

It is surely evident that the true home of music is among these ultimate immaterialities of thought, because it is the only one of the arts that can ever hope to express them. That home it will one day win. To my mind we have nowhere come so near to it as in the best of this music of Scriabine's. I care nothing for the theosophy that is tacked on to it by the composer and the annotators, and think that this is as likely as not to confuse or prejudice the hearer. But listening to it solely as music, only a congenitally unimaginative dullard, I fancy, or a musician sodden with the futile teaching of the text-books and the Conservatoires, could help feeling that here is music that comes as near as is at present possible to being the pure voice of Nature and the soul themselves. One needs no programme note to have the picture flashed upon one's brain of the soul of man slowly yearning into conscious being out of a primal undifferentiated world, torn by the conflict of emotions, violently purging itself of its grossnesses, and ultimately winning its way to the light.

And all this is done, not on the familiar "poetic" lines of the symphonic poem, but a stage further behind the veil, as it were; the wind that blows through the music is not the current stage and concert room formula, but the veritable wind of the cosmos itself; the cries of desire and passion and ecstasy are a sort of quintessential sublimation of all the yearning, not merely of humanity, but of all nature, animate and inanimate. No amount of criticism of the work in details can diminish the wonder of such an achievement as this. Its thematic texture may not always be distinguished, and the piano part may, as I believe, be mostly an error; but the fact remains that here is an imagination of extra-ordinary subtlety and scope, and a most remarkable faculty of musical expression. The only fear is lest the theosophist in Scriabine should overpower the artist in him.

(*Nation*, 1913.)

# Sibelius and the Music of the Future

## CONSTANT LAMBERT

*This Sibelius essay from the 1930s by British composer Constant Lambert (the culminating section of his delightful book* Music Ho!*) is the rare example of a sweeping judgment made about a living composer that turns out years later to be right on the money. Sibelius has always been the most difficult modern composer to classify and evaluate—he is regularly "revived" and dumped by the musical intelligentsia—yet Lambert puts him into exact and enduring perspective. Indeed, since Sibelius never composed another major work after this article was written (a thirty-year dry spell), the essay has a positively eerie exactitude. It is a portrait instantly and forever frozen in time; except for a few contemporary references, it could have been written yesterday. As this excerpt demonstrates, Lambert, who was Cecil Gray's colleague on the* Sackbutt *(see headnote on Cecil Gray) was both an erudite and wonderfully entertaining writer. The* New Grove *speaks accurately of his "almost insolent ease of writing and width of reference."*

Sibelius differs from all the other composers in this study in that it is impossible to attach any "label" to him. He is the only composer of today who enjoys both a popular and an intellectual esteem. His *Valse Triste* is as widely known and as vulgarized as anything by Puccini, yet his Fourth Symphony is as little known and as little comprehended as the work of Schönberg. Although already established as an important figure by the end of the nineteenth century, he does not strike us as belonging to the older generation of Elgar and Strauss. On the contrary, he is the only modern composer who has maintained a steady and logical progress, being forced neither into a mechanical repetition of his own mannerisms nor into an equally mechanical reaction against them. It is only recently indeed that he has been estimated at anything like his true worth. . . .

The great revolutionary figures of before the war, Debussy, Stravinsky, Schönberg and Bartók turned their back on the symphony and all that it stood for, and a pre-war critic, ignorant of Sibelius' work, might pardonably have thought that the symphony was as outmoded and antediluvian as the horse bus.

In Sibelius, however, we have the first great composer since Beethoven whose mind thinks naturally in terms of symphonic form. Coming at the end of the romantic movement, he is as far removed from the apex of the romantic past as Beethoven was from its future. His symphonies, then, though subjective in mood, are free from the tautological emotional repetitions of romantic music cast in the classic mould. Though their grim colouring clearly owes much to the composer's nationality and surroundings there is nothing in them that can be considered a folk song. Therefore, without being eclectic they address an international audience and are free from the conflict between local colour and construction which is to be observed in the Russian school. Finally, Sibelius is the one important figure of our times who has been uninfluenced by the Impressionist revolution— even *The Oceanides* though pointillist in orchestration and superficially Impressionist in form reveals on close analysis a construction as firmly knit as any of the symphonies. He has concentrated on the integration of form and has not wasted his energies on the disintegration of colour.

This formal strength explains why, unlike all other composers who belong equally to the pre-war and post-war periods of modern music, Sibelius' work does not split itself into two periods, and shows no sign of the definite reaction that we associate with the last ten years. One soon reaches the end to the possible dissection of technique and elaboration of vocabulary. This end was reached for all practical purposes in 1913, and since then the revolutionary composers having pulled the clock to pieces and being mentally incapable of putting it together again have taken to arranging the wheels and levers in neat little patterns.

Formalism is only the complementary reaction to formlessness, and montage follows naturally enough on disruption. But a sense of musical form, the power not only to arrange sounds tastefully but to think in them vitally, is a living and generative force which reaches no such dead end, and Sibelius' symphonies in consequence show a steady and logical process both formally and emotionally. The Olympian calm of *No. 7* may seem in contrast to the bitter and tragic quality of *No. 4* but technically speaking it is the logical result of the process of concentration and integration that is to be observed from the second symphony onwards. . . .

The first symphony hardly comes into a book on contemporary music. This opulently scored and virile work is the final flowering of the later nineteenth-century symphony, and though an excellent example of its genre it is constructed for the most part on recognized lines. Not until the second symphony are we faced with Sibelius's highly individual method of formal construction. The first movement of Sibelius's *No. 2* differs from any previous symphonic movement in that its undoubted continuity and formal balance are not established until the last bars. The exposition of a Beethoven symphony is by no means a complete statement, but it is logical enough as far as it goes. The exposition of this particular movement, a string of apparently loosely knit episodes, is completely incomprehensible at a first hearing, and it is only towards the end of the development and in the curiously telescoped recapitulation that the full significance of the opening begins to be apparent. Instead of being presented with a fait accompli of a theme that is then analysed and developed in fragments, we are presented with several enigmatic fragments that only become a fait accompli on the final page. It is like watching a sculptured head being built up from the armature with little pellets of clay or, to put it more vulgarly, it is like a detective story in which the reader does not know until the final chapter whether the blotting paper or the ashtray throws more light on the discovery of the corpse in the library. . . .

Sibelius has always been a figure apart from the rest of modern music. The lack of revolutionary vocabulary in his music has in the past led superficial critics to believe that he was apart through being behind the times. Now that the smoke of bombs and gunfire has cleared away we can see that his solitary position is really due to his having been in advance of the anarchists. Although, chronologically speaking, of the same generation as Strauss and Elgar, he is of all living composers the most interesting and stimulating to the post-war generation. . . .

Of all contemporary music that of Sibelius seems to point forward most surely to the future. Since the death of Debussy, Sibelius and Schönberg are the most significant figures in European music, and Sibelius is undoubtedly the more complete artist of the two. However much one may admire Schönberg's powerful imagination and unique genius, it is difficult not to feel that the world of sound and thought that he opens up—though apparently iconoclastic—is *au fond* as restricted as the academicism it has supplanted. Sibelius' music suffers from no such restriction, and it indicates not a particular avenue of escape but a world of thought which is free from the paralysing alternatives of escape or submission. It offers no material for the plagiarist, and is to be considered more as a spiritual example than as a technical influence. We are not likely to find any imitations of Sibelius' *No. 7*, such as we find of Stravinsky's *Symphonie des Psaumes,* because the spiritual calm of this work is the climax of the spiritual experience of a lifetime and cannot be achieved by any aping of external mannerisms.

Sibelius has had no direct influence on his generation, but if we compare the recent work of the revolutionary composers—Bartók's second Piano Concerto and Schönberg's *Orchestral Variations* for example—with that of ten years ago we can see that it represents an approach to the spirit of integration and artistic completeness that has always characterized his music. . . .

There is nothing in music which has really lost its meaning, no device of rhythm, no harmonic combination which the composer of vision cannot reanimate.

The music of the future, if it is to avoid the many psychological cul-de-sacs which have been examined in this volume, must inevitably be directed towards a new angle of vision rather than to the exploitation of a new vocabulary. This music will not be outwardly sensational, and though at times it may seem extremely unusual it will not be of the type that can be labelled "the new This" or "the new That." It will not truckle to topicality by pretending to be inspired by sporting events or by the opening of a wireless station, nor will it lose itself in a dream world of forgotten loves and vanished days. It is highly unlikely that it will be popular. But then we cannot pretend that the best music of any time was at all popular in the genuine sense of the word. Sibelius, it is true, has a popular following today but, like that of Beethoven, it is mainly a tribute to his worst works. His fourth symphony is as unappreciated now as were the later sonatas and quartets of Beethoven in their day. Nevertheless, just as the later quartets of Beethoven have influenced modern thought far more than the fashionable works of Hummel and Czerny, so will the symphonies of Sibelius have a more profound influence on future generations than the pieces d'occasion of his contemporaries. . . .

    (*Music Ho!* 1934.)

# Ives the Master

## GUY DAVENPORT

*Charles Ives, America's first great composer, inspired good prose by a number of other American composers, including several in this book (Leonard Bernstein, Aaron Copland, Virgil Thomson, Nicholas Slonimsky). Given Ives's innovativeness, influence, and uncompromising Americanness, this phenomenon is not surprising. What is not as celebrated is that Ives, far from being a remote, oddball figure, was part of a larger modernist stream in all the arts, a dimension that is captured by short story writer Guy Davenport, in language as crusty and powerful as Ives's own. Like his subject, Davenport is a master collagist, and thus an ideal commentator on Ives's uniquely disorienting sound world. He also writes with bitter eloquence on a broader subject of continuing relevance—America's neglect of its own best art and artists.*

At the end of Charles Ives' centennial year *The New York Times Book Review* devoted its December 1st issue to the important books of 1974. That it did not mention, either under Significant or Notable or Music or any rubric at all, David Wooldridge's *From the Steeples and Mountains: A Study of Charles Ives* (Knopf, $10.00) is an oversight (it probably wasn't an oversight, but out of courtesy to the Republic's most distinguished journal of literature we will take it as an oversight) comparable to omitting Lincoln from a list of the presidents. The *Times,* indeed, was in fashion in pretending that Mr. Wooldridge's book does not exist; the reviewers slept through its publication, and its publishers are under the impression that they have published a flop. They have, on the contrary, published the only book on Ives worthy of its subject, the first thorough study of Ives' music, the first biography of our greatest composer.

A hundred years ago last October 20th—on Rimbaud's twentieth birthday and while *Un Saison en Enfer* was going through the press of Poot et Cie. in Brussels—Charles Ives was born in Danbury, Connecticut. Naturally the site is now a parking lot; naturally the parking lot is owned by a bank. His country, whose greatest composer he was, and among its most distinguished patriots, issued no commemorative postage stamp, erected no monument, set no plaque, commanded no orchestra to play his music.

True, it was a year in which the country had to turn out a pack of scoundrels, porch climbers, thieves, bullies, liars, and bores from the Executive Branch of the government, a year in which the sludge of usury which forms the basis of our economy began to slither and lurch, a year indistinguishable from any other in the national contempt of the arts.*

Ives would not have been shocked. The government was simply living up to his opinion of politicians. He was born in the administration of Grant. He had his first heart attack after shouting at Franklin Roosevelt a principle of democracy which Roosevelt couldn't understand. He wanted to amend the Constitution so that two thirds of the states had to ratify a declaration of war. Ten years after his death we were capable of getting into a war that cost a million dollars a day and fifty thousand American lives without anybody in the government being able to say just how we got into war.

Perversely he read the London *Times* to find out the news. He did not listen to the radio, paid scant attention to books. He got through a long life without reading Robert Frost; he looked into Gertrude Stein and called her a Victorian. Like Pound, his junior by eleven years, he considered Browning to be the great modern poet, and wrote a handsome, majestic overture in his honor—in twelve-tone rows, a dozen years before Schoenberg invented them.

His creative life occupies only nineteen years, 1898 to 1917, of his seventy-nine. In that intense period, Mr. Wooldridge shows, with a depth of biographical detail and sharpness of critical attention, that Ives "wrote more music, of greater stature, than most composers in a lifetime."

By this time all literate people know the strange history of that

---

*The O. Henry Centennial was similarly denied a commemorative stamp, though not by the Union of Soviet Socialist Republics.

music, how Ives' reticence would have kept it from being played at all, how Nicolas Slonimsky played it in Boston, San Francisco, Paris; how German musicologists complained that it hurt their ears; how small groups heard some of the string works and songs; how John Kirkpatrick began his long task of teaching audiences to hear the *Concord Sonata* in Spartanburg, South Carolina, where a large cement apple sits on a pedestal in the Square. And Mr. Wooldridge has uncovered evidence that Mahler played the *Third Symphony* in Munich in 1910! . . .

Did Mann hear about Ives from Schoenberg and conceive of his *Doktor Faustus* then and there? Faustus is a rich composite, an allegory of the German spirit, but we still have to account for descriptions of imaginary music corresponding so eerily to the *Fourth Symphony*. Hearsay is a powerful instigation to the creative mind. What a symbol it would make, and what a closing of the circle: Goethe, Transcendentalism, Ives, Mann, Goethe.

June 1863: a bandmaster in shako and sash snaps out the cake-walk rhythms of "Dixie" while Lee rides ahead of the flags across the Mason and Dixon Line. The troops shout a great *Huzzah!* It is a moment: *iacta alea est.* Military music haunted Ives all of his career; it was the tangible memory of his father, it was an art that strangely went to war, where its presence was as right and congenial as singing in church. "When the cannonade was at its height," Col. Fremantle wrote in his account of Gettysburg, "a Confederate band of music, between the cemetery and ourselves, began to play polkas and waltzes, which sounded very curious, accompanied by the hissing and bursting of the shells." Before the line of tanks at El Alamein marched a line of highland pipers, Custer rode into Little Big Horn to "The Girl I Left Behind Me," Raleigh sailed into Cadiz harbor, *played an insulting fanfarol on the trumpet,* and sailed out again; the redcoats at Yorktown laid down their muskets, company by company, to a jig called "The World Turned Upsidedown"; D'Annunzio rode into Fiume at the head of his army of veteran *garibaldini* and Boy Scouts preceded by a symphony orchestra playing Verdi. Music is what the Ogboni call "words of power." It is both a spirit and a summoner of spirit; woe to those who trivialize words of power.

One way of beginning to hear Ives is to listen to how he summons spirits: his martial music incorporates the chains of the caissons, the rattle of gear, distant bugles, tolling bells of churchs near the battle. When he summons various songs and noises all at once, he is working the synergy of heightened quotation: the same effect Borges savors when he has a character drench himself in Cervantes' psychology and style until, after a lifetime of trying, he can write a page of the *Quixote.* The page is identical with one of Cervantes', but "much richer." The lines Eliot appropriates for *The Waste Land,* Pound for *The Cantos,* Wordsworth for *The Prelude* operate in this way. It is one of the century's modes. As value inheres in money alone, the arts shore up against their ruin.

Ives always quotes with perfect love and perfect contempt.

Ives has remained in classic American obscurity because:
He is ironic.
He is comic, satiric, lyric, contentious all at once.
His music is a matter of ideas.
Practically every composition is in a new form.
He despised music which beguiles, overpowers, or exists for itself: and this is our sole conception of music. It is practically impossible to discover people listening to music. We have it everywhere, dribbling, droning, booming. We converse to it, drive to it, wait to it, have our teeth drilled to it. It is simply another narcotic. A person who assumes a predilection for music finds himself dumbfounded before Ives, where listening is required. Conversely people who use music for sensual pleasure find Ives flat and unmoving. I see an analogy in Browning, where you have to keep awake line by line; you can't read him, as people manage to read Keats or Tennyson, "for the beauty of it."

The first American composer and the last great composer in the western tradition that descends from Bach, Ives is in the unique position of being a great inventor who ends rather than begins a series. He is therefore like R. Buckminster Fuller, fellow Transcendentalist and spiritual twin: their content goes back to archaic beginnings, their methods are profound inventions. Both have been repeatedly dismissed as cranks, though success thorough and indisputable vindicates their every venture. You can't argue with a geodesic dome or deny that Ives' *Fourth Symphony* is not as majestic as the Old Testament.

Ives aligns with the most significant art of his time: with Pound and Eliot in the reuse of extant compositions (Mann again, in ascribing to Leverkühn as to his own narrative prose the mode of exposition by serious parody as *the* mode of the Twentieth Century), with Joyce in the hermetic diffusion of symbolism throughout a work, with Picasso in exploring the possibilities of extending forms and techniques.

But practically all of Ives is like nothing else. There is beneath every passage a grasp of vision completely Ives'. I hear in it a lifelong grief for all that is tragic in our history: the caissons going into place at Shiloh, Foster's taking up the Abolitionist Cause in his songs, the primal force of music as a word of power (the black regiment that marched through a burning Richmond singing "The Day of Jubilo," the bagpipers who led the tank attack at El Alamein, the band that played "Nearer My God to Thee" as the *Lusitania* went down). Music, we are told, was born from tragedy; nearly all of Ives' grand themes allude to tragedies, particularly to that of the Civil War, and to his father's role in it as a musician.

The surface of Ives' music is music, just as the surface of Joyce's *Ulysses* is a tissue of clichés in one convention or another. Pound's *Cantos* was to have been an unbroken surface of voices from the past until at Pisa in the cage the design broke and the poet spoke in his own voice and in expectation of death before a firing squad.

Collage is retrospective in content, modern in its design. Kept up, it will recapitulate and summarize the history of its own being. One can go through Ives noting the voices (the Alcotts trying to speak Beethoven and Culture from Europe, Thoreau speaking through a hymn played on his flute against the voice of his woods, Fourth of July Bands speaking with a martial air beside the voice of Ragtime; Browning, Arnold, Whitman). Ives got as far as Isaiah asking *What is Man?* in the *Fourth Symphony*. History answers in the spiritual articulation of music, and finally a chorus of unidentifiable voices answers, in inarticulate words.

(*Parnassus*, Spring/Summer 1975.)

# Notes on Ravel

## NED ROREM

*A prolific and distinguished composer of songs and instrumental works, Ned Rorem is nevertheless likely to be remembered as much for his nonfiction writing as for his music. Since the 1960s, Rorem has been delighting and scandalizing readers with his gossipy, deliciously readable* Diaries *from Paris, New York, and other loci in the barely hidden world of politics and sexual aggrandizement that underlies the musical life as much as any other. Rorem's essays on music, contributed over the years to the* New York Review of Books *and other publications, resemble the* Diaries *in their chatty, feisty informality. They also display a high level of insight and originality, especially when the topic is twentieth-century music. Rorem simply sees things differently than anyone else and indulges in a degree of metaphorical risk-taking that few dare attempt. His article on Ravel— the composer who, against all expectations, has emerged as the most popular "serious" composer of this century—is both deeply personal and rigorously objective.*

Of those composers I most love, Ravel is the single one through whose sound I feel the man himself. The feeling can rise straight from a harmony hit in passing, evoking within a split second the vastly nonabstract realm of Paris before I was born: my heart beats in a *salon faubourien* during conversation with an artist I never met in a time that is not, and real tears well up for the unknown which is hyper-familiar. Time and again this happens as I'm seated at the piano playing Ravel, or hearing him in a concert hall. No other composer pulls quite the same trick.

A century ago (on the hundredth anniversary of Jane Austen's birth) Ravel was born of solvent and understanding parents in the village of Ciboure near the Spanish frontier. These few facts color all that he became. His art straddled the border as it straddled centuries, being in texture as opulent as a tourist's notion of Iberia, in shape as pristine as Rameau, in intent no less modern than ragas or group therapy, and in subject matter mostly antiromantic. Listen again to *Bolero*. ("It's my masterpiece," said the composer. "Unfortunately it contains no music.") French logic drenched in Basque mystery.

Mysterious for its lack of mystery was his worldly life: he didn't read much, didn't carouse, had avuncular crushes and a juvenile taste for enamel toys, heavy spices, mother figures, Siamese cats. Beneath garish shirts lay bland discretion.

But the unknown is good press. (Which is why a Maurice Sachs, dilettantish and mediocre, still holds the boards in France: his death was a publicized enigma, like Poe's, Lorca's, Desnos'.) The two most frequent questions on Ravel: Was he Jewish? Was he homosexual? (One assumes he couldn't be both.) Nobody knows so everyone cares. Beyond this—and beyond the details of his long, sad agony—the man was less absorbing than the artist. But the artist's method has been finely documented. What to add? This musician, who over the years brought me more than any other, now leaves me at a loss. What we love we long to share but need to hoard.

What we learn as children we question without question. That Ravel's music was standoffish, elegant, well made and casual I took as fact like the Oedipus complex or Eliot's genius, wondering uneasily why that special sound entered me like a heady draft of carnality throttling my Quaker frame to dwell on love and the pursuit of happiness.

It was the summer of 1936 that I first heard him, on the anti-macassared upright in Oberlin. While kohlrabi fumes floated from the pantry, my cousin Kathleen performed the *Sonatine*, which awakened me forever. Thinking the composer's name was Reville, I could locate no more of his music.

By 1937 I knew the spelling plus every work on record. I'd even begun composing a bit of Ravel myself.

On December 28, a Tuesday brimming with sunshine, Father (I still picture him there on the sofa) read aloud from the Chicago

*Tribune:* "French Composer Dies." (His name didn't yet merit a head-line.) Gershwin had gone that summer. Now this. Moved, I sat down and played the *Pavane.* "How obvious," snorted a fourteen-year-old pal when I told him later.

Like Minerva he emerged full-blown. Like Chopin he did not "ad-vance," have periods, grow more complex. He entered the world with the true artist's faculty for self-appraisal, and all his life wrote the same kind of music, consistently good. Goodness accounts, as with Chopin, for a proportionately short catalogue. Virginity ac-counts, as with Minerva, for concern about fertility through craft.

   Unlike Chopin he was no contrapuntalist. His canonic forays are abortive: those thousand examples of balanced clean lines are not counterpoints but harmonic shorthand. That fugue in *Le Tombeau de Couperin* is idiosyncratic.

A nation's music resembles its language in all respects, and since French is the only European tongue with no rhythm (no tonic ac-cent), any metricalization of a French phrase in music can be con-strued as correct. Lacking natural pulse, all French music becomes impressionist. French composers when they opt for rhythm exploit it squarely, like children. The spell of *Bolero* resides in its nonvariety, its contrast to Gallic speech which inherently rejects hypnosis, as op-posed to American speech which like jazz is pure monotony. (Not for nothing was hypnosis first documented by a Frenchman, Charcot. Where rhythm is a stranger, rhythm is a prophet.)

   *Bolero* has nothing to do with French music, yet only a French-man could have composed it.

Ravel's signatures are harmony and tune. His melodies are based on, and emerge from, chords. His identity (like Puccini's) lies in long line.

Melody is horizontal. No matter how brief or fragmental, melody necessarily unfolds, and so is experienced in time. Like sex and food, melody can be enjoyed in the Now. We react to a tune as it happens, although (unlike sex and food) we cannot judge the tune until it is over, whether the tune is three notes of Webern or three pages of liturgical chant.

   Harmony is vertical. Harmony too may exist in time (a single chord may be indefinitely sustained), although that is not its defining signal. (A shifting series or progression of chords is just that: chords, not *chord*—harmonies, not harmony.) Of course, a progression of simultaneous tunes—counterpoint, as it's named—produces at all moments harmony, that is, vertical noises that result from (but aren't specifically the purpose of) the juxtaposition of moving lines; but these moments are actually points in space rather than in time: no sooner sounded than they perish, or are retained like antimatter only in memory, in the past, while melody is experienced solely in the present, like a movie.

Debussy never, not once, even for violins, composed extended melody. His vocal writing, though tuneful, is glorified recitative, while the occasional *grande ligne* hints in his orchestral work are either cut short in mid-orgasm or exhaust themselves too soon for logic. (That brief outburst in *Iberia*'s middle movement brings no "expected" relief, merely dribbles off.) Such Debussyan tunes as are lengthy, like the vast ending of *La Mer* or in the soaring *Etudes*, are additive: literal repetitions piled up like pancakes.

Not that he couldn't melodize, but he had other fish to fry. The music of Debussy, that famed roué, leads somewhere, but not to sex. The music of Ravel, that presumed abstainer, usually emulates bodily fulfillment.

We know of Debussy's love-hate of Wagner. But how did a non-linear type like him react to such limitless ropes of silk as Ravel wove for his dragonfly fiddles in *L'Enfant et les sortilèges*, or to the endless opening theme of *Daphnis et Chloé*, or to that unbroken languor of the solo flute? Do we admire in others what we too can do, or what we cannot?

Ravel and Debussy each had a strong personality and so were inimitable; but they were contemporaries, after all, bearing the same age relationship as Liszt to Franck, or as Copland to Barber. (Satie, whom we think of as Papa, actually lay between them like Lucky Pierre.) Once we agree it's unfair to compare them, it's fun to compare them.

Their color is abundant and varied, but always pure. The difference between French and German orchestration is that the former uses no doubling. Reinforcement, yes; but where in Strauss a string tune is thickened with winds or brass, in Ravel the fat is skimmed off and held in abeyance. This makes for what is known as *transparent* instrumentation—a sound paradoxically opulent and lean. By extension the sound applies to his piano solo and vocal works. Sumptuous bones.

Another unchallenged *donnée:* Ravel's taste, the good taste—*son goût exquis*—which we accept at face value along with his "sophisticated" wit.

What *is* taste (or wit, for that matter) in music? For programmatic pieces it can be defined, but can the definition be extended (like the orchestral transparency of his piano works) to abstract pieces?

If taste means decorum, boundary, *mesure,* then Ravel's jeweled box holds jewels, Debussy's jeweled box holds a heart. But to a Mahler that heart is candy, to a Puccini it's gall.

Yes, he had taste. Like all Frenchmen Ravel was blinded by Poe, whose essay *The Philosophy of Composition* influenced him (he claimed) more than any music; yet he never actually envisaged setting Poe's fiction, as Debussy had planned with the "Fall of the House of Usher." Like all Frenchmen Ravel was approached by the gaudy Ida Rubinstein, whose spoken voice (that least musical of instruments, in contrast to the singing voice) was the requisite solo for the works she commissioned; yet he never succumbed to using that voice, as Debussy did in his *Martyre.*

Alone, subject matter determines taste in music. (Music without subject matter cannot be argued as tasteful or tasteless, there are no criteria.) Murder, war, and amorous passion being the texts for nine-tenths of lyric theater, and such texts being beyond taste, most opera is tasteless. Again, Ravel was tasteful there: his sonorous stories never grazed grown-up matters except in parody (licentious doings in *L'Heure espagnole*) or from a safe distance (slave revolt in *Chansons madécasses*). Otherwise he stayed close to home, which is to say close to the nonsexual side of Colette. Nor did he ever, save for a brief minute in the early song *Sainte* on a poem of Mallarmé, musicalize even a quasi-religious verse: the gods forbid such breech of taste.

Yet who does not forget himself at *L'Enfant et les sortilèges?* Colette's very stage directions are high poetry, and contribute to making this my single most preferred work of the century. Why? Because despite its length the quality of inspiration remains appropriately fevered while exploiting (no less adroitly than Bach's passions and Wagner's dramas do) each aspect of orchestral, and vocal expertise, both solo and choral.

(Ravel and Colette, as inevitable a pair as Gilbert and Sullivan, scarcely knew each other.)

How unfair to accuse him of taste! To hear *Daphnis et Chloé* is to hear great art (despite the hideous heavenly choirs, so copied by sound tracks that we hear the original now as a copy), but to see the score is to blush. Each "telling" tune illustrates a mawkish stage direction: the violas pose a question to which the shepherd opens his arms, the harp sweeps upward as the lovers reunite, etc.—what we call Mickey-mousing. . . .

His influence on others? On Poulenc it is obvious, though no one ever points out the harmonic progression of three chords in Ravel's *L'Indifférent* (1905) pilfered intact fifty years later to form the motto of Poulenc's *Carmélite* opera. More interestingly, no one ever points out the cadenza for two clarinets in Ravel's *Rapsodie espagnole* (1908) pilfered intact three years later to form the motto for Stravinsky's *Petrouchka* ballet. That bitonal *Petrouchka* sound outlined Stravinsky's harmony for the next decade, and by extension most Western music for the next half-century, yet the sound demonstrably stems from a few casual bars in the French musician's pseudo-Spanish idiom.

He evolutionized keyboard virtuosity more than anyone since Liszt, yet his complete solo piano works fit comfortably into one evening's program.

In his sixty-two years, Ravel, who worked constantly, didn't turn out more than eight hours' worth of music, as contrasted to Debussy's sixteen, Beethoven's thirty, Wagner's fifty, Bach's seventy, Ives's two thousand or Webern's two. Of those eight hours none is slipshod or routine. Not that he was a miniaturist; he was a perfectionist. So was Bach a perfectionist—different times, different mores—but a page of Ravel orchestration is twenty times busier than a page of Bach's. (Still, since Stravinsky was twice as busy as Ravel, yet twice as prolific, we draw no conclusions.)

He was a classicist, yes, sometimes, in those square-structured suites, concertos and pastiches with their recapitulations and so-called symmetrical melodies. (Symmetrical is a poor word, since time cannot have symmetry.) But so many other pieces are truly impressionist—all of *Gaspard de la nuit,* most of *Miroirs,* many of the straight orchestra numbers (though none of the thirty-three songs, curiously, since songs, being based on words, are by definition musically free). Such pieces are not so much heard as overheard, come upon, already transpiring before they start, evanescent. Made solely of middles, without beginnings or ends, they emerge from nowhere, from a mist, trouble us for a dazzling while, then without notice vanish like Scarbo, fade like Ondine. Any of these sparklers could be convincing shorter or convincing longer for they have been spinning always, and will always continue, though within human earshot only for those fugitive minutes. . . .

Even without his music the thought of him makes me feel good.

Nobody dislikes Ravel, and nobody disapproves. Can that be said of any other musician?

(*Commentary,* May 1975.)

# Varèse, Skyscraper Mystic

## PAUL ROSENFELD

*Paul Rosenfeld, in the words of Aaron Copland, was "first a music- lover, and second a music critic. . . . For once a critic completely involved himself in the music he was criticizing." In contrast to the alienating aloofness of many twentieth-century American music critics, especially in regard to music of their own age, Rosenfeld has a participatory approach that thrusts the reader into the center of the music. His style spares no adjectives or analogies when evoking the sensual qualities of a piece and connecting them to larger ideas. His vice, overwriting, is inextricably linked with his largeness of sensibility and his peculiarly visceral mode of insight. Although Rosenfeld was perfectly at home in old music (see "Bach the Colorist"), his specialty was the music of his contemporaries. In his early pieces for the* Dial, *the* Nation *and the* New Republic, *as well as in his later books, he championed the music first of Debussy and Ravel, later of American pioneers such as Ives, Ruggles, Copland, Sessions, and others long before their merit was widely recognized. For Rosenfeld, the ultimate American composer was French émigré Edgard Varèse, who not only made America his home but forged a fiercely uncompromising "New World" art. Verèse's thunderous "sound masses" find an ideal verbal complement in Rosenfeld's splendidly over- heated prose.*

The production of a piece such as [Varèse's] *Ionization* was indu-
bitably in the evolutionary order of things, predestined both by
the direction of Varèse's own development and by the development of musical feeling and musical resources during the last century and a half. Since Mozart, indeed, composers have almost stead-

ily been exhibiting an increasing sensitivity toward and an increasing appreciation of the musical possibilities of percussion and exploiting them ever more frequently and weightily. The romanticists laid ever larger quantities of pulsatile instruments under contribution. They associated snare and bass drums with the regular tympani and introduced xylophones, tom-toms, gongs, and bells of various kinds into the classic orchestra, steadily augmenting the once minute percussion choir in a ratio greater than the choirs of strings, woodwinds, and brasses, till at last it became the equal of the other three. The motive of this exploitation was first of all a desire for color. It was the desire for oriental and barbaric color that impelled some of the French and Russian composers to multiply the number of drums in their orchestra. It was also the desire for realistic effects: for this reason, Mahler introduced cowbells into his Sixth Symphony and Strauss whips into the orchestra of *Elektra.* Again, the motive for the augmentation of the percussion choir was the desire for dynamic expansion that culminated in the titanic ensembles of Mahler and Strauss, Holst, the younger Schoenberg, and Varèse. . . .

The feeling actually determinative of the general assault on the battery was, to begin with, primitivistic. An aftercrop of late romantic "barbarism," born both of the divided culture-being's yearning for the unindividualized, will-less condition of unity with nature which the European associates with the state of pre-Christian barbarian or African life, and of the threatening eruption of raw forces which culture subordinates or sublimates, it engendered dreams and ideas and pictures of Scythian and Negro worlds that, for reason of the excessive, subhuman indeterminacy of the sounds of percussive instruments, naturally found expression through frenetic and monotonous rhythms of the pulsatiles. Another source of the feeling making for the predominance of the battery lay in the astringent quality of life itself, creating an unlyrical disposition in composers as in other artists, a natural aversion from the more excessively vibratory and humanly singing instruments toward the both more brutishly and more mechanistically expressive ones. Still another is to be found in what may be termed "skyscraper mysticism." This is a feeling of the unity of life through the forms and expressions of industrial civilization, its fierce lights, piercing noises, compact and synthetic textures: a feeling of its immense tension, dynamism, ferocity, and also its fabulous delicacy and precision, that impels artists to communicate it through the portions of their mediums most sympathetic to it, and through forms partly imitative of those which excite their intuitions.

Varèse in particular among composers would seem to be subject to this feeling: he is somewhat the mystic of the sounds of sirens, horns, gongs, and whistles afloat in the air of the great industrial centers, in the sense in which Picasso is that of the city landscape with its house-wall, billboard, newspaper textures; and the pre-war Stravinsky, of the machine and its rhythms. That the other feelings, the primitivistic, the unlyrical, are also his, is not to be doubted: the first of his important compositions, *Amériques,* has affiliations with the extremely primitivistic *Sacre;* and, excessively austere, his music as a whole is almost bare of cantilena-like passages. But, himself one of the surviving members of the Guillaume Apollinaire group moved almost as a whole by the skyscraper mysticism, Varèse has pretty consistently retained its feeling; and thus spontaneously become one of the most audacious exploiters of the pulsatile and friction instruments, and of the medium's possibilities for high and piercing and shrill and brute dynamic sonorities. In this, he has undoubtedly been influenced by still another intuition, his vision of the perspectives of modern science. Those perspectives have been comprehending mindstuff in what hitherto had appeared the inanimate regions of life; events in the physical realm having come to show greater and greater resemblance to human expression and events in the psyche. The old antithesis between mind and matter has been proving more and more illusory; and Varèse, who was trained for engineering, would seem to have been standing before this new reality; finding it charged with emotion and generative of feelings of the relation between the forces known to physics and chemistry and those of the human psyche, and of ideas in the form of complexes and relations of the sounds and timbres of the instruments related to the whole realm of the semi-material. It may even be, as has been suggested, that he has in him something of the alchemist; that like the medieval scientists, he is moved by the desire to unveil god-nature and its divine or diabolic springs. Probably no chance cause is responsible for the affixion to his *Arcana* of an aphorism of Paracelsus of Hohenheim's.

In any case, his music gives us an overwhelming feeling of life as it exists in the industrial sites, and of the perspectives of recent science. Not that his art is in any way illustrative. His medium is independent, and if his expression is "metaphysical," like Wagner's and Scriabin's and Mahler's, and musically mythological, like theirs it addresses the senses, possibly with an unparalleled dynamism and aggressivity, but nonetheless beautifully and completely. Each of his pieces can be enjoyed sensuously for reason of its new, fabulously delicate and fabulously dynamic sonorities, its terrifically telescoped, concentrated, telegraphic form, its hard outlines, cubic bulks of brassy sound, powerful dissonances, subtle complex rhythmicality, golden screams; above all, for reason of its incredibly emotional tensity, that of the most characteristically modern life. He is thus the actual creator of the music the Futurists theoretically projected, but could not, for reason of their personal unmusicality, achieve. For what was theory in them, in him is feeling, and a musical one.

Take *Ionization,* the work for percussion alone. It is, as we have said, a complete piece of music: one is never conscious, during performances of it, of the limitation of the special medium the composer is exploiting. The performance creates, sustains, and finally releases a high nervous physical tension. The form which comprises the inordinate, delicate, overwhelming volumes of the piece is clear, apparently that of a three-part song, with distinct themes, developments, recapitulations. And still it is a myth: the representation of processes and the immanent creator. Subjected to it, one feels life wonderfully afresh in one of its apparently inhuman, excessively dynamic changes. By reason of their extreme hardness, extreme indeterminacy, and other points of dissemblance from the more humanly vibrating sounds of string and wind instruments, the tones of the forty-one percussion and friction pieces for which the composition is cast—triangles, Chinese blocks, rattles, snare drums, cymbals, lion roars, gongs, tom-toms, bells, piano (nonmelodic, playing only tone clusters), and the rest—in themselves somehow suggest the life of the inanimate universe. The illusion, if illusion it is, of an analogy between the subject of the music and events or processes in the physiochemical fields, is reinforced by the volumes of the extremely simplified, extremely skeletonized form, which, explosive, curiously timed and interrupted, and curiously related and responsive to one another, further suggest incandescent manifestations of material entities in stellar space. And the terrific conciseness of the style, telegraphically succinct in its themes, rapid in its mutation and developments, overleaping connective steps, and nervously alive with dialectically generated new ideas; and the acute high timbres, the abrupt detonations, and tremendous volumes of sound which figure almost incessantly, quite specifically suggest the spirit of some intensely dynamic process of the sort imperceptible to the senses but not to the penetrating organs of science. . . .

As for the process of the elevation and coronation of the battery as the king of the orchestra, leading to its autonomy, that may well have attained its term in *Ionization.* In music, we know how not only fashions but feelings change, and even if the skyscraper mysticism of Varèse should persist, as undoubtedly it will in himself, it may never again lead him to write for percussion and friction instruments alone. His very latest piece, *Equatorial,* is cast for an ensemble not wholly percussive in character, and the other composers who have recently taken to producing pieces for the battery alone have no claim on our consideration. But even if *Ionization* should prove a unicorn it would still maintain its place in the ranks of music. It is a little work of genius, born of the evolving life of music and its means, and the spirit of an individual and an epoch, a credit to its mother and its father. And it is both an individual and an epoch that are being denied in the stupid, extreme, entirely undeserved neglect— the most stupid, extreme, and entirely undeserved of all that are being inflicted by the musical world upon any living composer—that is still the part of the brilliant composer of *Ionization,* of *Hyperprism* and *Intégrales* and *Arcana* and all the rest of his powerful music.

(*Discoveries of a Music Critic,* 1936.)

# Contemporary Voyages: Benjamin Britten, Elliott Carter, Pierre Boulez

## ANDREW PORTER

*Andrew Porter, music critic for the* New Yorker *since 1972, writes reviews that blossom into expansive essays, not only on the performers, but on the works themselves—their histories, performance traditions, and acoustical peculiarities. A man of broad tastes, Porter makes illuminating connections with language and literature, linking such disparate artists as Berg and Melville, Mozart and Austen, in a supple prose style that recalls Hunt, Shaw, and other musical essayists who possessed freedom of language and largeness of sensibility. Porter's keenest enthusiasms are musical theater, pre–nineteenth-century opera and choral music, and contemporary music. In the latter field, his work has been particularly valuable in a culture that remains hostile to much that is new, whether nontonal and difficult or tonal and accessible. He has helped put Elliott Carter— surely one of America's major composers—on the map even as he has championed European revolutionaries such as Boulez and "conservative" masters such as Britten. As these excerpts demonstrate, adventure, along with joy and rapture, is his main esthetic yardstick. He is a critic from whom we can genuinely learn rather than to whom we simply react.*

## Benjamin Britten: Saved

The Metropolitan and the San Francisco productions of *Billy Budd* were complementary. Between them, they sustained a view long held by several of my friends but only recently mine, that *Billy Budd*, the sixth of Britten's fifteen operas, is musically the richest and most arresting of them all. Comparisons need not be odious: in brief, New York's version was scenically the more spectacular and emotionally the more romantic, while San Francisco's was musically in sharper focus—the clearest and keenest account of the opera I have ever heard. In both places, the conjunction of artists coming to the piece for the first time and artists who had long been associated with it resulted in performances of uncommon freshness, accuracy, and power. In New York, Captain Vere was sung by Peter Pears, who created the role, twenty-seven years ago, at Covent Garden. In San Francisco, Vere was Richard Lewis, who has been singing the part since 1964; the director was Ande Anderson, who worked on the original production, with the composer; and the designs derived from those John Piper created for the première. Outstanding among the new minds playing upon the piece and revealing new aspects of it were those of, in New York, James Morris, the Claggart, and, in San Francisco, David Atherton, who conducted, and Dale Duesing, the Billy.

The New York staging, directed by John Dexter and designed by William Dudley, is a big-house amplification of a version they put on in Hamburg in 1972. It is based on quick, penetrating appreciation of the work itself, of the Melville story on which it is based, and of differences between the story and the opera. Against a black back-cloth and wings, H.M.S. *Indomitable* (the opera was composed before Harrison Hayford and Merton Sealts established a definitive text of Melville's tale, in which the vessel is named the *Bellipotent*) is shown in lateral cross-section. Individually or all at once, its levels can rise and fall to create the different settings of the drama—main deck and quarterdeck, captain's cabin spanning the ship from side to side, berth deck. For the chase at the start of Act II, the whole structure rises hugely to reveal four decks fully manned for battle, and the towering visual effect mirrors the mounting excitement of the music. An illusion of five decks is created for Billy's soliloquy, and he lies in irons on the lowest of them. Here the designer has possibly erred. His scene does suggest Melville's "levels so like the tiered galleries of a coal mine"—but Billy should be on the second of them, just below the luminous night on the spar deck. His gun-deck Gethsemane is the most beautiful of Melville's many allegorically charged prison scenes. The gun bays suggest side chapels of a cathedral, branching from "the long dim-vistaed broad aisle between the two batteries." Flickering splashes of dirty yellow light from two swinging battle lanterns pollute the pale moonshine that struggles in through the open ports. Lying amid the black machinery of war, Billy in his "white jumper and white duck trousers, each more or less soiled, dimly glimmered in the obscure light of the bay like a patch of discolored snow in early April lingering at some upland cave's black mouth." The snow will soon melt. Billy's perfect beauty will soon be no more. Already it is smutched by his "generous young heart's virgin experience of the diabolical incarnate and effective in some men": "The skeleton in the cheekbone at the point of its angle was just beginning delicately to be defined under the warm-tinted skin. In fervid hearts self-contained, some brief experiences devour our human tissue."

In this last work of Melville's, left uncompleted at his death, in 1891, whiteness and blackness are symbols held more closely to their traditional values than they were in *Moby Dick*, forty years earlier. But nothing in Melville is quite unambiguous, and after Billy's funeral the *Indomitable* sails on under light airs into a whiteness so bleak, so blank, unmarked by good or ill, that it seems more chilling in its indifference than even the terrible Whiteness of the Whale. "The circumambient air in the clearness of its serenity was like smooth white marble in the polished block not yet removed from the marble-dealer's yard."

Not an image, not a word in Melville is lightly or carelessly chosen. (Vere's name tells of truth and also of vacillation; *Bili* and *Budd* were appellations of the Celtic Apollo; to *clag* is to adhere as with the touch of pitch or a spider's web.) Nor is a note, timbre, or harmony in Britten's score. And so discussion of any detail in a thoughtful, sensitive performance of *Billy Budd* leads toward speculation about the nature and meaning of the work. The design of Mr. Dudley's set obviates the five mid-act curtains—two in Act I, three in Act II—that Britten specifies; the scenes change before our eyes. Between scenes, Mr. Dexter has caught the principal characters— one, two, or all three of them—in shafts of light, on levels and in attitudes that brilliantly represent the ambiguities and changing tensions of the drama: Vere alone on his knees, invoking Authority; Billy and Claggart on the starry deck, each destined to be the other's destroyer, one carefree and the other racked; Vere between Billy and Claggart, a man caught between a Bright Angel and Lucifer; Billy between Claggart and Vere, innocent victim of, on one side, a passion that envy has perverted to hate and, on the other, a temperate judgment that—too late—is warmed by love. Explicatory tableaux uncalled for by the creators of an opera are usually to be deplored, but these added tableaux are not merely explicatory; they are at once dramatic and disturbing in the right way. On the surface, *Billy Budd*—Melville's or Britten's—is a fable of diagrammatic simplicity. The plot can be told in a few sentences—such as these from E. M. Forster's 1927 lectures published as *Aspects of the Novel:*

> The scene is on a British man-of-war soon after the Mutiny at the Nore. . . . The hero, a young sailor, has goodness. . . . On the surface he is a pleasant, merry, rather insensitive lad, whose perfect physique is marred by one slight defect, a stammer, which finally destroys him. . . . Claggart, one of the petty officers, at once sees in him the enemy—his own enemy, for Claggart is evil. . . . He accuses Billy of trying to foment a mutiny. The charge is ridiculous, no one believes it, and yet it proves fatal. For when the boy is summoned to declare his innocence, he is so horrified that he cannot speak, his ludicrous stammer seizes him . . . and he knocks down his traducer, kills him, and has to be hanged.

Yet by the force of Melville's imaginative thought and by the force of his language, both drawing vitality from Shakespeare and Milton, the simple black-and-white fable explodes in a bewildering moral rainbow. And, as the author exclaims in the course of his tale, "Who in the rainbow can draw the line where the violet tint ends and the orange tint begins?" *Billy Budd* is an unsettling opera to attend, and its power derives in the first place from Melville. To the writing desk on which Melville composed *Billy Budd* was attached the precept "Keep true to the dreams of thy youth." Those dreams were often terrible. In "Pierre, or, The Ambiguities," the tale of a nineteenth-century New York Hamlet, Melville observes how the trail of truth too far followed can lead to Hyperborean regions where "all objects are seen in a dubious, uncertain, and refracting light," to a barren pole, where the hitherto guiding compass points indifferently in all directions. No moral judgments are made in *Billy Budd*, but, in Forster's words, "Melville—after the initial roughness of his realism—reaches straight back into the universal, to a blackness and sadness so transcending our own that they are indistinguishable from glory." Such incandescent blackness is hard to distinguish from the whiteness that in *Moby Dick* strikes panic to the soul and in *Billy Budd* obliterates the temporal tragedy. In practical terms, one may regret the unrelieved blackness against which the drama is played at the Met; an unrelievedly white backcloth might serve as well—or as badly. What the opera needs (and received in San Francisco) is surely an evocation of the isolating sea, to define the *Indomitable* moving through night and days, through blackness and whiteness, as a "fragment of earth," and to affirm the important metaphor of the world in a man-of-war.

Forster's 1927 account of *Billy Budd* appears in a chapter titled "Prophecy." To illustrate that particular aspect of the novel, he cites Dostoyevsky, Melville, D. H. Lawrence, and Emily Brontë—and "Melville is at the center of our picture." Hardy, "a philosopher and a great poet," is excluded, because "Hardy's novels . . . do not give out sounds"—whereas in Melville "we catch the song" even when "we cannot catch the words of the song." Here Forster is speaking specifically of *Moby Dick*, but what he says is true of *Billy Budd:* "As soon as we catch the song in it," the easy yarn "grows difficult and immensely important." More than twenty years later, when an operatic collaboration between Britten and Forster was proposed, Melville's *Billy Budd*—P. N. Furbank tells us in his Forster biography—occurred to both men almost simultaneously as the ideal subject. Forster was unversed in operatic writing; Eric Crozier, the librettist of Britten's *Albert Herring*, was coopted to help with the stage mechanics. When he raised practical objections to the idea of an all-male opera, Britten and Forster swept them aside. The story filled some inner need in them. F. O. Matthiessen, at the close of the Melville section of his *American Renaissance* (1941), declared that "Melville could feel that the deepest need for rapaciously individualistic America was a radical affirmation of the heart." That chimes with Forster's famous remark "If I had to choose between betraying my country and betraying my friend, I hope I should have the guts to betray my country." Matthiessen says, "After all he had suffered, Melville could endure to the end in the belief that though good goes to defeat and death, its radiance can redeem life." That chimes with a belief proclaimed in many of Britten's works. It is a more optimistic reading of *Billy Budd* than mine, but is the reading expressed in the opera. Back in 1927, Forster wrote that in Melville, at last, "the balance righted itself, and he gave us harmony and temporary salvation." In the tale, Billy's death is signaled by a moment of temporary equilibrium—"The hull, deliberately recovering from the periodic roll to leeward, was just regaining an even keel when the last signal was given"—and is decked in the radiant imagery of redemption:

> At the same moment it chanced that the vapory fleece hanging low in the East was shot through with a soft glory as of the fleece of the Lamb of God seen in mystical vision. . . . Billy ascended; and, ascending, took the full rose of the dawn.

Britten and Forster seized on this theme and extended it. In Melville, Vere dies soon afterward, with Billy's name on his lips. In the opera, he lives on to become an old man, at peace with himself and the world, proclaiming that Billy "has saved me, and blessed me, and the love that passes understanding has come to me." It is a legitimate extension, perhaps, of the "salvation" implied by Melville's description and also by his bold stroke of sexual metaphor: when Billy was hanged, the customary spasm in the body was miraculously absent but, as if in mystic transference, Vere himself "stood erectly rigid as a musket." By Billy's sacrificial death Vere is saved, as Tannhäuser was saved by Elisabeth's, and Faust by Gretchen's. Forster gave up writing novels in 1924. He had protested "weariness of the only subject I both can and may treat—the love of men for women and vice versa." But Melville in the mid-nineteenth-century wrote fearlessly of passions in the all-male world he knew from his four years of seafaring, and at the end of the century—true to the dreams of his youth—he returned to that world. Of course, *Billy Budd* is not simply a homosexual yarn, but its imagery is strictly homoerotic. Billy is a glorious young Adam without an Eve. Claggart, a new Satan stirred by the sight of the paradise he cannot enter and is driven to destroy, sometimes watches the "cheerful sea-Hyperion" with feverish tears in his eyes and "a touch of soft yearning, as if [he] could even have loved Billy but for fate and ban." Even Captain Vere mentally strips Billy, as "a fine specimen of the genus *homo*, who in the nude might have posed for a statue of the young Adam before the Fall." For Melville, the tale continued his discoveries that *Lear*, *Hamlet*, and *Paradise Lost* were works relevant to life intensely lived on a whaler or a man-of-war, that he could treat again of their tremendous issues in terms of his own experience, and that he could reshape their high language to serve his expression. For more than thirty years (since *The Confidence*

*Man*, in 1857), he had published no prose. Like his own John Marr, a sailor stranded in a humdrum world, he was thrown "more and more upon retrospective musings . . . lit by that aureola circling over any object of affections in the past, for reunion with which an imaginative heart passionately yearns."

*Billy Budd* is a distillation of themes, thoughts, images, and characters encountered in *Redburn*, *White-Jacket*, and *Moby Dick*. It began as the ballad soliloquy of a sailor condemned to death for inciting a mutiny. A prose introduction then told of Claggart, the master-of-arms who preferred the charge against an innocent Budd. In a further expansion, Captain Vere was added, to complete the allegory of Innocence, Evil, and Responsibility—of Adam before the Fall, the envious and destructive Tempter, and an inadequate man called on to play the part of all-powerful Judge. Melville's last revisions, it seems, were concerned with dramatizing what was formerly narrated, thus leaving readers to draw their own conclusions. Forster and Britten completed the process, but they also made some significant changes. Melville does not judge Vere; he shows him. In *The Confidence Man*, he had already observed how "the moderate man" can be "the invaluable understrapper of the wicked man"; in a sense, Vere completes Claggart's unfinished work of destruction. But Melville allows Vere powerful arguments—the strict letter of the Articles of War, the danger of mutiny—to justify his action in condemning Billy to death. Forster rejected those arguments. He did judge Melville's Vere, and determined "to rescue Vere from Melville." In the book, Vere plays prosecutor and, by his speeches, sways a drumhead court that is inclined to acquit Billy. In the opera, he plays Pilate. He is silent when Billy cries "Captain Vere, save me!" He refuses to take responsibility, and, to his officers' "Grant us your guidance," answers, "No. Do not ask me. I cannot. . . . Pronounce your verdict." It adds a new mystery of human behavior. It complicates the drama. And it leads to the peripeteia of Vere's aria "I accept their verdict. . . . Beauty, handsomeness, goodness, it is for me to destroy you." We move into a drama of redemption and salvation. The stage remains empty as Vere goes off to tell Billy of the sentence, while a sequence of thirty-four common chords, differently scored and spaced, mystically represents Melville's "sacrament . . . wherever under circumstances at all akin to those here attempted to be set forth two of great Nature's nobler order embrace." In performances, this bold and wonderful stroke is sometimes nervously handled. The Metropolitan conductor, Raymond Leppard, underplayed the passage; the chords slipped by too easily. In San Francisco, David Atherton was eloquent—each chord did sound like a new statement, the gleam of a new possibility, in some close, solemn argument—but the director diminished the force of the sequence by leaving Vere onstage for the first half of it.

The opera makes its deepest statements through harmony. Those chords resolve into the untroubled, lapping F major of Billy's gun-deck ballad, and they recur at its close: "I'm strong . . . And I'll stay strong." The very opening bars of the work—introducing Vere as an old man, musing on the great crisis of his life—present a B-flat/B minor opposition that clears only in the long B-flat pedal at the very end of the work. These harmonic meanings are not at all obscure; audiences can appreciate them without any conscious analysis. And the whole work, for all its subtle, intricate networks of motivic relationships and developments, and its wondrously delicate, adventurous, and unconventional scoring, has a similar directness. In *Peter Grimes*, Britten created magnificent sea music—seascapes seen from the land. In *Billy Budd*, there is another kind of sea music, in which the movement of the ship—the sense of the long, straining timbers, of the vessel's living response to wind and wave—seems to live in the music itself. The absence of women's voices passes unnoticed; the score is often bright with clear, busy shipboard signals. Ship and sea provide a picturesque background—and foreground, too, for ship and sea enclose the action, to make intense the crisis set on "this fragment of earth, this floating monarchy" of which Vere is king. Britten thought that there was too much shipboard detail in Piper's 1951 settings. When Covent Garden revived the opera in 1964, they were stripped and simplified. I think the composer was probably wrong; the most powerful *Budd* décor I have seen—Roger Butlin's for the Welsh National Opera—was also the most realistic. But Piper's settings, further remodeled to Mr. Anderson's ideas, rebuilt in San Francisco on a larger scale and provided with projections of changing sea and skies, worked very well.

Since 1951, it has been customary to portray Claggart as a big, blustering bully. Forbes Robinson, who took the role in 1964, and then in the Welsh production, found more subtlety in the man, and in San Francisco he again gave a striking and impressive performance. But he is slightly too ponderous, in manner as well as appearance too conventionally a "heavy," to be altogether convincing. James Morris, at the Met, is the first Claggart of my experience to express fully the Lucifer-like beauty, sorrow, and passion of the Evil One, and to embody the occasional hint that in Billy and Claggart we have a final projection of the twinned bright and dark angels—Taji's Yillah and Hautia (in "Mardi"), Pierre's Lucy and Isabel—who recur in Melville's work. And Mr. Morris sang the role matchlessly. Except in the literal sense (for his low G and G-sharp were not strong), he plumbed Claggart's great monologue and made of it just what Forster hoped for:

> I want *passion*—love constricted, perverted, poisoned, but none the less *flowing* down its agonising channel: a sexual discharge gone evil. Not soggy depression or growling remorse.

No subsequent Billy has quite recaptured the freshness and naturalness of Theodor Uppman, who created the part and might have been born to play it. In Richard Stilwell's stage personality, there is usually a hint of patrician reserve; as Billy, at the Met, he doffed it almost too resolutely, and slightly forced the brightness and bounciness. But on the whole he was very good. Dale Duesing, in San Francisco, was even better. During the confrontation with Claggart, he expressed with marvelous intensity Billy's agony at this revelation of "the diabolical incarnate," and during the trial his further agony when Vere refuses to save him. Without exaggeration, he suggested the new understanding that comes to Billy, and carried the redemptive burden of the role as reshaped by Britten and Forster. In both places, *Billy Budd* proved overwhelming.

(Extracted by the author from the *New Yorker*, October 23, 1978.)

---

# Elliott Carter: Great Bridge, Our Myth

**M**uch American imagery is drawn together in Elliott Carter's latest composition, *A Symphony of Three Orchestras*, dedicated to the New York Philharmonic and its music director, Pierre Boulez, and first performed by them last month. The opening can be heard as an evocation in picturesque sound of the Brooklyn Bridge.

High on the violins, as one thin, shining, open-textured chord is laid
upon another, in shifting aeolian strains, it seems as if the cradle of
wires overhead may be sounding: "Sibylline voices flicker, waveringly
stream, As though a god were issue of the strings." The violins span
the stage from side to side. Between them, three piccolos then break
in with keen, bright bird cries, given added sharpness by small, high
hammer beats from piano and xylophone; clarinets and oboes swell
the shrill chorus to a brief tumult. In a program note, the composer
quotes the beginning of Hart Crane's *The Bridge:*

> How many dawns, chill from his rippling rest
> The seagull's wings shall dip and pivot him,
> Shedding white rings of tumult, building high
> Over the chained bay waters Liberty—

And a single trumpet wings out in long solo flight. Wheeling through
the faint, ethereal violin chords, it mounts, hovers, circles down,
soars again, swiftly plummets, stays for a moment poised low, traces a
final, sudden ascent and fall before coming to rest. A series of em-
phatic descending figures from each orchestra in turn ends the
introduction (in the Crane opening, "elevators drop us from our
day"), and the symphonic argument begins in earnest with a huge
span of sixths softly sustained by the strings of one orchestra and
*giocoso* chattering from two bassoons of another.

The piece lasts fifteen minutes. Orchestra I, on the left of the
platform, consists of brasses, strings, and kettledrums. Orchestra III,
on the right of the platform, consists of triple woodwinds (without
clarinets), two horns, strings (no cellos), and unpitched percussion,
mainly metallic. Orchestra II, central, is a smaller ensemble: three
clarinets, piano, vibraphone, xylophone, marimba, chimes, long
drum, tomtom, and a handful of strings. The violins of Orchestra I
and of Orchestra III, arranged across the front of the platform, provide a sonic balance like that of the first and second violins of a traditional orchestra traditionally seated; the differing wind and percussion complements give to each orchestra its distinctive timbre and
character. Orchestra II is a band of soloists, a concertante group set
against the twin-ripieno of the rest, and it is invited to phrase with
rubato.

The work plays without break but is not exactly a "one-move-
ment symphony." Between the introduction and an extended coda

there are twelve brief movements, four for each orchestra, and each orchestra plays its four movements twice, not in regular order. Each movement is altered when it returns. Each is based on a different three-note chord. Between movements, each orchestra falls silent for a few measures, and the silences and the lapping are so arranged that, for some moments at least, each movement can be heard by itself. But most of the time two or three movements are being played simultaneously. "The listener, of course," says Carter, "is not meant, on first hearing, to identify the details of this continually shifting web of sound . . . but rather to hear and grasp the character of this kaleidoscope of musical themes as they are presented in varying contexts." At fourth and fifth hearing, much of the detail still remained elusive. The movements most easily recognized are those of clear harmonic character: the piled-up sixths already mentioned, which form the first movement of Orchestra I; the pure, open fifths of Orchestra II's first movement; the 6–4 major and 6–3 minor triads (result of putting a major third above a perfect fourth, or vice versa) in the second movement of Orchestra III. Each of the twelve movements proceeds at its own distinct speed. The general effect, the "character of this kaleidoscope," is easy to enjoy. One kind of music breaks in upon another, comes to the fore, then recedes at the advance of yet another kind of music. Harmonic colors, instrumental timbres, varied textures, speeds, and kinds of figuration lap, clash, combine, cohere, then part. Perspectives shift. Foreground becomes middle or background. Image crowds upon image. It might have been chaos, but it is a disciplined dance of clearly formed ideas, defined in space by the siting of the three orchestras and defined in time by the composer's carefully balanced structure.

The structure recalls that of Carter's Third String Quartet, which is two independent, patterned duologues, one of four episodes each heard thrice, the other of six episodes each heard twice, concurrent but not synchronous, and so distributed that at some point each of the four episodes encounters and overlaps with each of the six. But the symphony is an "easier" work for the listener than the quartet, because its ideas are so colorful. Well before his ear has learned to spot and recognize the recurrent movements, he will have learned to find his way through the piece by sonic landmarks—besides those already mentioned, two rhapsodic violin solos; a peal of bells, clanging open fifths; a poignant melody from the bass clarinet; a sudden, insistent reiteration of G minor. Carter, as I have often remarked, is a "graphic" composer. To find words to describe the music of his Third Quartet and his Duo for Violin and Piano I turned to similes from nature. But the words for the symphony have already been written by Hart Crane. Since student days, Carter says, he has dreamed of making a musical work from Crane's *The Bridge*, and he calls the symphony in some sense a sketch for that work. Behind the jocund two-bassoon episode lies the Rip Van Winkle section of the poem. The pealing bells are partly a response to Columbus's prayer in *The Bridge*, partly an image from a later poem: "The bells, I say, the bells break down their tower; / And swing I know not where. Their tongues engrave / Membrane through marrow, my long-scattered score / Of broken intervals."

Anyone brought up, as I was, in the English choral tradition is brought up with Walt Whitman—set to music by Gustav Holst (Carter's teacher at Harvard), Delius, and Vaughan Williams—and comes to America prepared for long democratic vistas, primed with the poetic imagery of the New World, and ready for Crane. Long before I read *The Bridge*, I had walked to Brooklyn along that "path amid the stars crossed by the seagull's wing" and had ridden to Brooklyn on the IRT subway—had discovered with eyes and feet and feelings two of the most potent symbols in this city of romantic symbols. Some of them, such as Whitman's ferry to Brooklyn, have gone. Others, once visions, have become everyday sights: Whitman's view of the earth as a "vast Rondure swimming in space," which I sang of as a treble and have now seen through eyes transported by television's magic far out into space; Crane's day when "The soul, by naphtha fledged into new reaches, / Already knows the closer grasp of Mars." The new monuments have their own meanings. Since man is not allowed to set foot on the Verrazano-Narrows Bridge, it stands as a huge symbol of his slavery to the motorcar, while the Brooklyn Bridge continues to be celebrated. Alan Trachtenberg, in his monograph *Brooklyn Bridge: Fact and Symbol*, took the tale of what it has inspired up to 1965. Since then, Marianne Moore has hymned the "Caged Circe of steel and stone" (Elizabeth Bishop had invited Miss Marianne Moore over Brooklyn Bridge to come flying into Manhattan, "mounting the sky with natural heroism"), and now Elliott Carter has set sounding not only the "arching strands of song," the "humming spars," but Crane's transcendent vision of the bridge extending to span not just the East

River but all America from east to west. Far below the river runs the bridge's dark shadow, the subway—path amid the stars and swift passage tunneled through the earth. With Columbus, Cortés, and Pizarro, the poet voyages west, meets Pocahontas, dances with her, merges with the land and with the great flowing river. He travels now with the gait of a dreamer, lingering on the bridge itself while his mind voyages out in the clippers below to distant shores; then rushes swiftly by iron road across this huge land; then moves with the Mississippi, slow. Finally, he rides the subway home to Brooklyn—and Poe, his eyes like agate lanterns, is companion on that journey.

Carter's symphony is in no sense a musical "transcription" of *The Bridge,* but its different kinds of movement and its rich superimposition of image upon image produce something of the effect of that poem. And, because it compasses so much in fifteen minutes, other visions are recalled, other feelings stirred, while one listens—sights and sensations familiar to Carter's contemporaries but not to Crane's: the view of Manhattan from an airplane that has climbed steeply from La Guardia, when the huge, populous city shrinks to a small island in the river and its towers become play blocks heaped by a child; the sense, while flying west, that one is actually tracing through air and traversing the mythic span of Crane's bridge. Whitman hymned the linked Union Pacific and Central Pacific as "Bridging the three or four thousand miles of land travel, / Tying the Eastern to the Western sea . . . (Ah Genoese thy dream! thy dream!/ Centuries after thou art laid in thy grave, / The shore thou foundest verifies thy dream)," but flight has added a swifter metaphor-made-concrete to his vision. New York might be a hard city to live in were it not for the poets, painters, and musicians who teach us to see, to feel, and to dream here. Without them, a subway ride might be no more than a dirty, noisy, possibly dangerous way of getting from place to place—instead of a romantic adventure, symbolism experienced as fact. Without them, we might not see Hector, Orestes and the Furies, Faust, Don Quixote as through Manhattan's streets we saunter pondering. Pale, impassioned Norma, crazed Lucia, John of Leiden would stay locked inside the Met, and the vocalism of sun-bright Italy and German organ majestic not sound forth in the bold American day. Crane placed a sentence from Job at the start of *The Bridge*— "From going to and fro in the earth, and from walking up and down in it"—but it is not only Satan who stalks the city with him and with

us. Columbus, Cortés, and Pizarro, Pocahontas, Rip Van Winkle, and
Poe have been mentioned. Walt Whitman is ever at hand, a Virgil to
Crane's Dante. Marlowe, Blake, Melville, Isadora Duncan, and Emily
Dickinson appear, and Plato prefaces the final section with his "Music
is then the knowledge of that which relates to love in harmony and
system." That Carter should have found *The Bridge* an intractable
text to set as an oratorio is not surprising: Crane struggled for lucid
utterance; in Waldo Frank's words, "his attempt, with sound materials, to achieve poetic form was ever close to chaos." That Carter
should have been moved by the ideas and imagery of the poem to
compose this ordered symphony is not surprising, either. The techniques of time flow and overlapping discourse pursued in his earlier
works prepared him for the handling of so rich a theme.

We can praise *A Symphony of Three Orchestras* for its visionary
aspiration. We can praise it for its refined, very delicate, and subtle
workmanship. (Even the notation, designed to catch the differing
tempi within a single set of bar lines, so that one conductor can keep
time for all three orchestras, represents a triumph of musico-
mathematical ingenuity.) On the simplest but not least important
level, we can praise the expressive quality of the melodies and of the
instrumental colors (shimmering touches from a bell tree, warm cello
cantilenas, brass notes climbing one upon another like the courses of
some cyclopean wall—or of the "twin monoliths" that carry the
bridge). The symphony is of all Carter's scores the richest in sound.
But not aspiration, or good construction, or vivid orchestration is in
itself enough to produce a composition so moving and memorable as
this. All three combine. In a series of performances, Boulez and the
Philharmonic played it with ever-increasing mastery.

(Extracted by the author from the *New Yorker*, March 7, 1977.)

## Pierre Boulez: Chance, Death, and Mutability

When Pierre Boulez relinquishes the Philharmonic, at the end
of this season, and we try to draw up balance sheets of what
he brought to New York and what he failed to bring, the
second column can be headed by performances of his own music. For

Boulez is above all a great composer, and in most of his later works the act of composition continues during his conducting of them. With the Philharmonic he has not done *Pli selon pli,* that towering orchestral masterpiece of our day, or *Domaines,* or the early cantata *Le Soleil des eaux,* or *Le Marteau sans maître.* In fact, at subscription—or, for that matter, at Rug and at Prospective Encounter—concerts he had conducted none of his own music, except for two "Improvisations sur Mallarmé" (movements from *Pli selon pli*), until, this month, he introduced his *Rituel* to New York. During the four years that he was chief conductor of the BBC Symphony, Boulez performances of Boulez were frequent. He explains that of the BBC he was not music director, and that BBC concerts are not sold by subscription; at the Philharmonic, of which he *is* music director, he is unwilling to impose his own music on subscription audiences. It is an understandable decision. But as a result Philharmonic audiences have been cut off from a mainstream of contemporary music, and Boulez has wasted much of his and our time on routine and worse than routine executions of standard classics. Earlier this month, he conducted a deplorable performance of Beethoven's Fifth Symphony. A week later, with *Rituel,* he led us to the heights.

It is true that by means of phonograph records and sneak tapes of foreign performances an enthusiast can create his own Boulez performances. Yet where Boulez is concerned a recorded performance is likely to be in the nature of a snapshot of a work at just one stage of its life—better than nothing, but a poor substitute for living with, observing, being inspired by the progress of that marvelous musical mind, made manifest in individual compositions that themselves develop and grow from year to year, fold upon fold, and are so closely related one to the next that they seem to be parts of a single magnum opus in progress. Ideas from Boulez's Second Piano Sonata were reworked in his *Livre pour quatuor,* and that quartet, in turn, was reworked for string orchestra as *Livre pour cordes.* At the 1960 ISCM Festival, in Cologne, I heard him play a piano solo that was then a new addition to *Pli selon pli,* while *Pli* itself was still a work for chamber forces, not the great full-orchestra piece it is now. Four years later, that piano solo had grown into *Éclat,* for a glittery chamber ensemble, and was played by the BBC Symphony. The following year, there was a "world première" of *Éclat* in Los Angeles, in the form that excited Stravinsky's admiration (recounted in his *Themes and Episodes:* "*Éclat* is not only creative music but creative conducting as well, which is unique"). *Éclat* continued to expand, into *Éclat-Multiples*, a work now about thrice as long as the *Éclat* of 1964, and still open-ended. In rather similar fashion, Boulez's . . . *explosante/fixe* . . . began life, in 1972, as a page of musical ideas, clusters of instrumental monodies, followed by six pages of suggestions about how they might be assembled. It was one of seventeen "Canons and Epitaphs: In Memoriam Igor Stravinsky," by different composers, published in the magazine *Tempo*. That year, London heard a ten-minute version for flute, clarinet, and trumpet. Early in 1973, the Chamber Music Society of Lincoln Center presented a half-hour version, more elaborately scored, and intricately equipped with electronic spatial effects. Later that year, in Rome, members of the BBC Symphony under Boulez played a revised, longer version, and a few months after that, in London, they played one longer still.

From which it should be clear that a Boulez score as first set down contains ideas and possibilities that are then explored in performance, and that from such exploration there may result new ideas, for additional or more interesting and exciting ways of handling the original material. And that from a germ in one work another work may grow. Such practices are common enough in musical history. What Handel could do with one of his recurrent melodies, making it flower afresh in new forms through work after work, Boulez does with an "idea"—a structural device, a generative procedure, a way of organizing time or timbre. There is a parallel with Balanchine, who builds one work upon another, and is likely to change "finished" work, rethink passages of it, as he revives it in the living medium of performing artists.

*Rituel* (1975) bears the subtitle "In memoriam Maderna" and commemorates Bruno Maderna, the Venetian composer and conductor, who died in 1973. Boulez has described it as music "for an imaginary ceremony" that is at once a "ceremony of remembrance" in its constant return to the same ideas and a "ceremony of extinction, ritual of disappearance and survival" in its constant alterations of those ideas, which change as memories are apt to change. Like . . . *explosante/fixe* . . . , *Rituel* is a memorial composition. The works have other things in common, including a precedent in Stravinsky's *Symphonies of Wind Instruments*, Boulez's memorial to Debussy. *Symphonies* is a work that Boulez is close to (he conducted it at his first concert with the BBC Symphony and has several times conducted it with the Philharmonic), and in an introductory talk he gave about *Rituel* he explained that Stravinsky's block structure—and, in particular, the "idea" of long, complicated sounds followed by short ones—provided one stimulus for his own composition. The influence of *Symphonies* on *Rituel* is both sonic and formal, and it was not by chance that works by Debussy and Stravinsky completed the bill at the Philharmonic. . . . *explosante/fixe* . . . and *Rituel* also share a fixed point of reference—the note E-flat (which in German is Es, or S, Stravinsky's initial). In the score of the former, it sits at the center of the page, with an archipelago of six monody clusters scattered around it; alternative routes for moving about the page are provided. In the latter, a unison E-flat is the note of resolution for the chordal progressions that make up seven of the work's fifteen sections. This E-flat, on the first line of the treble staff, limns a kind of "horizon" above, below, or across which the events of the work can be heard to take place.

As a creator-performer, Boulez has long been concerned with opposed claims of chance and predetermination; with controlling instinct by intelligence; with giving order and lucidity to, while not clipping the wings of, imagination in full flight. Toward the end of his elegant but difficult Darmstadt lectures, published as *Boulez on Music Today*, he cites Baudelaire's attempted reconciliation of "lucidity" and "genius," and continues, "Imagination must stimulate intelligence and intelligence must anchor imagination." A thoroughly mastered modern technique is "an exalting mirror which the imagination forges for itself, and in which its discoveries are reflected." Once possessed of it, a musician can act freely and rationally. In the early fifties, Boulez began work on *Structures*, for two pianos, and the three pieces of Book I constitute perhaps the most rigidly controlled large composition of our day, in which the sequence of notes, their durations, their dynamics, and their modes of attack are determined by a set of rules and tables drawn up in advance. But in Book II, which appeared in 1961, there are passages where the tempo and spacing of events are left to the performers to decide. Boulez had entered his freer period. As an epigraph to the score of *Pli selon pli* he set a line of Mallarmé: "A throw of the dice will not abolish chance." Boulez has never been an *aleator*, a dice roller. His aim of "deducing multiple consequences from a certain number of rational points of departure" suggests something closer to chess. And . . . *explosante/fixe* . . . and *Rituel* are like games played with similar pieces but according to quite different sets of rules. The composer has compared the score of . . . *explosante/fixe* . . . to a city map: the journey from A to B can be made by many different routes, and each traveler can choose his own, but along the way there are signs—one way, no entry, no right turn—that must be obeyed in the interests of an orderly, controlled ensemble flow. *Rituel* is set out on the page in a more conventional fashion. The program note for a London performance last November said that "nothing is left to choice; the work is immutable." The New York program note, on the other hand, said of seven of the fifteen sections that it was "unlikely . . . that even in a thousand successive performances these sections would ever turn out exactly the same." The second statement is correct. *Rituel*, at this stage of its life, contains both an element of choice for the conductor and an element of chance—but choice and chance alike are held within narrow limits. On *this* map, everyone's route has been carefully plotted in advance. All that can happen is that along certain stretches members of the company may break step: some may straggle behind, others forge ahead and then wait at the next corner until the rest have caught up.

*Rituel* lasts about twenty-seven minutes. Seven is the recurrent number in its making. Seven odd-numbered sections are the chordal progressions with the final resolution on E-flat. In the first of them, there is one chord; in the second, two; and so on to seven in the seventh. The seven even-numbered sections, alternating with the chordal passages, are played by one or more of seven instrumental "groups," widely spaced on the platform. These groups are: one oboe, two clarinets, three flutes, four violins, five woodwinds, six strings, and seven woodwinds. The music they play is either elegiac lament or flickering, rapid figuration. The chordal sections are given out by a centrally stationed brass ensemble of twice-seven players, joined, after the first section, by whichever of the groups have been playing in the preceding section. This sounds schematic, and so it is: a well-planned, firm, and easily apprehended framework, on which Boulez has composed music of eloquence and beauty. A few sentences from one of my more lyrical London colleagues, written after last November's performance, may help to dispel any notion that *Rituel* is a dryly manufactured or unemotional work:

This odd, austere orchestral essay once again conjured, at second hearing, in a way that no other Boulez work seems to conjure, a multitude of references, echoes of other music faintly perceived: a swirl of instruments heard through the pink veil of Stockhausen's *Trans;* a sudden priestly cadence of Messiaen; delicate bubbles of Italianate texture, quickly punctured. And many insinuating moments: the dying-ember tones of gongs, woodblocks and dark-muted strings; nervous riffs of scraped and shaken percussion; the sudden shriek in pain of brass and clarinet.

I have not yet mentioned the percussion. At the back of the platform, two players, provided with seven gongs and seven tamtams, introduce each chordal section with a gong stroke and continue during it with a knell-like tolling rhythmically independent of the chords. Seven other percussionists, each of them with seven instruments (many of them exotic), are allotted one apiece to the seven groups, where they function as sub-conductors, giving the beat with tap, clack, tinkle, or tock. The element of chance enters here: although the rhythmic notation is precise, the meters are so tricky and the players so widely separated that at each performance the lapping of the different groups is bound to vary. The main conductor gives the signal to start the even-numbered sections and then leaves it to the individual percussion-conductors to carry on. He conducts the odd-numbered, chordal sections himself. When seven of one have alternated with seven of the other, all the forces unite in a long, elegiac final section, built on motifs that have been heard before. Then, one by one, the groups fall from the ensemble. The last note is a soft unison E-flat, over the tolling of a gong.

What else? Boulez gave his introductory talk at one of the informal Pre-Philharmonic Concert Lectures, and there he disclosed that practical considerations went into the making of *Rituel*. A work that calls for an unusual platform disposition, he decided, should be long enough, as well as good enough, to justify the disturbance it causes: an audience grows impatient when the reseating of an orchestra lasts almost as long as the music that follows. The idea of the seven solo percussionists came to him as he considered the difficulties his seven groups would have if there was no one to give them a beat; a single conductor would need seven arms. The element of choice was introduced at a late stage, because it proved difficult to secure unanimous attack on the chords. So now the conductor is invited to "spread" them, bringing in at will each group of instruments in turn until the full sonority is built up. The percussion is an integral and beautiful part of the piece; its manifold colors and the effect of clocks ticking away at different speeds are major expressive elements. But whether the spreading of the chords is a good idea I am unsure. Since most of these chords are prefaced by a brief appoggiatura-like anacrusis, a restless rat-a-tat of successive entries disturbs the grand solemnity of the original idea. However, the composer opined that the "analytical" effect of hearing timbre laid upon timbre was interesting. And so it was.

The traditional devices of funeral music are here: bell harmonies produced (as in the *Symphonies of Wind Instruments*) by sustained and complicated chords, the knell of the gong strokes, alternations as of versicle and response. After the very soft opening chord, the first sound heard is the solo oboe in lament. (The melody is close to the main theme of . . . *explosante/fixe* . . .) Gradually, the sections grow longer, and the textures denser, until a climax is reached. Then the long coda begins—solemn utterances broken by pauses during which the percussions, representing the varied ticks of time, become prominent. On all levels, *Rituel* seems to me a major work. It relates to earlier musical experience (Stravinsky; Messiaen; possibly the slow pageant of Harrison Birtwistle's *The Triumph of Time*, a work that Boulez has championed; Boulez's own *Domaines* and *Éclat* as well as . . . *explosante/fixe* . . .). It is at once complicated and lucid. The scoring is beautiful. After being stirred by this grave, passionate, and precisely ordered work, no one could call Boulez unemotional.

(Extracted by the author from the *New Yorker*, January 31, 1977.)

# PART III

## The Art

## of Music

# Music as Science and Sentiment

## HECTOR BERLIOZ

*For Hector Berlioz, music was not only an emotional and intellectual experience but an overpoweringly physical one as well. Several of his contemporaries have described how he would weep, jeer, curse, and convulse at performances. In this piece, newly translated for this volume by Jacques Barzun, he describes these symptoms himself, as well as other dimensions of how people create and respond to music. This opening section of* A travers chants *is his bold attempt to see the art whole. (For more on Berlioz, see headnote to "Weber and the Fantastic" and "Beethoven's Despair.")*

Music is, at one and the same time, a species of feeling and a science. It demands from anyone who cultivates it, whether as executant or composer, both natural inspiration and a range of knowledge only to be acquired by long study and profound meditation. This union of knowledge with inspiration constitutes the art. Failing these conditions a musician can only be an incomplete artist, supposing he deserves to be called an artist at all. The great question, which matters most, native gift without study, or study without native gift—a question which Horace did not venture to decide positively in the case of poets—seems to me equally difficult to settle in the case of musicians. Some persons quite unacquainted with the science have by sheer inspiration produced airs not only graceful, but even sublime; as for example, Rouget de l'Isle and his immortal "Marseillaise." But such flashes of inspiration light up only part of the realm of art while other parts equally important remain in shadow. It follows, given the complex nature of modern music, that these men cannot really be classified as musicians—THEY LACK KNOWLEDGE.

It is even more usual to find methodical minds, calm and cold, who, after having patiently studied theory and observed how things are done, have managed by long practice to squeeze the utmost out of incomplete faculties, and produced things that seem to fulfill the usual expectations people entertain about music. But these things satisfy the ear without giving delight and speak neither to the heart nor to the imagination. Now, the mere satisfaction of the ear is far from affording the exquisite sensations which that organ is capable of experiencing; and the delights of heart and imagination are not of a kind to be given up lightly; so that where both are combined with a sensuous pleasure of the most vivid sort—and this is true of the genuine musical works of any school—such incapable producers should also, as I think, be excluded from the class of those regarded as true musicians: THEY LACK FEELING.

What we call music is a new art; at least in the sense that in all probability it resembles but very slightly what the civilised nations of antiquity designated by that name. Moreover, it must be made clear from the outset that the word music anciently bore an acceptation of such extent that, far from merely signifying, as it does nowadays, the art of combining sounds, it was also applied to dance, mime, poetry, eloquence, and even to the whole range of the sciences.

If we assume the word *music* to be derived from *muse*, the extensive meaning assigned to it by the ancients is easily explained. It expressed, and was intended to express, *whatever was presided over by the Muses*. This accounts for the misinterpretations one finds in many commentators on ancient times. In our own speech we use an expression with a sense almost as general: we say *art* when referring to the various works of the mind, whether it acts alone or aided by certain organs, as well as to those exercises of the body which our intellect has poeticized. Thus it may happen that a reader two thousand years from now will come across in one of our books the phrase so often used as a title for some rambling essay: "On the state of Art in Europe during the nineteenth century." He will then have to interpret it: "On the state of poetry, eloquence, music, painting, engraving, sculpture, architecture, drama, acting, pantomime and dance during the nineteenth century." So with the exception of the exact sciences, to which it is not applied, our word *art* corresponds rather well to the word *music* as used by the ancients.

What musical art, properly so called, was among them, we know only imperfectly. Some isolated facts, related perhaps with the same exaggeration of which we have daily comparable examples; inflated ideas, often altogether absurd, found in certain philosophers, besides the often false interpretation of what they wrote—all this has tended to attribute to the ancients' music an immense power, indeed, such an influence upon manners and mores, that legislators were compelled, in the public interest, to control its progress and regulate its use.

Disregarding the causes that may have contributed to garbling the truth on this point, and assuming that the music of the Greeks may really have produced on some individuals an extraordinary effect—an effect due neither to the ideas expressed by the poetry nor to the facial expression and acting ability of the singer, but really to music and to music alone—we still need not see in the fact any proof that the art had attained among them a high degree of perfection. Who does not know what a powerful effect violent musical sound in the most ordinary composition may have upon nervous temperaments under certain circumstances? For example, when excited by the intoxicating acclamations of a crowd of devotees, by the remembrance of recent triumphs and the hope of new victories, by the sight of weapons as well as that of the beautiful slaves around him, by thoughts of voluptuous love, glory, power, immortality—the whole enhanced by the potent action of good fare and wine, Alexander the Great (whose temperament was so impressionable that he raved with admiration to ecstasy at the singing of Timotheus) can easily be imagined moved, without any great effort of genius being required from the singer, to produce this almost morbid state of sensibility.

Rousseau, in citing the modern example of Eric, King of Denmark, who killed his faithful servants while in a state of frenzy caused by certain songs, points out that these unfortunates must have been far less susceptible to music than their master; or the danger would have been mutual. But the philosopher's love of paradox shows again in this witty piece of irony. Of course the servants of the Danish king were not so susceptible to music as their master. Would it not seem strange had it been otherwise? We know that the musical sense develops by use; we know also that certain affections of the soul, very active in some persons, are much less so in others; that nervous sensibility is, in some degree, the heritage of the upper classes of society; and that the lower classes, whether on account of the manual labour which they perform or for whatever reason, are relatively deprived of it. It is because of this undeniable inequality in conformation that one is compelled to limit, for the present definition of music, the number of those upon whom it exerts its full force.

Nevertheless, Rousseau, although at times he ridiculed the accounts of marvels effected by ancient music, at other times he seemed inclined to believe them and to such an extent that he ranked much above modern music the ancient kind which we know very little about and which Rousseau knew no better than we. He ought to have been the last to depreciate the effects of our present music, for the enthusiasm with which he speaks of it shows that its effects upon him were of an intensity quite out of the common. Be that as it may, ordinary observation enables one to cite in favor of the power of our music certain facts which, to say the least, are of an authority equal to that of the ancient historians' doubtful anecdotes. How often we have seen at performances of masterpieces by our great masters, listeners agitated by dreadful spasms; crying and laughing at the same time, and manifesting all the symptoms of delirium and fever! One young musician from Provence, under the influence of the passionate emotion engendered by Spontini's *La Vestale*, could not endure the idea of returning to our prosaic world. On leaving the poetic paradise that had opened before him and after writing to his friends of his intention and once again hearing the work that was the object of his ecstatic admiration, he thought (rightly) that he had attained the maximum sum of happiness reserved to man on earth, and at the door of the Opera blew out his brains.

The celebrated singer Mme. Malibran, hearing for the first time, at the Conservatoire, the C minor Symphony of Beethoven, was seized with convulsions to such a degree that she had to be carried from the room. A dozen times we have seen on similar occasions, normally calm persons who had to leave the hall in order to conceal from the public the violence of their emotions. As to those which the author of this essay owes to music, he may at once affirm that no words can give an exact idea of the experience to those who have never had it. Without speaking of the spiritual results that music has produced in him, and only speaking of impressions received at the very moment of listening to works that he admires, he can say in all sincerity: On hearing certain works my vital strength seems first of all doubled; I feel a delightful pleasure in which reason plays no part;

the habit of analysis follows by itself to engender admiration. Emotion then increases in direct proportion to the energy or grandeur of the composer's ideas and soon produces a strange turmoil in the circulation of the blood; my arteries throb violently; tears which usually indicate the end of the paroxysm, may also show only a progressive stage soon to be exceeded. In such a case, spasmodic contractions of the muscles supervene; the limbs tremble; there is a total numbness of the hands and feet; a partial paralysis of the nerves of sight and hearing; I no longer see or hear perfectly, am seized with giddiness and am half swooning.

No doubt, sensations carried to such a degree of violence are somewhat rare; besides which they can be counteracted by a contrasting effect, that of bad music, which generates the opposite of admiration and pleasure. No music acts more strongly to this effect than that which appears to me to present the two main defects of platitude and false expression. I then blush as if for shame; indignation takes hold of me; and looking at me one might think that I had just suffered some outrage of the kind that is beyond forgiveness. In order to get rid of the impression thus received I feel a general upheaval, a rejection by the entire organism, similar to the effort of vomiting when the stomach seeks to relieve itself of some nauseous potion. It is disgust and hatred carried to the extreme: such music exasperates me and I seem to vomit it from every pore.

Of course, the habit of disguising and controlling feelings means that this response is rarely displayed. If since my youth, it has once or twice happened to me to give free reign to this reflex, it has been from lack of proper time to think—I was taken unawares.

Modern music has, therefore, no cause to envy that of the ancients with respect to the power it can exert.

(*A Travers Chants,* 1862; translated by Jacques Barzun.)

# The Condition of Music

## WALTER PATER

*This famous passage by Walter Pater, high priest of the "decadence" movement, appeared first in magazine format, later in a revised version in Pater's notorious* Studies in the History of the Renaissance, *a book described by Pater's disciple Oscar Wilde as "the very flower of the decadence: the last trumpet should have sounded the moment it was written." Although Pater has been labeled a dandified formalist, the most extreme exponent of "art for art's sake," his overall point here about the relationship between form and substance no longer seems eccentric. What is still striking is Pater's elegant, oddly sensible notion that music has a jump on the other arts.*

A*ll art constantly aspires towards the condition of music.* For while in all other kinds of art it is possible to distinguish the matter from the form, and the understanding can always make this distinction, yet it is the constant effort of art to obliterate it. That the mere matter of a poem, for instance, its subject, namely, its given incidents or situation—that the mere matter of a picture, the actual circumstances of an event, the actual topography of a landscape—should be nothing without the form, the spirit, of the handling, that this form, this mode of handling, should become an end in itself, should penetrate every part of the matter: this is what all art constantly strives after, and achieves in different degrees.

This abstract language becomes clear enough, if we think of actual examples. In an actual landscape we see a long white road, lost suddenly on the hill-verge. That is the matter of one of the etchings of M. Alphonse Legros: only, in this etching, it is informed by an indwelling solemnity of expression, seen upon it or half-seen, within the limits of an exceptional moment, or caught from his own mood perhaps, but which he maintains as the very essence of the thing, throughout his work. Sometimes a momentary hint of stormy light may invest a homely or too familiar scene with a character which might well have been drawn from the deep places of the imagination. Then we might say that this particular effect of light, this sudden inweaving of gold thread through the texture of the haystack, and the poplars, and the grass, gives the scene artistic qualities, that it is like a picture. And such tricks of circumstance are commonest in landscape which has little salient character of its own; because, in such scenery, all the material details are so easily absorbed by that informing expression of passing light, and elevated, throughout their whole extent, to a new and delightful effect by it. And hence the superiority, for most conditions of the picturesque, of a river-side in France to a Swiss valley, because, on the French river-side, mere topography, the simple material, counts for so little, and, all being very pure, untouched, and tranquil in itself, mere light and shade have such easy work in modulating it to one dominant tone. The Venetian landscape, on the other hand, has in its material conditions much which is hard, or harshly definite; but the masters of the Venetian school have shown themselves little burdened by them. Of its Alpine background they retain certain abstracted elements only, of cool colour and tranquillising line; and they use its actual details, the brown windy turrets, the straw-coloured fields, the forest arabesques, but as the notes of a music which duly accompanies the presence of their men and women, presenting us with the spirit or essence only of a certain sort of landscape—a country of the pure reason or half-imaginative memory.

Poetry, again, works with words addressed in the first instance to the pure intelligence; and it deals, most often, with a definite subject or situation. Sometimes it may find a noble and quite legitimate function in the conveyance of moral or political aspiration, as often in the poetry of Victor Hugo. In such instances it is easy enough for the understanding to distinguish between the matter and the form, however much the matter, the subject, the element which is addressed to the mere intelligence, has been penetrated by the informing, artistic spirit. But the ideal types of poetry are those in which this distinction is reduced to its *minimum;* so that lyrical poetry, precisely because in it we are least able to detach the matter from the form, without a deduction of something from that matter itself, is, at least artistically, the highest and most complete form of poetry. And the very perfection of such poetry often appears to depend, in part, on a certain suppression or vagueness of mere subject, so that the meaning reaches us through ways not distinctly traceable by the understanding, as in some of the most imaginative compositions of William Blake, and often in Shakespeare's songs, as preeminently in that song of Mariana's page in *Measure for Measure,* in which the kindling force and poetry of the whole play seems to pass for a moment into an actual strain of music.

And this principle holds good of all things that partake in any degree of artistic qualities, of the furniture of our houses, and of dress, for instance, of life itself, of gesture and speech, and the details of daily intercourse; there also, for the wise, being susceptible of a suavity and charm, caught from the way in which they are done, which gives them a worth in themselves. Herein, again, lies what is valuable and justly attractive, in what is called the fashion of a time, which elevates the trivialities of speech, and manner, and dress, into "ends in themselves," and gives them a mysterious grace and attractiveness in the doing of them.

Art, then, is thus always striving to be independent of the mere intelligence, to become a matter of pure perception, to get rid of its responsibilities to its subject or material; the ideal examples of poetry and painting being those in which the constituent elements of the composition are so welded together, that the material or subject no longer strikes the intellect only; nor the form, the eye or the ear only; but form and matter, in their union or identity, present one single effect to the "imaginative reason," that complex faculty for which every thought and feeling is twin-born with its sensible analogue or symbol.

It is the art of music which most completely realises this artistic ideal, this perfect identification of matter and form. In its consummate moments, the end is not distinct from the means, the form from the matter, the subject from the expression; they inhere in and completely saturate each other; and to it, therefore, to the condition of its perfect moments, all the arts may be supposed constantly to tend and aspire. In music, then, rather than in poetry, is to be found the true type or measure of perfected art. Therefore, although each art has its incommunicable element, its untranslatable order of impressions, its unique mode of reaching the "imaginative reason," yet the arts may be represented as continually struggling after the law or principle of music, to a condition which music alone completely realises; and one of the chief functions of aesthetic criticism, dealing with the products of art, new or old, is to estimate the degree in which each of those products approaches, in this sense, to musical law.

(*Studies in the History of the Renaissance,* 1893 edition.)

# Opera and Realism

## JOSEPH ADDISON

*As with so many kinds of periodical essay, music criticism gained a substantial boost in literary quality and sheer readability in the pages of the London* Tatler *and* Spectator *(1709–12), published by playwright and coffeehouse personality Richard Steele. Besides Steele himself, the most important contributor to the two papers was Joseph Addison, who combined eighteenth-century values of balance and moderation with an irrepressible gift for wit and raillery. The following disquisitions on the use and abuse of animals and other props on the musical stage anticipates Stravinsky's essay on* The Firebird *two centuries later, where Stravinsky recalls one of Diaghilev's live horses—a "better critic than an actor"— leaving a "malodorous calling card." The use of special effects, live or otherwise, is to this day a contentious issue, but no one has addressed it more shrewdly than Addison. It should be noted that Nicolini, the singer referred to in both essays, was a leading castrato, which perhaps will clarify the joke about how a lion "will not hurt a virgin," as well as other specimens of Addison's less-than-kind humor.*

An opera may be allowed to be extravagantly lavish in its decorations, as its only design is to gratify the senses, and keep up an indolent attention in the audience. Common sense, however, requires, that there should be nothing in the scenes and machines which may appear childish and absurd. How would the wits of King Charles's time have laughed to have seen Nicolini exposed to a tempest in robes of ermine, and sailing in an open boat upon a sea of pasteboard! What a field of raillery would they have been let into, had they been entertained [in a production of Handel's *Rinaldo*] with painted dragons spitting wildfire, enchanted chariots drawn by

Flanders mares, and real cascades in artificial landscapes! A little skill in criticism would inform us, that shadows and realities ought not to be mixed together in the same piece; and that the scenes which are designed as the representations of nature, should be filled with resemblances, and not with the things themselves. If one would represent a wide champaign country filled with herds and flocks, it would be ridiculous to draw the country only upon the scenes, and to crowd several parts of the stage with sheep and oxen. This is joining together inconsistencies, and making the decoration partly real and partly imaginary. I would recommend what I have here said to the directors, as well as to the admirers, of our modern opera.

As I was walking in the streets about a fortnight ago, I saw an ordinary fellow carrying a cage full of little birds upon his shoulder; and, as I was wondering with myself what use he would put them to, he was met very luckily by an acquaintance, who had the same curiosity. Upon his asking him what he had upon his shoulder, he told him, that he had been buying sparrows for the opera. Sparrows for the opera! says his friend, licking his lips; what, are they to be roasted? No, no, says the other; they are to enter towards the end of the first act, and to fly about the stage.

This strange dialogue awakened my curiosity so far, that I immediately bought the opera, by which means I perceived the sparrows were to act the part of singing birds in a delightful grove; though, upon a nearer inquiry, I found the sparrows put the same trick upon the audience, that [Dryden's] Sir Martin Mar-all practised upon his mistress; for, though they flew in sight, the music proceeded from a consort of flagelets and bird-calls which were planted behind the scenes. At the same time I made this discovery, I found, by the discourse of the actors, that there were great designs on foot for the improvement of the opera; that it had been proposed to break down a part of the wall, and to surprise the audience with a party of an hundred horse; and that there was actually a project of bringing the New River into the house, to be employed in jetteaus and waterworks. This project, as I have since heard, is postponed till the summer season; when it is thought the coolness that proceeds from fountains and cascades will be more acceptable and refreshing to people of quality. In the meantime, to find out a more agreeable entertainment for the winter season, the opera of *Rinaldo* is filled with thunder and lightning, illuminations and fire-works; which the audience may look upon without catching cold, and indeed without much danger of being burnt; for there are several engines filled with water, and ready to play at a minute's warning, in case any such accident should happen. However, as I have a very great friendship for the owner of this theatre, I hope that he has been wise enough to insure his house before he would let this opera be acted in it.

It is no wonder that those scenes should be very surprising, which were contrived by two poets of different nations, and raised by two magicians of different sexes. Armida (as we are told in the argument) was an Amazonian enchantress, and poor Signor Cassani (as we learn from the persons represented) a Christian conjuror (Mago Christiano). I must confess I am very much puzzled to find how an Amazon should be versed in the black art; or how a good Christian (for such is the part of the magician) should deal with the devil.

To consider the poets after the conjurors, I shall give you a taste of the Italian from the first lines of his preface: Eccoti, benigno lettore, un parto di poche sere, che se ben nato di notte, non è però aborto di tenebre, mà si farà conoscere figliolo d'Apollo con qualche raggio di Parnasso. "Behold, gentle reader, the birth of a few evenings, which, though it be the offspring of the night, is not the abortive of darkness, but will make itself known to be the son of Apollo, with a certain ray of Parnassus." He afterwards proceeds to call Mynheer Hendel the Orpheus of our age, and to acquaint us, in the same sublimity of style, that he composed this opera in a fortnight. Such are the wits to whose tastes we so ambitiously conform ourselves. The truth of it is, the finest writers among the modern Italians express themselves in such a florid form of words, and such tedious circumlocutions, as are used by none but pedants in our own country; and at the same time fill their writings with such poor imaginations and conceits, as our youths are ashamed of before they have been two years at the university. Some may be apt to think that it is the difference of genius which produces this difference in the works of the two nations; but to show there is nothing in this, if we look into the writings of the old Italians, such as Cicero and Virgil, we shall find that the English writers, in their way of thinking and expressing themselves, resemble those authors much more than the modern Italians pretend to do. And as for the poet himself, from whom the dreams of this opera are taken, I must entirely agree with Monsieur

Boileau, that one verse in Virgil is worth all the clinquant or tinsel of Tasso.

But to return to the sparrows; there have been so many flights of them let loose in this opera, that it is feared the house will never get rid of them; and that in other plays they make their entrance in very wrong and improper scenes, so as to be seen flying in a lady's bed-chamber, or perching upon a king's throne; besides the inconveniences which the heads of the audience may sometimes suffer from them. I am credibly informed, that there was once a design of casting into an opera the story of Whittington and his cat, and that in order to do it, there had been got together a great quantity of mice; but Mr. Rich, the proprietor of the playhouse, very prudently considered, that it would be impossible for the cat to kill them all, and that consequently the princes of the stage might be as much infested with mice, as the prince of the island was before the cat's arrival upon it; for which reason he would not permit it to be acted in his house. And indeed I cannot blame him: for, as he said very well upon that occasion, I do not hear that any of the performers in our opera pretend to equal the famous pied piper, who made all the mice of a great town in Germany follow his music, and by that means cleared the place of those little noxious animals.

Before I dismiss this paper, I must inform my reader, that I hear there is a treaty on foot with London and Wise (who will be appointed gardeners of the playhouse) to furnish the opera of Rinaldo and Armida with an orange-grove; and that the next time it is acted, the singing birds will be personated by tom-tits: the undertakers being resolved to spare neither pains nor money for the gratification of the audience.

(*Spectator*, March 6, 1711.)

There is nothing that of late years has afforded matter of greater amusement to the town than Signor Nicolini's combat with a lion in the Haymarket, which has been very often exhibited to the general satisfaction of most of the nobility and gentry in the kingdom of Great Britain. Upon the first rumor of this intended combat, it was confidently affirmed, and is still believed by many in both galleries, that there would be a tame lion sent from the Tower every opera night, in order to be killed by Hydaspes; this report, though altogether groundless, so universally prevailed in the upper regions of the playhouse, that some of the most refined politicians in those parts of the audience gave it out in whisper, that the lion was a cousin-german of the tiger who made his appearance in King William's days, and that the stage would be supplied with lions at the public expense, during the whole session. Many likewise were the conjectures of the treatment which this lion was to meet with from the hands of Signor Nicolini: some supposed that he was to subdue him in recitativo, as Orpheus used to serve the wild beasts in his time, and afterwards to knock him on the head; some fancied that the lion would not pretend to lay his paws upon the hero, by reason of the received opinion, that a lion will not hurt a virgin; several, who pretended to have seen the opera in Italy, had informed their friends, that the lion was to act a part in High-Dutch, and roar twice or thrice to a thorough bass, before he fell at the feet of Hydaspes. To clear up a matter that was so variously reported, I have made it my business to examine whether this pretended lion is really the savage he appears to be, or only a counterfeit.

But before I communicate my discoveries, I must acquaint the reader, that upon my walking behind the scenes last winter, as I was thinking on something else, I accidentally justled against a monstrous animal that extremely startled me, and upon my nearer survey of it, appeared to be a lion rampant. The lion, seeing me very much surprised, told me, in a gentle voice, that I might come by him if I pleased: "For," says he, "I do not intend to hurt anybody." I thanked him very kindly, and passed by him. And in a little time after saw him leap upon the stage, and act his part with very great applause. It has been observed by several, that the lion has changed his manner of acting twice or thrice since his first appearance; which will not seem strange, when I acquaint my reader that the lion has been changed upon the audience three several times. The first lion was a candle-snuffer, who being a fellow of a testy, choleric temper, overdid his part, and would not suffer himself to be killed so easily as he ought to have done; besides, it was observed of him, that he grew more surly every time he came out of the lion, and having dropped some words in ordinary conversation, as if he had not fought his best, and that he suffered himself to be thrown upon his back in the scuffle, and that he would wrestle with Mr. Nicolini for what he pleased, out of his lion's skin, it was thought proper to discard him; and it is verily believed, to this day, that had he been brought upon the stage another time, he would certainly have done mischief. Besides, it was objected against the first lion, that he reared himself so high upon his hinder paws, and walked in so erect a posture, that he looked more like an old man than a lion.

The second lion was a tailor by trade, who belonged to the playhouse, and had the character of a mild and peaceable man in his profession. If the former was too furious, this was too sheepish for his part; insomuch that after a short, modest walk upon the stage, he would fall at the first touch of Hydaspes, without grappling with him, and giving him an opportunity of showing his variety of Italian trips. It is said, indeed, that he once gave him a rip in his flesh-colored doublet; but this was only to make work for himself, in his private character of a tailor. I must not omit that it was this second lion who treated me with so much humanity behind the scenes.

The acting lion at present is, as I am informed, a country gentleman, who does it for his diversion, but desires his name may be concealed. He says, very handsomely, in his own excuse, that he does not act for gain; that he indulges an innocent pleasure in it; and that it is better to pass away an evening in this manner than in gaming and drinking: but at the same time says, with a very agreeable raillery upon himself, that if his name should be known, the ill-natured world might call him, "the ass in the lion's skin." This gentleman's temper is made out of such a happy mixture of the mild and choleric, that he outdoes both his predecessors, and has drawn together greater audiences than have been known in the memory of man.

I must not conclude my narrative, without taking notice of a groundless report that has been raised to a gentleman's disadvantage, of whom I must declare myself an admirer; namely, that Signor Nicolini and the lion have been seen sitting peaceably by one another, and smoking a pipe together behind the scenes; by which their common enemies would insinuate, that it is but a sham combat which they represent upon the stage: but upon inquiry I find, that if any such correspondence has passed between them, it was not till the combat was over, when the lion was to be looked upon as dead, according to the received rules of the drama. Besides, this is what is practised every day in Westminster Hall, where nothing is more usual than to see a couple of lawyers, who have been tearing each other to pieces in the court, embracing one another as soon as they are out of it.

I would not be thought, in any part of this relation, to reflect upon Signor Nicolini, who in acting this part only complies with the wretched taste of his audience; he knows very well, that the lion has many more admirers than himself; as they say of the famous equestrian statue on the Pont Neuf at Paris, that more people go to see the horse than the king who sits upon it. On the contrary, it gives me a just indignation to see a person whose action gives new majesty to kings, resolution to heroes, and softness to lovers, thus sinking from the greatness of his behavior, and degraded into the character of the London Prentice. I have often wished, that our tragedians would copy after this great master in action. Could they make the same use of their arms and legs, and inform their faces with as significant looks and passions, how glorious would an English tragedy appear with that action which is capable of giving a dignity to the forced thoughts, cold conceits, and unnatural expressions of an Italian opera! In the meantime, I have related this combat of the lion, to show what are at present the reigning entertainments of the politer part of Great Britain.

Audiences have often been reproached by writers for the coarseness of their taste; but our present grievance does not seem to be the want of a good taste, but of common sense.

(*Spectator,* March 15, 1711.)

# The Recording Angel

## EVAN EISENBERG

*Nothing in recent history has more profoundly influenced the way we experience music than recordings. An entire literature of short pieces on this phenomenon exists, stretching from writers such as Paul Rosenfeld and B. H. Haggin a half century ago to recent manifestos, pro and con, from performers such as Eric Leinsdorf, Arthur Rubinstein, and Glenn Gould. Yet until Evan Eisenberg's* The Recording Angel *appeared in 1987, we had no full-length study of the subject. Eisenberg, who contributes articles on music and culture to the* Nation *and other publications, makes clear that recordings are by no means an adjunct or representation of live music but a distinct, separate art form that has changed virtually every aspect of our musical life. Eisenberg's is a free-wheeling philosophical work of a kind that has become all too infrequent in our culture.*

However ersatz, however stratified, a musical architecture of time did exist in the nineteenth century. It was shattered by the phonograph. Before the phonograph any playing of music (with the single exception of a musician's playing for himself) was perforce a social event. People had to get together—Prince Leopold of Cöthen with his court orchestra. Count Rasumovsky with the rest of his amateur quartet, young Bernard Shaw with a thousand other Wagnerites, a hundred instrumentalists, a dozen singers, a conductor and sundry stagehands. So people got together, and to simplify matters they got together at regular intervals. Such practicalities had always supported music's link with ritual. When the phonograph arrived, much of that scaffolding collapsed.

For music was now an object that could be owned by the individual and used at his own convenience. There was no need to cooperate, coordinate or share with anyone else. Technically the musicians were still necessary; given the economics of production, so was the rest of the audience. But only technically. Once the record was owned they disappeared.

Now the *Symphony of a Thousand* could play to an audience of one. Now a man could hear nocturnes at breakfast, vespers at noon and the Easter Oratorio on Chanukah. He could do his morning crossword to the "One O'Clock Jump" and make love right through the *St Matthew Passion*. Anything was possible; nothing was sacred; freedom was (barring complaints from the neighbours and occasional desperate holding actions such as the Russian synod's 1912 ban on the recording of prayers) absolute. It was the freedom, once the cathedral of culture had been wrecked, to take home the bits you liked and arrange them as you pleased. Once again a mechanical invention had met capitalism's need to recreate all of life in its image. The cathedral of culture was now a supermarket.

My generation might be forgiven for harbouring a grudge against Glenn Gould, since he left the concert stage before we had a chance to hear him. In fact, we were too busy listening to his records to mind.* His records proved to us that classical music was not all sentiment and decorum, dressing up for concerts and pleasing one's teacher; that it could be sharp-boned and lonely, giving the same ecstasy as a chemistry set, a chess game, or rain rushing the breach of a car window. And his writings, if we had noticed them, could have given us a little more of that ecstasy, along with some hints on how it might be understood. . . .

It may be that some classical musicians will successfully follow his example, marketing themselves as personalities without appearing in person. But the economics of recording are not charitable to serious musicians, so most will probably have to keep concertizing. And Gould, in his heart of hearts, may not really have expected all the young musicians to follow him into the studio, any more than Thoreau expected America to follow him into the woods. His recitals had set an example for younger pianists, but the purifying of performance that he had begun could be completed only by an act of

*See headnote to "Scarlatti's Keyboard Quirks."—Ed.

negation. One could even say, without irony, that Gould served the concert stage best by leaving it: as he wrote of Schönberg, 'whenever one honestly defies a tradition, one becomes, in reality, the more responsible to it.'

But one never knows, or one knows only later. History may conclude that Gould was the one sane musician of the century; and his colleagues who work the continents like travelling salesmen, unpacking their hearts from Altoona to Vancouver, may seem as pathetic to our grandchildren as the bowing and scraping geniuses of the eighteenth century seem to us. In this sense, Gould may prove to have been our Beethoven. However that may be, it is too bad that Gould's morbid interest in the death of live music should have drawn attention from his tidings that a new art, the art of recorded music— what I call phonography—had been born. Gould was right to believe that the centre of musical gravity was now the spindle hole. He was right to insist that recorded music be viewed not as a reproduction of the concert but as an independent art, as distinct from live music as film is distinct from theatre.

The word 'record' is misleading. Only live recordings record an event; studio recordings, which are the great majority, record nothing. Pieced together from bits of actual events, they construct an ideal event. They are like the composite photograph of a minotaur. Yet Edison chose the word deliberately. He meant his invention to record grandparents' voices, business transactions and, as a last resort, musical performances. The use we put it to now might strike him as fraudulent, like doctoring the records. . . .

One is supposed to judge a stereo system by comparing its sound to live music. If the music one listens to is pure phonography—a pure studio product—that is impossible. One must either rely on laboratory measurements, or follow one's tastes without regard for accuracy. The first course is unsatisfying; the second is general among pop listeners and is said to have produced a vogue of 'artificial' sound—excessively bright, with an emphasis on the extreme treble and bass—among speaker manufacturers. But if producers use these as studio reference speakers, then these are the proper vehicles of their sonic intentions.

Even in the classical sphere, live music is only one touchstone of recorded sound. Fidelity itself is a vexatious concept. A producer might attempt to make a record in Carnegie Hall that, when played back in Carnegie Hall, would fool a blindfolded audience. To do this he would have to remove most of the hall's natural resonance from the recording, lest it multiply itself and muffle the music. The resulting record would sound dismal in a living room. The orchestra would not sound like an orchestra, because it would lack the associated ambience. Yet it would be faithful, in a sense, to the original. On the other hand, a record that captures all the resonance of Carnegie Hall may overwhelm the average living room. So most studio recordings try to strike a balance.

As much as Partch's chromelodeon or Nancarrow's Ampico,* the clavichord of Bach and the viol of Purcell fall outside the common language of piano and orchestra. We can play Bach and Purcell on modern instruments, and it is good that we can; but as we dig deeper into the past of music, that contortion feels more and more awkward. As the harmonic language becomes less familiar we become more apt to think of the music as sound, and more anxious to hear the sound of the original instruments. Now, if we had to depend on the proliferation of viols and clavichords, shawms and sackbuts in the small towns of the world, few of us would ever hear old music as it was meant to be heard. But we have records. The original-instrument movement is just as phonographic as the new-and-original-instrument movement. It is the other side of the coin. So one is not surprised to find in a 1955 essay by Varèse his wish 'to see revived the instruments for which Monteverdi, Lully and their predecessors wrote.' What are all these original-instrument recordings, after all, if not wish-fulfilment dreams dreamt by the phonograph? The ideal original-instrument recording of a Bach cantata is the one Bach would have made in the Thomaskirche.

'Under the charm of the Dionysian,' Nietzsche writes, 'nature which has become alienated, hostile or subjugated, celebrates once more her reconciliation with her lost son, man.' But if music might exist without a world, [as Schopenhauer asserts] surely it might exist without man. We ought to be modern enough by now to listen to music and hear a world in which the presence of man is contingent, even irrelevant.

*"New" instruments invented by these composers.—Ed.

Thanks to the atom bomb, we can hear the last movement of Vaughan Williams's Sixth Symphony as a peroration on the absolutely empty field of a future war. (The old composer's rumbling speech, so oddly appended to an early recording, may have been meant by Decca to relieve that emptiness.) But plenty of pre-atomic music can also be heard as non-human. Beethoven's outer-space music in the Ninth Symphony—the ascending minor thirds following the words 'über Sternen muss er wohnen'—never sounds quite right coming from woodwind players in dinner jackets; it sounds right coming from the blankness of a loudspeaker, preferably one perched on high. But the movement as a whole, to which Nietzsche refers us for a vision of Dionysian ecstasy, remains willfully human. Elsewhere Beethoven, instead of willing away his loneliness, lets it conduct him to icy, untenanted landscapes. The beginning of the Ninth Symphony suggests the creation of the world, an event no human was around to get emotional about. The slow movement of the second quarter in Opus 59 is like a barren planet, unvisited even by the artist who describes it, scattered with ruined porticos and the insteps of statues—or so it seems to me under the influence of the phonograph.

The standard outer-space music of today is electronic, the phonograph finding its own voice. It ranges from video game blips to the astral extravaganzas of Stockhausen (the first electronic work to be commissioned by a record company, Subotnick's *Silver Apples of the Moon*, falls plunk in the middle of the range). Varèse planned a dramatic work about an astronomer who exchanges signals with Sirius and who, when set upon by the uncomprehending masses, is translated there by 'radiation instantée.' The basis of this story was an American Indian folk-tale whose hero Varèse connected with the *Übermensch* of Nietzsche.

Let us follow this trail a little farther. Richard Strauss, one of several gray eminences impressed by the young Varèse, wrote his own more direct treatment of Nietzsche's theme. This was not overplayed until Stanley Kubrick used it in *2001: A Space Odyssey*, another story about a man who leaves mankind behind. Immediately the opening fanfare became (like Holst's *The Planets*) a standard audio demonstration piece. The drums and organ could be found in Mouret; what really counted was the sense of galaxies announcing themselves to their chosen one.

Intelligence from another planet is expected to manifest itself in simple geometric shapes. The monolith of *2001* is one such token; and it is easy to feel, as the mighty theme music springs from it, that the disc is another. As it happens, we have chosen the disc as our own envoy to the rest of the sapient universe, such as it may be. Accompanying each of the two Voyager spacecraft as they hurry to their appointments unspecified light-years away, is a gold-plated record encoded with human music—Bach, Beethoven, Chuck Berry, Javanese gamelan—spoken greetings and, somehow or other, photographs of life on earth. 'Billions of years from now,' Carl Sagan writes, 'our sun . . . will have reduced Earth to a charred cinder. But the Voyager record will still be largely intact . . . preserving a murmur of an ancient civilization that once flourished . . . on the distant planet Earth.'

Officially, the medium was chosen for its simplicity and permanence (a golden record is permanent if you don't play it). Deeper reasons are suggested by the cover art of the book *Murmurs of Earth*, which shows the golden record afloat in space, at home among the other orbs. A record is a world. It is the world scratched by man in a form that may survive him.

(*The Recording Angel: Explorations in Phonography*, 1987.)

# A Matter of Time and Space

## ANTHONY BURGESS

*Anthony Burgess has spent much of his career exploring the relationship between literature and music. A prominent novelist and literary essayist, he is also the composer of three symphonies and the lyrics to the Broadway show* Cyrano. *In novels such as* Napoleon Symphony, *he has experimented with musical form; in others such as* A Clockwork Orange, *he has used music (in this case, Beethoven's Ninth Symphony) as a central element in his themes and plots; in essays such as the following excerpt from* This Man and Music, *he tackles in a clear, no-nonsense way what he calls "the damnable problem of the meaning of music."*

Music and literature have this in common—that the dimension they work in is time. Having said that, I feel a twinge of dubiety about literature, whose very name celebrates a kind of subordination of time to space, since 'letters' freeze the temporal flux of speech into space-occupying symbols, and literature may be seen as the artistic disposition of these symbols. To carve on a stone slab some such line of verse as SVNT LACHRIMAE RERVM ET MENTEM MORTALIA TANGVNT looks like the victory of space over time: the flux, which carries everything away into oblivion, has been arrested; an object occupying space, deep incisions in a time-defying substance, proclaims the permanence of letters, as opposed to the transience of speech. But to think of literature in these terms is to confuse a reality with a mere appearance. The reality of literature, as opposed to its appearance in written or printed records, is the organization of speech sounds, and this makes literature a temporal art, a twin of music.

On the other hand, if we take the reality of literature to reside in a text, and not a performance, the art functions in the realm of the eye, and not of the ear, and this draws literature away from an art which, as is universally acknowledged, has no meaning except as an auditory experience. Shakespeare's plays are intended for performance. The playwright himself, as far as we know, had no interest in the printed text. If quartos of most of the plays were published in his lifetime, this was to protect the Lord Chamberlain's Men from the pirates. Shorthand writers would take down garbled versions of the plays at whose performance they assisted, and then sell these imperfect transcriptions to printers. If a 'bad' quarto of *Hamlet* circulated, the only thing to do was to publish the true text in a 'good' quarto. This had nothing to do with Shakespeare's desire to be an Ovid or Virgil and transmit his works to posterity. The play to him was less a text than the sum of the performances of the play. But posterity itself has decided that Shakespeare was wrong, and that the reality of Shakespeare resides in a printed book. *Hamlet* is not the sum of its performances: it is an ideal and hence unrealizable performance. No acted version of *Hamlet* can be much more than a partial, and hence imperfect, interpretation of that supreme reality the text.

The text is clearly as much a spatial artefact as a painting, a sculpture, or a work of architecture. The eye can travel freely through it and over it. The printed words symbolize the temporal flux of speech, but they are an improvement on speech because visual solidity has replaced the transience of the auditory experience. In a knotty sentence of *The Winter's Tale,* unintelligible in performance, the elements can be disentangled by the eye, the statement broken up and then reassembled. This is as much a spatial process as the repairing of an automobile engine. But clearly Shakespeare never intended us to do this. The reality was the performance, and perhaps the unintelligibility was part of the artistic intention. We have come to regard the text as the great visual reality because we confuse letters as art with letters as information.

The legal document, the scientific textbook, the theological discourse with sidenotes and footnotes—these do not pretend to be literature in the sense that literature is an appeal to the imagination. In taking in printed information, we engage only the reason, and the reason is best satisfied if it can regard words as visual counters and not auditory complexes. If I read a line of poetry, I cannot be unaware of its auditory content: there will be a rhythm close to that of music, and there will be sonic organization in the verbal statement. But it will be possible to treat that line as a spatial entity, since my eye can travel over it as with a painting or a sculpture. In reading a formula like $a + a + a = 3a$ or 'If a body is immersed in water the loss of weight of the body is equal to the weight of the water displaced,' the reason ignores the symbols as notations of speech sounds and concentrates on their semantic content. Works of literature, especially novels, are often treated in the same way. There is a confusion between the aesthetic and the didactic intentions, and we can end with the heresy that literature is a non-auditory art.

Now only to the highly rarefied musician will the text of a sonata or a symphony be the primal reality. Ernest Newman, the eminent music critic and Wagner scholar, held that there was more true artistic joy in the silent reading of a score than in going to a concert. After all, Beethoven was deaf when he composed his greatest works, and who could deny the reality of the inner auditory experience of that towering genius? Newman seemed to regard Beethoven's deafness as a victory of the musical imagination over the crass imperfections of the physical ear: let us all be like Beethoven—i.e. deaf. But Beethoven would have given his eyes in order to have the use of his ears. The Newmanian heresy was, for a time, quite widely diffused. In the twenties there was one work that everybody knew but nobody had heard—Bernard van Dieren's *Chinese Symphony*. There was no great urgency in the arrangement of a concert performance: everybody who counted knew what the music sounded like. Cecil Gray, another eminent musicologist, composed an oratorio based on Flaubert's *La Tentation de Saint-Antoine,* which he had no intention of having realized in performance. The work was there in the text, not to be freed from it, and the musical reality could be shut away in a cupboard. It was commonly believed by Newman and others that Bach, having completed a complex work like the *Art of Fugue,* had no other desire than to shove it into a drawer and forget about it. Music was a kind of purgation on which the chain could be pulled.

There is, one must admit, a large temptation to regard a musical text as a spatial territory for free wandering. An orchestral score, especially a complex one like that of Stravinsky's *Le Sacre du Printemps,* looks like a non-representational work of visual art, and it invites slow and silent poring. We can take an orchestral sound to pieces and then put it back together again. We can analyse texture and appraise instrumental balance. But all this is ancillary to the auditory experience of performance: it is an aspect of learning about music and not listening to it. Any musical work is what Shakespeare presumably thought a play to be—the sum of all its performances. The play and the poem and the novel have come to be regarded as primarily visual realities because of the supreme physical advantages of a printed text—portability, porability, privacy. Though we can now carry around a miniature cassette-reader and a recording of *Hamlet*, it is unlikely that literature for the eye will easily let itself be superseded. But it is essential that we retain the notion of literature as meaningful sound, art working through time not space.

It is of course somewhat drastic to make a division of art into two distinct categories, these spatial, those temporal. Spatial art, such as painting, sculpture and architecture, cannot be divorced from time: there is no such thing as rigid instantaneity of perception of a picture, statue or cathedral. The eye has to travel over and through the parts which add up to the whole of the two-dimensional structure which is a landscape or portrait or non-representational pattern of line and colour. With the three-dimensional art of sculpture, the body as well as the eye must move to take in successively the various planes. The appraisal of architecture involves a kind of circular travel, within and without. But the time attached to the spatial arts is of a special kind when compared with the time through which music operates. Music begins at the beginning and goes straight through to the end; it is a fixed pattern of successions. The visual arts make time truckle to spatial form: time is rhapsodic, unpatterned. Time is an unfortunate necessity, not the stuff of the art itself.

(*This Man and Music*, 1982.)

# Music and Sin

## H . L . MENCKEN

*That classical music has only recently come to be synonymous with the bland and the predictable is suggested by this biting Mencken article from only half a century ago. From Mozart to Richard Strauss, composers once unleashed erotic, subversive energies that generated controversy of a kind good for art and often for commerce as well (as Charles Rosen suggests above in "The Erotic Mozart.") Today, the "aphrodisiacal" works celebrated by Mencken are regarded as having about as much of an erotic charge as Muzak. Even jazz—as Mencken would undoubtedly be pleased to know—has been tamed for "lite" consumption. (For more on Mencken as music critic, see the headnote to "The Clarity of Haydn.")*

The delusion seems to persist that jazz is highly aphrodisiacal. I never encounter a sermon on the subject without finding it full of dark warnings to parents, urging them to keep their nubile daughters out of the jazz palaces on the ground that the voluptuous music will inflame their passions and so make them easy prey to bond salesmen, musicians and other such carnal fellows. All this seems to me to be nonsense. Jazz, in point of fact, is not voluptuous at all. Its monotonous rhythms and puerile tunes make it a sedative rather than a stimulant. If it is an aphrodisiac, then the sound of riveting is also aphrodisiac. What fetches the flappers who come to grief in the jazz parlors is not the music at all, but the alcohol. Drinking it out of flasks in the washrooms, they fail to keep the dose in harmony with their natural resistance, and so they lose control of their faculties, and what follows is lamentable. Jazz, which came in with Prohibition, gets the blame that belongs to its partner. In the old days, when it was uncommon for refined women to get drunk at dances, it would have been quite harmless. To-day even Chopin's funeral march would be dangerous.

The truth is that jazz is probably the least voluptuous variety of music commonly heard in Christendom. There are plenty of Methodist hymns that are ten times as aphrodisiacal, and the fact is proved by the scandals that follow every camp-meeting. In most parts of the United States, indeed, the Methodists have begun to abandon camp-meetings as subversive of morality. Where they still flourish it is not unusual for even the rev. clergy to be taken in Byzantine practices. But so-called good music is yet worse than the Methodist hymns. Has the world so soon forgotten James Huneker's story of the prudent opera mamma who refused to let her daughter sing Isolde, on the ground that no woman could ever get through the second act without forgetting God? That second act, even so, is much overestimated. There are piano pieces of Chopin that are a hundred times worse; if the Comstocks really had any sense, they would forbid their performance. And what of the late Puccini? If *La Bohème* is not an aphrodisiac, then what is? Yet it is sung publicly all over the world. Only in Atlanta, Ga., is there a law against it, and even that law was probably inspired by the fact that it was written by a Catholic and not by the fact that it has brought hundreds of thousands of Christian women to the abyss.

Old Ludwig himself was not without guilt. His "Egmont" overture is a gross and undisguised appeal to the *medulla oblongata.* And what of his symphonies and quartettes? The last movement of his "Eroica" is not only voluptuous to the last degree; it is also Bolshevistic. Try to play it with your eyes on a portrait of Dr. Calvin Coolidge. You will find the thing as impossible as eating ice cream on roast beef. At the time of its first performance in Vienna the moral sense of the community was so greatly outraged that Beethoven had to get out of town for a while. I pass over Wagner, whose *Tristan und Isolde* was probably his most decorous work, despite Huneker—think of *Parsifal!*—and come to Richard Strauss! Here I need offer no argument: his *Salome* and *Elektra* have been prohibited by the police, at one time or another, in nearly every country in the world. I believe *Der Rosenkavalier* is still worse, though the police leave it unmolested. Compare its first act to the most libidinous jazz ever heard of on Broadway. It is like comparing vodka to ginger-pop. No woman who hears it is ever the same again. She may remain within the law, but her thoughts are wayward henceforth. Into her ear the sirens have poured their abominable song. She has been beset by witches. There is a sinister glitter in her eye.

    (*Prejudices,* 1926.)

# Why Opera?

## JACQUES BARZUN

*In this provocative article, Jacques Barzun pinpoints the essence of opera—its meaning, appeal, historical significance, and peculiar separateness from the rest of music. As with his exploration of program music in "Literature in Liszt's Mind and Work" in this volume, Barzun sums up a complex phenomenon in clear language, taking on its own terms a form not always approved of by "intellectuals" and seeking out its value. An alternate title for this piece might be "Let Opera Be Opera."*

To the student of tastes and fashions (who at times dignifies his efforts by calling himself a cultural historian), the variable fate of opera presents some attractive puzzles. For example: Why did the genre take so long to develop—or was Greek tragedy an early fulfillment of operatic strivings, as Wagner believed? Again, why does opera divide music-lovers into two groups, one of them looking down its nose at the other, which meanwhile is looking through a lorgnette? Is this two-party system merely Eye versus Ear?

More topical is the question: Why has opera (other than Wagner's work) come back into repute among intellectuals? In my young time, fifty years ago, it took courage to say "Italian opera" except as a term of abuse. And for a final wonder, why is it that in opera the standard repertory, always and everywhere, consists almost wholly of works of the second rank? The great masterpieces are played occasionally, as a concession. It is as if the symphony orchestras fed on Dvořák and Grieg and Saint-Saëns, and the Great Books programs promoted Trollope and Dumas and Robert Louis Stevenson.

To hazard a single answer to the last two questions, I would suggest that opera is a form of art dedicated to central rather than elevated impulses. It supplies the touch of nature that makes us all kin and is neither noble nor profound. In fact, the true province of opera is Vanity and Violence. No one should find this truth unpalatable or think opera unworthy in consequence. In art that *is* art, nothing is to be scorned for what it portrays, though the same spectacle in the moral life might incur blame.

If opera does indeed concentrate on something universal and *common,* then it is clear why intellectual opinion between, say, 1890 and 1940 was hostile to the genre: its very virtues repelled. Symbolists and aesthetes loathed anything large, loud, public and decisive. Only a lucky accident made them accept Wagner as a cultural hero about that time and permitted his works to satisfy their operatic desires without shaming the partakers. Wagner's message and musical system occupied their delicate minds while his powerful thrills coursed through their gratified bodies. But in Donizetti, Verdi, Gounod and the rest there was—or appeared to be— no similar mind-stuff, so the prevailing snobisms abandoned them to the use of an inferior order of being, the opera-lover.

Now all is changed, and the sensitive freely discourse on the fine points, in any and every opera, of interpretation, setting and score. The experience of the Second World War, it would seem, reconciled artists and thinkers to the permanency of Vanity and Violence and to their expression in art. Indeed, all the arts have adopted for themselves the violent, the grotesque, the implausible. But even this obvious transformation will doubtless fall short of convincing. I must therefore explain what I mean by the pair of words I have used. Vanity is pomp, show, the ego asserting itself not meanly but in magnificence, in costume—the ego royal, the *Dongiovann'ego.*

Whether individual or collective, this ego animates the operatic soul and pushes it always in one direction—toward violence. Dueling, assassination, suicide and war are the normal activities of the operatic population, regardless of age or sex. For vanity on the grand scale cannot be patient or conciliatory; it is not the haughty pride that is content with self-approval. Because the operatic life is lived in public, face must be saved. Consequently, the occupational disease of an operatic hero is death. Consult the plots of the familiar operas and you find the enemy invariably defied, not argued with. The obstacle is removed, not negotiated out of the way. Even love is conducted in a take-it-or-leave-it style that fittingly ends in poisoned cups and signals to the executioner over the head of the weeping (and scheming) she.

To be sure, tender and gentle persons are often worked into the fabric of operas, but this innocence is there to heighten the contrast—or to feed vanity's contempt for the feeble. Think of poor Ottavio, trailing his useless sword well behind the fierce skirts of Donna Anna. Yet even he can think of no principle of action but "vendicar," because her grief "morte mi dà"—words that Mozart underlines with martial notes of ludicrous effect, being uttered by a forcible-feeble avenger. To rank as an operatic hero he should have unsheathed at the first opportunity and, at the very least, dispatched Leporello. This requirement explains why the unworldly composers, such as Brahms and César Franck, cannot be imagined as driving their muse to write an opera. As for the masterly inactivity of *Pelléas*, it is a *tour de force* that will not bear repetition. Violence is there, but muted—though no beholder will forget the extensive vanity of Mélisande's wig.

The artistic justification for this perpetual violence rooted in vanity is that grand opera is a visual art for a large audience. Obviously, subtle gestures and facial expressions will not carry to such an assembly eager for spectacle. But opera is not merely spectacular, it is verbal and musical too; and while the ears are occupied it is difficult to follow light or rapid movements on the stage. Hence a perfect logic dictates the combination of strong, simple feelings with large, unmistakable manifestations. The amateur of chamber music or *théâtre intime* calls them respectively crude feelings and blatant manifestations; he is applying the criteria of one genre to the features of another, which is to be thoroughly *un*critical. In opera, the sympathetic and educated ear detects and enjoys the subtleties, the refinements, with which the composer has decorated and deepened the gross goings-on of his puppets.

The wise man therefore accepts the conventions of opera (even while he laughs at them) instead of getting indignant like Tolstoy in his famous critique. In opera it is both funny and quite right that declarations of love, like tender reproaches and useless pleas, should be addressed to the back of the other person twenty feet away. Both parties need plenty of air and room for the limbs. If at some point they *must* embrace, they do so side by side, like Siamese twins, once again in the interests of free play for the diaphragm. Similar management is needed for the struggle over that leaden goblet containing the poison unknown to science. Firmly grasped by the two contestants, it must be tugged at semi-rhythmically regardless of the dynamics of liquids: those of the music are far more important.

To generalize, in opera—as in all public displays—convention rules and petty realism does not matter. Ritual makes clear the intention, which is why a good opera calls for gorgeous costume, costume magnified beyond credibility and the power to sit down, as in the real life of the eighteenth century. It is true that *Wozzeck* and *Louise* almost manage with department-store clothes, but I predict that future directors of those operas will jealously preserve and gradually exaggerate the period look, for just the reason I advance. Opera wants gold braid and bright reds, sequins and long trains and tiaras: they are half the action, the other half being the scenery. To clinch the point, one need only appeal to experience: the acme of fulfillment for the Idea of Opera is the horse. The horse is the ostentatious and military animal, the visible animal easily identified, the animal that connotes grandeur and expense, the only animal that dresses well. Man on top of horse is the implacable conqueror, the symbol of vain and violent human nature. As a meal on the stage is to a comedy of manners, so is a horse to an opera.

You may argue that opera also gives us the undistinguished peasants and the beggar who is a prince in disguise. Yes, but how in fact are they dressed? They never wear any garment acknowledging a single source of material, but always those amazing confections made of innumerable bits of differently colored cloth, like the décor of a yacht club, hung in bunches at various points of the body. And that is the correct rendering for opera of the appropriate phrase "a peasant, a beggar, in rags."

The true lover of opera, then, is the man whose soul responds with "Ha Ha" to the sound of trumpets. He is not ashamed to recognize within himself the operatic emotions, and he is happy to suspend disbelief about their contrived occasions. He accepts those cruel edicts of bearded royalty, needless sacrifices of tremulous vestals, implausibly mistaken identities in darkened colonnades, absurd displays of trust in patent villains, life-and-death decisions turning on a harsh modulation, and protracted harangues in which lovers turn from banter to ferocity because for eight bars the orchestra has been smoldering with suspicion.

The opera-lover willingly pays the price of his own transient skepticism because he knows how fundamental all this madness is to the life of mankind. He knows that what he beholds transfigured in opera is the essence of government and the state, the façade and parade of public life. He knows that in earlier centuries, and notably in the age of Shakespeare, the playhouse used to afford this same spectacle of gorgeousness, violence and the flourish of trumpets. A thinning of the blood of taste on the one hand, and an *embourgeoisement* of manners on the other, removed this great element from the theater, leaving only the tragedies of domesticated men and women in dark suits and short dresses. Perhaps the last horse seen on the legitimate stage was in *The Italian Straw Hat,* and he is there as a joke. . . .

There remains the paradox that I mentioned at the outset, of the greatest operas seeming to be less fit for common use than those of the second rank. When the operas of Mozart, Weber, Handel, Boito, Gluck, Beethoven, Spontini, Berlioz, Mussorgsky or Montemezzi are played from time to time, it is with an air of bestowing a favor on the demanding few among the regular audience, which prefers its heavy dose of Verdi and Puccini year in and year out, content to compare one singer with another. The so-called standard works are evidently the solid, nourishing part of the diet; the others are like a rich dessert not to be overindulged in. Some are tempted to explain the difference by the superior dramatic force of the works that have, as the phrase goes, won a place in the repertory. If this were true, we should have *Don Giovanni* once a week the world over; for it is surely the best of all librettos allied to the greatest of all operatic music. And *Carmen* would come next in popularity. No, if drama were indispensable to public favor, Wagner's works would still be unperformed. With the exception of a very few works, for example *Euryanthe* and *The Magic Flute,* a bad libretto has never harmed an opera. For opera, as I hope to have shown, is spectacle—not drama, not even theater.

This truth perhaps explains why the operas generally called great are not the most popular: they distract by some excess—of music, of drama, of idea, of variety, of wit, of fancy, of tender feeling.

In a word, they are not pure show and brilliant surface, but lead our souls into something darker and deeper or finer and gayer than vanity and violence. Beethoven's *Fidelio,* for example, or Weber's *Oberon,* moves in a realm of poetry unknown to Puccini, a realm that Verdi entered only with *Otello* and *Falstaff,* and this is true even though the stories of *Fidelio* and *Oberon* are silly enough for any opera—or were until dramatic music transfigured them.

To illustrate the difference, one need only compare what Gounod makes of the Faust legend with what Goethe, Berlioz, Boito or Busoni made of it. In the admirable *Faust* of Gounod there is the show of everything and the meaning of nothing. Mephisto is devilishly like the Devil, Gretchen is a model of purity, Faust the public notion of a philosopher-rake, and Valentin what any brother would want to be. When a daring director makes the Walpurgisnacht resemble the kind of orgy that would bring in the police, the Idea of Opera is satisfied. For these notions and facsimiles are realities too, the common kind, which we should not deny or scoff at merely because there are other, stranger realities for art to embody. The musical *Fausts* of the three B's I have named are perhaps disqualified as operas by their meddling with those stranger truths; certainly Berlioz' *Damnation de Faust* should never be staged, its own fit form having to be mangled when staging is attempted.

But the form is not the point here so much as the dramatic and poetic conception of the music; it is this conception that makes the great operas differ from the standard ones. To illustrate by yet another comparison, the death of Valentin in Gounod is operatically perfect; that of Boris in Mussorgsky, or of Pompeo in Berlioz' *Benvenuto Cellini,* is death in the spirit of tragedy, not of opera, and it is accordingly disturbing.

The great operas thus require a special mood, induced by long familiarity or by special study, as happened for Wagner. His works overlap the two realms of what I might venture to call pure opera (the standard works) and tragic opera (the great works). *Carmen* also bridges the distance between them, and so does the little-known but exquisite *Roi d'Ys* by Lalo. And doubtless there are others; it is a further peculiarity of the operatic genre that its riches are not present to the mind of any but the specialized scholar. At the close of his excellent *Short History of Opera,* Donald Grout says, "It is sad to think that so much beauty lies buried in the silence of the past, that all these things which so mightily pleased our forefathers have become old things of yesterday."

This fate does not arise from perverse neglect. The forms and tones that convey the spectacle of life's surface are bound to be more changeable than other forms and tones; like fashions themselves, the vanity of yesterday does not invite us to the imaginative effort of re-creation that we willingly make in order to recapture the quite different spirits of tragedy and comedy in *their* antiquated forms. Opera is a show of the time and for the time, which is why at any time the repertory is so severely small, why the charm of those many Italian pieces that delighted Stendhal is irrecoverable, why all of Meyerbeer is gone into limbo, and why we periodically come back to the few great operas. For reasons extrinsic to the genius of opera they put us in a quasi-religious mood of wonder and exultation, mindful of what an opera proposes to our sensual natures, but also lifted above pure opera's absorption in the vanity and violence of earthly life.

(*Opera News,* January 28, 1967.)

# PART IV

## Memoirs and

## Portraits

# The Damnation of Faust: From Triumph to Ruin
# On Hearing Beethoven's C-Sharp Minor Quartet

## HECTOR BERLIOZ

*The Berlioz* Memoirs *is a larger-than-life portrait of a man and an age— "perhaps the most arresting autobiography ever written," in the words of the* New Yorker's *Andrew Porter. The* Memoirs *is hard to rival for drama, narrative drive, and sheer power of personality, qualities all apparent in this excerpt documenting the roller-coaster story behind the production of* The Damnation of Faust, *offered here in a vigorous translation from 1969 by David Cairns. Also included is a remarkable paragraph from Berlioz's biography of Beethoven, a passage revealing that resistance to "modern music" is hardly new and that subjective responses to difficult new art have always been stubbornly mysterious and unpredictable.*

A Viennese amateur well up in the ways of the country I was about to visit had come to see me, bringing a volume of old airs. "If you want the Hungarians to like you," he said, "write a piece on one of their national tunes. They will be delighted, and when you come back you can tell me what you thought of their *eljen* (bravos) and their applause. Just choose something from this collection." I took his advice and chose the Rákóczy theme, on which I wrote the march that you know.

No sooner had the announcement of a new piece of *hony* music gone up all over Pesth than the national imagination began to ferment. People speculated as to how I had treated the famous, nay the sacred melody which for so long had set the hearts of Hungarians aflame with a holy passion for liberty and glory. There was even some anxiety about it, a fear of profanation. Far from being offended by such an attitude, I admired it. It had, besides, only too much justification in the many execrable medleys and catchpenny arrangements in which the noblest strains were submitted to every kind of wanton outrage. Perhaps, too, there were Hungarian music-lovers who had been in Paris and had seen how we drag the immortal Marseillaise through the gutter on our national holidays.

At length one of them, a M. Horváth, editor of a Hungarian newspaper, unable to contain his curiosity, called on the publisher who was dealing with the arrangements for my concert, found out from him the address of the copyist who was making the orchestral parts, went straight there, asked to see the manuscript, and examined it attentively. He was not reassured by this inspection, and next day could not disguise his anxiety.

"I have seen your score of the Rákóczy March," he said uneasily.

"Well?"

"Well—I'm nervous."

"Nonsense!"

"You state the theme piano; we, on the contrary are used to hearing it played fortissimo."

"Yes, by the gipsies. In any case, is that all? Don't worry, you shall have such a forte as you have never heard in your life. You can't have read it properly. One must always consider the end."

All the same, on the day of the concert, I felt a tightening of the throat when the moment came for this devil of a piece to be produced. After a trumpet fanfare based on the rhythm of its opening bars, the theme, you may remember, is announced piano by flutes and clarinets accompanied by pizzicato strings. The audience remained calm and judicious during this unexpected exposition. But when a long crescendo ensued, with fragments of the theme reintroduced fugally, broken by the dull strokes of the bass drum, like the thud of distant cannon, the whole place began to stir and hum with excitement; and when the orchestra unleashed its full fury and the long-delayed fortissimo burst forth, a tumult of shouting and stamping shook the theatre; the accumulated pressure of all that seething mass of emotion exploded with a violence that sent a thrill of fear right through me; I felt as though my hair were standing on end. From that moment I had to give up all thought of my peroration. The thunders of the orchestra were powerless against such a volcano in eruption; nothing could stop it. We had to repeat the piece, of course. The second time, the audience could scarcely contain itself a few seconds longer to hear a bar or two of the coda. Horváth in his box was throwing himself about like one possessed. I could not help laughing as I shot him a glance which said: "Well—are you still nervous, or are you satisfied with your forte?" It was a good thing that I had placed *Rákóczy-induló* (the Hungarian title of the piece) at the end of the programme, for anything we had tried to play after it would have been lost.

These stirring events, it may readily be surmised, left me in a state of some excitement. They had a curious sequel. I was mopping my face in a little room behind the stage when a shabbily dressed man entered without warning, his face shining and working strangely, and on seeing me fell on my neck and embraced me passionately, his eyes filling with tears, and barely managed to stammer out:

"Ah, monsieur—me Hungarian—sorry fellow—no speak French—*un poco l'italiano*—forgive—my rapture—ah! understand your cannon—yes, yes—big battle—German dogs!—in heart of me" (striking his chest vehemently) "I keep you—ah, Frenchman—republican—know to make music of revolution!" I cannot attempt to describe the man's alarming exaltation. He wept and gnashed his teeth. It was sublime. . . .

The day after my arrival in Breslau, I had attended a concert at which the audience sat coldly unresponsive throughout the entire proceedings; to my astonishment, the performance of a work as sublime as the C minor Symphony of Beethoven was followed by total silence. I had never met anything like it; but when I expressed surprise and ventured to protest at Beethoven's being received in this manner, a lady, in her own way a devotee of the master, corrected me. "You're mistaken," she said. "They admire this great work as much as anybody, and if they don't applaud, it's out of *respect.*" This work, which would have a profound significance in Paris and wherever the claque is traditionally active, gave me, I confess, the liveliest anxiety. I was terribly afraid of being respected. Happily nothing of the sort occurred. At my concert, the audience (to whose respect I must have lacked sufficient claim) saw fit to treat me according to the vulgar convention in use for favoured artists throughout the rest of Europe, and I was applauded most irreverently.

It was during this journey through Austria, Hungary, Bohemia and Silesia that I began composing my *Faust* legend, which had long been taking shape in my mind. As soon as I had made up my mind to do it, I had also to resolve to write most of the libretto myself; for the fragments from Gérard de Nerval's translation which I had set to music twenty years earlier and which I intended to rework and include in the score, plus two or three other scenes written to my instructions by M. Gandonnière before I left Paris, together amounted to less than one-sixth of the work.

So, as I bowled along in my old German post-chaise, I attempted to write the verses that were to be set to my own music. I began with Faust's invocation to Nature, seeking neither to translate nor yet to imitate Goethe's original but simply to take my inspiration from it and extract the musical essence it contained. . . .

Once launched, I wrote the verses that I lacked as and when the musical ideas came to me; and I composed the score with an ease such as I have very rarely experienced with any of my other works. I wrote it when and where I could: in coaches, in trains, on steamboats, even in the towns that I visited (this despite all the various responsibilities that my concerts entailed). Thus I wrote the introduction, "Le vieil hiver a fait place au printemps," in an inn at Passau on the Bavarian frontier. The scene on the banks of the Elbe, Mephistopheles' aria "Voici des roses" and the dance of the Sylphs, were written in Vienna. I have said how and on what occasion, in the course of a night—in Vienna again—I wrote the Hungarian march on the Rákóczy theme. The extraordinary impression it produced in Pesth induced me to incorporate it in my score; I took the liberty of locating my hero in Hungary when the action begins, and of making him witness the passage of the Hungarian army across the plain where he wanders, wrapped in his thoughts. A German critic professed to find it most irregular that I should have done so, and said I had no business putting Faust there. I cannot see why. I would have had no hesitation in taking him anywhere in the world if the work would have benefited. I was under no compulsion to keep to Goethe's story. A person like Faust may after all have any journey ascribed to him, no matter how outlandish, without violence being done to plausibility. Later the same strange argument was taken up more vehemently by other German critics. They attacked me for the changes my libretto had made to the text and plot of Goethe's masterpiece—as if no other

*Faust* but his existed,* and as if in any case it were possible to set such a poem to music complete and unchanged. I was stupid enough to answer them in the preface to the score. I have often wondered why these same critics have never lectured me about the libretto of my *Romeo and Juliet* symphony, which differs considerably from the immortal tragedy. No doubt it is because Shakespeare *was not a German.* Patriotism! fetishism! cretinism!

The choral refrain of the Peasants' Dance was written by the light of a shop's gas-jet in Pesth, one evening when I had lost my way in the town. In Prague I got up in the middle of the night to set down a tune that I was afraid of forgetting, the angelic chorus in the scene of Margaret's apotheosis: "Remonte au ciel, âme naïve, que l'amour égara." The students' song "Jam nox stellata" was written, words and music, in Breslau. The big trio, "Ange adoré dont la céleste image," I composed near Rouen at the country place of the Baron de Montville, where I spent a few days on my return to France.

The rest was written in Paris, but always in odd moments, unpremeditatedly—at home, at the café, in the Tuileries Gardens, even on a milestone in the Boulevard du Temple: I did not have to search for ideas; I let them come, and they presented themselves in the most unpredictable order. Finally, when the whole score was sketched out, I set myself to work carefully over it again, to polish the various sections, to join and knit them together with all the tenacity and patience I am capable of, and to complete the orchestration, which had only been roughly indicated here and there. I regard this work as one of the best things I have done. The public naturally shares this opinion of it.

To have written it was nothing: it had to be performed. It was then that my frustrations and tribulations began. The copying of the orchestral and vocal parts cost me an enormous sum; the numerous rehearsals which I required of the performers, and the exorbitant fee of 1,600 francs for the hire of the Opéra-Comique (the only place then available to me) further committed me to an enterprise that could not fail to be my ruin. But I went on. As any one else would have done in my place, I fortified myself with plausible arguments. "When I performed *Romeo and Juliet* for the first time," I reasoned,

*Marlowe's, for example, or Spohr's opera, neither of which resembles Goethe's *Faust.*

"public interest ran so high that 'corridor tickets' had to be issued to accommodate the people who could not get into the hall; and despite the enormous cost of putting on the work, I made a small profit. Since then my stock has risen in the public estimation and the fame of my successes abroad has given it a prestige in France that it did not have before. As a subject *Faust* is at least as well known as *Romeo*, and generally considered to suit me; I am thought likely to have treated it well. All in all, there is every reason to hope that people will be extremely curious to hear this new work, which is on a larger scale and more varied in colour than its predecessors. I should at least cover my expenses." Delusion! Some years had gone by since the first performance of *Romeo and Juliet,* and in that time the apathy of the Paris public towards all that pertains to art and literature had made impressive strides. Already people were no longer sufficiently interested, least of all in music, to sit cooped up in the middle of the day (I could not give my concerts in the evening) and in the Opéra-Comique, a theatre which the smart world is not given to frequenting. It was the end of November (1846) and snowing; the weather was terrible. I had no star singer for the part of Marguerite. Roger, who sang Faust, and Herman Léon, the Mephistopheles, could be heard any day in the same theatre, and they were not smart either. The result was that *Faust* was given twice before a half-empty house. The fashionable Paris audience, the audience which goes to concerts and is supposed to take an interest in music, stayed comfortably at home, as little concerned with my new work as if I had been the obscurest Conservatoire student. For all the number of people that came to those two performances, it might have been the most footling opera in the company's repertory.

Nothing in my career as an artist wounded me more deeply than this unexpected indifference. The disillusionment was cruel, but it was useful. I learnt my lesson, and since then have not staked twenty francs on the popularity of my music with the Parisian public. I hope I never will, if I live to be a hundred.*

I was ruined. I owed a considerable sum of money which I had

*I did not stick to my resolve. Having written *The Childhood of Christ*, I could not resist having it performed in Paris. Its success was immediate, and so great as to be positively insulting to my earlier works. I gave several performances in the Salle Herz which, instead of ruining me as *Faust* had done, made a profit of several thousand francs. (*1858*).

not got. After two days of unutterable depression, I thought I saw a way out of my entanglement: I would go to Russia. But to do so would again require money, the more so as I did not want to leave any of my outstanding debts unpaid. It was then that my friends came to the rescue, with a kindness that was a wonderful solace to me in my difficulties. As soon as it became known that I was driven to go to St. Petersburg in an attempt to make good the loss in which my latest work had involved me in Paris, I had offers of help from all sides. M. Bertin got the cashier of the *Journal des débats* to advance me a thousand francs. Some of my friends lent me five hundred, others six or seven hundred. A young German named Friedland, whom I had got to know on my recent journey to Prague, produced twelve hundred. Sax, though himself in difficulties, did the same. Finally Hetzel the publisher, who has since played a distinguished part in the Republican government, made me a loan, although he was only an acquaintance at the time. We met by chance in a café.

"I hear you're off to Russia," he said.

"Yes, I ———"

"It's a very expensive journey, particularly in winter. If a thousand-franc note would be any help, please take it."

I accepted it as unreservedly as the excellent Hetzel had offered it. Thus I was able to face the world and fix the day of my departure.

I think I have said before, but do not mind repeating, that if I have come across a good many rogues and knaves in my life, I have been extraordinarily lucky in the opposite respect. Few artists have encountered such generosity of spirit and ungrudging loyalty as I.

Dear and excellent men! You have no doubt long forgotten the noble way you treated me. Let me here remind you and most warmly thank you for it, and tell you how profoundly happy it makes me to think of all you did for me!

(*Memoirs*, 1870; translated by David Cairns.)

## On Hearing Beethoven's C-Sharp Minor Quartet

The writer is speaking of a recent concert at which the C-sharp Minor Quartet was given by Baillot's ensemble:

About two hundred persons were in the hall listening religiously. After a few minutes, the audience grew restless; people began to talk, each telling his neighbor of his increasing discomfort and boredom. Finally, unable to stand such weariness of spirit, nine tenths of the audience got up and left, complaining aloud that the music was unbearable, incomprehensible, ridiculous—the work of a madman defying common sense.

Silence was at last restored at the request of a few, and the quartet was concluded. Thereupon the voice of condemnation broke out again. M. Baillot was accused of making fools of the public by presenting extravagant nonsense. A few Beethoven devotees apologized, pleading the composer's mental derangement. "What a pity that such a great man should have produced deformities after all his masterpieces!"

Yet in one corner of the room there was a small group—and I must confess, whatever one may say, that I was among them—whose thoughts and feelings were altogether different. This tiny fraction of the audience, suspecting what was going to happen, had huddled together so as not to be bothered in their contemplation. After a few bars in the first movement, I did indeed fear I might be bored, though I kept listening. Shortly the chaos seemed to unwind, and just when the public's patience gave out mine revived, and I fell under the spell of the composer's genius. . . . Here is music, then, which repels almost all those who hear it and which, among a few, produces sensations wholly out of the ordinary. Whence this enormous discrepancy?

(From a biography of Beethoven by Berlioz in *Le Correspondant*, 1837; translated by Jacques Barzun.)

# A Ramble among the Musicians of Germany

## EDWARD HOLMES

*Published anonymously in 1828,* A Ramble among the Musicians of Germany *is perhaps the only musical travelogue comparable in sharpness and color to the travel sections of Charles Burney's* History *(see headnote to "Purcell, England's Master"). Seldom has any book described music in relation to its setting with greater ease, humor, and pungency. The author of this evocative "ramble"— one influenced by Hazlitt and the Lambs—was Edward Holmes, an English man of letters in the circle of Keats and Shelley. Like his contemporary Leigh Hunt, Holmes was a literary man and musician (his compositions have now fallen into neglect) who also wrote a regular music column. Beginning in 1826, Holmes contributed regular music criticism to the* Atlas *as well as occasional pieces on music to the* Spectator *and* Fraser's Magazine. *He became a great champion of Berlioz (who mentions him in the* Memoirs) *after an initial period of skepticism. His 1845* Life of Mozart *was the first full-length biography of a composer whose music, as these excerpts from* A Ramble *indicate, was singularly able to soften Holmes's barbed wit.*

## Munich

Catholic music flourishes in Munich because the abominations of the Scarlet Lady are unceasing in that city; and there is perhaps no place in which the Pope, were he to leave Rome, might sooner domiciliate. One of the greatest musical curiosities to be heard in their church performance, was the accompaniment of Gregorian tones, in a manner which I believe to have been hitherto unimagined in any other part of the world. Some of these melodies were taken as *canto fermo* subjects, and accompanied with three vocal parts in free song, and with very florid orchestral additions. I found much musician-like skill in the treatment of this idea, but am not prepossessed in favour of the taste which could countenance this extravagant union of styles that are void of all assimilation. The Gregorian tones should be preserved as they were in the time of the elder monks, severe and awful: these Gothic melodies are the only unclothed tunes which are welcome to a musician's ear in that state; on their rude sublimity, which contains the foundation of church harmony, have Handel and Leo piled their glorious superstructures—habitations fit for the gods.

In the cathedral I heard Haydn's mass in B flat, No. 8, performed as usual with a full band. The choruses struck me as being very dignified in their effect, but many movements were played in a time utterly distinct from that which is generally received in London as the correct one. The Benedictus, which is a soprano solo, with an *obligato* accompaniment for the organ, was taken much too fast; but it is more likely that the priests might be blameable for hurrying the music, than that the director misunderstood its character. In the last-mentioned piece, though not well sung, there was opportunity to observe the mastery of Haydn, and his extraordinary skill in every mode of combination; and though the damning fault of an incorrect time was committed, I found plenty of leisure for admiration. The soft stops of the organ blended charmingly with the stringed instruments; but the organist was rather deficient in taste, and his playing made me lament the polished and exquisite manner in which I have heard the same thing executed on a pianoforte in England. The Agnus Dei, with the expression of the words "dona nobis pacem," were well sung; but it is so difficult to preserve entire silence in these spacious buildings, that the fine subsiding of tone, the delicacy and refinement necessary in this sort of music, is greatly injured. Every time the host is elevated, the priests ring a large bell so violently, that it shatters the nerves, and frightens one out of the agreeable trance into which the mind is lulled. This is the only drawback (though a great one) to the pleasure their services give in the hearing.

# Vienna

This morning I visited the Abbé Stadler, who was so kind as to show me the manuscript of Mozart's last and greatest work, the Requiem, which is in his possession. There is a three-fold interest about this gentleman—that he is a learned church composer, that he is extremely amiable, and that he was the young and dear friend of Mozart. If the reader chooses to accompany me in this interview, he must picture to his fancy the abbé as a slight and venerable figure, rather short than otherwise, enveloped in a morning gown, and wearing a little brown wig; his hands are somewhat tremulous with age, but his face, smooth almost as an infant's, tells of a life passed in serenity; and one may soon perceive that suavity and gentleness are constitutional with him. Talk with the kind abbé of Mozart, and he warms into rapture, tells of an inspired being, who within a short space put forth more exquisite works than have been ever devised in the longest life, of a being full of affection, sensibility, and sociality, who was once his intimate and associate; and as he lingers fondly over old scenes, he may say, as he did to me, "All these things have long passed away, but I am here still." In the Abbé Stadler I saw the *real* tomb of Mozart; and few of those who have lived in marble for two hundred years may boast such honour as to have their remembrance last fresh and ardent in the warm bosom of a human being for forty. The acquaintance of the Abbé Stadler with Mozart commenced when the latter was nine years old. The score of the original MSS. was produced, or rather part of it, from the *Dies Irae* to the *Sanctus* (the rest being in the custody of Eybler, the Hof capellmeister): its appearance, and the melancholy history connected with its composition, which I believe every one knows took place while the author was hurrying to the grave, filled me with a crowd of emotions. One of them was like that which a devotee would experience on seeing an undoubted relic of his favourite saint—the thin, sickly fingers that had pressed that paper, the pale anxious face that had been bending over it—how must Mozart have looked, and how felt, when penning the *Lachrymosa* and the *Rex tremendae*—his being sublimating to an essence, to his fingers' ends and in his feet must he have felt the intense pleasure of creating, his mortality all the time wrestling with the deity within. No one of sensibility could have written the Requiem without a great shock to his physical strength; he must have lived in a fever of thought, have trodden the air unclogged by "this vile body;" nay, I think that even if a ruddy Devonshire farmer could have produced it, *knowing* what he was doing, it would have made a ghost of him. The notes are small and clear, but there is a hurry and dash in the strokes by which they are joined together, which show the ardour and completeness of the author's design. There are no alterations, and it is the first transcript of Mozart's mind. In some of the passages I thought I could discern a tremulousness in the marks, which seemed as if he apprehended life would be gone before he could make his thoughts eternal; or did he tremble from contact with their extreme beauty, as the bee seems to do when he grapples with a flower? The *Recordare* appears most carefully written; the score is not full; wherever there is a duplicate part, it is filled up by an assistant, but the figures are carefully marked in Mozart's own hand. Two observations are suggested by the sight of this work: first, how by a few strokes a great genius goes farther in the result than the most painful elaboration of thought will arrive at, and also how certain habits of thinking allow a man in the hastiest composition to defy with safety the sternest and most unrelenting criticism to find a fault, and to which indeed, were it the subject of a lecture, the professor's exordium might be, "This is perfection of its kind." The Abbé Stadler also possesses the desk at which Mozart *stood* when engaged in composition; it is a deal one, painted, but its coat is the worst for wear.

In less than forty years so completely has every bodily trace of Mozart vanished from the minds of the people of Vienna, that there is not a soul there who can even tell the place in which he was buried: by some strange accident the Abbé does not even know it. The answer to every inquiry is, "Nobody knows—the register of St. Stephen's must be consulted for the information." There is no rude memento, no sculptured stone, to indicate that the divine Mozart once sojourned in Vienna; and as for the spot of his interment, it may not be thought too fanciful to suppose, that Earth, the general mother, jealous of her production, has hidden him again in her womb, lest celestial beings should claim him as their own. This is perhaps a poetical apology for what is in fact a piece of neglect everlastingly disgraceful to the Viennese, who, I am afraid, have more joy in the pageant of a funeral, than they have sorrow for the loss of great men.

The Abbé Stadler showed me some lessons in composition

which Mozart had given to his niece; and we observed the method he adopted to try her abilities in music by first giving her a melody without a bass, then a bass without a melody, then by degrees requesting her to add the inner parts. I also saw Mozart's own early exercises, some of which consisted of canon in all the intervals (most adroit in the seventh, that apparent contradiction), with fugues, &c., a ground-work in harmony, which, coupled with his fine invention, made him the great master he was. Mozart's *extempore* playing was so exquisitely regular and symmetrical in design, that it was impossible for judges who heard him not to imagine that the whole had been written before—which is the ultimatum of praise. The Abbé Stadler observed, that it was impossible to take a minuet out of a quartett or quintett of Mozart, and not to discover that he was a great master of fugue; but his admirable fancy was ever found "taming its wildness to the loving hand" of Nature. As a player, his left hand, the weakest and most uncertain part of "human mortals," never missed fire when he levelled it at a passage.—Mozart's widow, who has been married to a gentleman in Copenhagen, has lately lost her second husband: one of his sons is a musical teacher and composer of no great eminence, the other is a merchant at Milan.

The German opera is not much patronized by the Viennese, who doat upon those things which are *foreign,* and despise their own good writers. Both the Italian and German opera are played at the same house; but the latter is considered by the public as a mere foil to the former, and by the managers as a mere stop-gap. Weber's *Freischütz* was produced during my stay, a circumstance which pleased me extremely, because I wished to remark the difference between our own adaptation and the original. The transposition of situation in the music, and (in some parts) its alteration for our own theatres, is not favourable to Weber. Much beautiful concerted music is omitted among us, particularly the last *finale,* which, with its imitations and fugued passages, is extremely good. The German singers are now so familiar with the opera, that the choruses go with a joviality and spirit beyond all imagination, for their parts have not the appearance of having been studied, and in a romantic opera it is essentially necessary that the music should flow as it were spontaneously from the mouths of the singers, leaving them to get into the thick of the scene with untaxed memories. The incantation scene is not managed with that fine accumulation of horror that it is in London; all intercourse with the fiend takes place in the decayed and hollow trunk of a tree. The devil is not allowed to appear on the Austrian stage; for priestly despotism will not allow that lovely bugbear to make his appearance before the public, lest good Catholics should get used to him, and in time begin to dandle and cocker him as they do their favourite saints, and then how would the argument of terror be weakened, which has hitherto been found so beneficial in improving people's lives and in lightening their consciences and purses? . . .

The flippancy of taste displayed by the more fashionable concert-goers in Vienna may be imagined from an exhibition of instrumental playing with which they were entertained on one occasion when I was present, the prominent parts of which were variations for the violin, performed by Madame Parravacini, and the first movement of Hummel's pianoforte concerto in B minor played by Frederic Wörlitzer, of Berlin, a boy thirteen years old. The lady's violin performance required much politeness and self-command to restrain laughter, it was so extremely bad, and particularly in some rapid *staccato* passages near the bridge, where the defiance of tune was droll; the boy, though well tutored, got through his task without conveying the slightest pleasure. Both these performers seemed to attract in proportion as the individuals were unfit to manage their instruments—the lady to *fiddle*, or the boy to play on the pianoforte. We have had so much of child's play lately in England, that it is to be hoped the fashion is on the decline; for if extremes be good, how much better would it be to employ those "whose tops are bald with dry antiquity," and to let the superannuated have a chance; because, if we did not there get rapidity we might get sentiment, which is a better thing. Common listeners frequently imagine, that provided the mere notes are played, the end of music is accomplished, forgetting that the mind of the performer should show itself in the light in which he understands a passage, and then, instead of being a mere automaton, with a number of ready-made graces bestowed upon his mechanism, we should have the emanation of his feeling and sensibility struck out in a momentary impulse. Too many lads have been made players and singers because they have elastic fingers or loud voices, who are wholly destitute of the musical gift, perhaps even of ear. If physical advantages as well as genius be necessary to make a player, it is a pity wholly to discard the latter ingredient, and to let the former shift for itself. Weber's overture to *Euryanthe* was not so well played as at Darmstadt; the opera orchestra in Vienna has correctness, but less of tone than others of Germany. The last piece of this concert was a *scena*, the composition of Cadolini; it was accompanied by a chorus, and intended to display the powers of Mademoiselle Lalande to advantage. I had hoped to leave Vienna with a pleasurable recollection of this lady, who really *can* sing well, but my chronicle would not be faithful if I were not to say that the affair was most silly and frivolous. About twenty men in black came streaming in with much solemnity as a chorus, but more for the purpose of making a half circle round Madame Lalande, who stood radiant in smiles and whiteness, the centre of attraction, and screamed one of the vilest compositions I ever heard. The audience of the opera at Vienna, with its worthless overheaped applause, its *bravoes* ever bestowed in the wrong place, would destroy the modesty and discretion of the best singer that ever appeared on this earth. The Viennese are for their pains heartily welcome to the enjoyment of those whom they have thus schooled; Lablache is the only actor and singer of whom I would' rob them: but to those in England who expect discrimination and judgment in a metropolitan audience, I would say, seek it rather among Austrian boors. . . .

Every music lover who visits Vienna will like to know that Mozart lived in the Rauhenstein Gasse, a narrow street leading down to the cathedral, in a house now a tavern or drinking-house, which, by some remarkable coincidence, wears on its front a badge of fiddles and other musical instruments. No one must be so deluded as to imagine, that when Mozart arrived at his own home he knocked at a street door as ordinary mortals do; no, he walked under a gateway, and thence up stairs to his ordinary apartments. That Mozart gave his Sunday evening concerts, and enchanted people in a room on the first floor with a bow window to it, is a fact not to be despised, for if we fancy the human being, we must give him a local habitation, else he is a spirit, and not one of ourselves. We do not wish to know the great performances of great men, we wish to know their *little* actions, how they walked, looked, and spoke, their crooked habits and peculiarities; and to know that Mozart had a restless and nervous fidgetiness in his hands and feet, and seldom sat without some motion of them, makes him more present to us than the most laboured picture. And here lived Mozart; he who has thrown a fresh grace around the ideal of womanliness, who *could* "paint the rose and add perfume to the violet"; and in love, while the subtle and metaphysical poets are trying to get at the heart of its emotions, gives us straight a language for sighs and tears, for tenderness and rapture. The difference between Mozart and other great composers, such as Haydn for instance, is, that while the latter economize their subjects, he could ever trust to the wealth of his feelings, he saved nothing on paper; he took rural excursions, not to look for thoughts but to enjoy sensation, and began to write when the throng of ideas became insupportable to him. Music was with him, as a certain poet said of verses, a secretion. There is one melancholy of the style of Gluck, and another melancholy of Mozart; that of the first seems like the despondency of a lover who parts with his mistress for ever, the other has more of the caressing pensiveness which one may imagine in a being who enjoyed in a summer arbour by moonlight the song of nightingales, with his head all the time resting in the lap of his mistress. What an enviable perfection must have been Constance Weber's in filling such a mind as Mozart's with beautiful images, in suggesting such an air as "Porgi Amor," or in creating the bitter sweet regrets of "Dove sono." Almost the whole of the songs in Mozart's operas are a continuation of the same spirit which made him in infancy ask his friends, "Do you love me?" and they show that he who asked for affection could return it with interest. As the excess of the passion in a man of genius ever helps him in the completion of the greatest designs, let it be to the praise of women, that besides that one element in which he reigned supreme, Mozart was of all musicians at once the best lover, and the most refined, various, and intellectual composer that the world has produced.

(*A Ramble among the Musicians of Germany*, 1828.)

# Paganini

## LEIGH HUNT

*Although Leigh Hunt's opera articles provide the most sumptuous amalgam of his musical, theatrical, and political views, (see "Mozart's Noisy Ghost"), he was also an astute admirer of instrumental music. An accomplished pianist, flutist, and lutenist, Hunt regaled Keats, Shelley, and other friends with music wherever he happened to be—including jail, where he was thrown for two years for his subversive* Examiner *attacks on the Prince Regent. This is the first of Hunt's "remarks" on Paganini, the legendary fiddle player allegedly possessed by the devil. In a later piece, Hunt tempered his astonishment at Paganini's technical genius with the caveat that "science and force" are "the predominant qualities of his playing. If he is supposed to be making love, we should say that he did it with more fervor of the senses than with entireness of heart." Nevertheless, it is Hunt's initial bedazzlement that is most striking, a masterpiece of musical description that creates the illusion not only of hearing the music but of seeing Paganini's strings "shiver with pleasure." Like so much of the best nineteenth-century musical journalism, this essay begins as a review but expands into a character sketch, one in which the personality of the performer becomes indistinguishable from the ecstasy of the music.*

Let us not belie the effect . . . which this extraordinary player had upon us last night. To begin with the beginning, he had a magnificent house. We though at first we were literally going to *hear* him, without seeing his face; for the house was crammed at so early an hour that, on entering it, we found ourselves fixed on the lowest of the pit stairs. It was amusing to see the persons who came in after us. Some, as they cast up their eyes, gaped amazement at the huge mass of faces presented in all quarters of the house; others looked angry; others ashamed and cast a glance around them to see what was thought of them; some gallantly smiled, and resolved to make the best of it. One man exclaimed, with unsophisticated astonishment, "Christ Jesus!" and an Italian whispered in a half-execrating tone, "Oh, Dio!"

Meantime we heard some interesting conversation around us. We had been told, as a striking instance of the effect that Paganini has produced upon the English musical world, that one eminent musician declared he could not sleep the first night of his performance for thinking of him, but that he got up and walked about his room. A gentleman present last night was telling his friends that another celebrated player swore that he would have given a thousand guineas to keep the Italian out of the country, he had put everybody at such an immeasurable distance. These candid confessions, it seems, are made in perfect good-humour, and therefore do honour to the gentlemen concerned. The truth is, as a late writer observed, that men of real pretensions are not apt to grudge higher pretensions in others, if they are of a very genuine surpassing nature. Envy is lost in admiration. . . .

As it was the first time we had seen the great player, except in the criticisms of our musical friends, which had rendered us doubly curious, we looked up with interest at him from our abysm in the pit. A lucky interval between a gentleman's head and a lady's bonnet favoured our endeavour, and there we beheld the long, pale face of the musical marvel, hung, as it were, in the light, and looking as strange as need be. He made divers uncouth obeisances, and then put himself in a masterly attitude for his work, his manner being as firm and full of conscious power when he puts the bow to the instrument as it is otherwise when he is not playing. We thought he did not look so old as he is said to be; but he is long-faced and haggard, with strongly-marked prominent features, wears his black hair flowing on his neck like an enthusiast, has a coat of ancient cut which astonishes Fop's Alley; in short, is very like the picture of him in the shops. He is like a great old boy, who has done nothing but play the violin all his life, and knows as much about that as he does little of conventional manners. His face at the same time has much less expression than might be looked for. At first it seemed little better than a mask; with a fastidious, dreary expression, as if inclined to despise his music and go to sleep. And such was his countenance for a great part of the evening. His fervour was in his hands and bow. Towards the close of the performances, he waxed more enthusiastic in appearance, gave way to some uncouth bodily movement from side to side, and seemed to be getting into his violin. Occasionally also he put back his hair. When he makes his acknowledgments, he bows like a camel, and grins like a goblin or a mountain-goat.

His playing is indeed marvellous. What other players can do well, he does a hundred times better. We never heard such playing before; nor had we imagined it. His bow perfectly talks. It remonstrates, supplicates, answers, holds a dialogue. It would be the easiest thing in the world to put words to his music. We heard an enthusiastic violin player assert once, in the heat of argument with a painter, that it would be as possible to call for a chop at a tavern by playing, as by painting it. Last night we almost began to think that this hyperbole was hardly a fiction. We are sure that with a given subject, or even without it, Paganini's best playing could be construed into discourse by any imaginative person.

Last night he began a composition of his own (very good, by the way)—an *Allegro Maestoso* movement (majestically cheerful) with singular force and precision. Precision is not the proper word; it was a sort of peremptoriness and dash. He did not put his bow to the strings, nor lay it upon them; he struck them, as you might imagine a Greek to have done when he used his plectrum, and "smote the sounding shell." He then fell into a tender strain, till the strings, when he touched them, appeared to shiver with pleasure. Then he gave us a sort of minute warbling, as if half a dozen humming birds were singing at the tops of their voices, the highest notes sometimes leaping off and shivering like sprinkles of water; then he descended with wonderful force and gravity into the bass; then he would commence a strain of earnest feeling or entreaty, with notes of the greatest solidity, yet full of trembling emotion; and then again he would leap to a height beyond all height, with notes of desperate minuteness, then flash down in a set of headlong harmonies, sharp and brilliant as the edges of swords; then warble again with inconceivable beauty and remoteness, as if he was a ventriloquizing-bird; and finally, besides his usual wonderful staccatos in ordinary, he would suddenly throw handfuls, as it were, of staccatoed notes, in distinct and repeated showers over his violin, small and pungent as the tips of pins.

In a word, we never heard anything like *any* part of his performance, much less the least marvel we have been speaking of. The people sit astonished, venting themselves in whispers of "Wonderful!"—"Good God!"—and other unusual symptoms of English amazement; and when the applause comes, some of them take an opportunity of laughing, out of pure inability to express their feelings otherwise.

(*Examiner,* June 23, 1831.)

# Berlioz, Liszt, Chopin

## HEINRICH HEINE

*Berlioz, Liszt, and Chopin were not only great composers and performers but also charismatic personalities, with all the attendant scandals, mob scenes, and sex appeal we associate in our time with rock stars. The most witty and exuberant reporter on these figures—and on the splashy nineteenth-century Paris musical scene in general—was Heinrich Heine. Like all masters of musical portraiture, Heine was always careful to connect the personality with the music, the sex appeal with the artistry, making his pieces considerably more than gossip. (See headnote to "Rossini and Meyerbeer.")*

**B**erlioz and Liszt are quite the most remarkable phenomena of the Parisian musical world. I say remarkable, not the most beautiful, nor the most agreeable. From Berlioz we shall soon have an opera. The subject is an episode in the life of Benvenuto Cellini, the casting of "Perseus." Something very much out of the common is expected, for this composer has already produced uncommon things. The bent of his mind is towards the fantastic, blent not with sentiment but with sentimentality; there are marked analogies between him and Callot, Gozzi, and Hoffman. It is even apparent in his outward appearance. What a pity it is that he has cut his great antediluvian locks, the bristling hair that rose from his forehead like a forest about a steep escarpment of rocks! It was thus I saw him for the first time, six years ago, and thus he will always remain in my memory. It was at the *Conservatoire de Musique*, when a big symphony of his was given, a bizarre nocturne, only here and there relieved by the gleam of a woman's dress, sentimentally white, fluttering to and fro—or by a flash of irony, sulphur yellow. The best thing in the composition is a Witches' Sabbath wherein the devil reads the mass, and church music is parodied with the most terrible and savage buffoonery. It is a farce wherein all the hidden vipers we carry in our hearts hiss joyously aloud. My neighbour in my box, a communicative young man, pointed out to me the composer, who was sitting at the extremity of the hall in a corner of the orchestra, playing the kettle-drum. For the kettle-drum is his instrument. "Do you see that stout Englishwoman in the proscenium? That is Miss Smithson; for nearly three years Berlioz has been madly in love with her, and it is this passion that we have to thank for the wild symphony to which we are listening to-day."

There, in one of the stage-boxes, sat the celebrated Covent Garden actress; Berlioz had his eyes fixed on her, and every time that her look met his, he struck his kettle-drum like a maniac. Since then Miss Smithson has become Madame Berlioz, and it is also since then that her husband has allowed his hair to be cut. When at the Conservatoire this winter I again listened to his symphony, he again sat as kettle-drum player at the back of the orchestra, the stout Englishwoman was again in the stage-box, again their looks met, . . . but he no longer struck his kettledrum with mad fury.

It is Liszt who of all composers has the most elective affinity with Berlioz, and it is he also who is the best executant of his music. I need not discourse to you about his talent: his fame is European. He is incontestably the artist who found the greatest number of enthusiasts in Paris, if, also, the most vehement detractors. It is a significant sign that no one speaks of him with indifference. Without a positive value it is impossible in this world to evoke either partisan or hostile passions. Fire is needed to enflame men, whether to love or to hatred. The best witness in Liszt's favour is the personal esteem in which friends and foes alike hold him. He is a man of eccentric character, but noble, disinterested and guileless. The tendencies of his mind are most remarkable. Speculation has the greatest fascination for him; and still more than with the interests of his art he is engrossed with all manner of rival philosophical investigations which are occupied with the solution of all the great questions of heaven and the earth. For long he was an ardent upholder of the beautiful Saint-Simonian idea of the world. Later the spiritualistic or rather vaporous thoughts of Ballanche enveloped him in their mist; now he is enthusiastic over the Republican-Catholic dogmas of a Lamennais who has hoisted his

Jacobin cap on the cross . . . Heavens knows in what mental stall he will find his next hobby-horse!

But this unquenchable thirst for light, for the divine, is ever laudable, and is a witness to his leanings towards holiness, towards religion. That so restless a brain, driven distracted by all the sufferings and all the doctrines of the day, impelled to concern itself with all the needs of mankind, inclined to poke its nose into every pot wherein the good God cooks the future:—that Franz Liszt cannot be a placid player of the piano to peaceable citizens in comfortable nightcaps, is easily understood. When he sits down to the piano, when, after having stroked back his hair from his forehead several times, he begins to improvise, it often happens that he storms all too madly over the ivory keys, and there resounds a chaos of heaven-high thoughts whence here and there the sweetest flowers breathe out their perfume; so that the hearer is at once agonised and enchanted, yet none the less agonised.

I confess to you that, much as I like Liszt, his music does not affect my inner self pleasantly, more especially as I am a Sunday child, and so see the spectres that other people hear only. For, as you know, at each tone drawn forth by his hand, the corresponding figure is evoked in my mind, and becomes visible to my inner vision. My brain still trembles at the recollection of the last time I heard Liszt play at a concert. It was a concert in aid of the unfortunate Italians at the *hôtel* of that beautiful, noble, and suffering princess who so beautifully represents the country of her body and that of her spirit, Italy and heaven . . . (you certainly must have seen her in Paris, that ideal figure, which nevertheless is only the prison-house wherein the holy angel-soul is confined. . . . But the prison-wall is so beautiful, that whosoever stands before it and gazes is as one bewitched. . . .) It was at the concert in aid of the most deserving of the unfortunate Italians that one day, during the bygone winter, I last heard Liszt play. I no longer know what he played, but I could swear that it was variations on a theme out of the Apocalypse. At first I could not see them distinctly, those four mystic animals, I could hear their voices only, especially the roaring of the lion, and the screeching of the eagle. The ox with the book in his hand I saw distinctly enough. What Liszt played best of all was his rendering the Valley of Jehoshaphat. There were lists as at a tournament, and around the immense enclosure the people pressed as spectators, deathly white and trembling. First, Satan galloped into the lists, in black armour, mounted on a milk-white horse. Slowly behind him, Death caracolled on his pale horse. Last of all rode Christ in armour of gold on a black horse. With his sacred spear he straightway thrust Satan to earth, and thereafter Death, and the onlookers shouted with joy. . . . A storm of applause was awarded to this performance of the valiant Liszt, who rose from the piano exhausted, and bowed to the ladies. On the lips of the most beautiful among them there dawned the sweet mournful smile at once reminiscent of Italy, and a presage of heaven.

This same concert had another interest for the public. You doubtless know to satiety, from the newspapers, of the unfortunate estrangement which exists between Liszt and the Viennese pianist Thalberg, and of the commotion which an article by Liszt against Thalberg created in the musical world, also of the *rôle* which lurking enmities and gossipings have played alike to the detriment of the critic and the criticised. At the very height of this scandalous strife the two heroes of the day determined to play at the same concert, one after the other. They both set aside their wounded private feelings in the furtherance of a scheme of benevolence; and the public, to whom they thus gave the opportunity of contemporaneously recognising and appreciating their particular diversities, accorded to them a generous and merited approbation.

It is, indeed, sufficient to make a single comparison between the musical temperament of each composer, to be convinced that there is as much of hidden malice as of narrowness of mind in the endeavour to praise one at the expense of the other. Their technical proficiencies counterbalance one another; and as regards their spiritual character, no more striking contrast could be imagined than the noble, soulful, intelligent, good-natured German, or, rather, Austrian Thalberg, face to face with the wild, lightning-flashing, volcanic, heaven-storming Liszt!

Comparison between two virtuosi is usually based upon a mistake, such as once also flourished in the domain of poetry, that is to say, comparison based on the principle of difficulties overcome. But now it is generally admitted that metrical form has quite another importance than merely to demonstrate the artistic skill with which a poet can manipulate language, nor do we admire a beautiful poem merely because its production is at the cost of much labour. In the same manner it will soon be perceived that it suffices if a musician can communicate by means of his instrument all that he feels and thinks, or what others have felt and thought; and that all the *tours de force* of the virtuoso, which testify merely to difficulties vanquished, ought to be proscribed as useless noise, and relegated to the domain of conjurers, of tumblers, of sword-swallowers, and dancers on tight ropes and on eggs.

It suffices, in a word, that a musician be absolute master of his instrument in order that the listener may wholly forget the mechanical means, and that the spirit alone is made audible. . . .

It would be an injustice on my part were I on this occasion to omit mention of a pianist who, with Liszt, is at present more fêted than any other. I allude to Chopin, who shines as virtuoso, not merely on account of his technical perfection, but also as a composer of the highest order. He is a man of the first rank. Chopin is the favourite of the *élites* who in music seek the highest spiritual enjoyment. His fame is of an aristocratic kind, perfumed with the praises of good society; it is as distinguished as his personality.

Chopin was born in Poland of French parents, but received part of his education in Germany. The influences of the three nationalities affect his personality to an extent that is very remarkable. He has, in short, appropriated the best characteristics of each: Poland has bequeathed to him chivalrous tendencies, her historical sorrows; France, her delicate grace, her charm; Germany, her profound romanticism. . . . For the rest, nature has given him a slender elegant figure, somewhat fragile, a noble heart, and genius. Yes, genius, in the full acceptation of the term, must be allowed to Chopin. He is not virtuoso only, he is also a poet; he can make us apprehend the poetry which lives in his heart; he is a "tone-poet," and no enjoyment is equal to that which he bestows upon us when he sits down at the piano and improvises. Then, he is neither Polish, nor French, nor German; he betrays a higher origin, he is of the kindred of Mozart, of Raphael, of Goethe; his true fatherland is the dream kingdom of Poetry.

("Letters on the French Stage," 1837; translated by Elizabeth A. Sharp.)

# Memories of Great Composers

## ETHEL SMYTH

*Dame Ethel Smyth was one of the first respected female composers in our century. Among the admirers of her chamber and operatic works were Tchaikovsky, Dvořák, and Clara Schumann. Dame Ethel's most lasting contributions, how-ever, (her music having fallen into oblivion) may well be her nonfiction prose. The most notable of her five autobiographical books is the two-volume* Impressions That Remained. *Among many other vividly depicted subjects, these volumes contain portraits of late-nineteenth-century composers that are extraordinarily shrewd, touching, and powerful—some of the most memorable musical portrai-ture in English. It is hoped that the following samples will bring a new audience for these* Impressions, *which have recently fallen into undeserved obscurity.*

## Grieg

Throughout the greater part of the winter of 1887–88 the Griegs were in Leipzig and it is then that my real friendship with them began. When Grieg appeared on a platform, whether alone or accompanying his wife's superb rendering of his songs, the audience went mad, but there was a simplicity and purity of spirit about them that success could not tarnish. Out of action, these two tiny people looked like wooden figures from a Noah's Ark, the transfiguration which ensued when they got to work being all the more astonishing. Frau Grieg sang in Norwegian of course and one often had only a vague idea as to the meaning of the words, but her performance was, as Vernon Lee once said about someone else's singing, 'explosive literature,' and one wept, laughed, and thrilled with excitement or horror without knowing why. The song over, she again became Noah's wife. Grieg is one of the very few composers I have met from whose lips you might hear as frank a confession as he once made concerning one of his later works. I had been so enthusiastic, and he was always so keen to get at honest impressions, that I ventured to say the coda of one of the movements seemed not quite up to the level of the rest. 'Ah yes!' he said, shrugging his shoulders, 'at that point inspiration gave out and I had to finish without!'—I remember too on a certain occasion his being invited for a huge sum to conduct not only his own work but the whole programme, and refusing on the ground that he was too bad a conductor. 'But the public won't mind that,' pleaded the manager, 'they'll come to *see* you conduct: besides which, as you conduct your own music you surely can get along with other people's well enough for all purposes?' At this remark Grieg shook his pale yellow mane angrily: 'My own music?' he snapped, 'any fool can conduct his own music but that's no reason for murdering other people's'—and the manager had to drop the subject.

## Tchaikovsky

Of all the composers I have known the most delightful as personality was Tchaikovsky, between whom and myself a relation now sprang up that surely would have ripened into close friendship had circumstances favoured us; so large-minded was he, that I think he would have put up unresentingly with all I had to give his work—a very relative admiration. Accustomed to the uncouth, almost brutal manners affected by many German musicians as part of the make-up and one of the symptoms of genius, it was a relief to find in this Russian, who even the rough diamonds allowed was a master on his own lines, a polished cultivated gentleman and man of the world. Even his detestation of Brahms's music failed to check my sympathy—and that I think is strong testimony to his charm! He would argue with me about Brahms by the hour, strum passages on the piano and ask if they were not hideous, declaring I must be under hypnotic influence, since to admire this awkward pedant did not square with what he was kind enough to call the soundness of my instinct on other points. Another thing that puzzled him was my devotion to Marco, of whom he was secretly terrified, but this trait he considered to be a form of English spleen and it puzzled him less than the other madness. For thirty years I have meant to enquire whether dogs play no part in the Russian scheme of life or whether Tchaikovsky's views were peculiar to himself; anyhow it amused me, reading his Memoirs, to find Marco and Brahms bracketed together as eccentricities of his young English friend.

On one point we were quite of one mind, the neglect in my school, to which I have already alluded, of colour; 'not one of them can instrumentate' he said, and he earnestly begged me to turn my attention at once to the orchestra and not be prudish about using the medium for all it is worth. 'What happens,' he asked, 'in ordinary conversation? If you have to do with really alive people, listen to the inflections in the voices . . . there's instrumentation for you!' And I followed his advice on the spot, went to concerts with the sole object of studying orchestral effects, filled notebook upon notebook with impressions, and ever since have been at least as much interested in sounds as in sense, considering the two things indivisible.

## Brahms

Early in 1879, I think some time in January, Brahms came to Leipzig to conduct his Violin Concerto—played of course by Joachim, who had just been introducing it at Amsterdam, and was much upset at having to tune down his ears again to normal pitch, after having learned, as he said, to play it apparently in D ♯ major in Holland—a hard feat! I understood then why pitch always has a tendency to rise, for, wedded as Joachim was to orthodoxy in all things, I nevertheless caught a few remarks about 'increased brilliancy,' and so on. That Concerto, which has never been among my favourite Brahms's works, may for aught I know be child's play to students nowadays; at that time however the technique was unfamiliar and not considered favourable to the instrument. Wags called it 'Concerto *against* (instead of *for*) the Violin.' But I fancy my musical sensibility was blurred in the wild excitement of at last getting to know the great man himself. During the following years I saw a good deal of him, on and off, and here follows the summing-up of my impressions for what they are worth.

Some people, I believe, have youthful enthusiasms, even in their own branch of art, that wane as years go on, but I can remember no musical recantations. A favourable judgment seems to me to imply a satisfied need; you may have many needs, but why should one interfere with the other? Why, when you come to know and admire, say, Anatole France, should you delight less in someone at the opposite pole, for instance Dickens? From the very first I had worshipped Brahms's music, as I do some of it now; hence was predisposed to admire the man. But without exactly disliking him, his personality neither impressed nor attracted me, and I never could understand why the faithful had such an exalted opinion of his intellect. Rather taciturn and jerky as a rule, and notoriously difficult to carry on a conversation with, after meals his mind and tongue unstiffened; and then, under the stimulus of countless cups of very strong black coffee, he was ready to discuss literature, art, politics, morals, or anything under the sun. On such occasions, though he never said anything stupid, I cannot recall hearing him say anything very striking, and when his latest pronouncement on Bismarck, poetry, or even music was ecstatically handed round, it generally seemed to me what anyone might have said.

Once only do I remember his taking an exceptional line. A portrait of the old Kaiser by Lenbach, recently exhibited at the Museum, had aroused such a storm of indignation that it was withdrawn, and I believe ended by being 'verboten' as far as public galleries were concerned. The reason was that whereas all other portraits of Wilhelm I. represented a martial-looking veteran of about sixty, of whom the Press stated that he swung himself on to his horse without the aid of a mounting block, Lenbach had painted a very tired old man of eighty-four, with pale, flabby cheeks, and sunken, lack-lustre eyes—in short the fine old wreck he was, of whom it was whispered that, as a matter of fact, he had to be lifted on to his horse in the recesses of the stable yard in order to make his daily appearance in the Thiergarten. This picture was infinitely pathetic and even beautiful; so, it seemed to me, was the idea of the old warrior determined to sally forth as long as he could sit on a horse's back, no matter how he got there. But the people who manufacture public opinion in Germany saw in this record of human decay something detrimental to monarchical prestige, some going so far as to declare the picture should be publicly destroyed and the painter arraigned for *lèse-majesté*—in short the incident opened one's eyes to the gulf that lies between German and Anglo-Saxon mentality. There was a minority of another way of thinking, but these kept pretty quiet, and I was delighted to find that Brahms, who always had the courage of his opinions and truckled to no one, thought the whole outcry preposterous, and said so.

I think what chiefly angered me was his views on women, which after all were the views prevalent in Germany, only I had not realised the fact, having imagined 'mein Mann sagt' was a local peculiarity. Relics of this form of barbarism still linger in England, but as voiced by a people gone mad on logic, worshippers of brute force, and who visualise certain facts with the hard stare of eyes devoid of eyelashes, these theories would, I fancy, repel even our own reactionaries. George III., himself a German, might have subscribed 150 years ago to William II.'s famous axiom about women being out of place anywhere except in the kitchen, nursery, and church, but you often heard it quoted with complete assent by German women themselves in my day.

Brahms, as artist and bachelor, was free to adopt what may be called the poetical variant of the 'Kinder, Kirche, Küche' axiom, namely that women are playthings. He made one or two exceptions, as such men will, and chief among these was Lisl, to whom his attitude was perfect . . . reverential, admiring, and affectionate, without a tinge of amorousness. Being, like most artists, greedy, it specially melted him that she was such a splendid Hausfrau; indeed as often as not, from love of the best, she would do her own marketing. During Brahms's visits she was never happier than when concocting some exquisite dish to set before the king; like a glorified Frau Röntgen she would come in, flushed with stooping over the range, her golden hair wavier than ever from the heat, and cry: 'Begin that movement again; that much you owe me!' and Brahms's worship would flame up in unison with the blaze in the kitchen. In short he was adorable with Lisl.

In his relations with her husband, who completely effaced himself as musician in the master's presence, he took pains to be appreciative, but could not disguise the fact that Herzogenberg's compositions did not greatly interest him. Once when he had been in a bad temper and rather cruel about them, Lisl rated him and wept, and Brahms kissed her hand and nearly wept too, and it appears there was a most touching scene; but the thing rankled in her bosom for a long time.

To see him with Lili Wach, Frau Schumann and her daughters, or other links with his great predecessors was to see him at his best, so gentle and respectful was his bearing; in fact to Frau Schumann he behaved as might a particularly delightful old-world son. I remember a most funny conversation between them as to why the theme of his D major Piano Variations had what she called 'an unnecessary bar tacked on,' this being one of the supreme touches in that wonderful, soaring tune. She argued the point lovingly, but as ever with some heat, and I thought him divinely patient.

His ways with other women-folk—or to use the detestable word for ever on his lips 'Weibsbilder'—were less admirable. If they did not appeal to him he was incredibly awkward and ungracious; if they were pretty he had an unpleasant way of leaning back in his chair, pouting out his lips, stroking his moustache, and staring at them as a greedy boy stares at jam-tarts. People used to think this rather delightful, specially hailing it, too, as a sign that the great man was in high good-humour, but it angered me, as did also his jokes about women, and his everlasting gibes at any, excepting Lisl of course, who possessed brains or indeed ideas of any kind. I used to complain fiercely to her about this, but her secret feeling was, I expect, that of many Anti-Suffragist women I have known, who, for some reason or other on the pinnacle of man's favour themselves, had no objection to the rest of womenkind being held in contempt—the attitude of Fatima, the Pride of the Harem. To be fair to Lisl I never heard her express definite sentiments on the subject, about which I had never thought myself, but as she was of her epoch and intensely German, her instinct was probably that of Fatima.

A delightful trait in Brahms was his horror of being lionised. He had a strong prejudice against England which he would jocularly insist on for my benefit, but what chiefly prevented his going there was dread of our hero-worshipping faculties: 'I know how you went on with Mendelssohn,' he said. What with their own embarrassment and his total lack of ease—or, as the Italians put it, lack of education—ordinary mortals who humbly tried to convey to him their admiration for his music had rather a bad time. The only person who sailed gaily through such troubled waters was Consul Limburger, but this again did not please Brahms and outraged the elect. After some performance, Limburger once remarked in his airy way: 'Really, Herr Doctor, I don't know where you mean to take us in the slow movement, whether to Heaven or Hell!' and Brahms replied with a mock bow: 'Whichever you please, Herr Consul,' which was quoted as a brilliant piece of repartee that ought to have crushed the audacious Limburger. But one retort of his was really rather good. The first subject in one of his Chamber works is almost identical with a theme of Mendelssohn's, and when some would-be connoisseur eagerly pointed out the fact, Brahms remarked: 'Ganz richtig—und jeder Schafskopf merkt's leider sofort!' ('Quite so—and the worst of it is every blockhead notices it directly.')

I am bound to say his taste in jokes sometimes left much to be desired, and can give an instance on the subject of my own name, which all foreigners find difficult, and which, as I innocently told him, my washerwoman pronounced 'Schmeiss.' Now the verb 'schmeissen,' to throw violently, is vulgar but quite harmless; there is however an antique noun, 'Schmeiss,' which means something unmentionable, and a certain horrible fly which frequents horrible places is called 'Schmeiss-Fliege.' As Brahms was for ever commenting on the extreme rapidity of my movements he found the play upon words irresistible and nicknamed me 'die Schmeiss-Fliege,' but Lisl was so scandalised at this joke that he had to drop it.

Among his admirers it was the fashion to despise Wagner, but to this he demurred, and a remark he often made 'His imitators are monkeys (*Affen*) but the man himself has something to say' was cited as proof of his noble, generous disposition. People like Joachim and Herzogenberg considered Wagner a colossal joke, and I remember their relating how as a sort of penance they sat through a whole act of *Siegfried,* keeping up each other's spirits by exchanging a 'Good morning' whenever a certain chord, let us say a diminished ninth, occurred in the score—a very provoking pleasantry even to hear about.

I like best to think of Brahms at the piano, playing his own compositions or Bach's mighty organ fugues, sometimes accompanying himself with a sort of muffled roar, as of Titans stirred to sympathy in the bowels of the earth. The veins in his forehead stood out, his wonderful bright blue eyes became veiled, and he seemed the incarnation of the restrained power in which his own work is forged. For his playing was never noisy, and when lifting a submerged theme out of a tangle of music he used jokingly to ask us to admire the gentle sonority of his 'tenor thumb.'

One of his finest characteristics was his attitude towards the great dead in his own art. He knew his own worth—what great creator does not?—but in his heart he was one of the most profoundly modest men I ever met, and to hear himself classed with such as Beethoven and Bach, to hear his C minor Symphony called 'The Tenth Symphony,'* jarred and outraged him. Once, when he turned up to rehearse some work of his, Reinecke had not yet finished rehearsing one of Mozart's symphonies—I forget which—and after the slow movement he murmured something to Lisl that I did not catch. She afterwards told me he had said: "I'd give all my stuff (*Kram*) to have written that one Andante!"

Among desultory remarks of his which remained in my mind, I remember his saying that he had given up predicting what a young composer's development would be, having so often found that those he thought talented came to nothing and *vice versa;* and in this connection he pointed out that all the work of Gluck's that still lives was written after he was fifty. I have never looked up Gluck in a Lexicon to see if this opinion would still hold good.

To me personally he was very kind and fatherly in his awkward way, chiefly, no doubt, because of the place I held in his friend's heart; but after a very slight acquaintance I guessed he would never take a woman-writer seriously, and had no desire, though kindly urged by him to do so, to show him my work. At last one day, without asking my leave Lisl showed him a little fugue of mine, and when I came in and found them looking at it he began analysing it, simply, gravely, and appreciatively, saying this development was good, that modulation curious, and so on. Carried away by surprise and delight I lost my head, and pointing out a constructive detail that had greatly fussed Herzogenberg—the sort of thing that made him call me a bad pupil—asked eagerly: 'Don't you think if I feel it that way I have a right to end on the dominant?' Suddenly the scene changed, back

---

*The implication was that it equalled, or surpassed, Beethoven's Ninth Symphony.

came the ironic smile, and stroking his moustache he said in a voice charged with kindly contempt: 'I am quite sure, dear child, you may end when and where you please!' . . . There it was! he had suddenly remembered I was a girl, to take whom seriously was beneath a man's dignity, and the quality of the work, which had I been an obscure male he would have upheld against anyone, simply passed from his mind.

Now let us suppose a publisher had been present—and they swarmed at the Herzogenbergs—what would have been the effect of this little scene on a budding inclination to print for me later on? And does the public realise that unless it is published music cannot possibly get known? . . .

　　　　.　.　.　.　.　.

One day I had a small triumph over Brahms. Among my exercises for Herzogenberg were two-part 'Inventions' in the Bach manner, and Lisl played him one of these as a new find unearthed by the Bach Society. In it was a certain harmonic turn not of Bach's time, but which he, who anticipated most things, might quite well have used, and Brahms's remark, which I must quote in the original, was 'Dem Kerl fällt doch immer wieder was Neues ein!' ('That fellow is always hitting on something new'). When the truth came out, the composer was warmly commended—and this time did not deserve it. It was just a bit of successful mimicry that any fairly clever musician might pull off.

But my greatest success with Brahms—who by the by held that everyone resembles some orchestral instrument and called me 'the Oboe'—had nothing to do with music. Piqued by his low estimate of my sex, I wrote a little sarcastic poem the last verse of which ran:

Der grosse Brahms hat's neulich ausgesprochen:
'*Ein g'scheidtes Weib, das hat doch keinen Sinn!*'
D'rum lasst uns emsig uns're Dummheit pflegen,
Denn nur auf diesen Punkt ist Werth zu legen
　　Als Weib und gute Brahmsianerin!
*Translation*
As the great Brahms recently proclaimed,
'*A clever woman is a thing of naught!*'
So let us diligently cultivate stupidity,
That being the only quality demanded
　　Of a female Brahms admirer!

That night he was at a supper given in his honour, and the mouth of everyone who approached him to talk about his music was stopped by his taking the poem out of his breast pocket and insisting on the unfortunate person reading it. This characteristic proceeding went on, I was told, throughout the evening and must have maddened the admirers.

In post-Leipzig days I saw little of him, but once when I was passing through Vienna and called on him, he was more than kind and cordial and begged me to fix up a meal at his house on my way back. Alas, when the time came he was away.

In jotting down these various impressions I am quite aware they do not do him justice. Even then I knew all about his wonderful generosity to poor musicians and old friends fallen on evil days. I noticed, too, that even the cynicism about women was belied by the extreme delicacy and tenderness of his work, and more especially by his choice of words to set to music. But all I can say is that this poetical insight did not determine his working theory (ascribed by some foolish persons to an early disappointment in love); and the point of memoirs—so it seems to me—is to relate what you saw yourself, not what other people, books, or subsequent reflections tell you. I saw integrity, sincerity, kindness of heart, generosity to opponents, and a certain nobility of soul that stamps all his music; but on the other hand I saw coarseness, uncivilised-ness, a defective perception of subtle shades in people and things, lack of humour, and of course the inevitable and righteous selfishness of people who have a message of their own to deliver and can't run errands for others. When Wagner died he sent a wreath and was bitterly hurt at receiving no acknowledgement. A friend of the Wagners told me gloatingly that Cosima had said: 'Why should the wreath be acknowledged? *I understand the man was no friend to Our Art'*—and my informant added: 'It was a mistake to send it at all.' . . . Of such was the Kingdom of Wagner.

The accounts that reached the world of his cruel illness and death were infinitely tragic, for he fought against his doom, they say, and like a child when bedtime comes, wept and protested he did not want to go. The only consolation is to believe, as I for one do, that his best work was behind him, and that perhaps Nature did well to ring down the curtain.

(*Impressions That Remained,* 1919.)

# Memories of Great Performers

## GARY GRAFFMAN

*In his enchanting memoirs,* I Really Should be Practicing, *(1981), as well as in his articles for publications such as the* New York Times *and* Connoisseur, *Gary Graffman has joined the ranks of Charles Rosen, Glenn Gould, and other pianists who are gifted with words as well as music. (See "The Erotic Mozart" and "Scarlatti's Keyboard Music.") Graffman is a master of the musical anecdote whose writing is as pungent and incisive as his playing. Whether recounting the treacherously unpredictable personalities of pianos, the hair-raising logistical mishaps of tours, or the eccentric personalities of conductors, Graffman has a vitality and irreverence that make even the grittiest details of music-making irresistibly dramatic. Especially endearing are his portraits of musical artists who influenced his life, which become an entertaining means of advancing his own seasoned perceptions about musical performance.*

By far the most lasting effect of my slight brush with Toscanini was that, thanks to the Weisses' friendship, I was invited to attend, with Piero,* the famous concerts and—even more importantly—rehearsals with the NBC Symphony, then in its heyday. This was extremely lucky because although the concerts were free, tickets were almost impossible to obtain, as NBC's Studio 8-H, where they took place, didn't seat many people. And entry to the rehearsals was truly an achievement, for NBC employed a bouncer to remove those unfortunates who somehow managed to sneak in and whose credentials didn't pass muster. The tight security at re-

*Piero Weiss, whose family was close to Toscanini.

hearsals was understandable, for Toscanini's temper made Vengerova's* chair-throwing sessions seem like tea parties. The legends about his tirades and baton-breakings are not exaggerated; and, in addition to expanding my musical understanding, I emerged from those rehearsals with a lifetime supply of shockingly foul Italian obscenities, for which Piero had obligingly provided simultaneous translation.

We went to these rehearsals a couple of times a month over a period of several years. Toscanini was certainly the major conductorial influence on me then, as I assume he was on many musicians and music lovers of my generation in the United States. I imagine that his strict adherence to the composers' instructions, in most cases without any feeling of pedantry (in fact, quite the opposite: a feeling of great excitement, since he was the most exciting of all the great conductors), had an extremely salutary influence on all of us who came in contact with him, no matter how peripherally.

Heifetz was also a major influence on me. His perfection seemed nothing short of magic, and I felt—as I still do—that there is no pianist who has such unearthly control over his instrument as that incredible violinist. He never smiled, he never moved (Vengerova would have been happy if I'd imitated *his* stage deportment), and I don't think I ever heard him make one slip of any kind. He always knew just what he wanted to do, and it always came out. The most remarkable thing about all of this, for me, was that nothing ever sounded planned or overworked. The phrases that he would spin out so voluptuously (but with such fantastic varieties of sound!), the daredevil feats that he would toss off so lightly (and with such perfect intonation!) had such vitality and spontaneity that a blasé teenager like myself came away with goose pimples.

But by far the greatest number of concerts I attended during those years involved pianists. Pianists in recital, pianists with orchestra, pianists playing sonatas and chamber music, pianists playing with other pianists, sometimes even pianists accompanying singers. There was no shortage of pianists. (There never is.) But what is surprising was how many truly great pianists were performing regularly then.

Hofmann was the first of the giants I heard, and that was a few

*Madame Isabelle Vengerova, Graffman's piano teacher at the Curtis Institute.

years before the time of which I'm writing, at the famous Jubilee Concert that he gave at the Metropolitan Opera House in 1937. Even though I was only nine, I remember it vividly. Perhaps the fact that I'd recently played for him at Curtis (and, having *tutoyéd* him, our resulting intimacy) had something to do with it. Nevertheless, the remarkable sound he effortlessly charmed out of the instrument, with never a hint of harshness, is with me still.

I heard Rachmaninoff a few times at Carnegie Hall. He died when I was fourteen, so the last time was probably shortly before that; but I was old enough to appreciate the extraordinary rhythmic propulsion that underscored his performances and the utter clarity of his playing, with those infinite nuances and gradations of sound that meant the difference between life and death to Vengerova.

I also heard others of that era, but it was Rachmaninoff and Hofmann who exerted some influence on me. I really mean "some," because the overwhelming piano influence that I felt was unquestionably from Horowitz, Rubinstein, Serkin and Schnabel. I attended almost every performance they gave in New York during those years.

These were the artists who made me lose myself completely in the music. Their playing was very, very different one from the other, and yet I would be so convinced by the way each of them played—actually, carried along by his thoughts—that it seemed, when listening to any one of them, that there was no other possible way of performing that work at that moment. This, of course, is what artistry is all about. Each pianist in his own particular way utilized the little black spots that the composer put on the paper as more than simply a point of departure. For, as freely as he may have played, he was really trying to re-create through himself what he passionately believed the composer's wishes to be.

I began to realize that the performer of a Beethoven sonata had a relation to the composer similar to that of an actor to Shakespeare, and although a great artist must have something unique to offer and must play his music or role with such authority, devotion and abandon that the audience will be utterly convinced, it must be within the boundaries of the composer's or playwright's instructions. Shakespeare used words and Beethoven, notes. But Shakespeare actually gave fewer instructions as to how to read one of his sentences, let alone paragraphs, than Beethoven did within a single phrase of his music, not to mention an entire section of a work. For example: in bars 4, 5 and 6 of the last movement of his A-flat Sonata, Opus 110, Beethoven gives no less than eighteen admonitions pertaining to mood and attitude, tempo changes, dynamic changes and quality of sound. . . .

And to make things more difficult, the performer, rather than appearing to be confined in a straitjacket by these injunctions, must, while respecting all of the above, seem to be improvising freely under some divine inspiration. Yet I came to understand that, miraculous as it may have seemed, there were as many different great performances of these three bars as there were great performers.

One razzle-dazzle artist whose irresistible charms won him a secure spot in Rosalie Leventritt's chastely Schubertian heart was a gangling Juilliard student from Texas named Van Cliburn. He was nineteen when he played at the Leventritt Competition. Word had gotten around that he was very gifted, but nobody really knew what to expect. And he looked so different. He was so tall—and, well, so *American*. . . . At the time Van entered the Leventritt, however, pianists were Central or Eastern European, or at least of that extraction. It looked so odd to see a *cowboy* play the *piano*. But when Van took over the keyboard, all visions of bucking broncos vanished instantly. The Leventritt jury—and the audience, of which I was one—were astonished by his relaxed yet seemingly limitless virtuosity, and when he finished an electrifying performance of a Liszt rhapsody, there was a good moment's stunned silence before the judges could gather the temerity to ask him to play a little something else. He was still sitting at the piano, awaiting instructions, and I remember that he turned to them at that moment, before beginning the next piece, and shyly asked, "Would y'all mahnd if Ah went and got a glass of WAWtuh?"

The few moments he was gone from the stage gave us all a much-needed breather and the opportunity to shake our heads in wonderment. The jury scribbled busily on little index cards provided for their comments, doodles and reminder notes about each contestant—not that they were likely to forget this one. At the end of the afternoon, after victorious Van had been borne away in triumph, Naomi and I noticed a forgotten note pad on the floor beneath the chair where Talent Scout Arthur Judson . . . had been sitting and scribbling busily. We pounced on it and read his sage assessment of the winner's potential: "Not now; perhaps another year." . . .

Rosalie Leventritt was often called upon to provide solace for wounds inflicted on some of her great friends by one of her greatest friends, George Szell. Although she shared his impeccable, uncompromising standards, her bronze core was cloaked in soft celadon-green velvet, while his was armored with steely porcupine quills, which could pierce deeply and painfully. He was aware and, I think, even proud of his ogre-like reputation. The day that *Time* magazine appeared on the newsstands with his picture on the cover and an exhaustive profile inside displaying his foibles—warts and all—his delight was boundless. "It's official! It's official!" he crowed. "It's in print—I'm a bastard!"

George Szell had a reputation for being fierce. It is said that his bite was even worse than his bark. He was completely intolerant of anything he deemed wrongdoing, and this was particularly true when the transgression concerned music. Once, jokingly, someone who knew him well enough to dare it mentioned to him that he treated the interpretation of one short phrase of music as a matter of life or death. "But don't you see," he replied, impaling the speaker with his laser-beam eyes, frighteningly magnified behind ice-cube-thick spectacles, "it is. It *is*."

(*I Really Should be Practicing*, 1981.)

# Conversations with Arrau

## JOSEPH HOROWITZ

*Joseph Horowitz, former music critic for the* New York Times, *program editor and principal annotator for the Kaufmann Concert Hall of the 92nd Street Y, and author of* Understanding Toscanini *(chosen by the National Book Critics Circle as one of the most distinguished books of 1987), is a probing commentator on the contemporary musical scene. His elegantly composed book on Claudio Arrau, one of the last Romantic pianists, juxtaposes Arrau's burning integrity against the chilly ambience of the modern concert hall. In sketching Arrau, Horowitz manages to capture a worldview, a sensibility "actually susceptible to exaltation" that seems to be fading from the pseudoglamorous, "supra-personal scheme" of today's jet-set performer.*

Not long after meeting Claudio Arrau for the first time, in 1976, I was invited to watch him rehearse Beethoven's Third Piano Concerto at New York's Avery Fisher Hall. Dapper in a three-piece suit and gravely composed, Arrau at the keyboard made the orchestra seem a vulgar backdrop to affairs of the soul. Afterward, in Arrau's dressing-room, there were complaints about the listlessness of the musicians. They will play better for the concert, Arrau said; in rehearsal, they are always casual. Does Claudio Arrau ever play casually? someone asked. "I *can't!*" he answered, his eyes aghast, his face burning with feeling.

This glimpse of the artist at the mercy of his emotions has been renewed many times in the course of our acquaintance. His mere salutations are delivered with devouring honesty. He seems as incapable of lapsing into mere amenity as into rudeness. Notwithstanding his eminence, and the ponderous undertow of his visceral energies, he is an endearingly gracious man.

Neither his English, which bears traces of Spanish and German, nor his changeable physiognomy defines his origin. In fact, Arrau made his way strangely into the world. Chillán, Chile, where he was born in 1903, was a small city many hours from Santiago. His mother, who was already 43 and had been married 21 years, taught piano. He never knew his father. He seems to have learned to read music mainly on his own, and before he could read words. When he was eight, he went abroad to study, supported by a stipend awarded by the Chilean Congress. In Berlin, where he settled with his mother, brother, and sister, he became the favourite pupil of Martin Krause, an imperious pedagogue who himself had studied with Liszt. His early celebrity continued: he played for kings and queens, and under Arthur Nikisch and Fritz Steinbach. Then, in 1918, Krause died, and Arrau's progress halted. Abandoned in post-war Berlin, he lacked the cunning to promote his career, even to support himself and his family. An abbreviated American tour in 1923–24 sent him home penniless. On the verge of giving up, he sought help in psychoanalysis. Gradually, his reputation was remade, and his adulthood consolidated. In 1935–36, in a heralded feat of memory and endurance, he performed the complete solo clavier works of Johann Sebastian Bach in 12 recitals. In 1937, he married Ruth Schneider, a mezzo-soprano from Frankfurt, and moved out of the flat he had shared with his mother and sister. The Second World War drove the Arraus to the United States in 1940–41.

His arduous itinerary, generous programmes, and catholic repertoire have long been trademarks. He still plays more than 70 concerts a season. He makes his home in suburban Douglaston, New York, a half-hour's drive from Manhattan, but is rarely there. He has a summer house in southern Vermont, four miles outside the village of Weston (population 500), but spares even less time for it. His entourage is surprisingly small . . .

Two overlapping character types permeate his identity: the man-child and the artist. The first is rooted in his prodigy years and evokes images of the pianist in knee pants, his feet dangling above the pedals. In Chile, escorted by his mother, he played for the President. In Europe, under Krause's supervision, he sat in the laps of duchesses and queens. Early photographs suggest a shy, silent child with soft features and strangely experienced eyes.

The autocratic Krause, with his goatee and twirled moustache, might almost have been one of E.T.A. Hoffmann's Svengali-like music masters. Most of the authority figures from Arrau's early years, however, were maternal, beginning with his hovering mother, who dressed in black for decades after her husband's death, and who lived to be 99.

Arrau's enduring innocence is partly a legacy of his childhood eminence. He remains the least cynical, least devious of men. He does not drink or smoke. He distrusts machines: he cannot drive a car, boil an egg, or even operate a phonograph. I have seen him struggle for minutes, with mounting exasperation, to disengage three locks on the front door of his home in Douglaston.

A second portion of his innocence arises from his vocation. He guards the purity of his environment. He shuns parties and loses track of small talk. He spends time alone with music and—especially in Vermont, where he weeds and plants—with nature. In conversation, as at the piano, he discloses emotional strife with startling frankness. He plainly embodies the nineteenth-century model of the artist as solitary, suffering hero.

Arrau's concentrated life style suits his stark concentration of mood. He is not an ironist, and knows no puns. Even at its gentlest, his presence registers with palpable force.

He is a small man—about five and a half feet tall—and when he is tired his outsized head can seem an archaic burden for old, brittle legs. His hands, also large for his frame, are prepossessing. The fingers are individually articulate, the fingertips cushioned and slightly spread. The ranginess of his thumbs, resulting from the peculiar elasticity of the joints, makes them seem longer than they are.

Because every mood consumes his features, he has many faces. His flaring nostrils and prominent cheekbones, dapper moustache and shiny hair at times still connote the dark good looks of a South American cosmopolite. When he is suddenly pensive, his hazel-green eyes cloud over and his gaze wanders. At the piano, his profile is chiselled, the flesh stretched taut and marked with lines of pain. In repose, he is round-faced and cherubic; his eyes crinkle, his cheeks soften and inflate.

His voice is a gentle baritone, used softly and expressively. The words themselves are often ancillary, for in terms of language Arrau is an effortful speaker. Sometimes, before answering a question, he will draw a breath and look away. His sentences break down when a phrase or name will not come, and the ensuing silences can seem dangerous. Even when the verbal stream is steady, it is usually short: four or five sentences materialise, then the engine runs down.

Especially when music obtrudes, Arrau's words tend to dissipate. In fact, music is so distant from his social self that to play the piano for students or friends would be inconceivable. It is really not far-fetched to surmise that for Arrau words and music occupy distinct personal realms, and that the pronounced civility of the first moderates the instinctual abandon of the second. His gentle manners, his fastidious attire ("Time" magazine once likened him to "a fugitive from a Man of Distinction ad"), the artifacts that embellish his work environment—these suggest a striving for order whose musical equivalent is his absolute fidelity to the text, and whose adversary is a substratum of fire and ice.

To witness Arrau performing the Liszt sonata is to know how thoroughly this substratum can obliterate his normal self-awareness. Even while asleep, the demons cast a trembling glow from behind his mildest public face. And they penetrate the timbre of his voice.

Arrau listens to his own recordings with visible discomfort; he perceives the clothes of civility being stripped away.

(*Conversations with Arrau*, 1982.)

# Perfect Pitch

---

## NICOLAS SLONIMSKY

---

*Of all the thousands of musical lives chronicled by lexicographer Nicolas Slonim-sky, none is more colorful or bizarre than his own. It takes in everything from the Russian Revolution to the McCarthy blacklists, from music lessons in 1919 with Glière to jam sessions in 1981 with Frank Zappa. In his various careers as composer, conductor, raconteur, biographer, and musical detective, Slonimsky has lived enough lives for two or three men. At 93, he finally set it all down in* Perfect Pitch *(1988), in witty, neurotically precise Slonimskian prose. Reprinted here are two excerpts from that volume. The first is from a chapter called "Paris," where Slonimsky settled after a harrowing escape from Russia via Constantinople and where he served Stravinsky, Koussevitsky, and other luminaries as "piano banger" and musical arranger. The second is from "Three Places in New England," where he offers firsthand accounts of Ives, Ruggles, and other American revolutionaries he championed in the 1930s as an iconoclastic conductor before being run out of the Hollywood Bowl by outraged dowagers and reactionary music critics (the norm then, as now). Although Slonimsky claims he has "failed dismally" at his various careers, he has clearly succeeded in one thing. As these charming reminiscences attest, he is one of the greatest musical chroniclers of our time.*

The gift of music is a compartmentalized faculty. A composer of genius may be a poor performer and may not even possess that talisman of precocious genius, the sense of perfect pitch. Ravel was completely helpless in spotting wrong notes in his own compositions when he conducted. Alfredo Casella told me that even Debussy let pass the most horrendous mistakes in his orchestral works, and in one instance failed to notice that the clarinet player used a clarinet in B-flat instead of one in A; one could only imagine what heterophony resulted from such an unintended transposition of a semitone.

Stravinsky had a very limited sense of pitch. I recall an embarrassing episode wherein Stravinsky conducted his *Ragtime* for eleven players, a work which calls for the Hungarian keyboard instrument, cimbalom. Since there was no cimbalom to be found in Paris, I was hired to play the part on the piano. At a rehearsal, Koussevitzky turned the pages for me (I would dearly love to have a photograph of that scene!). Towards the end of the rehearsal I noticed that the left hand of the cimbalom part was written in the treble clef, an obvious error, I thought, for the hands crossed all the time. Koussevitzky also noticed this incongruity; we both came to the conclusion that the clef in the left hand should have been a bass clef, and I blithely played on. During the intermission I pointed out this apparent error to Stravinsky. Perspiring profusely, as he always did during conducting, and wiping the sweat from his neck with a towel, he said, 'No, the treble clef in the left hand is right, because the part was written for the upper manual of the cimbalom, which sounds an octave higher.' I was perplexed. There I was, in effect transposing the piece in the double counterpoint of the 13th, right under Stravinsky's nose, and he was never the wiser for it.

Stravinsky was also a poor proof-reader. When his *Symphony of Psalms* was being engraved in Koussevitzky's publishing house, Prokofiev, who was in Paris at the time, happened to look at the proofs. He told me with obvious glee that he had found fifty-three gross errors on the very first page of Stravinsky's score. 'You will not find such errors in my music!' he boasted. It so happened that his *Sinfonietta* was also being engraved at the time, and Prokofiev carried the proofs with him. Seized with a diabolical temptation, I asked him to let me look at the proofs. He agreed, but warned me that I would be wasting my time trying to find errors. This was a supreme challenge to my vanity. There were no wrong notes, but to my delight I found the wrong clef in one of the parts in the score. Prokofiev was visibly annoyed when I showed it to him. He fixed the clef, and the score was published without this embarrassing mistake.

Stravinsky was above all a man of rhythm, and in his orchestral works he extended the rhythm section to an integral part of the score, coequal with strings and winds. He also favoured the dry and hard timbre of the drums. Conducting a rehearsal of *Les Noces*, he asked the drummer to use a harder stick: 'Plus dur, plus dur!' he cried, until the exasperated musician exclaimed: 'Vous voulez que je fasse ça avec ma queue!' and obscenely pointed to his crotch, suggesting that his ithyphallic drumstick would be hardest, whereupon the players erupted in canonic counterpoint. 'Tu te flattes, tu te flattes!' Stravinsky remained unruffled.

In all my lengthy association with Koussevitzky I never saw him read a book, and yet in his younger days in Moscow he was surrounded by writers, poets, and multifarious deep-thinkers, among them the philosopher Medtner, a brother of the composer. Koussevitzky was also fortunate in his friendship with Skriabin, who himself read infrequently. Skriabin's brother-in-law, Boris de Schloezer, tells of Skriabin's lifelong wrestling with the concepts of divinity, eternity, and destiny. The titles of his works, such as *Divine Poem, Poem of Ecstasy*, and *Poem of Fire*, had a personal meaning for him. The opening of the *Divine Poem* was to him a declaration of self-being, 'I am', which Skriabin added to the manuscript at Schloezer's suggestion. Skriabin wrote in his diary: 'I want to conquer the world the way a man takes a woman.' At the Moscow Conservatory Skriabin was indeed known as a passionate 'woman-taker'.

Koussevitzky was the first fully to appreciate the genius of Skriabin. He went to see him in Switzerland and offered him a publishing contract with the Éditions Russes on generous financial terms. It came as a lifesaver to Skriabin who, living with Tatiana Schloezer as his common-law wife, was in such financial straits that he sometimes did not have money for a postage stamp. To Skriabin, Koussevitzky was a messenger heaven-sent to serve his messianic destiny. To Koussevitzky, Skriabin was the medium serving to project his own genius as a music-maker. Two messiahs could not exist on the same terrestrial plane, and their relationship gradually deteriorated into an ugly series of mutual recriminations. In the end, Skriabin could not bear to hear Koussevitzky's name even mentioned, and referred to him as 'the unspeakable one'.

Skriabin died in 1915 at the age of 42, of an abscess that could have been cured in twenty-four hours with a few injections of penicillin. Alas, those wonder drugs were not available in his time.

Stravinsky remarked acidly in one of his published dialogues that Skriabin's early death was to be lamented, but that one shuddered to think what kind of music Skriabin would have written had he lived longer. Indeed, Skriabin's elfin spirit would not have fitted into the era of Stravinsky and Schoenberg with their set systems. Modern music followed bifurcated roads, retrospective on the fringes of neo-classicism, introspective among the followers of the New Vienna School. The mystical direction of Skriabin, perpendicular to both dimensions, and asymptotic to an astral plane, had lost its audience. I recall an episode at Koussevitzky's Paris villa in 1925; Prokofiev was there for lunch; he picked up the score of Skriabin's *Divine Poem* lying on the piano top, and played over a few pages with a condescending smile on his lips. 'What ought to be done with this music,' he finally declared, 'is to liven it up with a bass drum.' And he demonstrated where he would have used the drum in the score. Skriabin with a bass drum! What blasphemy!

It was through Henry Cowell that I met Charles Ives. In 1928 Ives invited Cowell and me to his brownstone on East 74th Street in New York, and Mrs Ives, providentially named Harmony, graciously served us lunch. They had adopted a girl named Edith. At the time I met him Ives was only 54 years but looked frail, suffering from a variety of ailments, as a result of a massive heart attack in 1918, and he had practically ceased composing. I learned to admire the nobility of his thought, his total lack of selfishness and his faith in the inherent goodness of mankind. There was something endearingly old-fashioned in his way of life; he spoke in trenchant aphorisms, akin to the language of Thoreau and Emerson, and he wrote in a similarly forceful manner. He possessed a natural wisdom combined with an eloquent simplicity of utterance. Amazingly enough, he started his career as a successful insurance man. His achievements in business were postulated, so he explained, on his respect for people at large. Yet Ives was capable of great wrath. He inveighed mightily against self-inflated mediocrity, in politics and art alike. The most disparaging word in his vocabulary was 'nice'. To him it signified smugness, self-satisfaction, lack of imagination. He removed himself from the ephemeral concerns of the world at large. He never read newspapers. He did not own a radio or a phonograph, and he rarely, if ever, attended concerts. The only piece of modern music he ever heard was Stravinsky's *Firebird;* reports differ whether he also heard *La Mer* of Debussy.

Ives was extremely biased in his opinions. Toscanini was a 'nice old lady' and Koussevitzky a 'soft seat'. Some of his aphoristic utterances are fit for an anthology. 'Dissonance is like a man . . .' 'Music is the art of speaking extravagantly . . .' 'A song has a few rights, the same as other ordinary citizens . . .' 'What has sound got to do with music? . . .' 'Beauty in music is too often confused with something that lets the ears lie back in an easy chair . . .' And he urged people to 'stretch their ears'. He was impatient with copyists who questioned rough spots in his manuscript. 'Please don't try to make things nice!' he would admonish. 'All the wrong notes are right!'

Ives was a transcendental rebel in politics. He once circulated a proposal to amend the Constitution of the United States and establish a system of direct vote for President. When Harding was elected President in 1920, Ives gave vent to his indignation in a song damning politicians who betrayed the ideals of the nation. He never participated in active political campaigns; his politics were those of mind and soul. So far removed was he from the reality of the world that he was not aware of the rise of the Nazis. When I told him what evil things Hitler was doing in Germany, Ives rose from his chair to the full height of his stature and exclaimed with rhetorical emphasis: 'Then why does not someone *do* something about this man!'

I told Ives about my chamber orchestra and asked if he could give me one of his works. He suggested *Three Places in New England.* As I looked over the score, I experienced a strange, but unmistakable, feeling that I was looking at a work of genius. I cannot tell precisely why this music produced such an impression on me. The score possessed elements that seemed to be mutually incompatible and even incongruous: a freely flowing melody derived from American folk-songs, set in harmonies that were dense and highly dissonant, but soon resolving into clearances of serene, cerulean beauty in triadic formations that created a spiritual catharsis. In contrast, there were rhythmic patterns of extreme complexity; some asymmetries in the score evoked in my mind by a strange association of ideas the elegant and yet irrational equations connecting the base of natural logarithms and the ratio of the circumference of a circle to its diameter with the so-called imaginary number, a square root of a negative quantity. The polytonalities and polyrhythms in the Ives score seemed incoherent when examined vertically, but simple and logical when viewed horizontally.

The more I absorbed the idiom of *Three Places in New England* the more I became possessed by its power. After conducting the score numerous times in public I felt total identification with the music, so much so that years later, when it became extremely popular, I would turn it off when I heard it on the radio, mumbling, 'It is mine, it is mine.'

The original scoring of *Three Places in New England* exceeded the dimensions of my chamber orchestra, but fortunately most orchestral music of Ives was scored for a 'theatre orchestra', capable of different arrangements. In fact, Ives called *Three Places in New England* an 'orchestral set', implying optional instrumentation. I asked if he could possibly arrange the score to accommodate my chamber orchestra. Yes, he could, and would. In fact, the resulting arrangement became the last orchestral score that Ives wrote out, at least in part, in his own handwriting; later he was unable to handle a pen.

I gave the world première of *Three Places in New England* at the Town Hall in New York on 10 January 1931. Ives was present; it was one of the few occasions that he came to a concert. By that time my conducting had improved considerably so that I was no longer preoccupied with its technical aspect. And I was also able to control my nerves. I was not disturbed by the whispered refrain of the leader, 'So far, so good,' after each movement. The rest of the programme included Henry Cowell's *Sinfonietta, Men and Mountains* by Carl Ruggles, and a couple of simpler pieces intended to mollify sensitive ears. The final number was Mozart's *Ein musikalischer Spass,* the 'joke' of the title being a polytonal coda. I put it on as if to say, 'Look, listen, Mozart did it too.'

There were a few boos and hisses after the Ruggles piece. I was told that Ives stood up and said to a person who grumbled against Ruggles: 'You sissie, you don't realize that this is a piece of real strong masculine music.' This report found its way into the Ives literature, but I cannot very well believe it. It would have been utterly out of character for him to make such a public display of himself.

(*Perfect Pitch*, 1988.)

# The Religion of the Pianoforte

## GEORGE BERNARD SHAW

*In this "fragment of autobiography," the ideal finale for this book, Shaw sums up his philosophy of music, the most participatory and "active" of the arts. Taking it as established that life "is a curse unless it operates as pleasurable activity," Shaw shows why "high feeling"—much more so than abstract thought—is the way into the arts, especially music. Most people, Shaw fears, view "classical" music as a "web of learnedly and heavily decorative sound patterns, and never as containing a delicious kernel of feeling." As an antidote to this unfortunate notion, Shaw insists that we become "skilled voluptuaries," an ideal that is surely more attainable through the reading of writers like himself.*

The other day somebody went to Rubinstein and said, "Is the pianoforte a musical instrument?" That is just the sort of question people put nowadays. You call on the Prince of Wales to ask, "Is England a republic?" or on the Lord Mayor with, "Is London a city?" or on Madame Calvé to take her opinion, as an expert, on "Is Cavalleria Rusticana an opera?" In treating such questions as open ones you have already achieved a paradox; and even if the Prince of Wales should have the presence of mind to simply say No, and the Lord Mayor and Madame Calvé, Yes, and have you immediately shewn out, still you are in a position to fill the contents bill of one of our weekly scrap papers with, "Is England a republic?—What the Prince of Wales says"; and so sell off an edition to people who cannot bring themselves to think that the plain explanation of the mystery is that you are a foolish person.

Yet it will not do to reply to "Is the pianoforte a musical instrument?" by a simple Yes. That would be an understatement of a quite extraordinary case. The pianoforte is the most important of all musical instruments: its invention was to music what the invention of printing was to poetry. Just consider the analogy for a moment. What is it that keeps Shakespear alive among us? Is it the stage, the great actors, the occasional revivals with new music and scenery, and agreeably mendacious accounts of the proceedings in the newspapers after the first night? Not a bit of it. Those who know their Shakespear at all know him before they are twentyfive: and that there is no time—one has to live instead of to read; and how many Shakespearean revivals, pray, has an Englishman the chance of seeing before he is twentyfive, even if he lives in a city and not in the untheatred country, or in a family which regards the pit of the theatre as the antechamber to that pit which has no bottom? I myself, born of profane stock, and with a quarter-century of play-going, juvenile and manly, behind me, have not seen as many as a full half of Shakespear's plays acted; and if my impressions of his genius were based solely on these representations I should be in darkness indeed. For what is it that I have seen on such occasions? Take the solitary play of Shakespear's which is revived more than twice in a generation! Well, I have seen Mr Barry Sullivan's Hamlet, Mr Daniel Bandmann's Hamlet, Miss Marriott's Hamlet, Mr Irving's Hamlet, Signor Salvini's Hamlet, Mr Wilson Barrett's Hamlet, Mr Benson's Hamlet, Mr Beerbohm Tree's Hamlet, and perhaps others which I forget. But to none of these artists do I owe my acquaintance with Shakespear's play of Hamlet. In proof whereof, let me announce that, for all my Hamlet-going, were I to perish this day, I should go to my account without having seen Fortinbras, save in my mind's eye, or watched the ghostly twilight march (as I conceive it) of those soldiers who went to their graves like beds to dispute with him a territory that was not tomb enough and continent to hide the slain. When first I saw Hamlet I innocently expected Fortinbras to dash in, as in Sir John Gilbert's picture, with shield and helmet, like a medieval Charles XII, and, by right of his sword and his will, take the throne which the fencing foil and the speculative intellect had let slip, thereby pointing the play's most characteristically English moral. But what was my first Hamlet to my first Romeo and Juliet, in which Romeo, instead of dying forthwith when he took the poison, was interrupted by Juliet, who sat up and made him carry her down to the footlights, where she complained of being very cold, and had to be warmed by a love scene, in the middle of which Romeo, who had forgotten all about poison, was taken ill and died? Or my first Richard III, which turned out to be a wild *potpourri* of all the historical plays, with a studied debasement of all the best word music in the lines, and an original domestic scene in which Richard, after feebly bullying his wife, observed, "If this don't kill her, she's immortal"? Cibber's Richard III was, to my youthful judgment, superior to Shakespear's play on one point only, and that was the omission of the stage direction, "Exeunt fighting," whereby Richmond and the tyrant were enabled to have it out to the bitter end full in my view. Need I add that it was not through this sort of thing, with five out of every six parts pitiably ill acted and ill uttered, that I came to know Shakespear? Later on, when it was no longer Mr Blank's Hamlet and Miss Dash's Juliet that was in question, but "the Lyceum revival," the stage brought me but little nearer to the drama. For the terrible cutting involved by modern hours of performance; the foredoomed futility of the attempt to take a work originally conceived mainly as a long story told on the stage, with plenty of casual adventures and unlimited changes of scene, and to tight-lace it into something like a modern play consisting of a single situation in three acts; and the commercial relations which led the salaried players to make the most abject artistic sacrifices to their professional consciousness that the performance is the actor-manager's "show," and by no means their own or Shakespear's: all these and many other violently anti-artistic conditions of modern theatrical enterprise still stood inexorably between the stage and the real Shakespear.

The case of Shakespear is not, of course, the whole case against the theatre: it is, indeed, the weakest part of it, because the stage certainly does more for Shakespear than for any other dramatic poet. The English drama, from Marlowe to Browning, would practically not exist if it were not printed. To extend the argument to literature in general it is only necessary to imagine the nation depending for its knowledge of poetry and romance on the recitations of elocutionists and the readings with which some of our sects replace the "lessons" of the Church of England. Such a conception dies of its own absurdity. Clearly, the literature which the private student cannot buy or borrow to take home and puzzle out by himself may be regarded as, at best, in a state of suspended animation.

But what has all this to do with the pianoforte? Well, can anything be more obvious? I decline to insult the intelligence of the public by explaining.

Let me, however, do an unsolicited service to thousands of fellow creatures who are huddling round the fire trying to kill time with such sensations as they can extract from novels, not suspecting a far more potent instrument stands dumb by the wall, unthought of save as one of those expensive and useless pieces of show furniture without which no gentleman's drawing room is complete. Take a case by way of illustration. You are a youth, let us suppose, poring over The Three Musketeers, or some romance of Scott's. Now, in the name of all that is real, how much satisfaction do you get out of mere *descriptions* of duels, and escapes, and defiances, and raptures of passion? A good deal, you think (being young); but how if you could find a sort of book that would give you not merely a description of these thrilling sensations, but the sensations themselves—the stirring of the blood, the bristling of the fibres, the transcendent, fearless fury which makes romance so delightful, and realizes that ideal which Mr Gilbert has aptly summed up in the phrase, "heroism without risk"? Such a book is within your reach. Pitch your Three Musketeers into the waste-paper basket, and get a vocal score of Meyerbeer's Huguenots. Then to the piano, and pound away. In the music you will find the body and reality of that feeling which the mere novelist could only describe to you; there will come home to your senses something in which you can actually experience the candor and gallant impulse of the hero, the grace and trouble of the heroine, and the extracted emotional quintessence of their love. As to duels, what wretched printed list of the thrusts in *carte* and *tierce* delivered by D'Artagnan or Bussy d' Amboise can interest the man who knows Don Giovanni's duel in the dark with the Commandant, or Romeo's annihilation of Tybalt (not Shakespear's, but Gounod's Romeo), or Raoul's explosion of courage on the brink of the fight in the *Pré aux Clercs*. And mark, it is only at the piano that that *Pré aux Clercs* fight is really fought out— that Maurevert comes out of the darkness with his assassins to back San Bris, and that Marcel, in extremity, thunders his *Eine feste Burg* at the door of the inn, and brings all the Huguenot soldiers tumbling out to the rescue with their rataplan. Go to the theatre for that scene, and there is no sense in what passes: Maurevert is cut; Marcel is cut; everything that makes the scene grow and live is cut, because the opera is so long that even with the fourth act omitted it is impossible to present it unmutilated without an ungentlemanly curtailment of the waits between the acts. Besides, it is a curious circumstance that operatic stage managers never read operas, perhaps because, since they never conceive cause and effect as operating in the normal way, the composer's instructions would only lead them astray. At all events, we have Meyerbeer at the same disadvantage on the stage as Shakespear.

Here I can conceive our Musketeer-loving youth interrupting me with some impatience to explain that he cannot play the piano. No doubt he cannot: what of that? Berlioz could not play the piano; Wagner could not play the piano; nay, I myself, a musical critic of European reputation, *I* cannot play. But is any man prevented from reading Othello by the fact that he cannot act or recite? You need not be able to play your Huguenots: if you can read the notes and bungle over them, that is sufficient. This only leads our youth to put his difficulty more precisely: he cannot even read the notes. Of course not; but why? Because he has never discovered that they are worth learning. Pianism has been presented to him as a polite accomplishment, the object of which is to give pleasure to others—an object which has not been attained, he has observed, in the case of his sisters. To him, therefore, I seem to propose that he shall, in pure and probably unsuccessful altruism, spend so many hours a day for a year over Czerny's, Plaidy's, or Cramer's exercises in order that he may be able to play Beethoven's Pathetic Sonata slowly and awkwardly, but note-accurately, to the manifest discomfort and disturbance of all within earshot. Now, he does not care two straws about the Pathetic Sonata, and would not spend twelve hours, much less twelve months, over Czerny to save all Beethoven's works from destruction, much less to oblige me. Therefore, though he will learn to smoke, to skate, to play billiards, to ride, to shoot, to do half-a-dozen things much more difficult than reading music, he will no more learn his notes than a sailor will learn ploughing. Why would he, since no pleasure can come of it for himself? As to giving pleasure to others, even sisterless youths know, first, that there are not ten men in Europe among the most gifted and arduously-trained professionals whose playing gives pleasure to enough people to fill St James's Hall; and second, that the effect of ordinary amateur playing on other people is to drive them almost mad. I learnt my notes at the age of sixteen or thereabouts; and since that time I have inflicted untold suffering on my neighbors without having on a single occasion given the smallest pleasure to any human being except myself. Then, it will be asked, Why did I begin? Well, the motive arose from my previous knowledge of music. I had been accustomed all my life to hear it in sufficing quantities; and the melodies I heard I could at least sing; so that I neither had nor desired any technical knowledge. But it happened one day that my circumstances changed, so that I heard no more music. It was in vain now to sing: my native woodnotes wild—just then breaking frightfully—could not satisfy my intense craving for the harmony which is the emotional substance of music, and for the rhythmic figures of accompaniment which are its action and movement. I had only a single splintering voice; and I wanted an orchestra. This musical starvation it was that drove me to disregard the rights of my fellow lodgers and go to the piano. I learnt the alphabet of musical notation from a primer, and the keyboard from a diagram. Then, without troubling Czerny or Plaidy, I opened Don Giovanni and began. It took ten minutes to get my fingers arranged on the chord of D minor with which the overture commences; but when it sounded right at last, it was worth all the trouble it cost. At the end of some months I had acquired a technique of my own, as a sample of which I may offer my fingering of the scale of C major. Instead of shifting my hand by turning the thumb under and fingering $\frac{C\,D\,E\,F\,G\,A\,B\,C}{1\;2\;3\;1\;2\;3\;4\;5}$, I passed my fourth finger over my fifth and played $\frac{C\,D\,E\,F\,G\,A\,B\,C}{1\;2\;3\;4\;5\;4\;5\;4}$. This method had the advantage of being applicable to all scales, diatonic or chromatic; and to this day I often fall back on it. Liszt and Chopin hit on it too; but they never used it to the extent that I did. I soon acquired a terrible power of stumbling through pianoforte arrangements and vocal scores; and my reward was that I gained penetrating experiences of Victor Hugo and Schiller from Donizetti, Verdi, and Beethoven; of the Bible from Handel; of Goethe from Schumann; of Beaumarchais and Molière from Mozart; and of Mérimée from Bizet, besides finding in Berlioz an unconscious interpreter of Edgar Allan Poe. When I was in the schoolboy-adventure vein, I could range from Vincent Wallace to Meyerbeer; and if I felt piously and genteelly sentimental, I, who could not stand the pictures of Ary Scheffer or the genteel suburban sentiment of Tennyson and Longfellow, could become quite maudlin over Mendelssohn and Gounod. And, as I searched all the music I came across for the sake of its poetic or dramatic content, and played the pages in which I found drama or poetry over and over again, whilst I never returned to those in which the music was trying to exist ornamentally for its own sake and had no real content at all, it followed that when I came across the consciously perfect art work in the music dramas of Wagner, I ran no risk of hopelessly misunderstanding it as the academic musicians did. Indeed, I soon found that they equally misunderstood Mozart and Beethoven, though, having come to like their tunes and harmonies, and to understand their mere carpentry, they pointed out what they supposed to be their merits with an erroneousness far more fatal to their unfortunate pupils than the volley of half-bricks with which they greeted Wagner (who, it must be confessed, retaliated with a volley of whole ones fearfully well aimed).

Now, in this fragment of autobiography, what is it that stands as the one indispensable eternal condition of my musical culture? Obviously, the pianoforte. Without it, no harmony, no interweaving of rhythms and motives, no musical structure, and consequently no opera or music drama. But on the other hand, with it nothing else was needed, except the printed score and a foreknowledge of the power of music to bring romance and poetry to an enchanting intimacy of realization. Let a man once taste of the fruit that brings that knowledge, and no want of technical instruction will prevent him from doing what I did, if only he can get access to a piano and ten shillings' worth of cheap editions of operas and oratorios. I had not the key to the instrument, but I picked the lock by passing my ring finger over my little finger, driven as I was to that burglarious process by my craving for the booty within. It was easier than learning to read French; and how many of us learn to read French merely to satisfy our craving for a less reticent sort of novel than England produces! It is worth anyone's while to do likewise for the sake of Meyerbeer, Gounod, and Verdi alone—nay, for the sake of Offenbach and the Savoy operas. For one must not affright people of moderate capacity by promising them communion with the greatest men, whom they are apt to find dry. On the other hand, let me not lead those older and abler souls to whom the heroics of Verdi, the seraphic philanderings of Gounod, and the pseudo-historical effect-mongering of Meyerbeer are but children's entertainments, to suppose that there is no music at their level. Music is not always serenading Jessica and

Lorenzo: it has higher business than that. As one of those swaggering bronzes from the furniture-shops—two cavaliers drawing their swords at one another from opposite ends of the mantelpiece—is to a statue by Praxiteles, so is an opera by Meyerbeer to one by Mozart. However you may despise romantic novels, however loftily you may be absorbed in the future destiny of what is highest in humanity, so that for mere light literature you turn from Dante to Goethe, or from Schopenhauer to Comte, or from Ruskin to Ibsen—still, if you do not know Die Zauberflöte, if you have never soared into the heaven where they sing the choral ending of the Ninth Symphony, if Der Ring des Nibelungen is nothing to you but a newspaper phrase, then you are an ignoramus, however eagerly you may pore in your darkened library over the mere printed labels of those wonders that can only be communicated by the transubstantiation of pure feeling [into] musical tone. The greatest of the great among poets, from Aeschylus to Wagner, have been poet-musicians: how then can any man disdain music or pretend to have completed his culture without it?

Thus to the whole range of imaginative letters, from the Bab Ballads to Prometheus Unbound, you have a parallel range of music from Trial by Jury to Tristan and Isoldè, conveying to your very senses what the other could only suggest to your imagination. Only, to travel along this higher range rather than along the lesser one, you must use your piano. This is the mission of the pianoforte, to assert which adequately is such an answer to "Is the pianoforte a musical instrument?" as will send the questioner away an abashed idiot.

Now let us consider the drawbacks to culture by pianoforte as opposed to culture by ordinary reading. To begin with, people do not read aloud; consequently half-a-dozen persons can sit in the same room and enjoy six different books by the light of the same lamp. Imagine these people going to six pianos and simultaneously striking up The Mikado, Dinorah, Faust, Aïda, Fidelio, and Götterdämmerung. Nay, imagine them doing it, not in the same room, but even in the same house, or in the same square, with the windows open in summer! In German towns they have a music curfew, and will not let you play after a stated hour in the evening. When Liszt was teaching at Weimar, playing the pianoforte with the window open was a public misdemeanor punishable by fine. The only wonder is that the piano is permitted at all except in lighthouses and other detached residences. At present unmusical people get used to the noise of a piano just as they get used to the noise of cabs clattering past; but in the end the pianos will make most people musical; and then there will be an end of the present anarchic toleration. For just in proportion as you like bungling on a piano yourself does the bungling of others offend and disturb you. In truth, just as the face a man sees when he looks in the glass is not his face as his neighbor sees it, so the music we hear when we play is not what our neighbors hear. I know no way out of this difficulty just at present. We cannot go back to the clavichord unless we listen to it through a microphone; for though you can play Bach fugues on a clavichord, you cannot play *Suoni la tromba*, or *Di quella pira*, or the Rákóczy March, or the Ride of the Valkyries—at least, not to your heart's content. Even good playing and good pianos are eternally impossible. For the laws of nature forbid good playing with our keyboard, which defies the human hand and only gives us the run of the twelve keys on condition that they are all perceptibly out of tune. And the laws of nature equally seem, so far, to decree that the pianoforte string which gives the most beautiful tone and the pianoforte action which gives the most perfect touch will not last; so that if you get an ideal piano at a cost of some hundreds of pounds, in five years you will want a new one. But you are far more likely, as the income-tax returns prove, to be compelled to put up with a twentyfive pound piano on the three years' system; and though excellent French pianets (considering) are to be had at that price, the ordinary British householder prefers a full-sized walnut piano of the sort that justifies the use of dynamite. Thus we appear to be driven to this lamentable alternative: either to give up the best part of our culture or else make it a curse to the people downstairs or next door. We seem hardly to have the right to hesitate; for now that the moral basis of pianism as a means of giving pleasure to others is exploded, and shewn to correspond to the exact opposite of the facts of the case, it appears to be our plain duty to forbid amateur music altogether, and to insist on romance and poetry being restricted to their silent, incomplete, merely literary expression.

But this, I submit, we dare not do. Without music we shall surely perish of drink, morphia, and all sorts of artificial exaggerations of the cruder delights of the senses. Asceticism will not save us, for the conclusive reason that we are not ascetics. Man, as he develops, seeks constantly a keener pleasure, in the pursuit of which he either destroys himself or develops new faculties of enjoyment. He either strives to intensify the satisfaction of resting, eating, and drinking, the excitement and exercise of hunting, and the ardor of courtship, by "refining" them into idleness, gluttony, dipsomania, hideous cruelty, and ridiculous vice, or else he develops his feeling until it becomes poetic feeling, and sets him thinking with pleasure of nobler things. Observe, if you please, the order of development here: it is all-important, as I shall shew, even at the cost of a digression. It is feeling that sets a man thinking, and not thought that sets him feeling. The secret of the absurd failure of our universities and academic institutions in general to produce any real change in the students who are constantly passing through them is that their method is invariably to attempt to lead their pupils to feeling by way of thought. For example, a musical student is expected to gradually acquire a sense of the poetry of the Ninth Symphony by accumulating information as to the date of Beethoven's birth, the compass of the *contra fagotto*, the number of sharps in the key of D major, and so on, exactly analogous processes being applied in order to produce an appreciation of painting, Greek poetry, or what not. Result: the average sensual boy comes out the average sensual man, with his tastes in no discoverable way different from those of the young gentleman who has preferred an articled clerkship in a solicitor's office to Oxford or Cambridge. All education, as distinct from technical instruction, must be education of the feeling; and such education must consist in the appeal of actual experiences to the senses, without which literary descriptions addressed to the imagination cannot be rightly interpreted. Marriage, for instance, is admittedly an indispensable factor in the education of the complete man or woman. But in educational institutions appeals to the senses can only take the form of performances of works of art; and the bringing of such performances to the highest perfection is the true business of our universities.

This statement will surprise nobody but a university man. Fortunately there is no such thing as an absolutely pure specimen of that order. If it were possible to shut off from a boy all the influence of home, and to confine him absolutely to public-school life and university life, the resultant pure product of what we call "education" would be such a barbarous cub or insufferable prig as we can only conceive by carefully observing the approaches to these types which are occasionally produced at present. But such a complete specialization is not possible. You cannot wholly shut art out now, even with the assistance of modern architects. Though my name is to be found on the books of no Oxford college, I have enjoyed all the real education which the university has to offer by simply walking through the university and looking at its beautiful old quadrangles. I know fairly-educated Oxford men—though, to be sure, they are all truants and smugglers, connoisseurs of the London theatres and galleries, with pictures, pianofortes, and beautiful things of one kind or another in their rooms, and shelves upon shelves of books that are never used as textbooks. I remember conversing once with the late Master of Balliol, an amiable gentleman, stupendously ignorant probably, but with a certain flirtatious, old-maidish frivolity about him that had, and was meant to have, the charm of a condescension from so learned a man. In Oxford he was regarded as a master educator. I would ask what right he had to that distinction in a country where Hallé had made, and was conducting, the Manchester band; where August Manns, with Sir George Grove, had created the Crystal Palace orchestra; and where Richter was teaching us what Wagner taught him? Sir Frederick Burton, as master of the National Gallery, Sir Augustus Harris, as master of the Royal Italian Opera, were and are worth to England, educationally, forty thousand Masters of Balliol. Which is the greater educator, pray—your tutor when he coaches you for the Ireland scholarship or Miss Janet Achurch when she plays Nora for you? You cannot witness A Doll's House without *feeling,* and as an inevitable consequence, thinking; but it is evident that the Ireland scholarship would break up Oxford unless it could be won without either feeling or thinking. I might give a thousand illustrations, if space permitted, or if criticism of the university system were my main purpose instead of my digression.

Taking it, then, as established that life is a curse to us unless it operates as pleasurable activity, and that as it becomes more intense with the upward evolution of the race it requires a degree of pleasure which cannot be extracted from the alimentary, predatory, and amatory instincts without ruinous perversions of them; seeing, also, that the alternative of "high thinking" is impossible until it is started by "high feeling," to which we can only come through the education of the senses—are we to deliberately reverse our Puritan traditions and aim at becoming a nation of skilled voluptuaries? Certainly. It may require some reflection to see that high feeling brings high thinking; but we already know, without reflection, that high thinking brings what is called plain living. In this century the world has produced two men—Shelley and Wagner—in whom intense poetic feeling was the permanent state of their consciousness, and who were certainly not restrained by any religious, conventional, or prudential consider- ations from indulging themselves to the utmost of their oppor- tunities. Far from being gluttonous, drunken, cruel, or debauched, they were apostles of vegetarianism and waterdrinking; had an utter horror of violence and "sport"; were notable champions of the inde- pendence of women; and were, in short, driven into open revolution against the social evils which the average sensual man finds ex- tremely suitable to him. So much is this the case that the practical doctrine of these two arch-voluptuaries always presents itself to ordi- nary persons as a saint-like asceticism.

If, now, relieved of all apprehensions as to the social safety of allowing the world to make itself happy, we come to consider which of the arts is the most potent to this end, we must concede that eminence to music, because it alone requires for its enjoyment an artistic act on the part of its reader, which act, in its perfection, becomes such an act of re-creation as Wagner found in Liszt's playing of Beethoven's sonatas. There is no need in this account to set up the musician above the painter, the masterbuilder, or the sculptor. There are points at which all rivalry between the arts vanishes. When you are looking at the Turner water-colors in the National Gallery, the poetic feeling which they so exquisitely and sufficingly express com- pletely delivers you from that plane on which mere hero-worshipers squabble as to whether the painter or the composer of music is the better man. None the less, in the National Gallery the feeling is expressed by the painter and not by you, although your feeling, too, struggles for expression, sometimes almost painfully. You stand dumb, or at best you turn to your neighbor and say, "Pretty, aint it?" of which remark most art criticism is but an elaboration.

Now suppose the feeling were aroused, not by a picture, but by a song! At once your tongue is loosed: you sing the song, and thereby relieve one of your deepest needs—strange as that may sound to peo- ple who sing songs solely to gain the applause of others. Further, you gain by practice the power of expressing feeling, and with that power the courage to express it, for want of which power and courage we all

go miserably about today, shrinking and pretending, misunderstanding and misunderstood, making remarks on the weather to people
whose most nourishing sympathy or most salutary opposition we
might enjoy if only we and they could become fully known to each
other by a complete self-expression. Music, then, is the most fecund
of the arts, propagating itself by its power of forcing those whom it influences to express it and themselves by a method which is the easiest
and most universal of all art methods, because it is the art form of that
communication by speech which is common to all the race.

This music wisdom has been urged on the world in set terms by
Plato, by Goethe, by Schopenhauer, by Wagner, and by myself. As a
rule, when, in order to obtain concreteness, I couple my teachings
with the name of any individual who enjoys opportunities of carrying
out my ideas, he threatens me with legal proceedings, on the ground
that I have taken him seriously. And indeed the commonsense of the
country under present circumstances feels that to take music as
seriously as religion, morals, or politics is clear evidence of malicious
insanity, unless the music belongs to an oratorio. The causes of this
darkness are economic. What is the matter with us is that the mass of
the people cannot afford to go to good concerts or to the opera.
Therefore they remain ignorant of the very existence of a dramatic
or poetic content in what they call "classical" or "good" music, which
they always conceive as a web of learnedly and heavily decorative
sound patterns, and never as containing a delicious kernel of feeling,
like their favorite Annie Laurie. Consequently they do not crave for
pianos; and if they did they could not afford to buy them, and would
perforce fall back on the poor man's piano—the German concertina
or accordion. At the same time, our most gifted singers, instead of
getting ten or fifteen pounds a week and a pension, have to be paid
more than Cabinet Ministers, whose work turns them prematurely
grey, or officers in the field, or musical critics. All this must be altered
before any serious advance in culture can be effected. The necessity
for change in the social structure is so pressing that it drives the
musician into the political arena in spite of his own nature. You have
Wagner going out in '48 with the revolutionists because the State
declined to reform the theatre, just as I am compelled, by a similar
obtuseness on the part of our own Governments, to join the Fabian
Society, and wildly masquerade as a politician so that I may agitate for
a better distribution of piano-purchasing power.

If I were now to string all these points in their logical order on the thread of a complete argument, to prove that the future of humanity depends at present on the pianoforte, I should render my case repugnant to the British mind, which sensibly objects to be bothered with logic. But let me, in allowing the British mind to jump at its conclusion, plead for a large construction for the word pianoforte. An organ, an harmonium, a vocalion, an aeolion, an orchestrion, or any instrument upon which the full polyphony of an opera or symphony can be given, may obviously replace the pianoforte; and so far as the playing can be done, wholly or partly, by perforated cards, barrels, or other mechanical means of execution, by all means let it be so done. A fingering mechanism so contrived as to be well under the *artistic* control of the operator would be an unspeakable boon. Supply me with such a thing and I will make an end of Paderewski.

Finally, let no one suppose that because private readings and performances are better than nothing, they are therefore an efficient substitute for complete dramatic and orchestral representations. Far from it; they are makeshifts, and very miserable makeshifts too. In Italy, when you go from the picture gallery to the photograph shop, you are revolted by the inadequacy of the "reproductions" which turn Carpaccio's golden glow into sooty grime. At Bayreuth when, on your way back of an evening from the Festival Playhouse, you hear someone strumming a pianoforte arrangement of the overture to Die Meistersinger, you wonder how the wretch can bear to listen to himself. Yet, after a few months in England, when you pull out your photograph, or sit down to the pianoforte score of Die Meistersinger, you are very pleasantly and vividly reminded of Carpaccio or Wagner. Also, however diligently you may read your Shakespear or your Ibsen, you must date your full acquaintance with any work of theirs from the time when you see it fully performed on the stage as they meant you to. The day will come when every citizen will find within his reach and means adequate artistic representations to recreate him whenever he feels disposed for them. Until then the pianoforte will be the savior of society. But when that golden age comes, everybody will see at last what an execrable, jangling, banging, mistuned nuisance our domestic music machine is, and the maddening sound of it will thenceforth be no more heard in our streets.

(*Fortnightly Review*, February 1894.)

# Suggestions for Further Reading

Included are authors represented in this book as well as selected works by others whose words on music are worth seeking out. To make the reader's search easier, I have emphasized recent over obscure editions. Originally published in newspapers, journals, and concert programs, the work of many of the most worthwhile writers on music has unfortunately never been collected in book form.

Barzun, Jacques. *Berlioz and His Century*. Chicago: Univ. of Chicago Press, 1956; adapted from *Berlioz and the Romantic Century*, 1949.
———, ed. *Pleasures of Music*. Chicago: Univ. of Chicago Press, 1951; abridged, 1977.
Berlioz, Hector. *Evenings with the Orchestra*. 1852. Reprint. Translated by Jacques Barzun. New York: Knopf, 1956.
———. *Memoirs*. 1870. Reprint. Translated by David Cairns. New York: Knopf, 1969.
Bernstein, Leonard. *Findings*. New York: Simon and Schuster, 1982.
———. *The Infinite Variety of Music*. New York: Simon and Schuster, 1962.
———. *The Joy of Music*. New York: Simon and Schuster, 1959.
Boulez, Pierre. *Notes of an Apprenticeship*. Translated by Herbert Weinstock. New York: Knopf, 1968.
———. *Orientations*. Translated by Martin Cooper. Cambridge: Harvard Univ. Press, 1986.
Burgess, Anthony. *This Man and Music*. New York: McGraw-Hill, 1982.
Burney, Charles. *Dr. Charles Burney's Continental Travels*. London: Blackie & Son, 1927.
———. *A General History of Music*. 1776, 1789. Reprint. New York: Dover, 1957.
Busoni, Ferruccio. *The Essence of Music*. 1922. Reprint. Translated by Rosamond Ley. London: Rockliff, 1957.
Capell, Richard. *Schubert's Songs*. New York: Basic, 1957.
Chorley, Henry. *Thirty Years' Musical Recollections*. 1862. Reprint. Edited by Ernest Newman. New York: Knopf, 1926.
Copland, Aaron. *Copland on Music*. New York: Doubleday, 1960.
———. *The New Music*. 1941. Rev. ed. New York: Norton, 1968.
———. *What to Listen for in Music*. New York: McGraw-Hill, 1957.

Craft, Robert. *Prejudices in Disguise.* New York: Knopf, 1974.

Debussy, Claude. *Debussy on Music.* Translated by Richard Langham Smith. 1977. Reprint. Cornell: Cornell Univ. Press, 1988.

Eisenberg, Evan. *The Recording Angel.* New York: McGraw-Hill, 1987.

Gilman, Lawrence. *Orchestral Music: An Armchair Guide.* New York: Oxford Univ. Press, 1951.

Gould, Glenn. *The Glenn Gould Reader.* Edited by Tim Page. New York: Knopf, 1984.

Graffman, Gary. *I Really Should Be Practicing.* New York: Doubleday, 1981.

Gray, Cecil. *Contingencies.* New York: Oxford Univ. Press, 1947.

———. *The History of Music.* New York: Barnes and Noble, 1925.

———. *A Survey of Contemporary Music.* New York: Oxford Univ. Press, 1924.

Hale, Philip. *Great Concert Music.* New York: Doubleday, 1935.

Hanslick, Eduard. *The Beautiful in Music.* 1854. Reprint. Translated by Gustav Cohen. New York: Bobbs-Merrill, 1957.

———. *Music Criticisms.* Translated by Henry Pleasants. Harmondsworth, Middlesex: Penguin, 1950.

Henderson, W. J. *Modern Musical Drift.* New York: Longmans, Green, 1904.

Holmes, Edward. *A Ramble among the Musicians of Germany.* 1828. Reprint. New York: Da Capo, 1969.

Horgan, Paul. *Encounters with Stravinsky.* New York: Farrar, 1972.

Horowitz, Joseph. *Conversations with Arrau.* New York: Knopf, 1982. Reprint. New York: Limelight, 1984.

———. *Understanding Toscanini: How He Became an American Culture-God and Helped Create a New Audience for Old Music.* New York: Knopf, 1987. Reprint. St. Paul, Univ. of Minnesota Press, 1988.

Huneker, James. *Chopin: The Man and His Music.* New York: Scribner's, 1900.

———. *Franz Liszt.* New York: Scribner's, 1911.

———. *Mezzotints in Modern Music.* New York: Scribner's, 1899.

———. *Variations.* New York: Scribner's, 1921.

Ives, Charles. *Essays before a Sonata.* 1920. Reprinted in *Three Classics in the Aesthetic of Music.* New York: Dover, 1962.

Lambert, Constant. *Music Ho!* 1934. Reprint. London: Hogarth, 1985.

Liszt, Franz. *The Life of Chopin.* 1852. Reprint. Translated by John Broadhouse. London: William Reeves, 1913.

Mellers, Wilfrid. *Music in a New Found Land.* 1964. Reprint. New York: Oxford Univ. Press, 1987.

Mencken, H. L. *H. L. Mencken on Music.* Edited by Louis Cheslock. New York: Knopf, 1961.

Newman, Ernest. *From the World of Music.* 1956. Reprint. New York: Coward, McCann, 1957.

———. *A Musical Motley.* 1919. Reprint. New York: Knopf, 1925.

———. *Testament of Music.* New York: Knopf, 1963.

Nietzsche, Friedrich. *The Case of Wagner; Nietzsche contra Wagner.* 1888. In *The Complete Works of Friedrich Nietzsche,* translated by Anthony M. Ludovici, 1909–11, vol. 8. Reprint. New York: Russell & Russell, 1964.

Porter, Andrew. *Musical Events.* New York: Summit, 1987.

———. *A Musical Season.* New York: Viking, 1974.

———. *Music of Three More Seasons.* New York: Farrar, 1981.

———. *Music of Three Seasons.* New York: Farrar, 1978.

Rolland, Romain. *Beethoven the Creator.* New York: Harper, 1929.

———. *Handel.* Translated by A. Eaglefield Hull. New York: Holt, 1916

———. *Musicians of Today.* 1908. Reprint. Translated by Mary Blaiklock. Freeport, N.Y.: Books for Libraries Press, 1969.

———. *Some Musicians of Former Days.* Translated by Mary Blaiklock. London: Trubner, 1915.

Rorem, Ned. *An Absolute Gift.* New York: Simon, 1974.

———. *The Nantucket Diary.* Berkeley: North Point, 1987.

———. *The Paris and New York Diaries of Ned Rorem.* Berkeley: North Point, 1983.

———. *Settling the Score.* New York: Harcourt, 1988.

Rosen, Charles. *The Classical Style.* New York: Norton, 1972.

Rosenfeld, Paul. *Discoveries of a Music Critic.* 1936. Reprint. New York: Vienna House, 1972.

———. *Musical Impressions.* New York: Hill & Wang, 1969.

Schumann, Robert. *Music and Musicians.* 2 vols. Translated by Fanny Raymond Ritter. London: William Reeves, 1880 (more complete than the Rosenfeld edition).

———. *On Music and Musicians.* Translated by Paul Rosenfeld. New York: Pantheon, 1946.

Schweitzer, Albert. *J. S. Bach.* 2 vols. Translated by Ernest Newman, 1911. Reprint. New York: Dover, 1966.

Shaw, George Bernard. *G. B. S. on Music.* Harmondsworth, Middlesex: Penguin, 1962.

———. *The Great Composers.* Edited by Louis Crompton. Berkeley: Univ. of California Press, 1978.

———. *How to Become a Music Critic.* Edited by Dan Laurence. New York: Hill & Wang, 1961.

———. *London Music in 1888–89.* London: Constable, 1937.

———. *Music in London, 1890–94.* London: Constable, 1932.

———. *The Perfect Wagnerite.* 1898. Reprint. New York: Dover, 1967.

———. *Shaw on Music.* Edited by Eric Bentley. New York: Doubleday, 1955.

Slonimsky, Nicolas. *The Lexicon of Musical Invective.* 1953. Univ. of Washington Press, 1969.

———. *Perfect Pitch.* New York: Oxford Univ. Press, 1988.

Smyth, Ethel. *Impressions That Remained.* 2 vols. London: Longmans, Green, 1919.

Thomson, Virgil. *American Music Since 1910.* New York: Holt, 1971.

———. *The Art of Judging Music.* New York: Knopf, 1948.

———. *The Musical Scene.* 1945. Reprint. New York: Greenwood, 1968.

———. *Music Reviewed: 1940–54.* Reprint. New York: Vintage, 1967.

———. *Music Right and Left.* 1951. Reprint. New York: Greenwood, 1969.

———. *Music with Words.* New Haven: Yale Univ. Press, 1989.

————. *The State of Music.* New York: William Morrow, 1939.

————. *The Virgil Thomson Reader.* Edited by John Rockwell. Boston: Houghton Mifflin, 1981.

Tovey, Donald Francis. *Beethoven.* New York: Oxford Univ. Press, 1945.

————. *Essays and Lectures on Music.* New York: Oxford Univ. Press, 1949.

Wagner, Richard. *Richard Wagner's Prose Works.* Translated by William Ashton Ellis. 1896. Reprint. New York: Da Capo, 1964 (selections only).

Wolf, Hugo. *The Music Criticism of Hugo Wolf.* Translated by Henry Pleasants. New York: Holmes, 1978.

For centuries, distinguished writers have taken on the challenge of describing great music and its significance in their lives. From Joseph Addison to Virgil Thomson, writers in and out of the music field have used their most vivid language to conjure the sounds and emotions of the music that mattered most to them. Yet until this book, no single volume has ever collected the best of this writing in one place. Scattered in magazines, essay collections, and program notes, this literature is largely unknown to the general reader—who often thinks that music essays are for musicians only—and even to the musician—who often reads only narrow specialty publications.

*Words on Music* is thus the first book of its kind. Covering instrumental and vocal music from the eighteenth through the twentieth centuries, it features essays distinguished by their literary quality, their readability, and their appeal to a wide audience. Included is writing by novelists, essayists, composers, performers, cultural historians, and others who have written about music with precision and passion.

Here is George Bernard Shaw on Handel, Albert Schweitzer on Bach, Glenn Gould on Scarlatti, E. T. A. Hoffman on Beethoven, Heinrich Heine on Rossini, Aaron Copland on Mozart, George Eliot on Wagner, G. K. Chesterton on Gilbert and Sullivan, Leonard Bernstein on Mahler, Guy Davenport